GODZILLA

DARK HORSE COMICS®

ゴジラ

東宝怪獣

ゴジラ

ゴジラ・シリーズ

PUBLISHING CREDITS

afterword
Robert V. Conte

original miniseries &
first edition editor
Randy Stradley

second edition editor
Robert V. Conte

collection editor
Lynn Adair

collection designer
Brian Gogolin

Mike Richardson
publisher

Neil Hankerson
executive vice president

David Scroggy
vice president of publishing

Lou Bank
vice president of sales & marketing

Andy Karabatsos
vice president of finance

Mark Anderson
general counsel

Diana Schutz
editor in chief

Randy Stradley
creative director

Cindy Marks
director of production & design

Mark Cox
art director

Sean Tierney
computer graphics director

Chris Creviston
director of accounting

Michael Martens
marketing director

Tod Borleske
sales & licensing director

Mark Ellington
director of operations

Dale LaFountain
director of m.i.s.

なんだ!!

GODZILLA

CREATOR & ADAPTATION CREDITS

script & art
Kazuhisa Iwata

Adapted by
Randy Stradley
Mike Richardson

cover painting
Bob Eggleton

lettering
Dan McKinnon
Jean Simek
David Jackson

art touchups
Jim Bradrick
Chris Chalenor
Chris Warner
Jerry Prosser

DARK HORSE COMICS®

GODZILLA®

ISBN: 1-56971-063-5

Based on the Toho Co. motion picture The Return of Godzilla (a.k.a., Godzilla 1985).
Originally published in Japan by Shogakukan, Inc.
English translation and publication is made possible through the services of Viz Communications, Inc.

Godzilla® 2nd edition. Published by Dark Horse Comics, Inc., 10956 SE Main Street, Milwaukie, OR 97222. The name "Godzilla" and his likeness are registered trademarks of Toho Co. Ltd.

This book collects issues 1-6 of the Dark Horse comic-book miniseries Godzilla, published in 1988 and 1989.

Published by Dark Horse Comics
10956 SE Main Street
Milwaukie, OR 97222

Second edition: May 1995

10 9 8 7 6 5 4 3 2

Printed in Canada

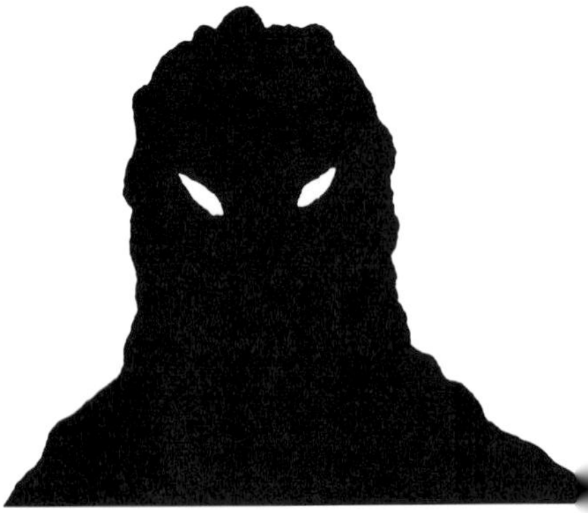

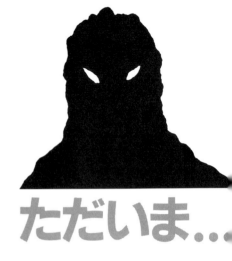

ただいま…

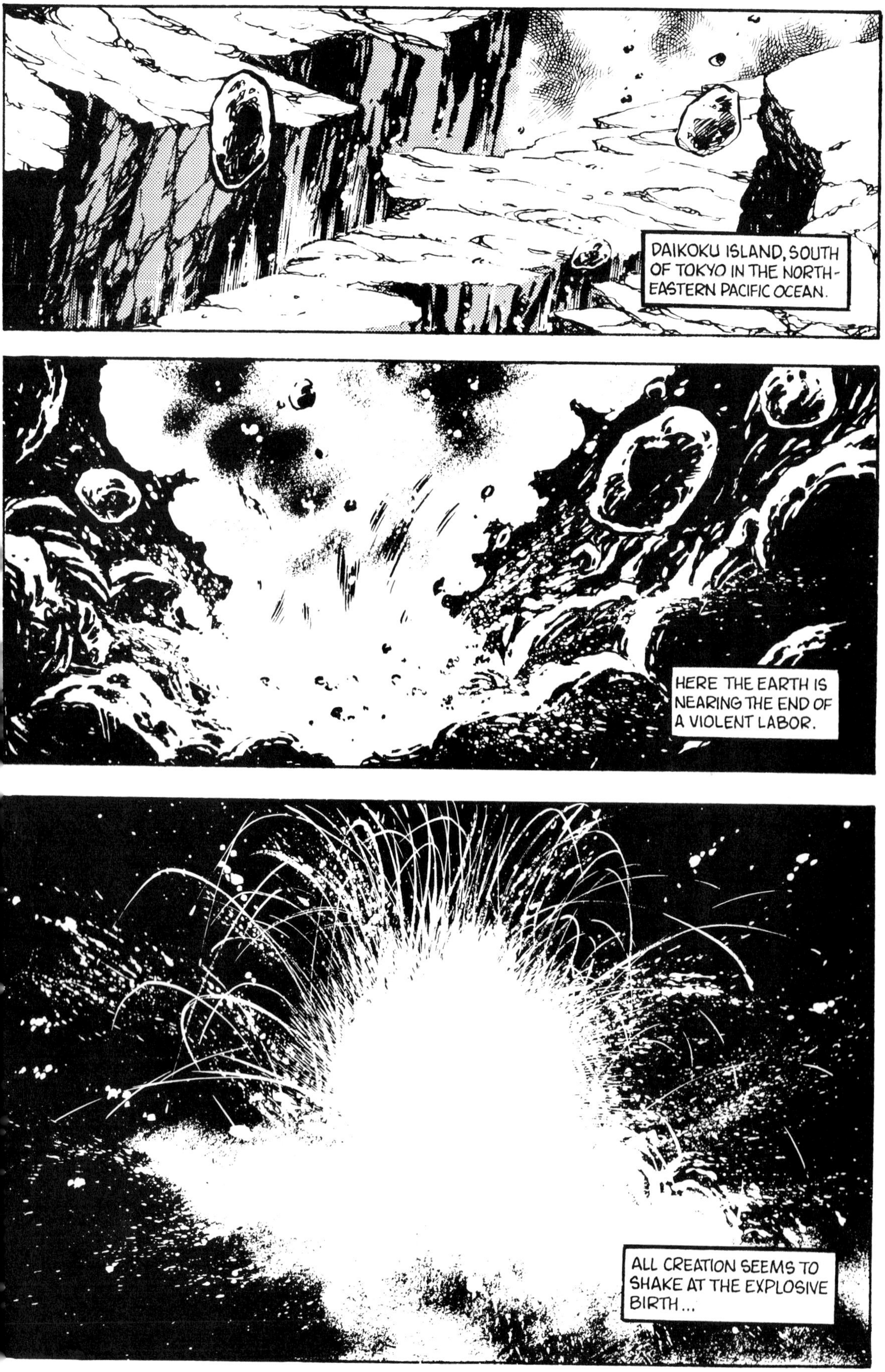
DAIKOKU ISLAND, SOUTH OF TOKYO IN THE NORTH-EASTERN PACIFIC OCEAN.
HERE THE EARTH IS NEARING THE END OF A VIOLENT LABOR.
ALL CREATION SEEMS TO SHAKE AT THE EXPLOSIVE BIRTH...

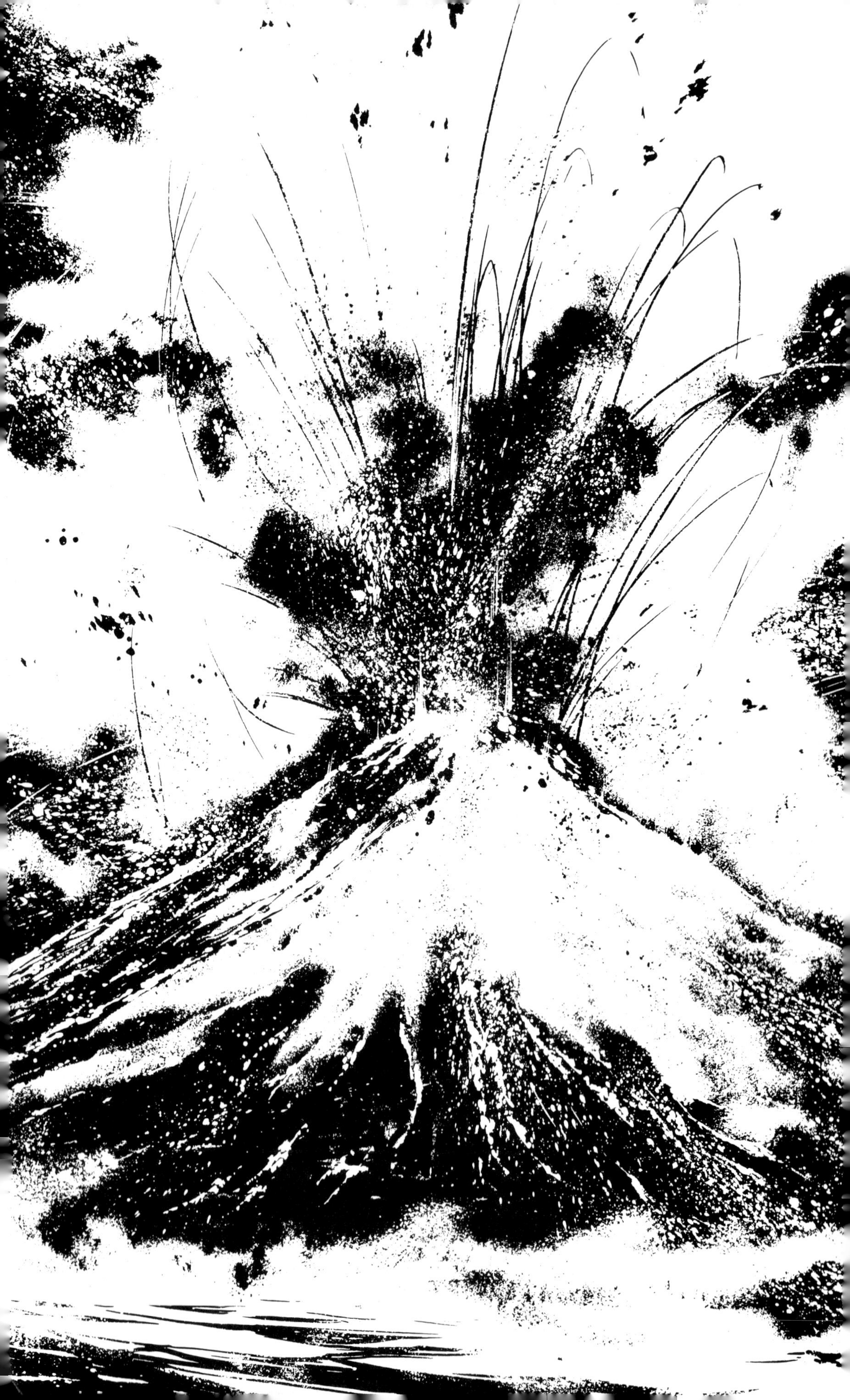

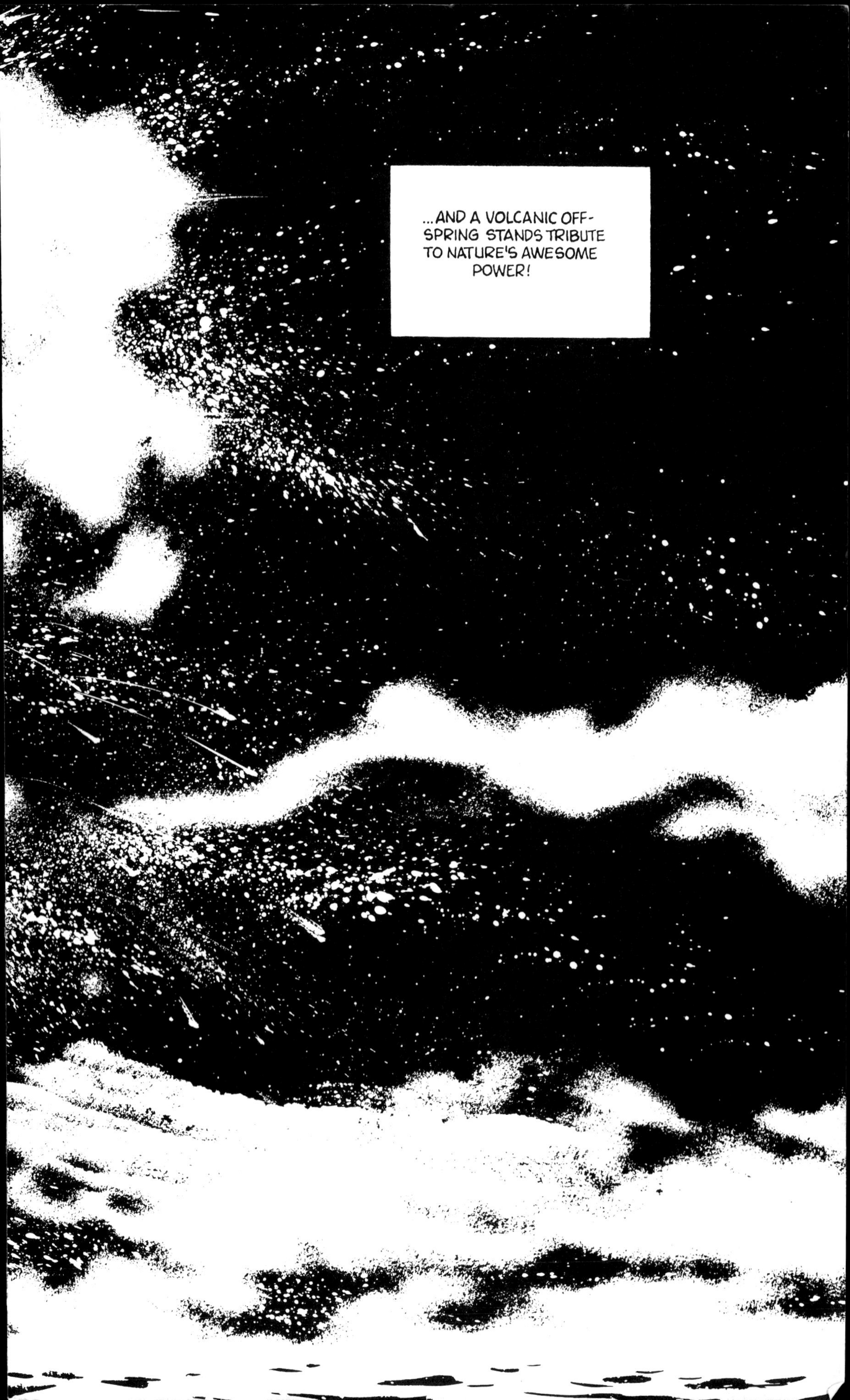
...AND A VOLCANIC OFF-SPRING STANDS TRIBUTE TO NATURE'S AWESOME POWER!

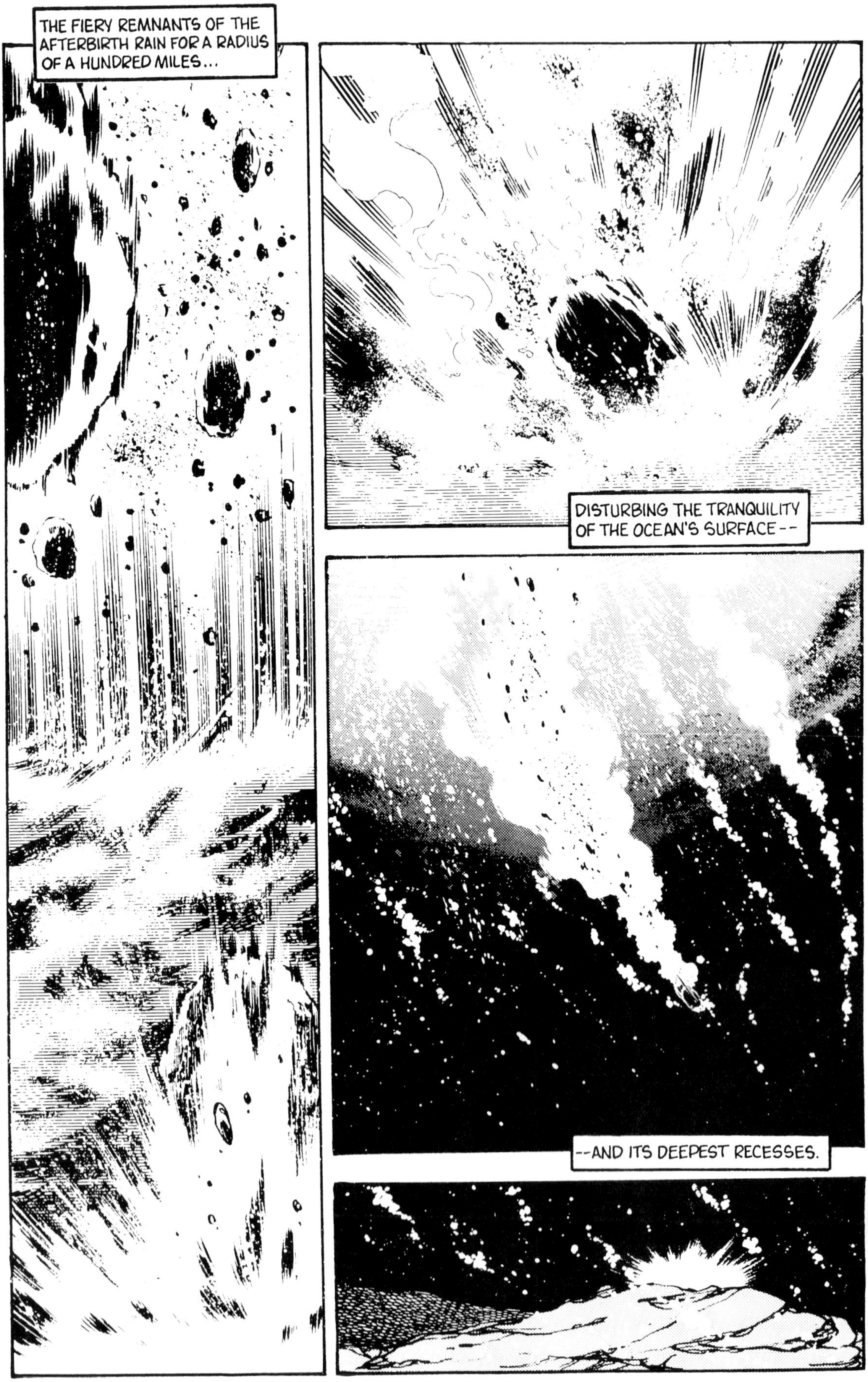
THE FIERY REMNANTS OF THE AFTERBIRTH RAIN FOR A RADIUS OF A HUNDRED MILES...
DISTURBING THE TRANQUILITY OF THE OCEAN'S SURFACE--
--AND ITS DEEPEST RECESSES.

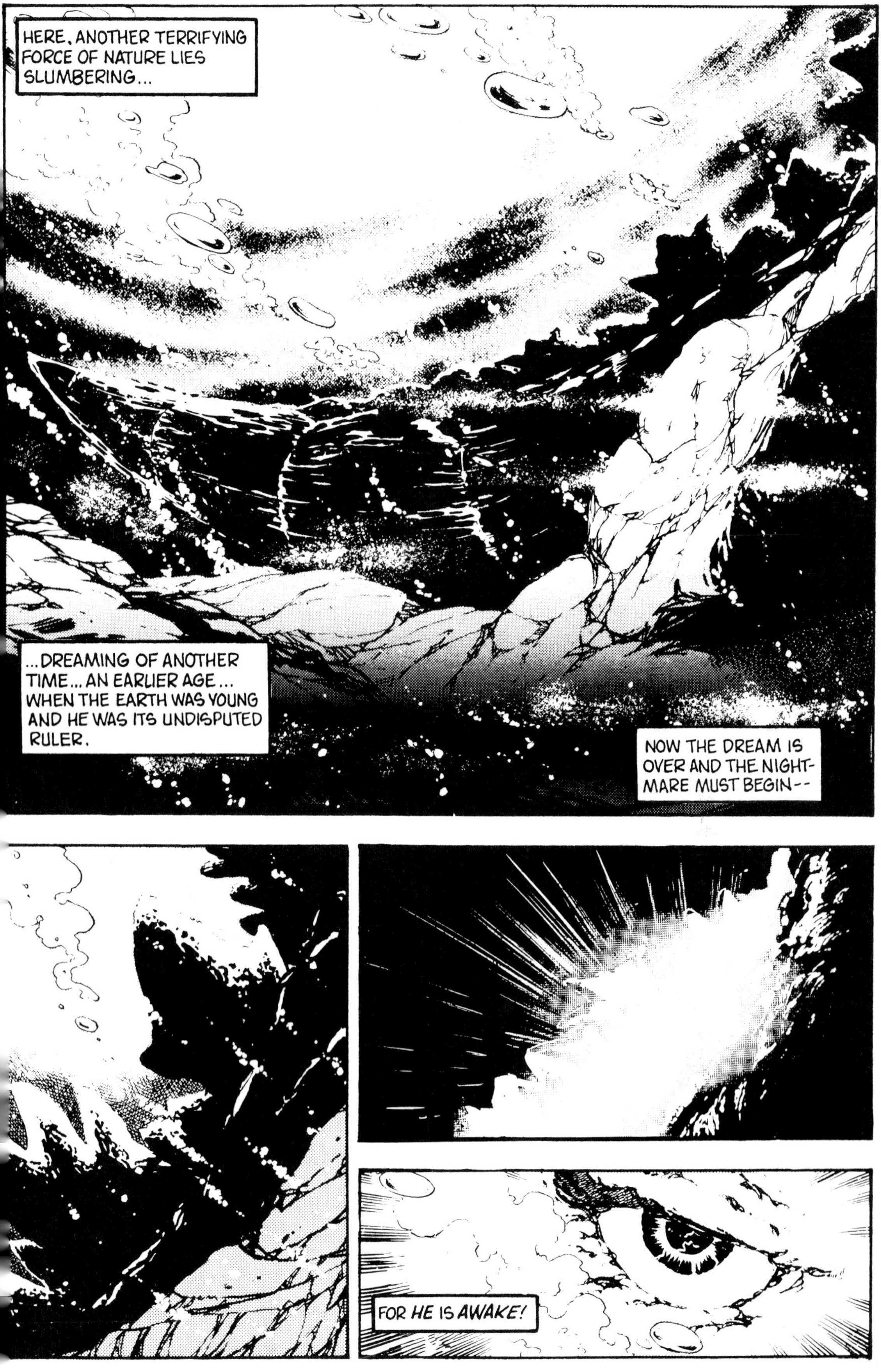
HERE, ANOTHER TERRIFYING FORCE OF NATURE LIES SLUMBERING...
...DREAMING OF ANOTHER TIME... AN EARLIER AGE... WHEN THE EARTH WAS YOUNG AND HE WAS ITS UNDISPUTED RULER.
NOW THE DREAM IS OVER AND THE NIGHT-MARE MUST BEGIN--
FOR HE IS AWAKE!

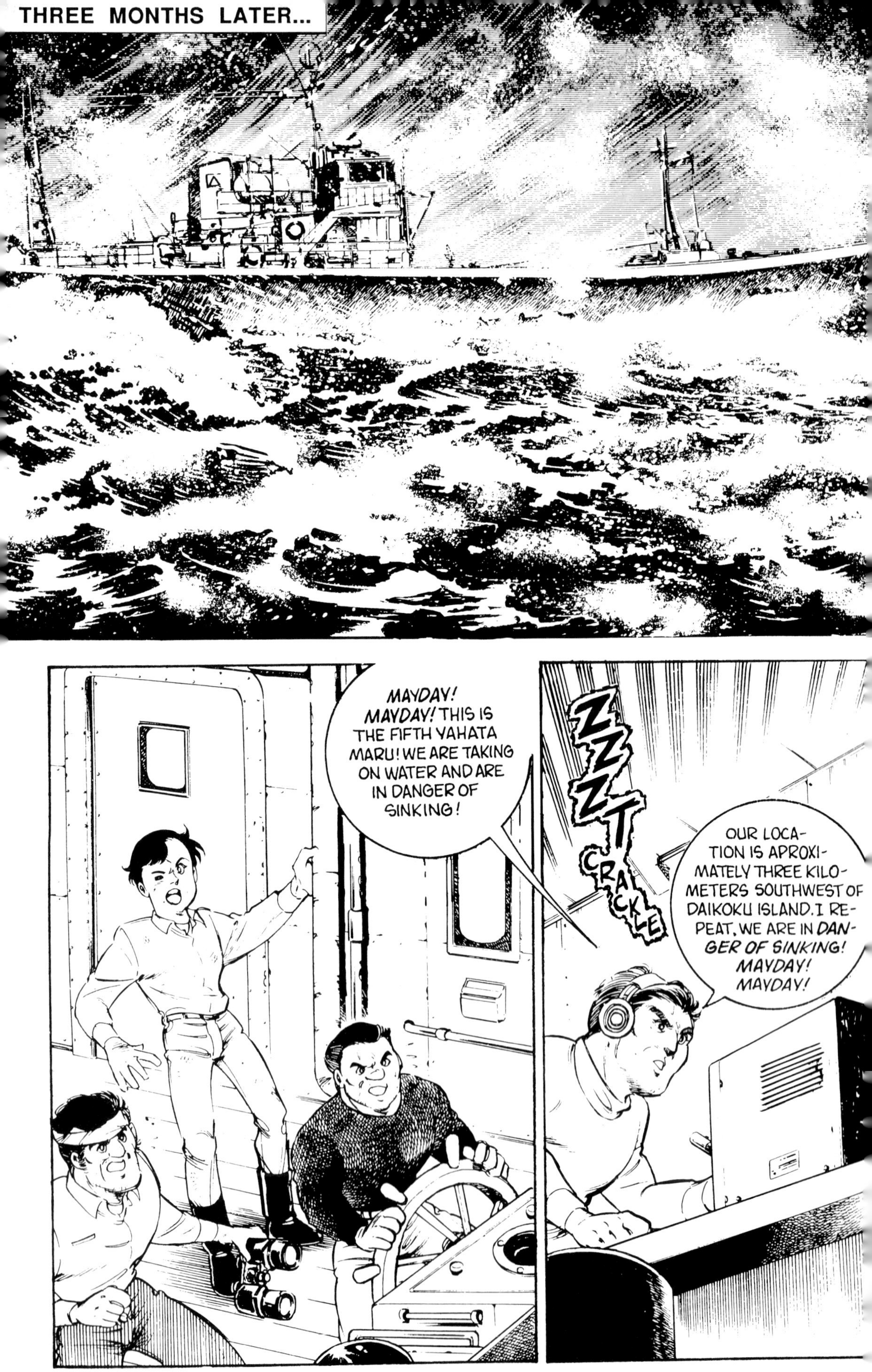
THREE MONTHS LATER...
MAYDAY! MAYDAY! THIS IS THE FIFTH YAHATA MARU! WE ARE TAKING ON WATER AND ARE IN DANGER OF SINKING!
ZZZT CRACKLE
OUR LOCATION IS APROXIMATELY THREE KILOMETERS SOUTHWEST OF DAIKOKU ISLAND. I REPEAT, WE ARE IN DANGER OF SINKING! MAYDAY! MAYDAY!

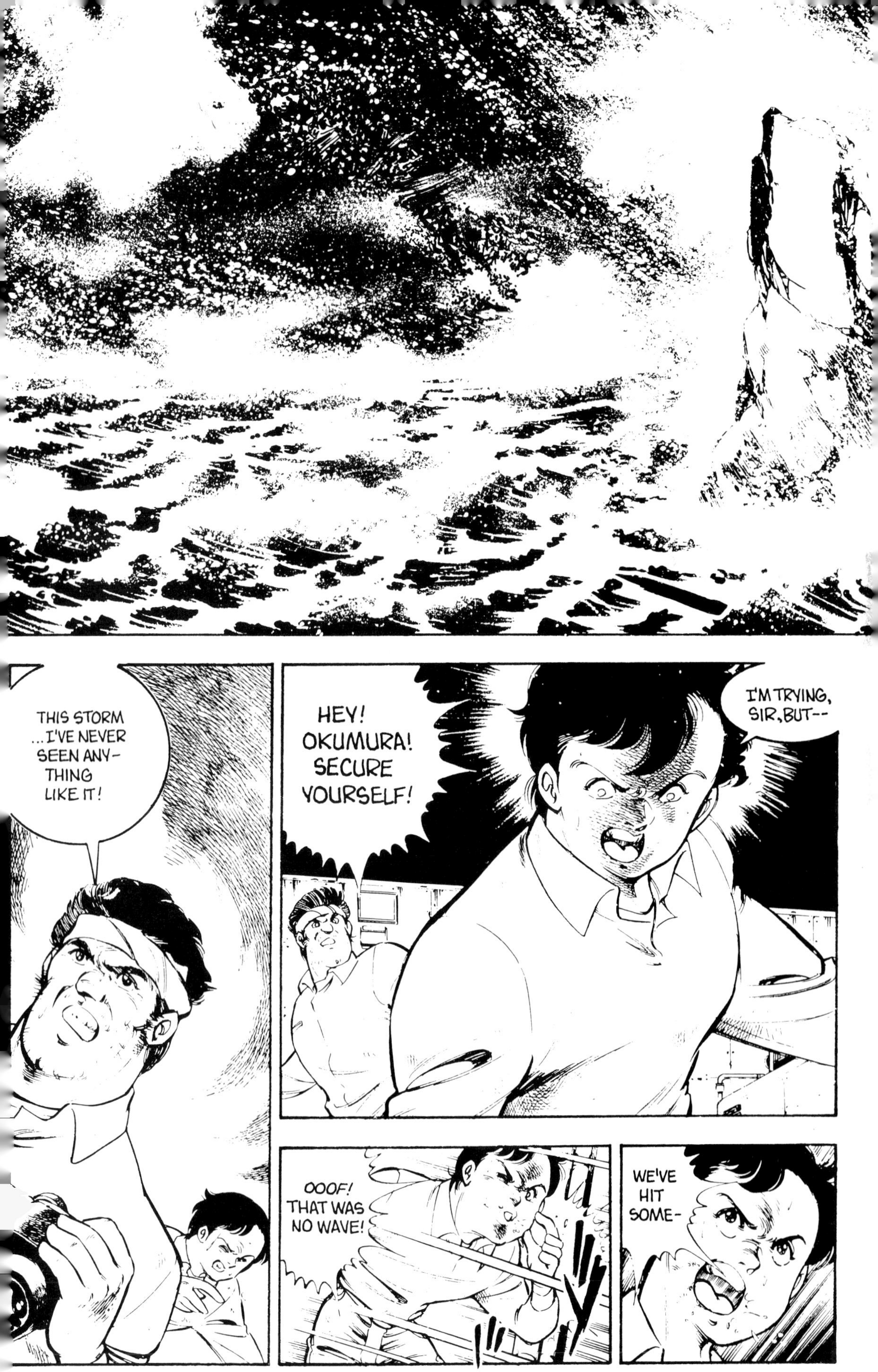
THIS STORM ...I'VE NEVER SEEN ANY-THING LIKE IT!
HEY! OKUMURA! SECURE YOURSELF!
I'M TRYING, SIR, BUT--
OOOF! THAT WAS NO WAVE!
WE'VE HIT SOME-

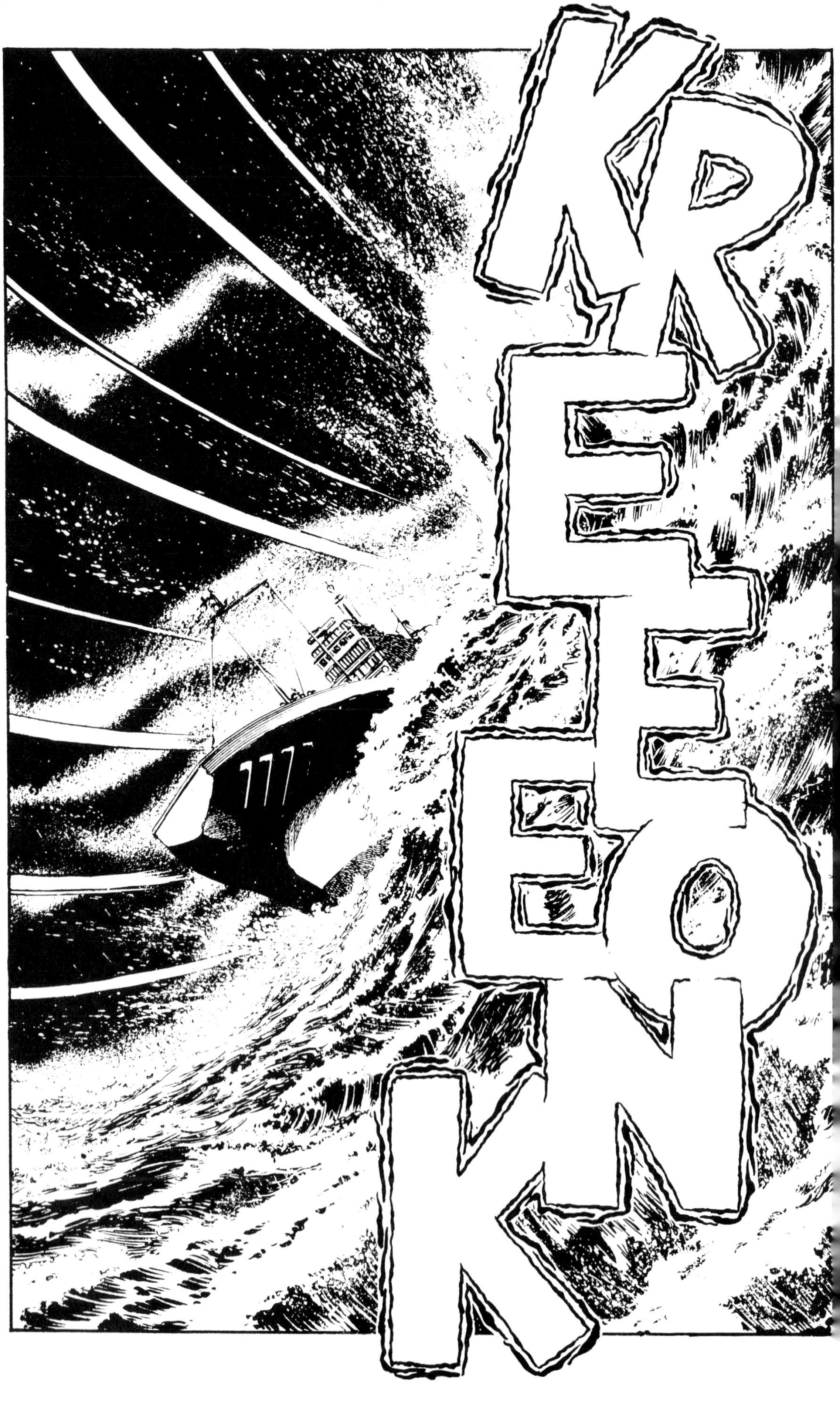
KREEEONK

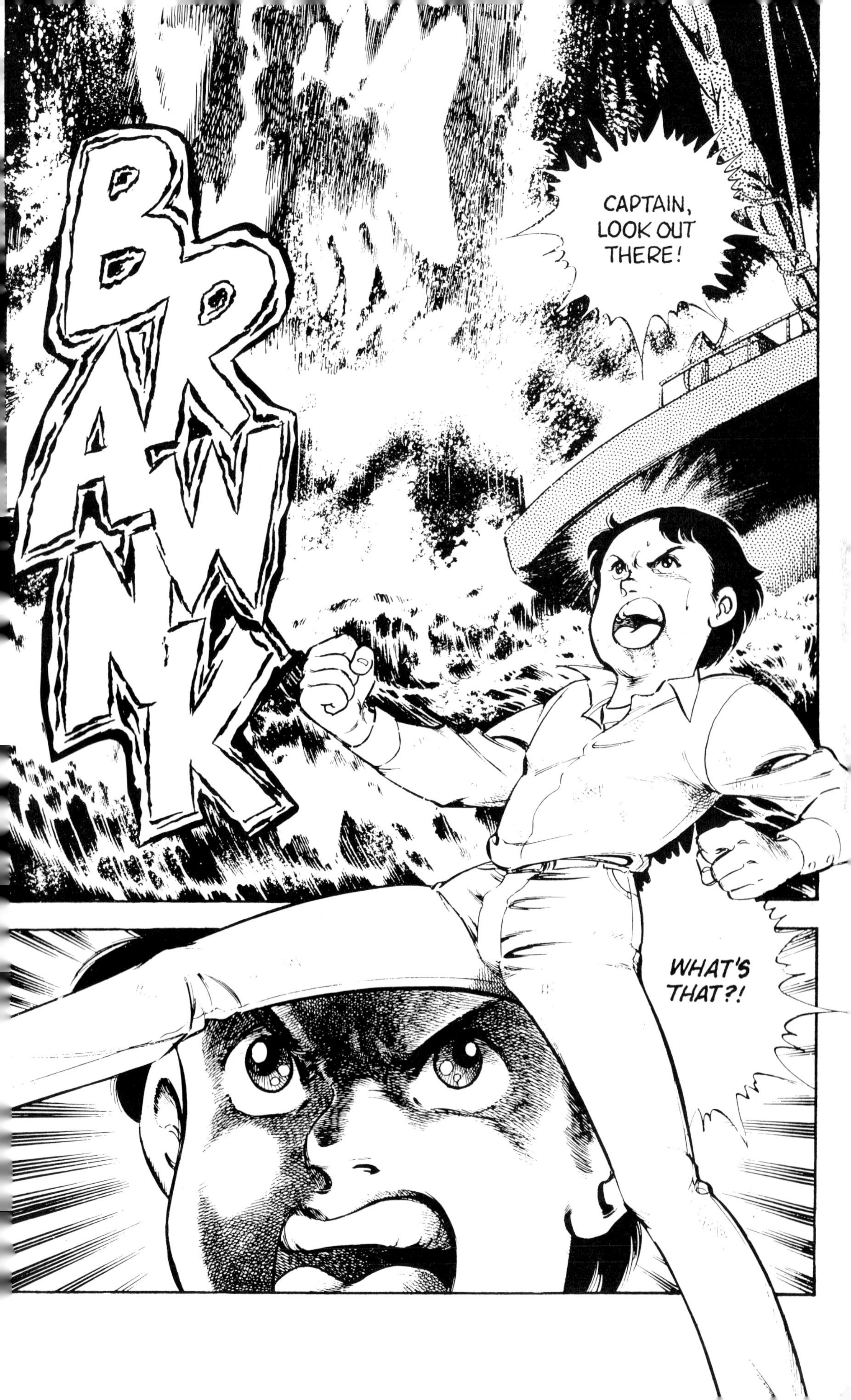
BRAWNK
CAPTAIN, LOOK OUT THERE!
WHAT'S THAT?!

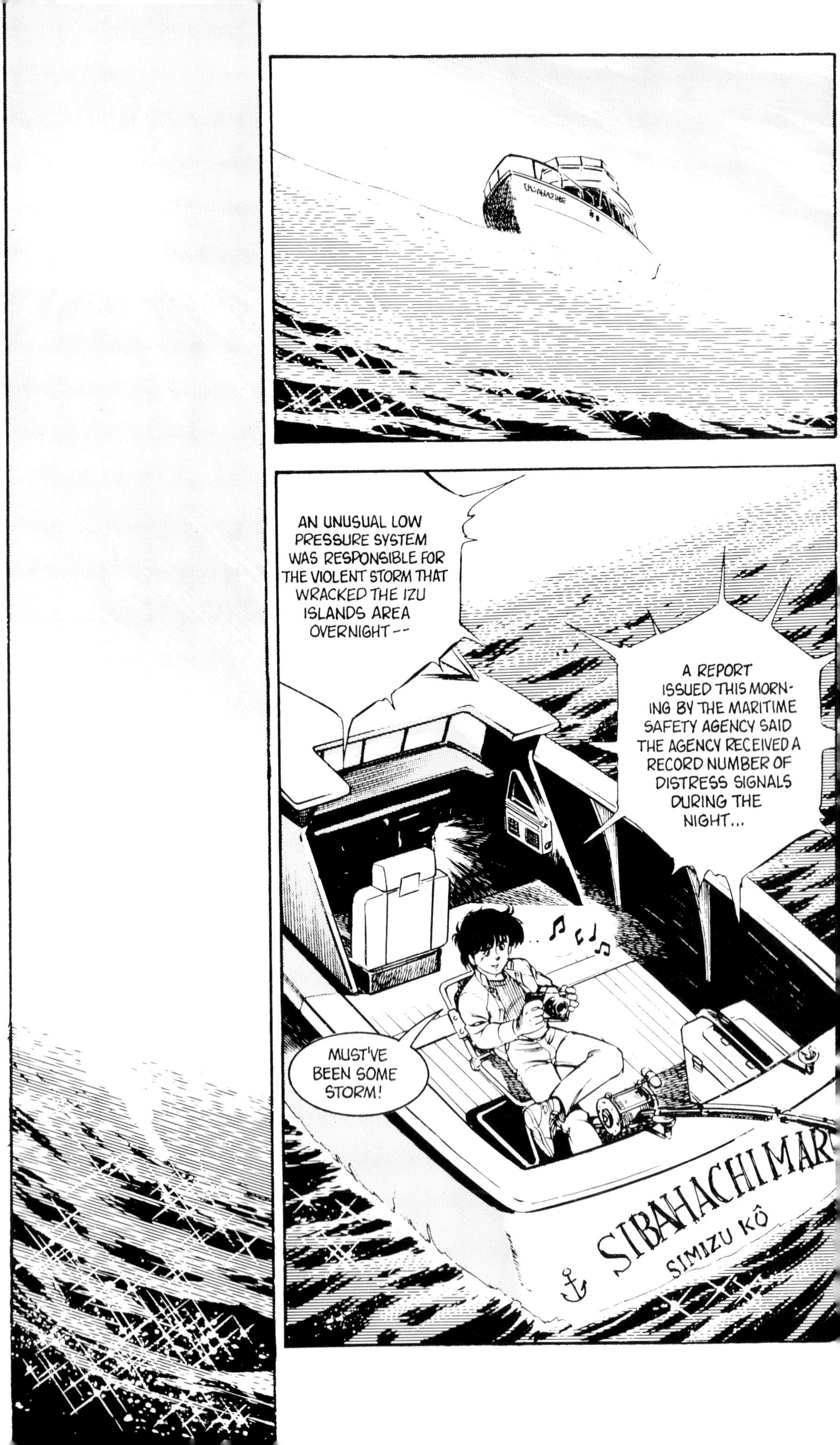
AN UNUSUAL LOW PRESSURE SYSTEM WAS RESPONSIBLE FOR THE VIOLENT STORM THAT WRACKED THE IZU ISLANDS AREA OVERNIGHT --
A REPORT ISSUED THIS MORNING BY THE MARITIME SAFETY AGENCY SAID THE AGENCY RECEIVED A RECORD NUMBER OF DISTRESS SIGNALS DURING THE NIGHT...
MUST'VE BEEN SOME STORM!
SIBAHACHI MAR
SIMIZU KÔ

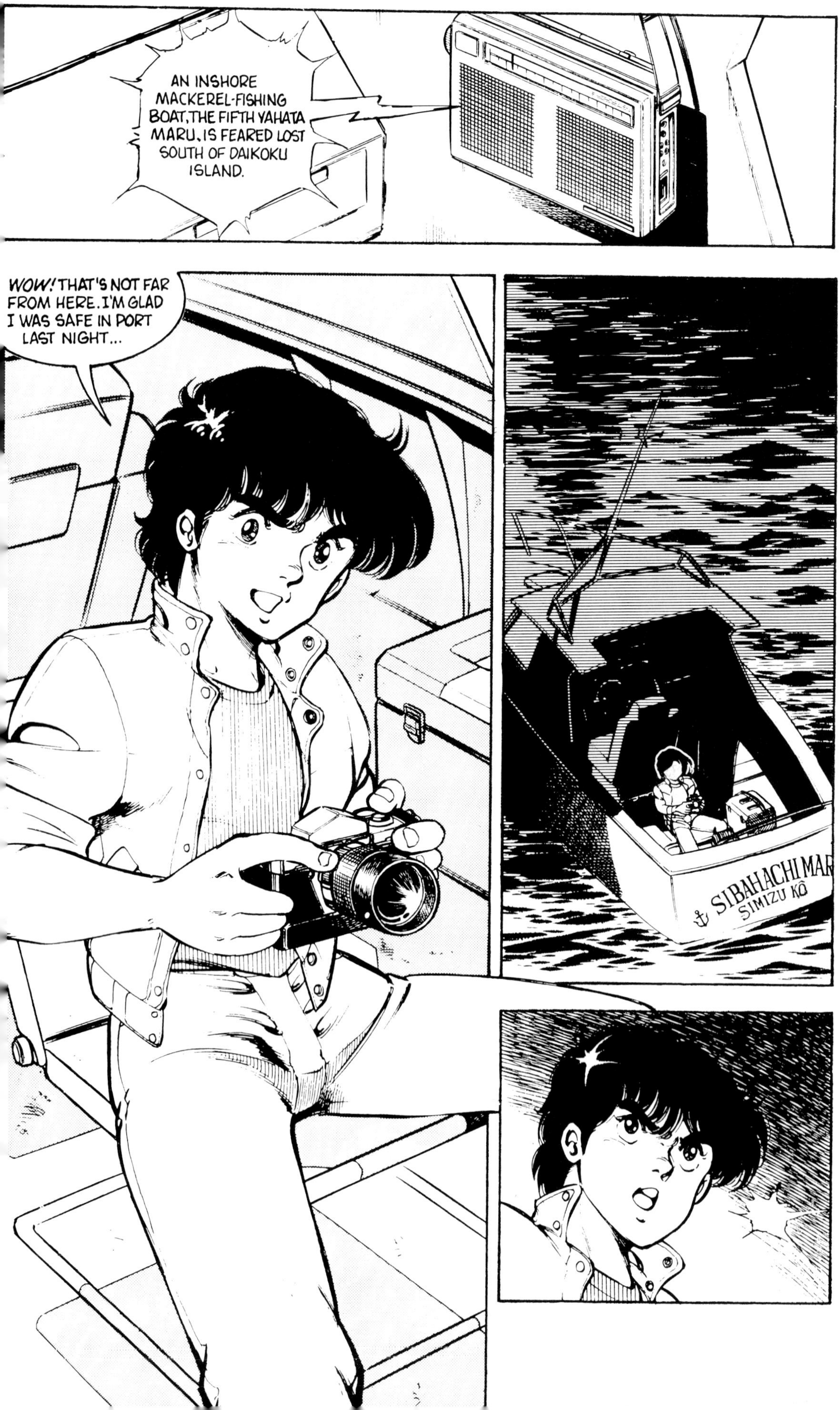
AN INSHORE MACKEREL-FISHING BOAT, THE FIFTH YAHATA MARU, IS FEARED LOST SOUTH OF DAIKOKU ISLAND.
WOW! THAT'S NOT FAR FROM HERE. I'M GLAD I WAS SAFE IN PORT LAST NIGHT...
SIBAHACHI MAR
SIMIZU KÔ

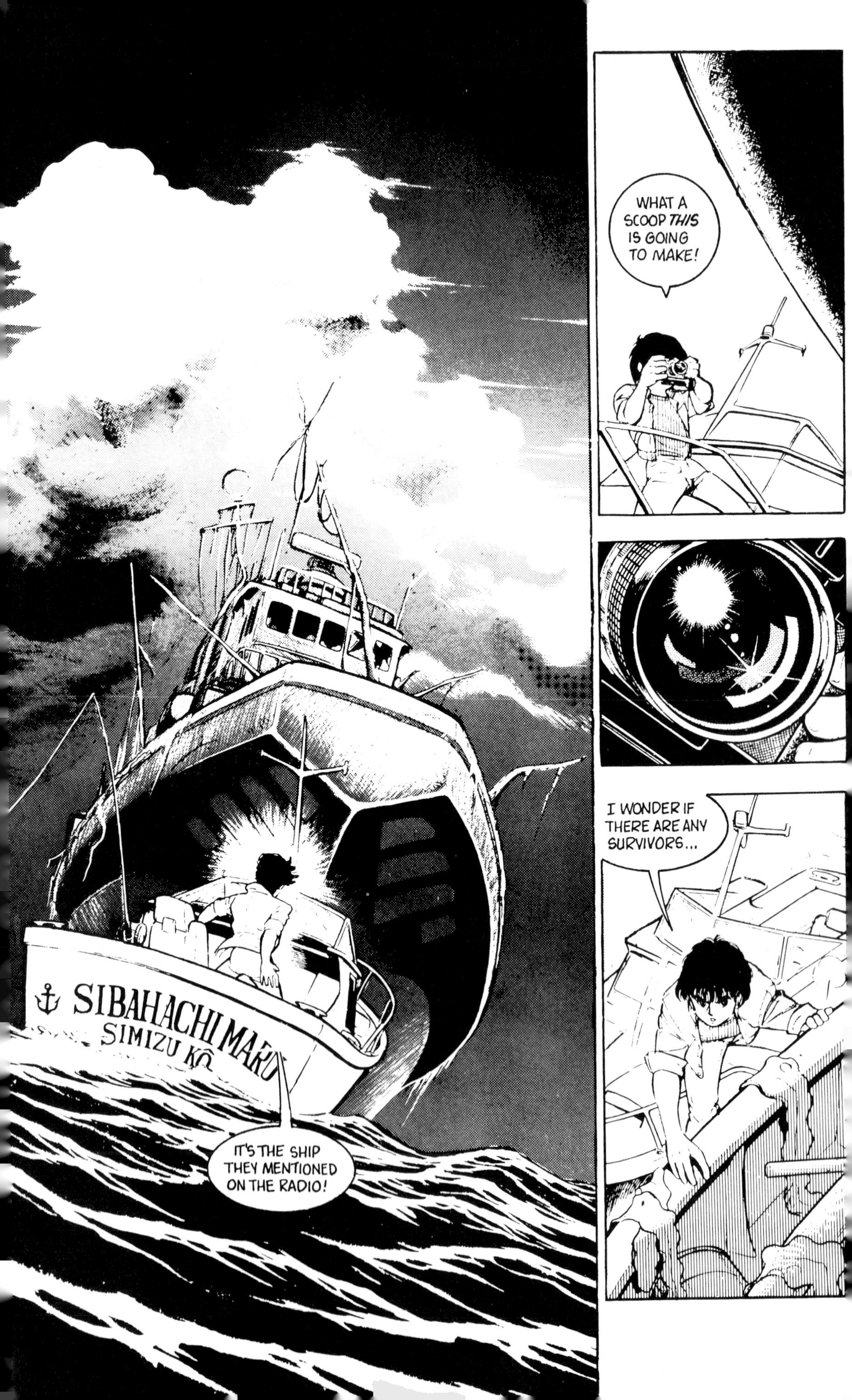
SIBAHACHI MAR
SIMIZU KŌ
IT'S THE SHIP THEY MENTIONED ON THE RADIO!
WHAT A SCOOP *THIS* IS GOING TO MAKE!
I WONDER IF THERE ARE ANY SURVIVORS...

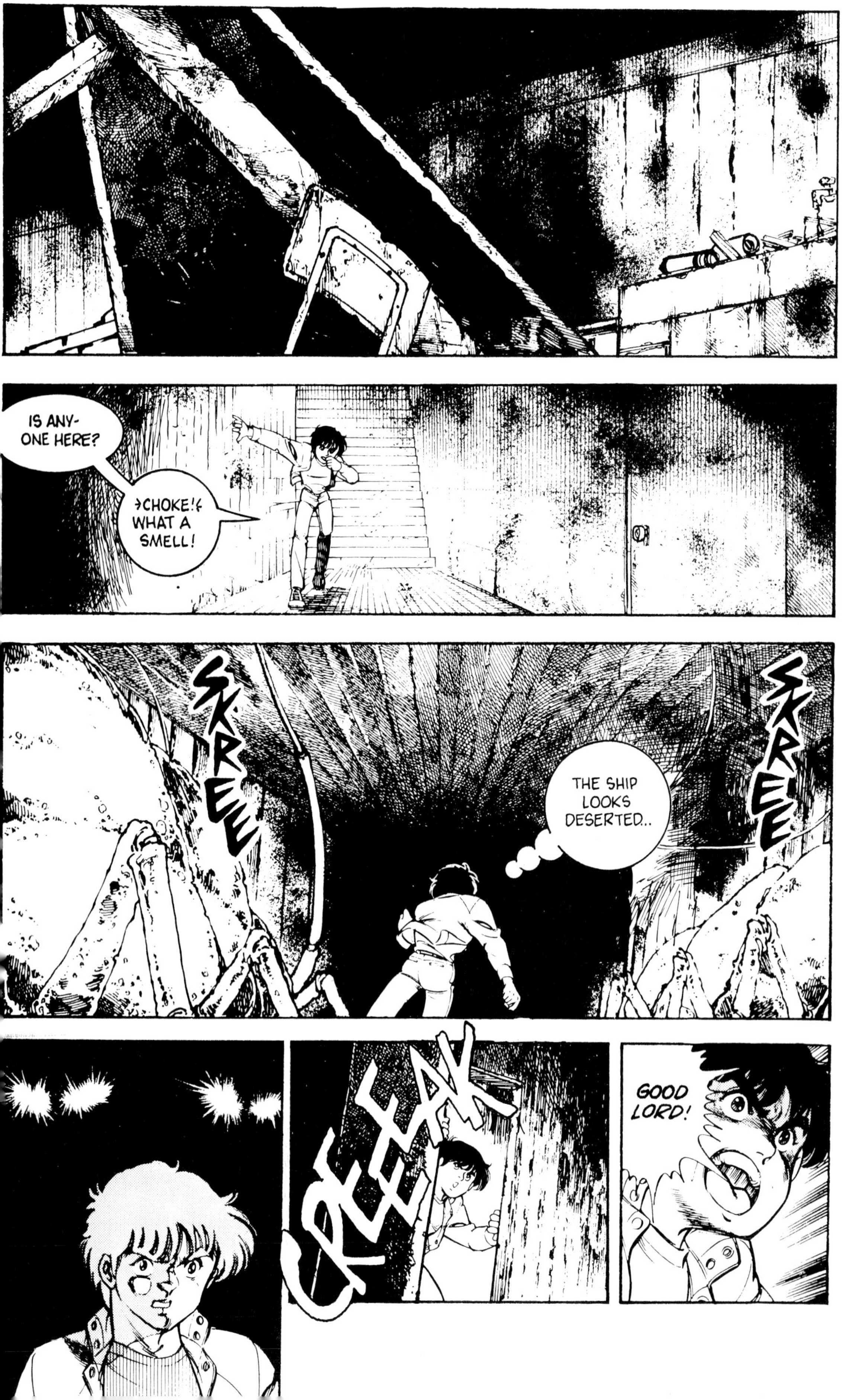
IS ANY-
ONE HERE?
≯CHOKE!≮
WHAT A
SMELL!
SKREE
THE SHIP
LOOKS
DESERTED..
SKREE
CREEAK
GOOD
LORD!

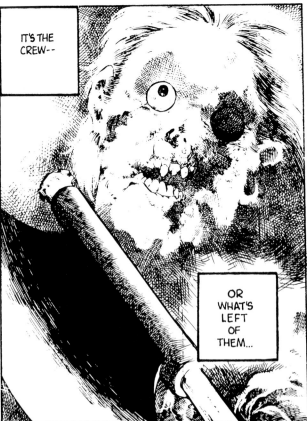

IT'S THE
CREW--

OR
WHAT'S
LEFT
OF
THEM...

ULP...

IT'S LIKE
THEY WERE
EATEN ALIVE!
WHAT COULD'VE
DONE THIS
TO THEM?

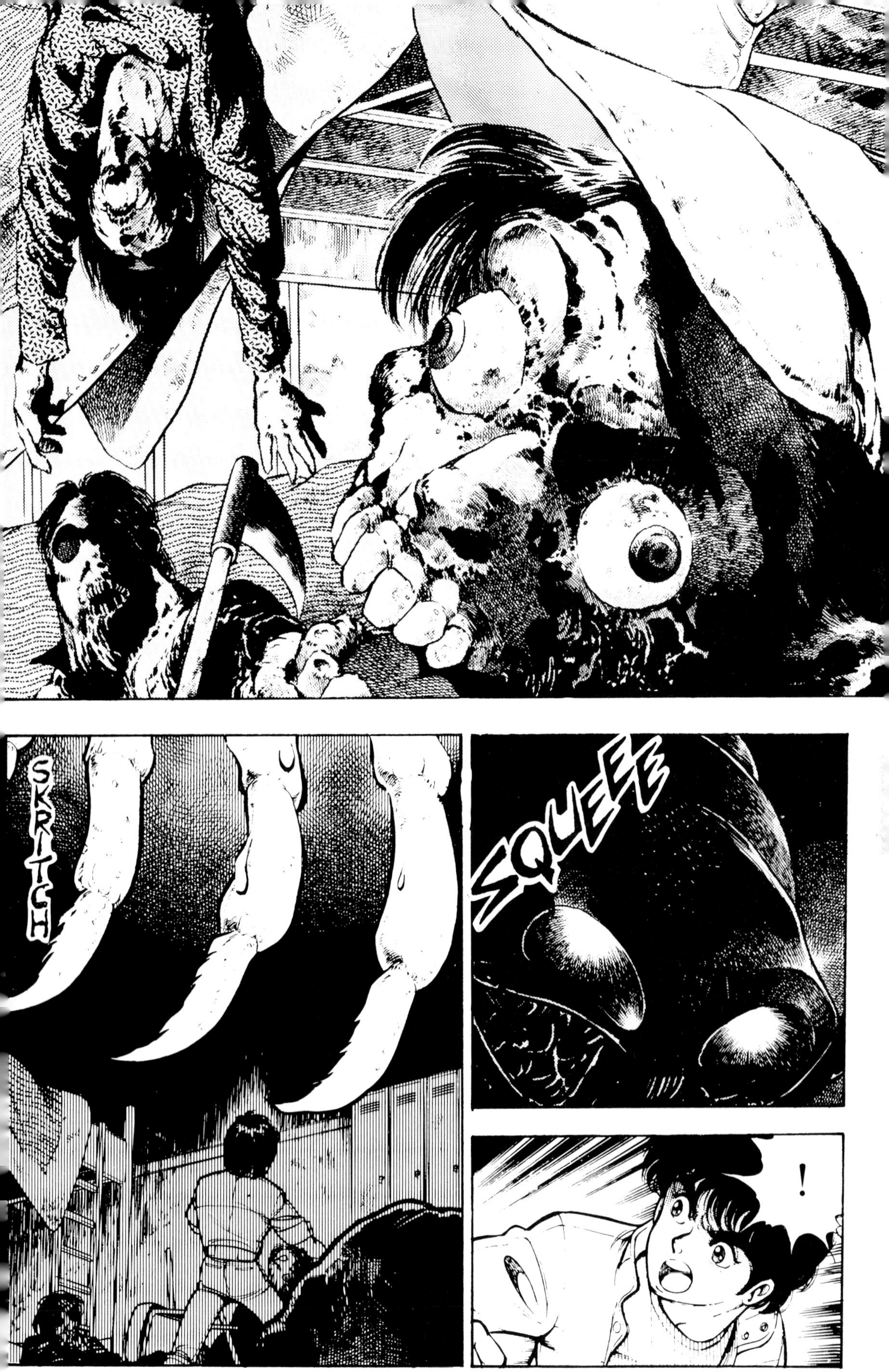
SKRITCH
SQUEEE
!

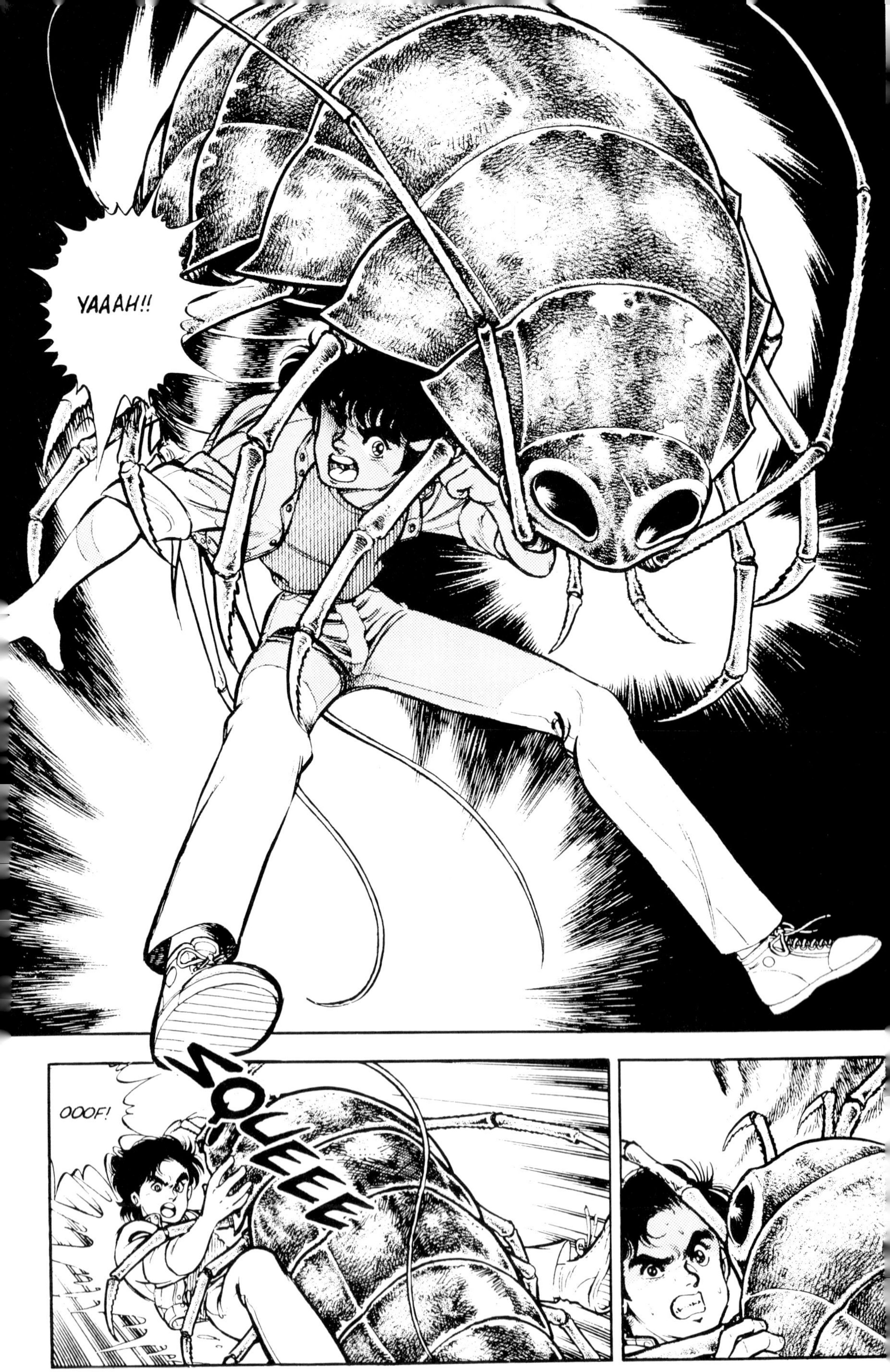
YAAAH!!
OOOF!
SQUEEE

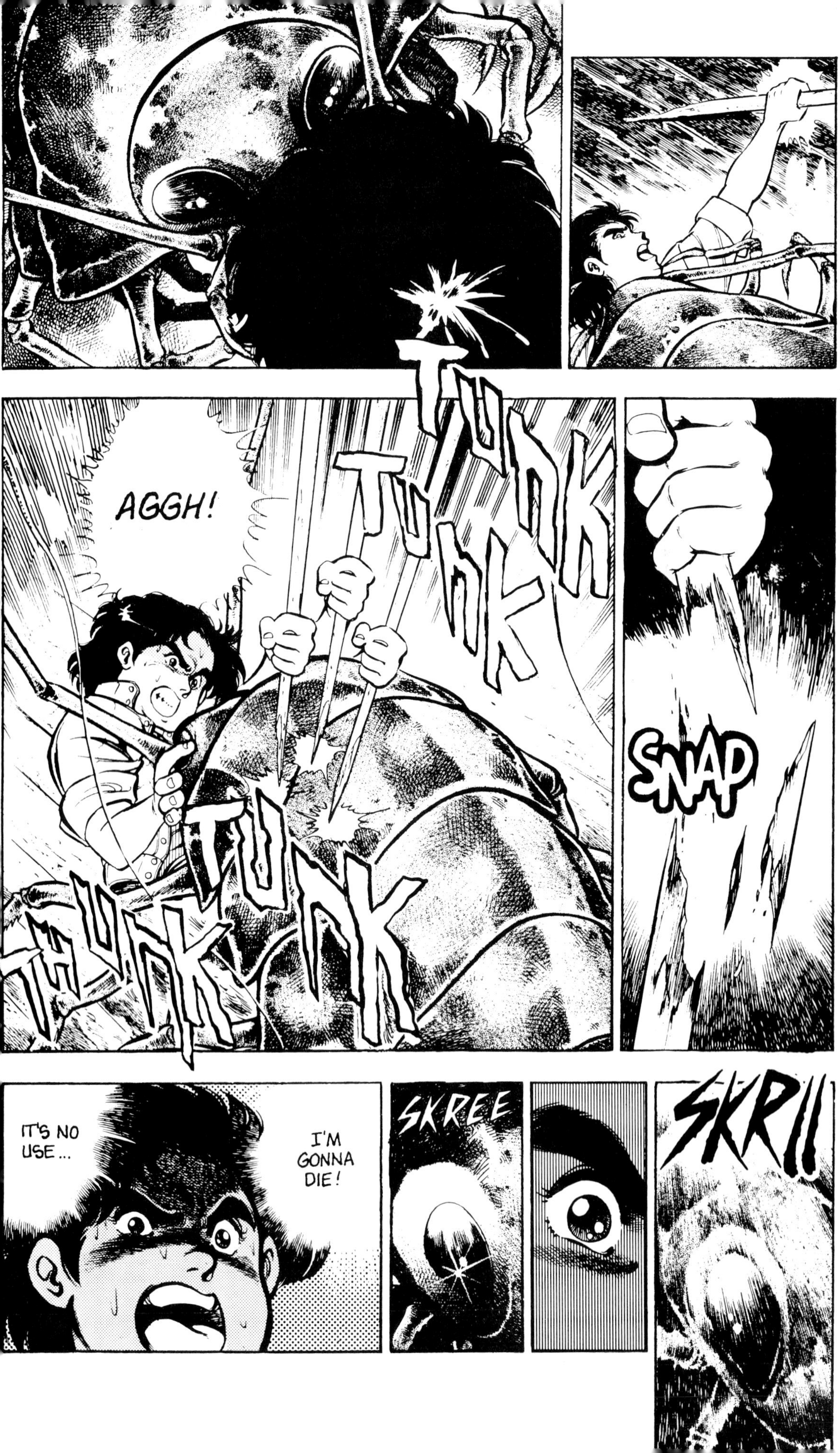

TUNK
TUNK
AGGH!
SNAP
TUNK
THUNK
IT'S NO USE...
I'M GONNA DIE!
SKREE
SKRII

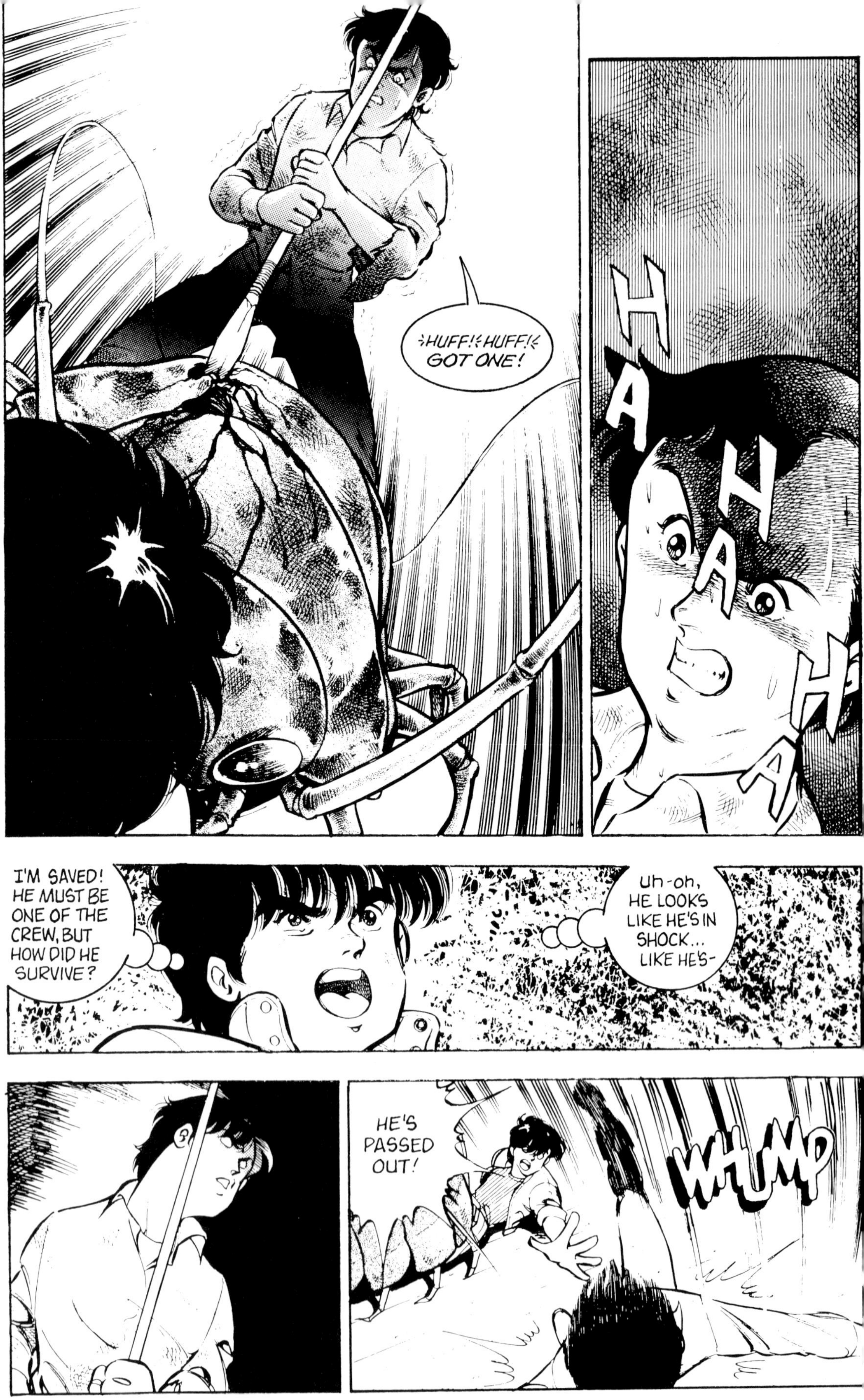
HUFF! HUFF! GOT ONE!
HAHAHAHA
I'M SAVED! HE MUST BE ONE OF THE CREW, BUT HOW DID HE SURVIVE?
Uh-oh, HE LOOKS LIKE HE'S IN SHOCK... LIKE HE'S-
HE'S PASSED OUT!
WHUMP

HEY, BUDDY! WAKE UP! YOU ALL RIGHT?

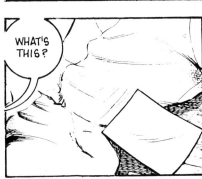

WHAT'S THIS?

A PHOTOGRAPH...

WELL, WHOEVER YOU ARE, I'LL SEE THAT YOU GET BACK TO YOUR FAMILY AND FRIENDS. YOU SAVED MY LIFE.

I'D BETTER GET US BOTH OFF THIS SHIP BEFORE MORE OF THOSE THINGS --WHATEVER THEY ARE --COME CRAWLING AROUND!

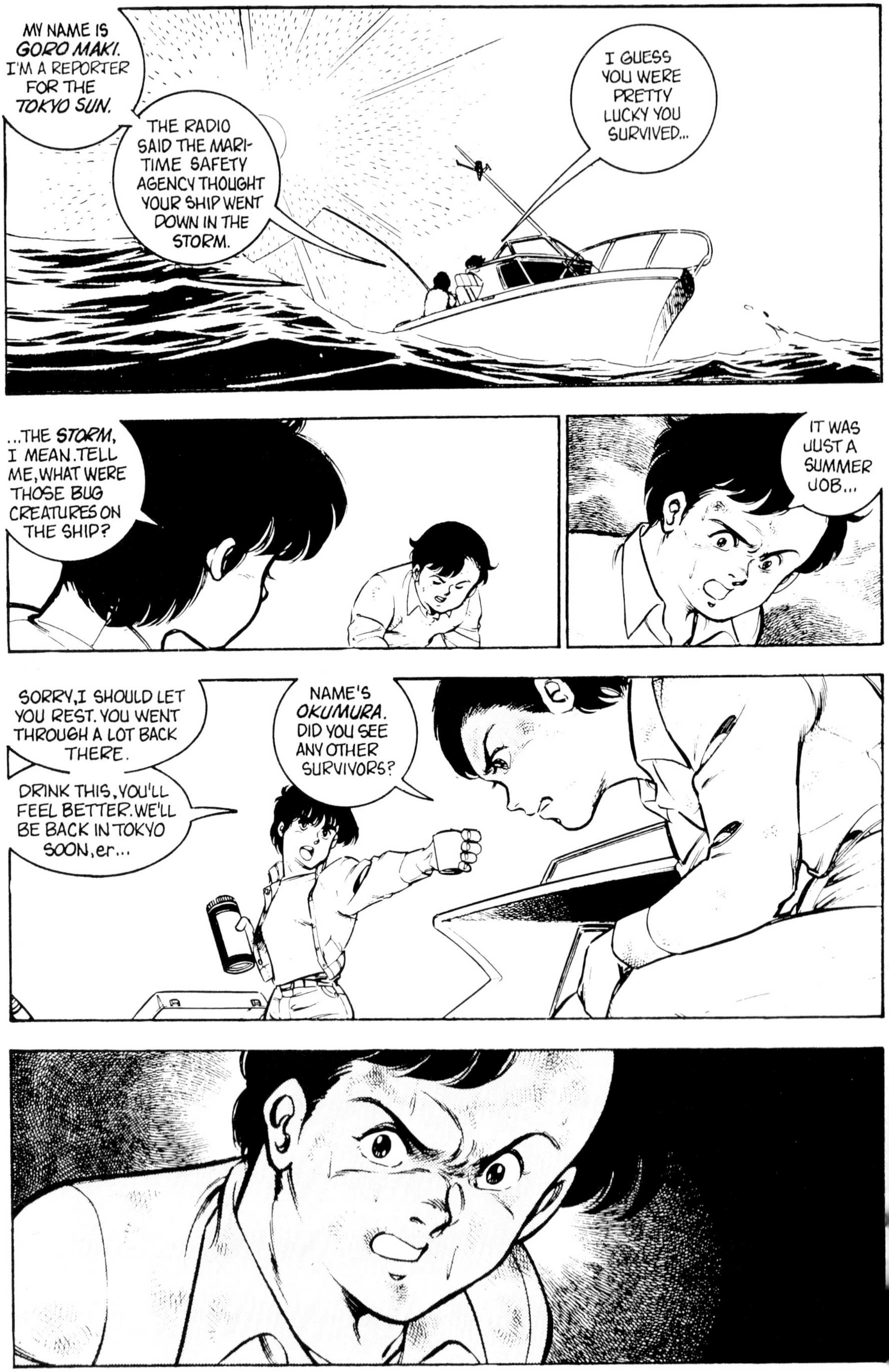
MY NAME IS GORO MAKI. I'M A REPORTER FOR THE TOKYO SUN.
THE RADIO SAID THE MARITIME SAFETY AGENCY THOUGHT YOUR SHIP WENT DOWN IN THE STORM.
I GUESS YOU WERE PRETTY LUCKY YOU SURVIVED...
...THE STORM, I MEAN. TELL ME, WHAT WERE THOSE BUG CREATURES ON THE SHIP?
IT WAS JUST A SUMMER JOB...
SORRY, I SHOULD LET YOU REST. YOU WENT THROUGH A LOT BACK THERE.
DRINK THIS, YOU'LL FEEL BETTER. WE'LL BE BACK IN TOKYO SOON, er...
NAME'S OKUMURA. DID YOU SEE ANY OTHER SURVIVORS?

UH, LOOK, OKUMURA, WHEN WE GET BACK THE AUTHORITIES ARE GOING TO HAVE QUESTIONS...

YOU KNOW, ABOUT THE SHIPWRECK-

SHIPWRECK! THERE WAS NO SHIPWRECK.

IT WAS A MONSTER!

A MONSTER!?

IT CAME OUT OF THE SEA—LIKE A LIVING MOUNTAIN!

ARE YOU TALKING ABOUT THOSE BUGS THAT ATTACKED ME?

NO, NOT THE BUGS-- IT WAS A MONSTER! GIGANTIC! BIGGER THAN THE SHIP!

IT BREATHED BLUE FIRE...ITS ROAR WAS LOUDER THAN THE STORM ...WE THOUGHT IT WAS THE END OF THE WORLD!

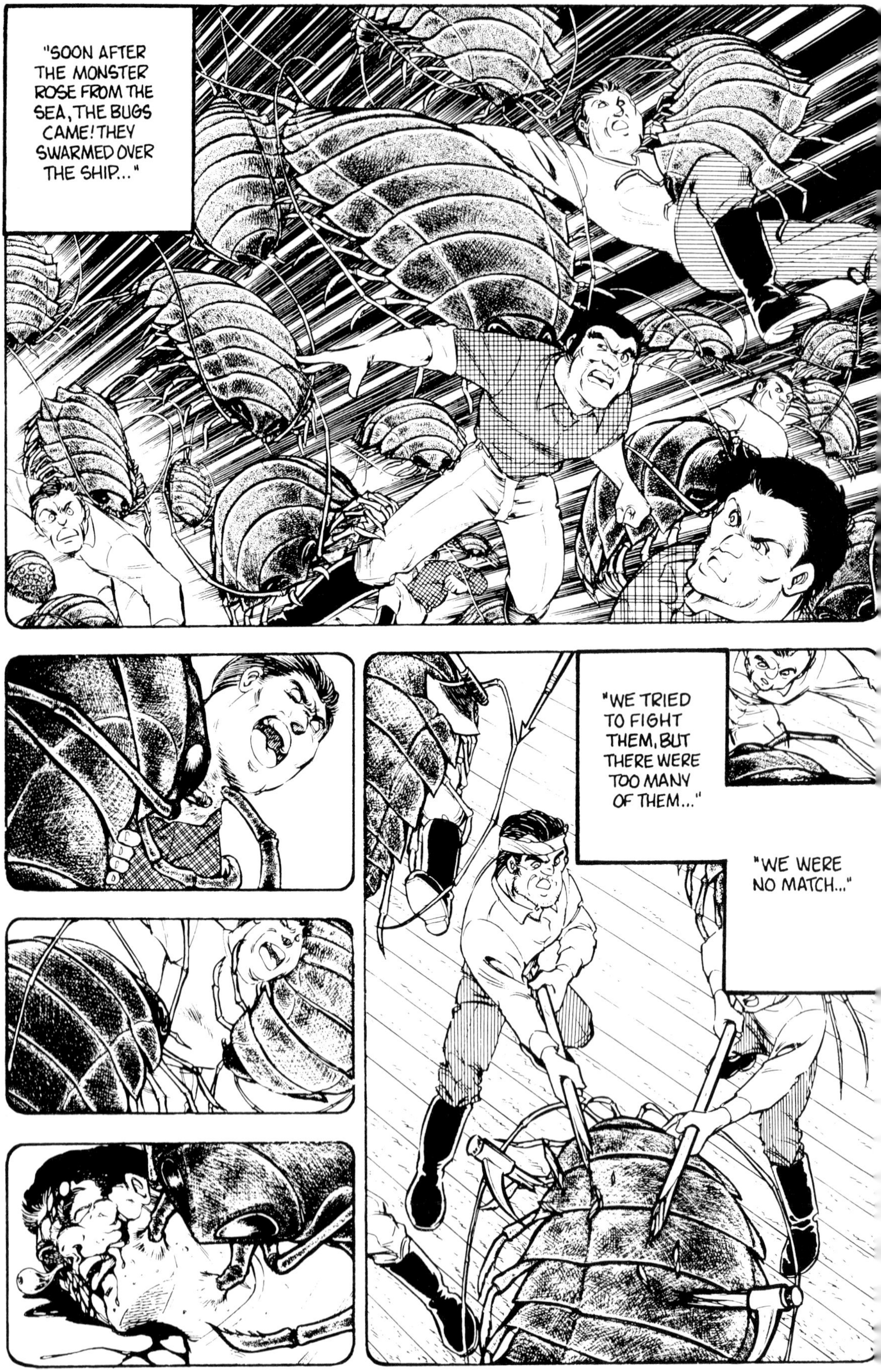
"SOON AFTER THE MONSTER ROSE FROM THE SEA, THE BUGS CAME! THEY SWARMED OVER THE SHIP..."
"WE TRIED TO FIGHT THEM, BUT THERE WERE TOO MANY OF THEM..."
"WE WERE NO MATCH..."

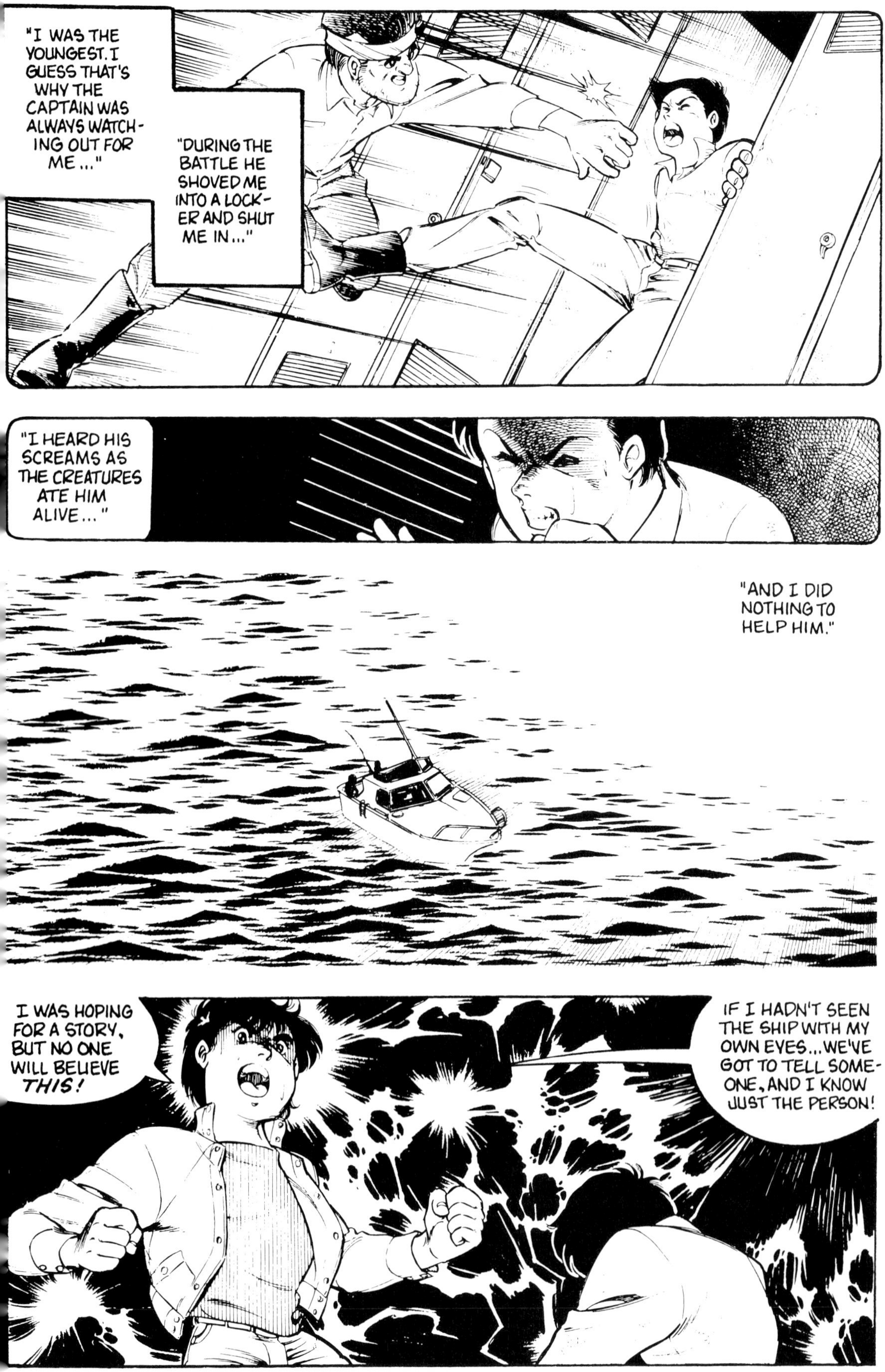
"I WAS THE YOUNGEST. I GUESS THAT'S WHY THE CAPTAIN WAS ALWAYS WATCHING OUT FOR ME..."
"DURING THE BATTLE HE SHOVED ME INTO A LOCKER AND SHUT ME IN..."
"I HEARD HIS SCREAMS AS THE CREATURES ATE HIM ALIVE..."
"AND I DID NOTHING TO HELP HIM."
I WAS HOPING FOR A STORY, BUT NO ONE WILL BELIEVE *THIS!*
IF I HADN'T SEEN THE SHIP WITH MY OWN EYES... WE'VE GOT TO TELL SOMEONE, AND I KNOW JUST THE PERSON!

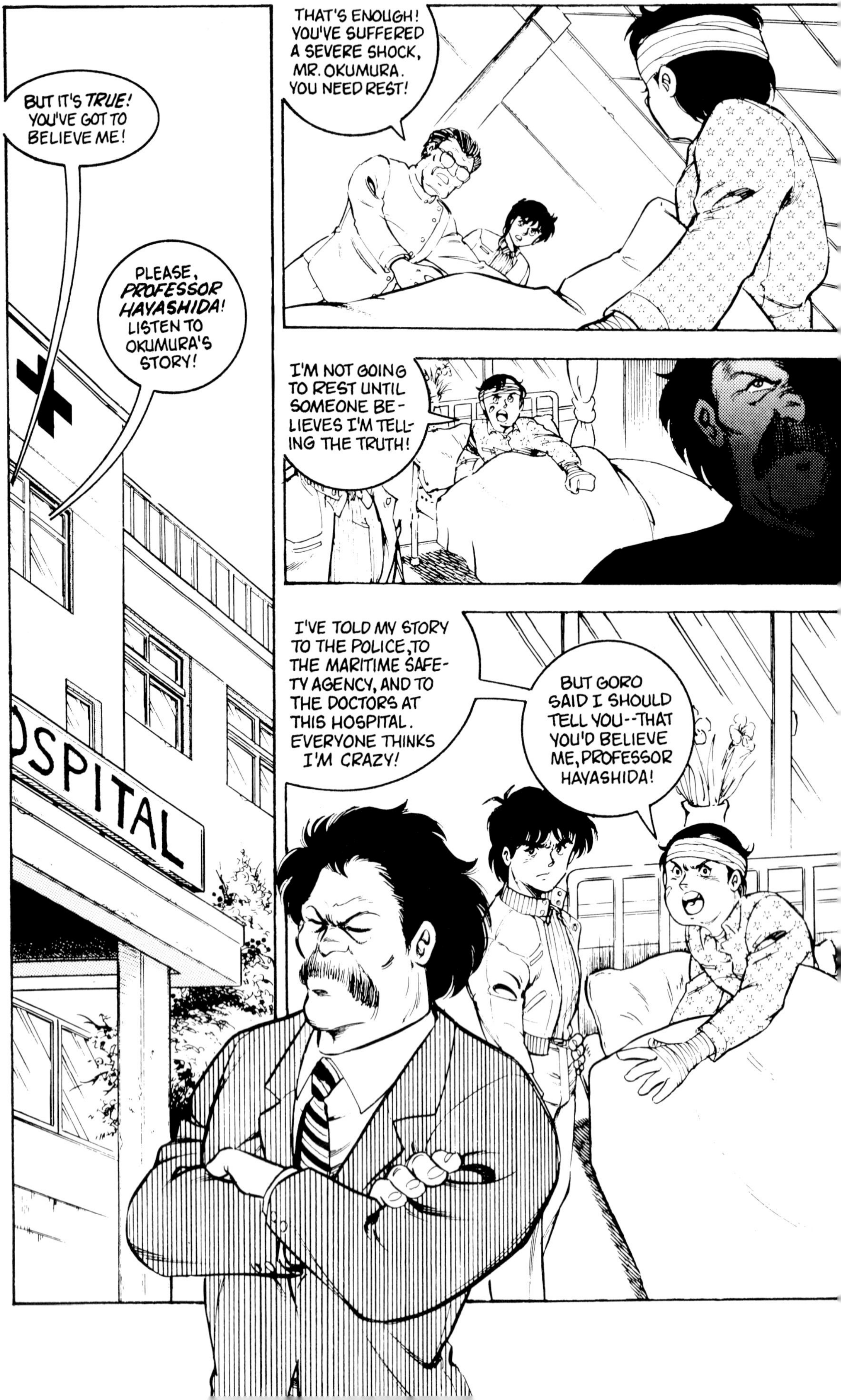
BUT IT'S TRUE! YOU'VE GOT TO BELIEVE ME!
PLEASE, PROFESSOR HAYASHIDA! LISTEN TO OKUMURA'S STORY!
THAT'S ENOUGH! YOU'VE SUFFERED A SEVERE SHOCK, MR. OKUMURA. YOU NEED REST!
I'M NOT GOING TO REST UNTIL SOMEONE BE-LIEVES I'M TELL-ING THE TRUTH!
I'VE TOLD MY STORY TO THE POLICE, TO THE MARITIME SAFE-TY AGENCY, AND TO THE DOCTORS AT THIS HOSPITAL. EVERYONE THINKS I'M CRAZY!
BUT GORO SAID I SHOULD TELL YOU--THAT YOU'D BELIEVE ME, PROFESSOR HAYASHIDA!
HOSPITAL

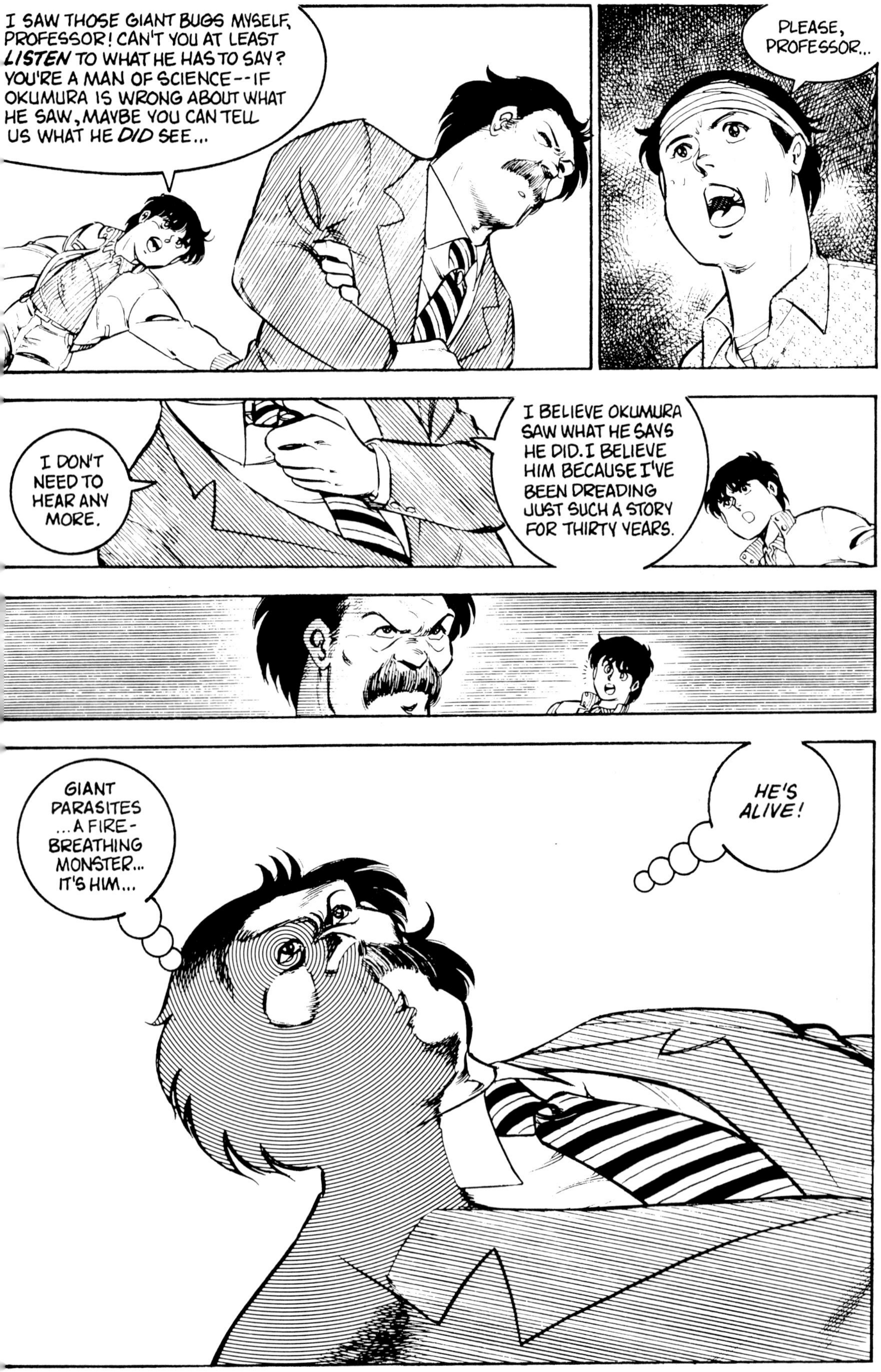
I SAW THOSE GIANT BUGS MYSELF, PROFESSOR! CAN'T YOU AT LEAST LISTEN TO WHAT HE HAS TO SAY? YOU'RE A MAN OF SCIENCE--IF OKUMURA IS WRONG ABOUT WHAT HE SAW, MAYBE YOU CAN TELL US WHAT HE DID SEE...
PLEASE, PROFESSOR...
I DON'T NEED TO HEAR ANY MORE.
I BELIEVE OKUMURA SAW WHAT HE SAYS HE DID. I BELIEVE HIM BECAUSE I'VE BEEN DREADING JUST SUCH A STORY FOR THIRTY YEARS.
GIANT PARASITES ...A FIRE-BREATHING MONSTER... IT'S HIM...
HE'S ALIVE!

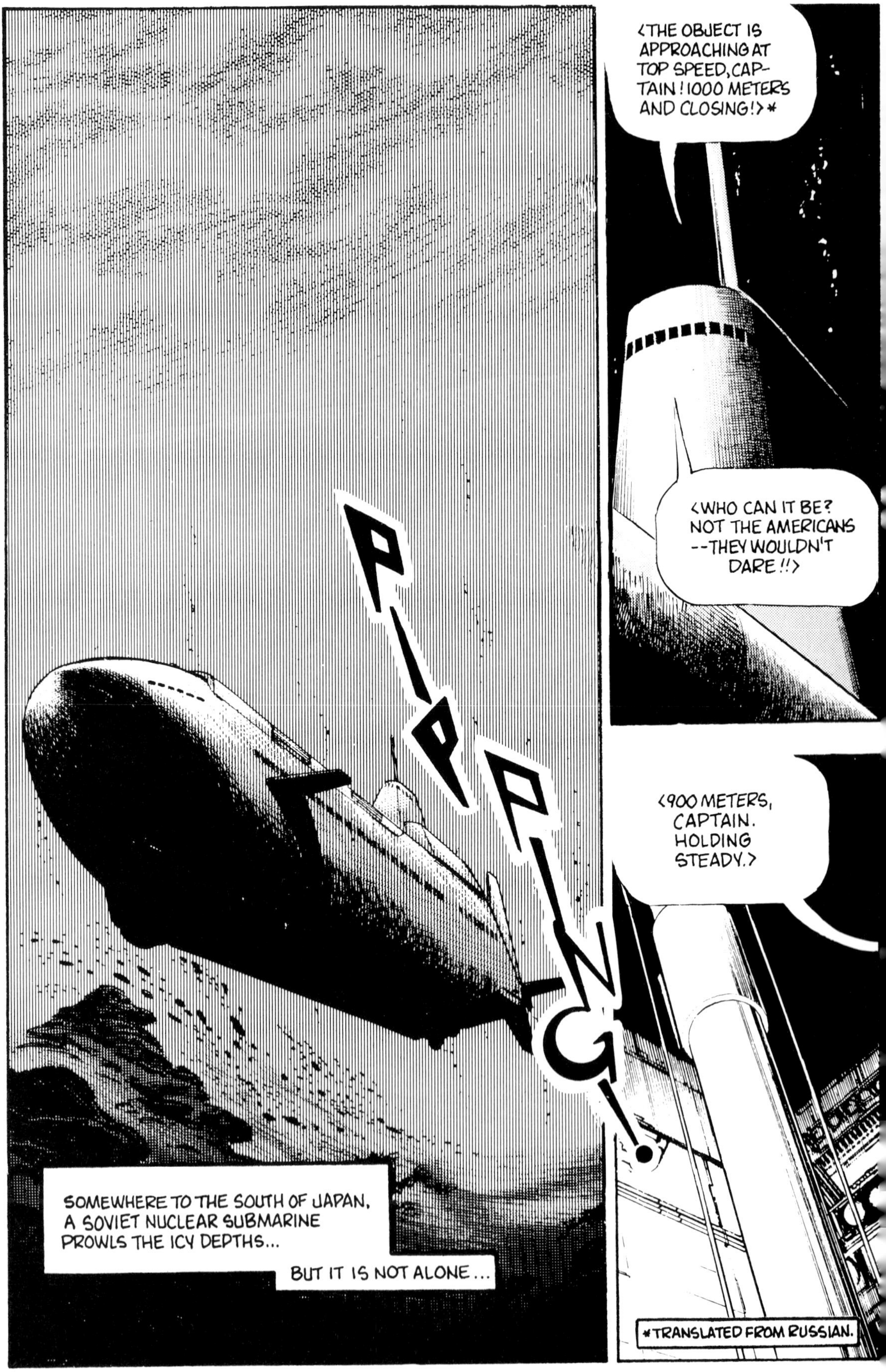
SOMEWHERE TO THE SOUTH OF JAPAN, A SOVIET NUCLEAR SUBMARINE PROWLS THE ICY DEPTHS...
BUT IT IS NOT ALONE...
PIPPING!
<THE OBJECT IS APPROACHING AT TOP SPEED, CAPTAIN! 1000 METERS AND CLOSING!>*
<WHO CAN IT BE? NOT THE AMERICANS --THEY WOULDN'T DARE!!>
<900 METERS, CAPTAIN. HOLDING STEADY.>
*TRANSLATED FROM RUSSIAN.

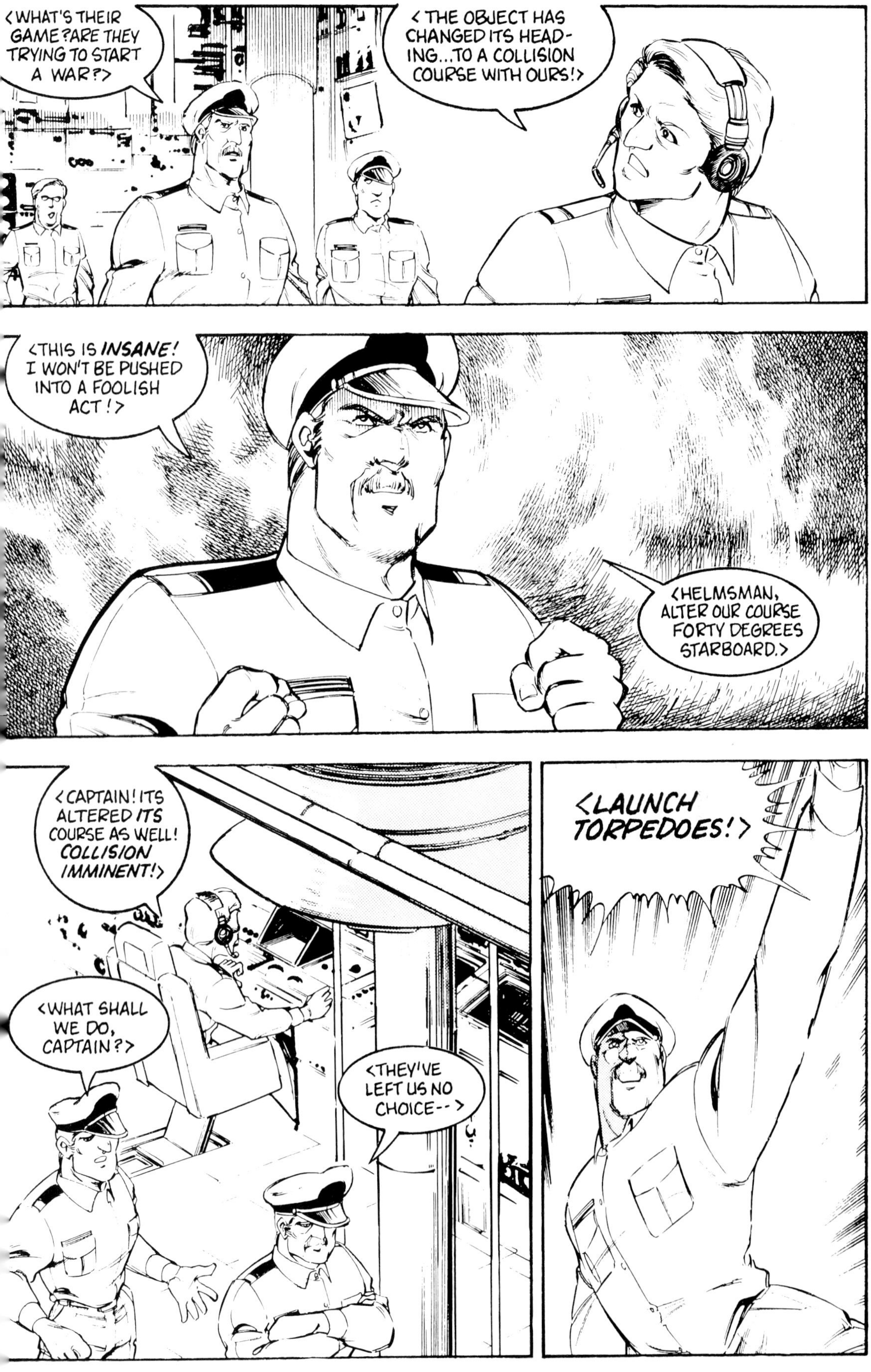
<WHAT'S THEIR GAME?ARE THEY TRYING TO START A WAR?>
<THE OBJECT HAS CHANGED ITS HEAD-ING...TO A COLLISION COURSE WITH OURS!>
<THIS IS INSANE! I WON'T BE PUSHED INTO A FOOLISH ACT!>
<HELMSMAN, ALTER OUR COURSE FORTY DEGREES STARBOARD.>
<CAPTAIN! ITS ALTERED ITS COURSE AS WELL! COLLISION IMMINENT!>
<WHAT SHALL WE DO, CAPTAIN?>
<THEY'VE LEFT US NO CHOICE-->
<LAUNCH TORPEDOES!>

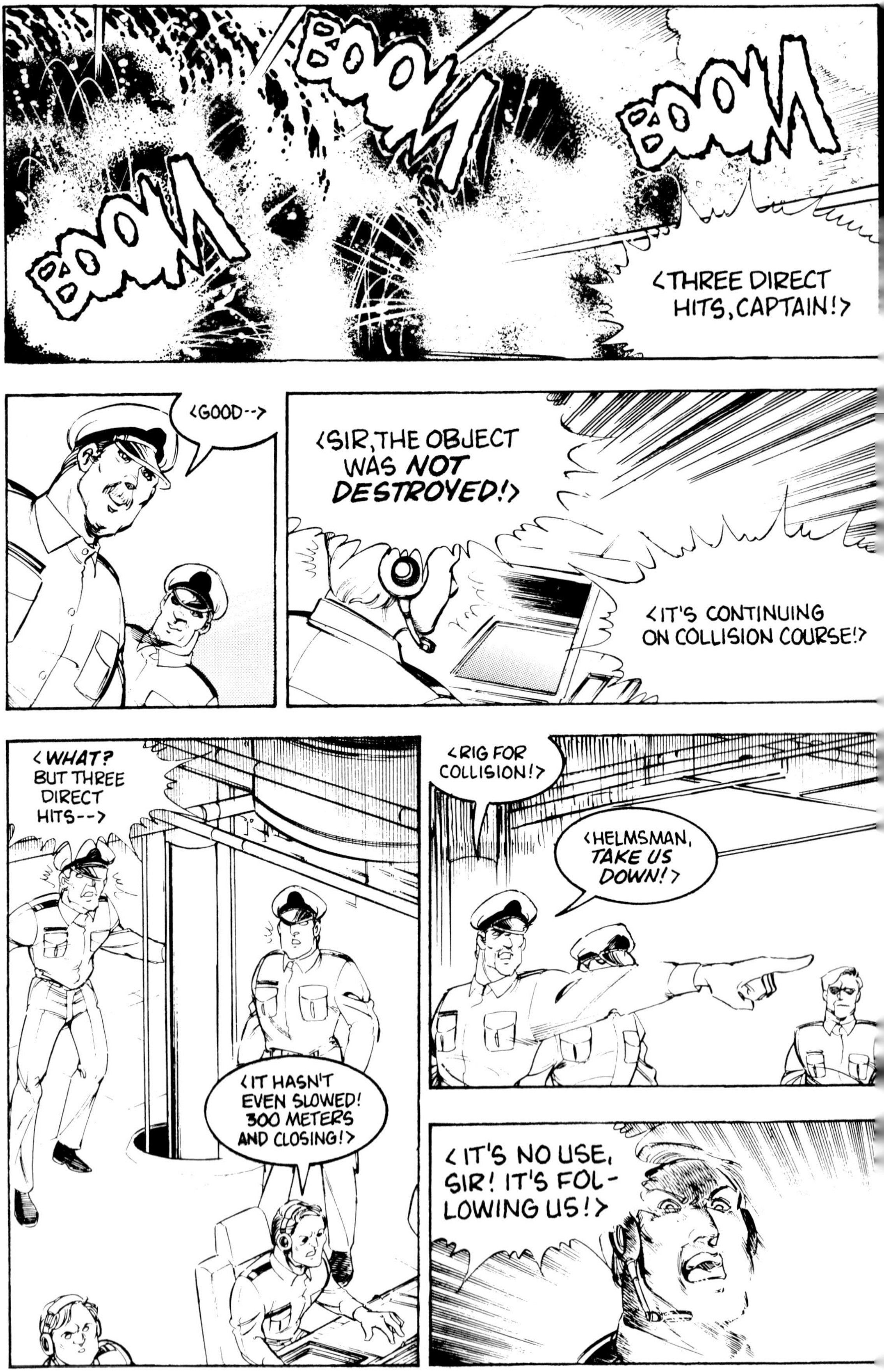
BOOM
BOOM
BOOM
<THREE DIRECT HITS, CAPTAIN!>
<GOOD-->
<SIR, THE OBJECT WAS NOT DESTROYED!>
<IT'S CONTINUING ON COLLISION COURSE!>
<WHAT? BUT THREE DIRECT HITS-->
<IT HASN'T EVEN SLOWED! 300 METERS AND CLOSING!>
<RIG FOR COLLISION!>
<HELMSMAN, TAKE US DOWN!>
<IT'S NO USE, SIR! IT'S FOL-LOWING US!>

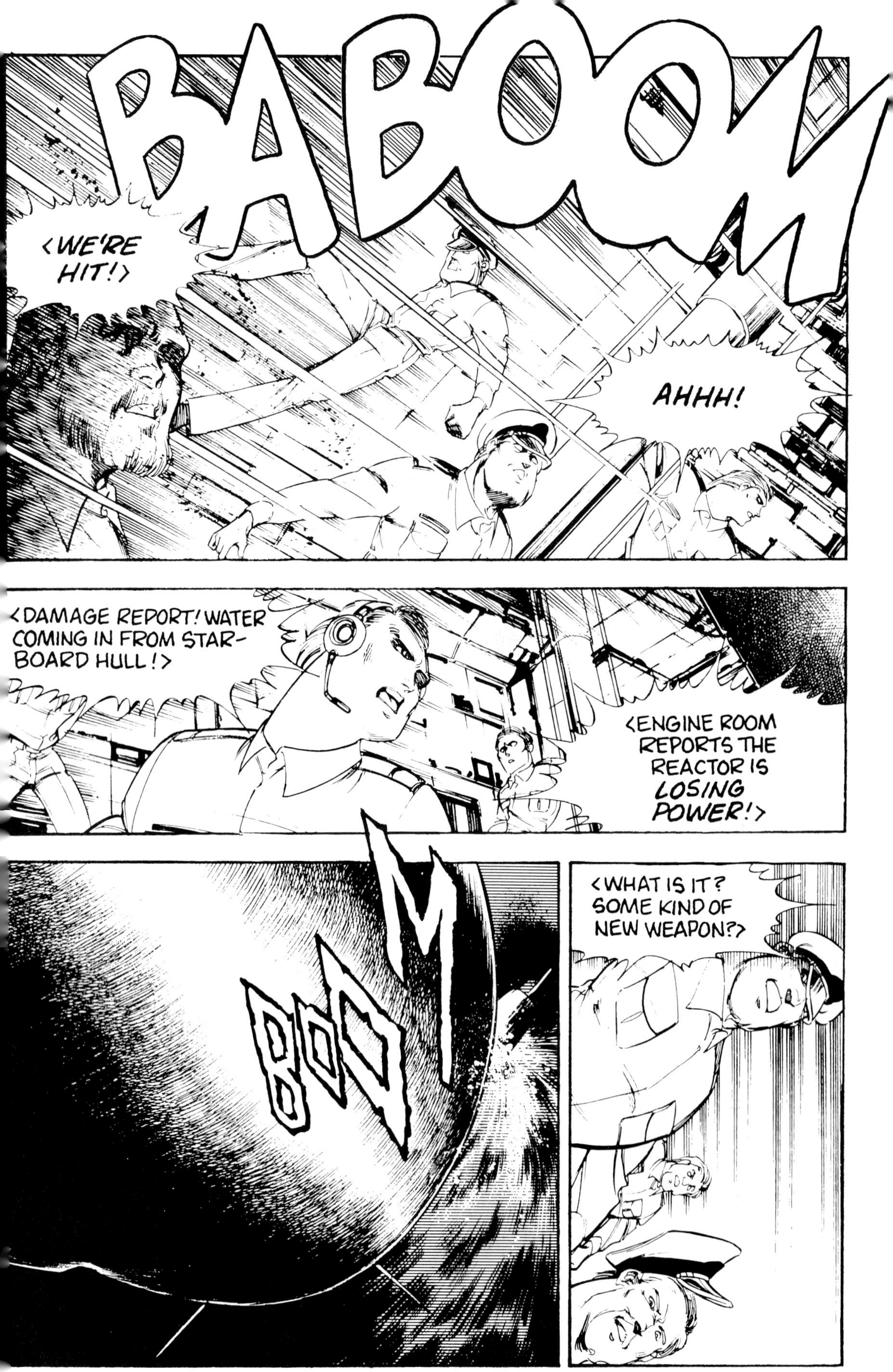
BABOOM
<WE'RE HIT!>
AHHH!
<DAMAGE REPORT! WATER COMING IN FROM STAR-BOARD HULL!>
<ENGINE ROOM REPORTS THE REACTOR IS *LOSING POWER!*>
BOOM
<WHAT IS IT? SOME KIND OF NEW WEAPON?>

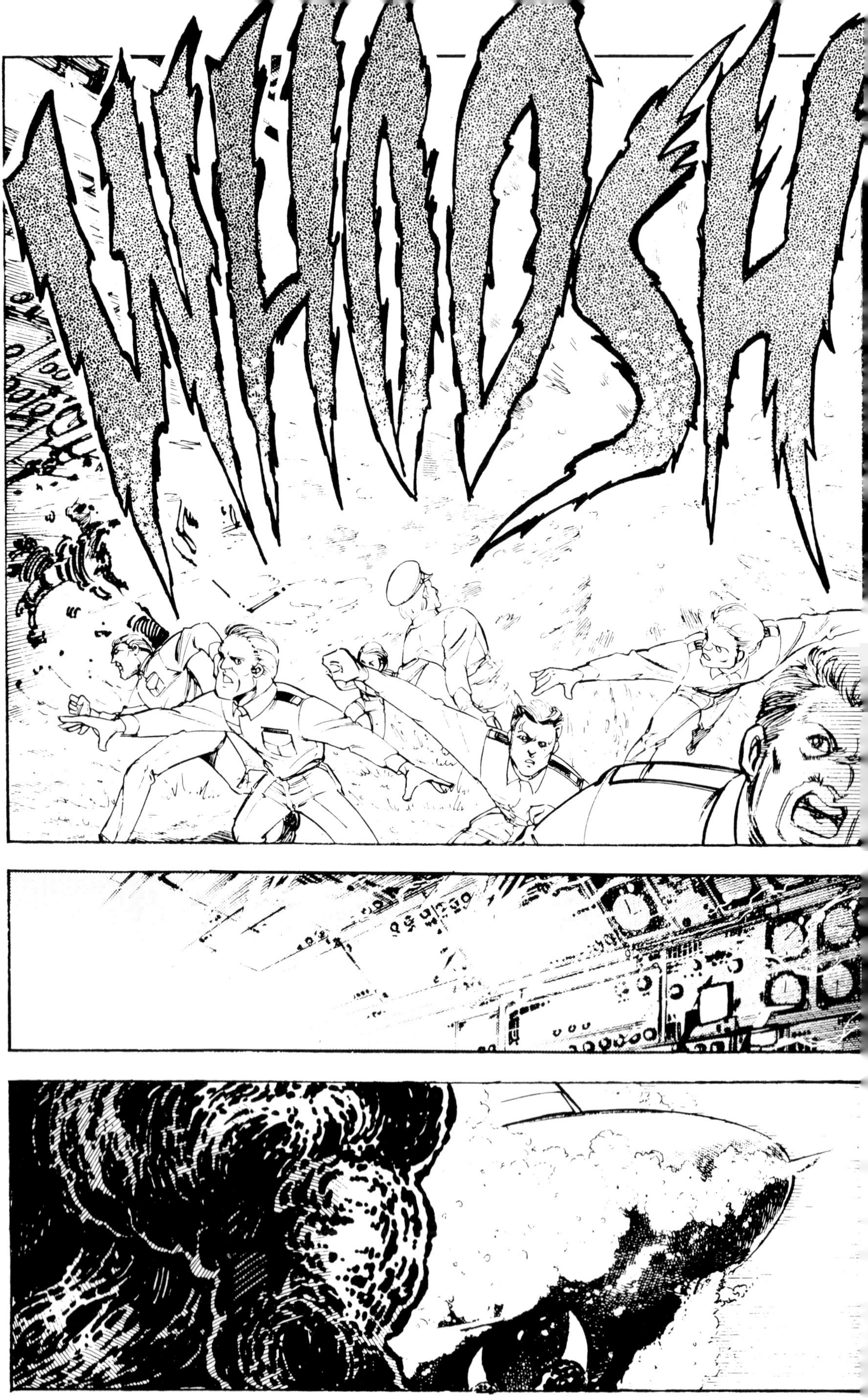
WHOOSH

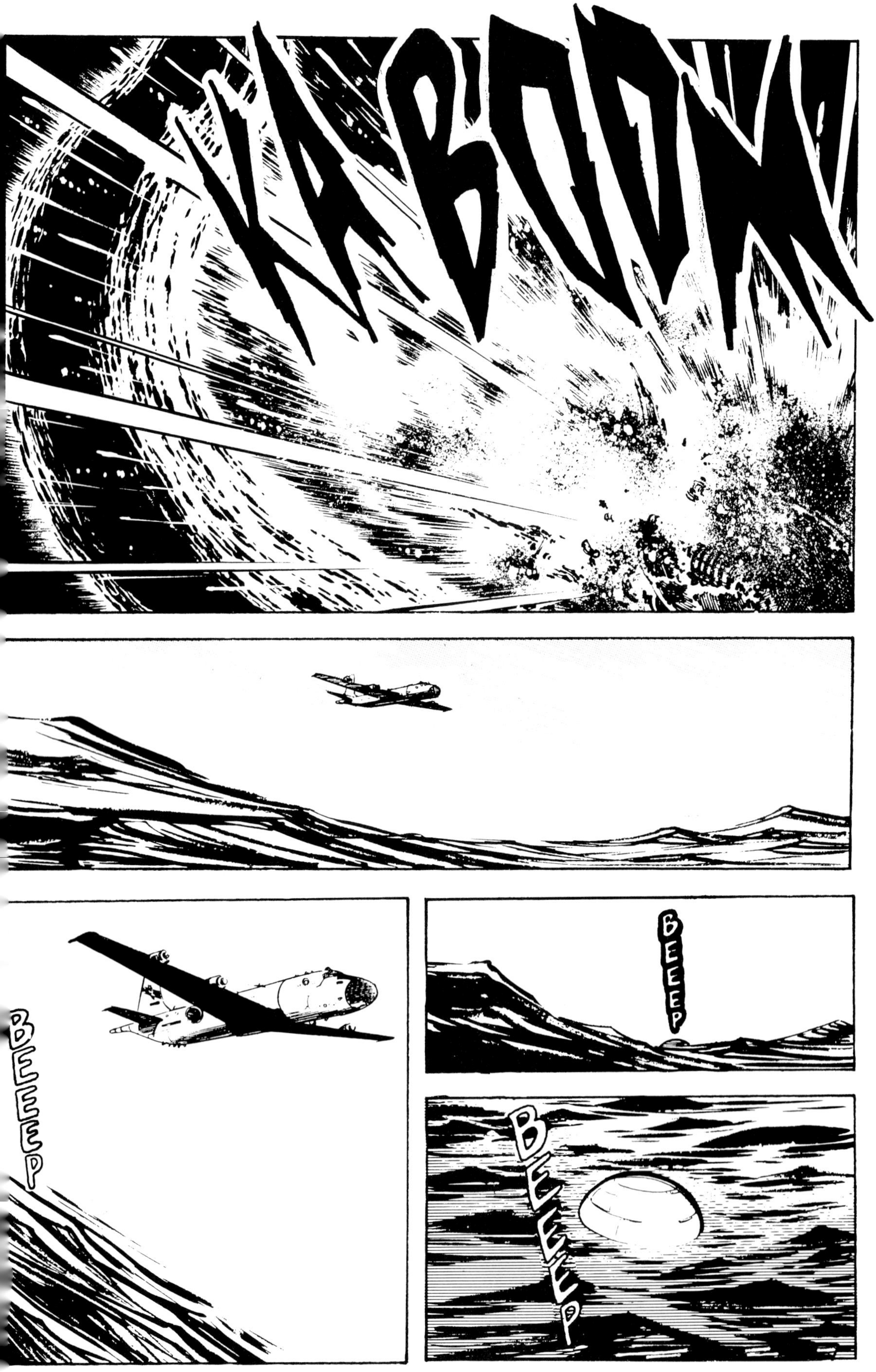
KABOOM
BEEEEP
BEEEP
BEEEEP

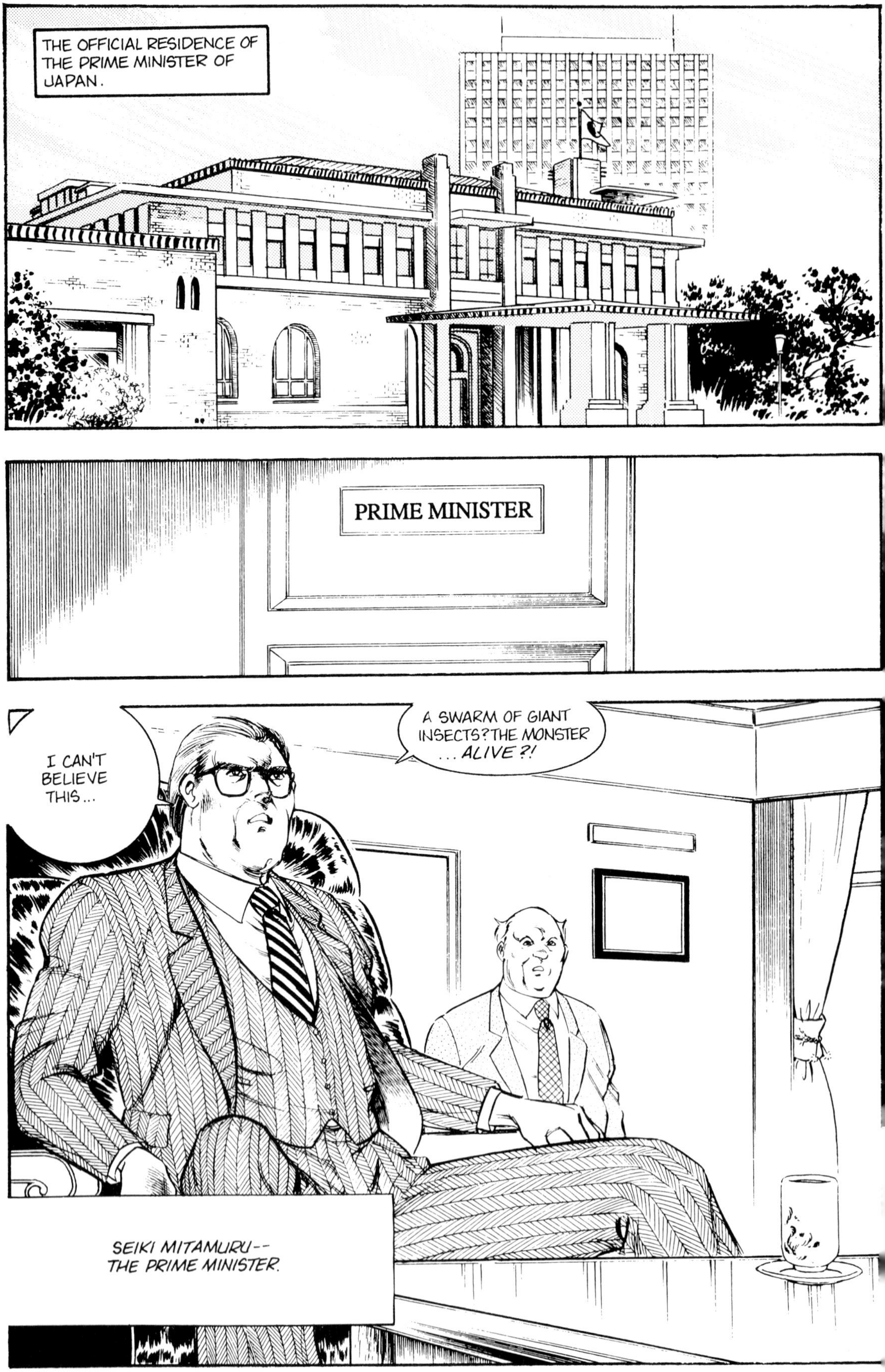
THE OFFICIAL RESIDENCE OF THE PRIME MINISTER OF JAPAN.
PRIME MINISTER
I CAN'T BELIEVE THIS...
A SWARM OF GIANT INSECTS? THE MONSTER ... ALIVE?!
SEIKI MITAMURU-- THE PRIME MINISTER.

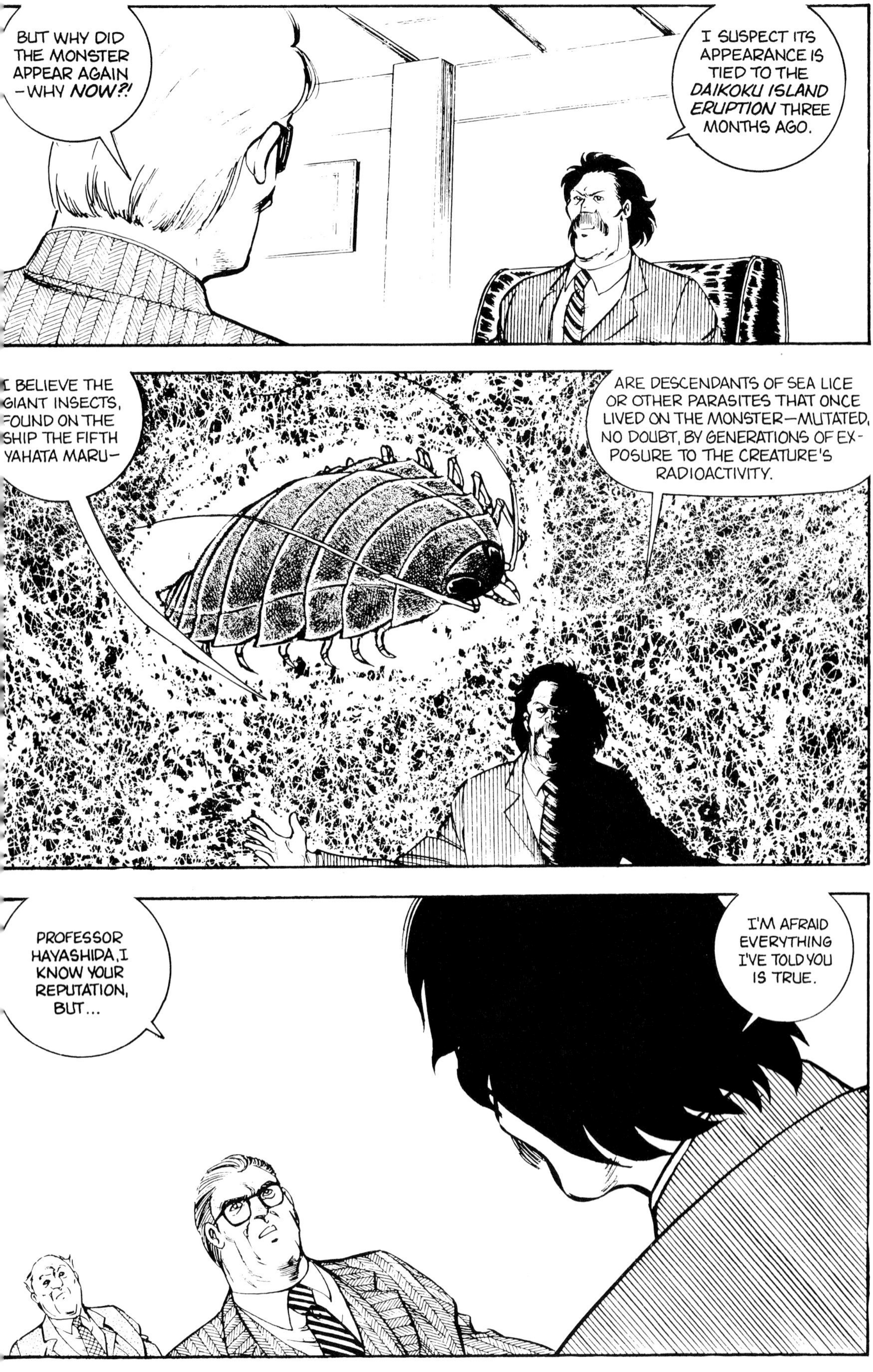
BUT WHY DID THE MONSTER APPEAR AGAIN —WHY NOW?!
I SUSPECT ITS APPEARANCE IS TIED TO THE DAIKOKU ISLAND ERUPTION THREE MONTHS AGO.
I BELIEVE THE GIANT INSECTS, FOUND ON THE SHIP THE FIFTH YAHATA MARU—
ARE DESCENDANTS OF SEA LICE OR OTHER PARASITES THAT ONCE LIVED ON THE MONSTER—MUTATED, NO DOUBT, BY GENERATIONS OF EXPOSURE TO THE CREATURE'S RADIOACTIVITY.
PROFESSOR HAYASHIDA, I KNOW YOUR REPUTATION, BUT...
I'M AFRAID EVERYTHING I'VE TOLD YOU IS TRUE.

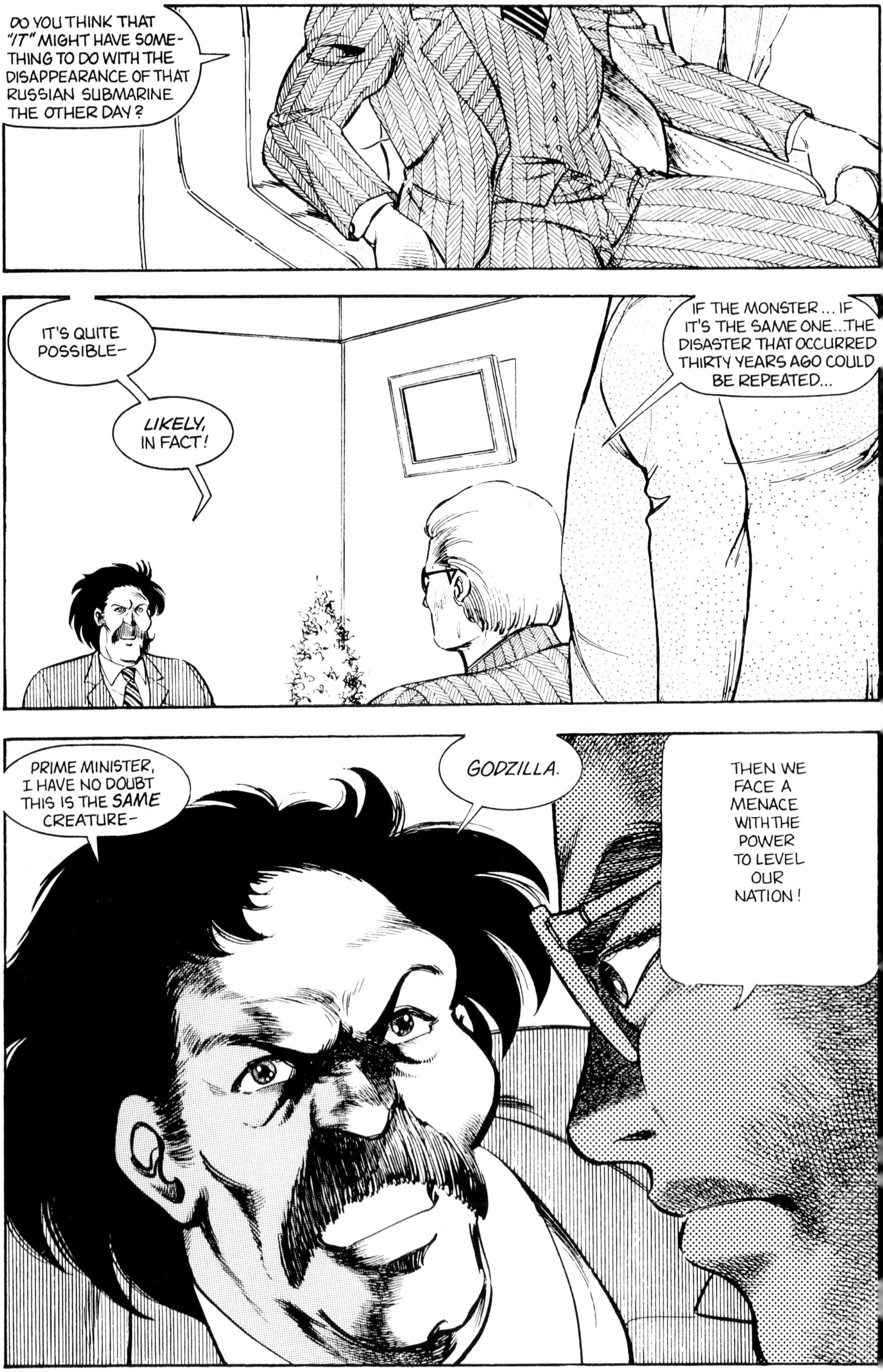
DO YOU THINK THAT "IT" MIGHT HAVE SOMETHING TO DO WITH THE DISAPPEARANCE OF THAT RUSSIAN SUBMARINE THE OTHER DAY?
IT'S QUITE POSSIBLE-
LIKELY, IN FACT!
IF THE MONSTER... IF IT'S THE SAME ONE...THE DISASTER THAT OCCURRED THIRTY YEARS AGO COULD BE REPEATED...
PRIME MINISTER, I HAVE NO DOUBT THIS IS THE SAME CREATURE-
GODZILLA.
THEN WE FACE A MENACE WITH THE POWER TO LEVEL OUR NATION!

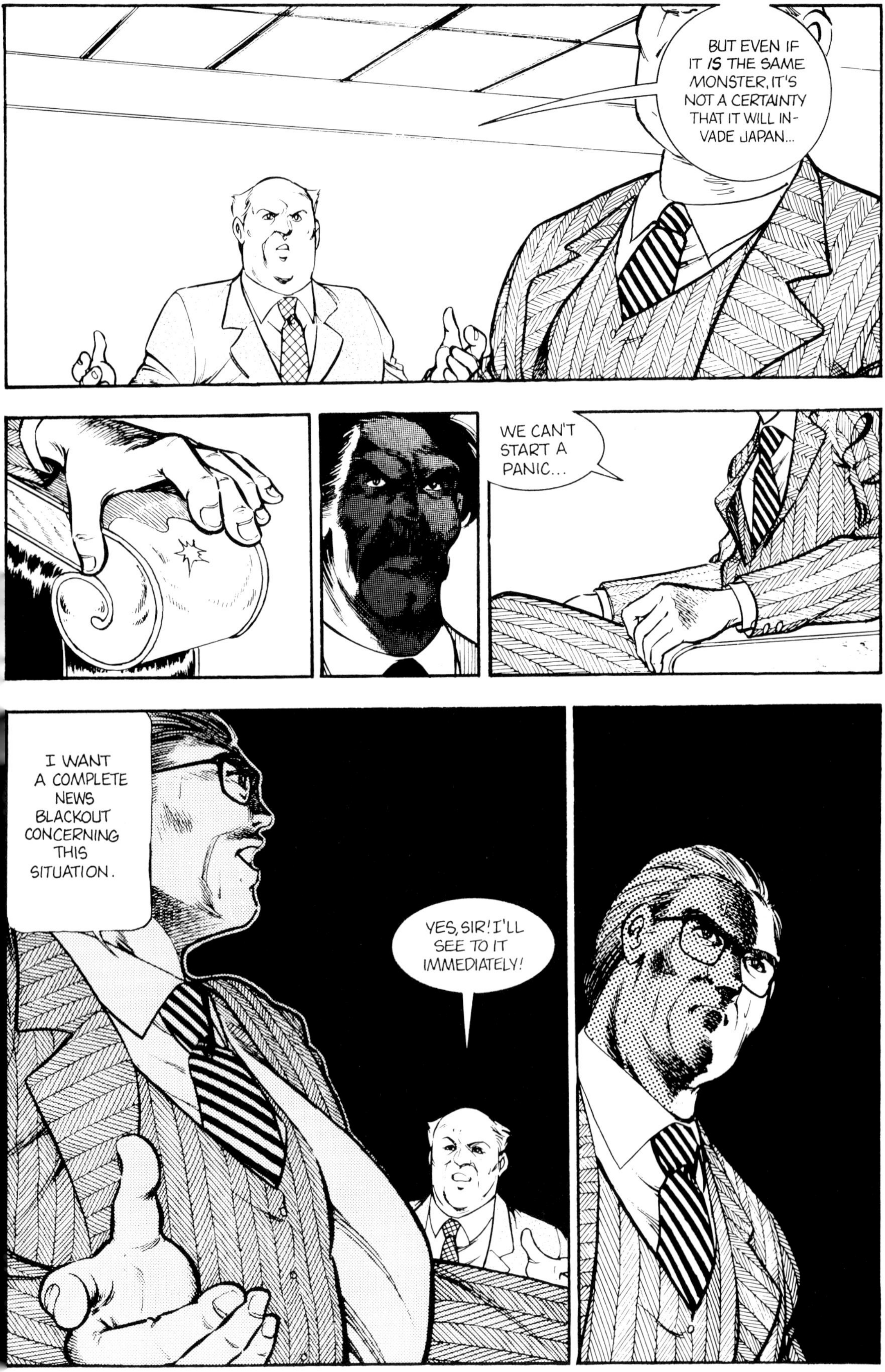
BUT EVEN IF IT IS THE SAME MONSTER, IT'S NOT A CERTAINTY THAT IT WILL IN-VADE JAPAN...
WE CAN'T START A PANIC...
I WANT A COMPLETE NEWS BLACKOUT CONCERNING THIS SITUATION.
YES, SIR! I'LL SEE TO IT IMMEDIATELY!

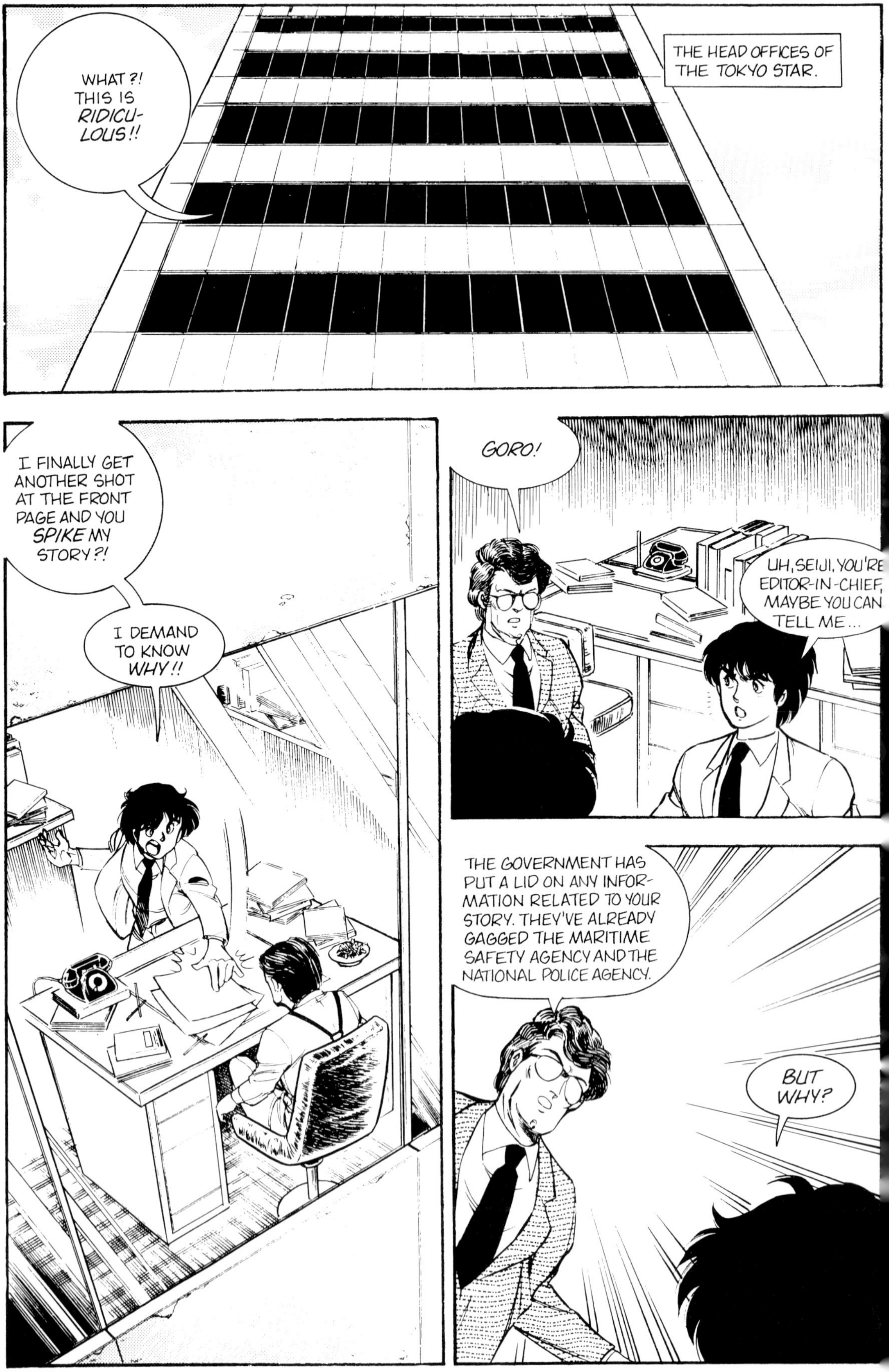
THE HEAD OFFICES OF THE TOKYO STAR.
WHAT?! THIS IS RIDICULOUS!!
I FINALLY GET ANOTHER SHOT AT THE FRONT PAGE AND YOU SPIKE MY STORY?!
I DEMAND TO KNOW WHY!!
GORO!
UH, SEIJI, YOU'RE EDITOR-IN-CHIEF, MAYBE YOU CAN TELL ME...
THE GOVERNMENT HAS PUT A LID ON ANY INFORMATION RELATED TO YOUR STORY. THEY'VE ALREADY GAGGED THE MARITIME SAFETY AGENCY AND THE NATIONAL POLICE AGENCY.
BUT WHY?

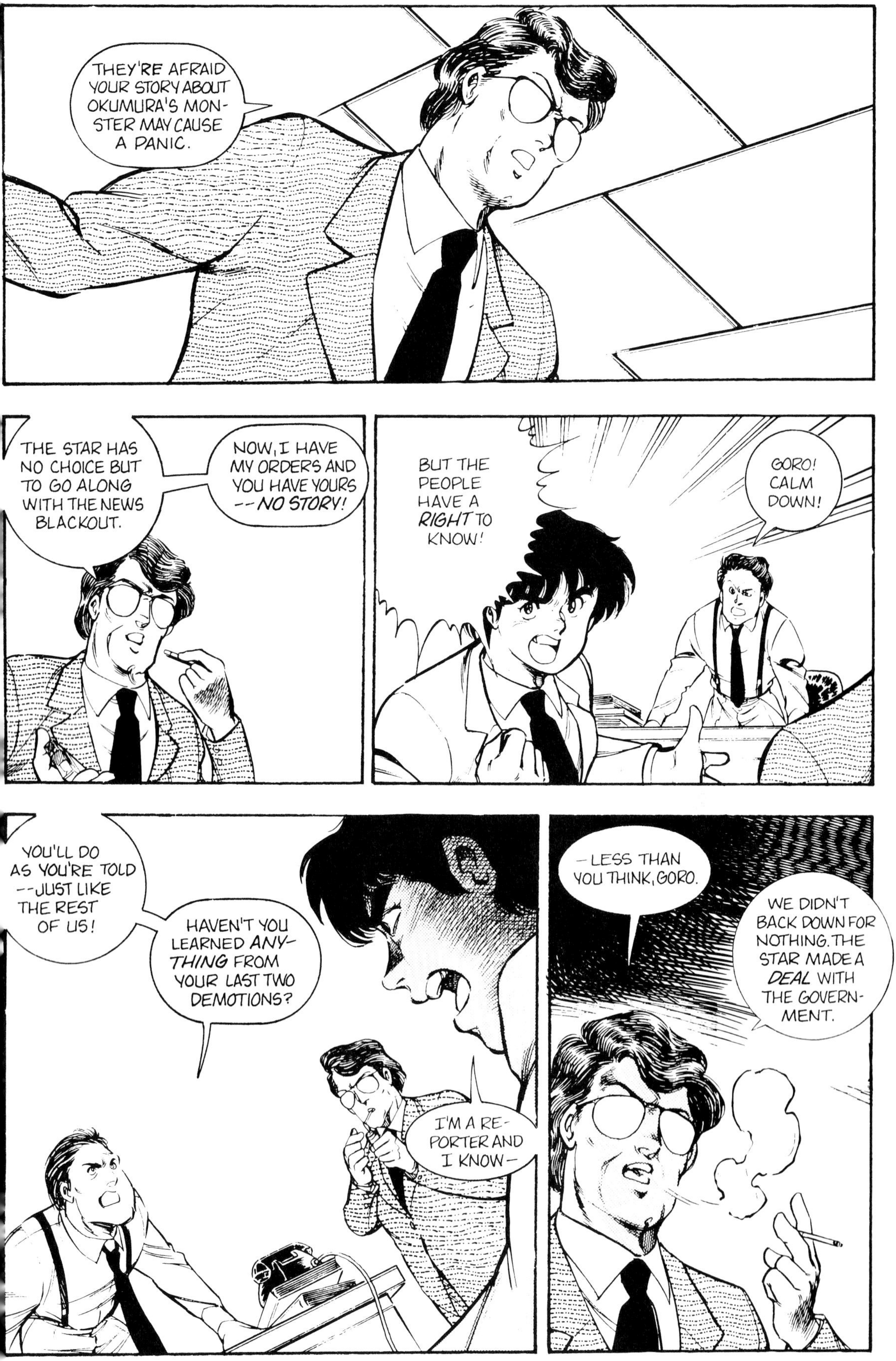

THEY'RE AFRAID YOUR STORY ABOUT OKUMURA'S MONSTER MAY CAUSE A PANIC.
THE STAR HAS NO CHOICE BUT TO GO ALONG WITH THE NEWS BLACKOUT.
NOW, I HAVE MY ORDERS AND YOU HAVE YOURS --*NO STORY!*
BUT THE PEOPLE HAVE A *RIGHT* TO KNOW!
GORO! CALM DOWN!
YOU'LL DO AS YOU'RE TOLD --JUST LIKE THE REST OF US!
HAVEN'T YOU LEARNED *ANYTHING* FROM YOUR LAST TWO DEMOTIONS?
I'M A REPORTER AND I KNOW—
—LESS THAN YOU THINK, GORO.
WE DIDN'T BACK DOWN FOR NOTHING. THE STAR MADE A *DEAL* WITH THE GOVERNMENT.

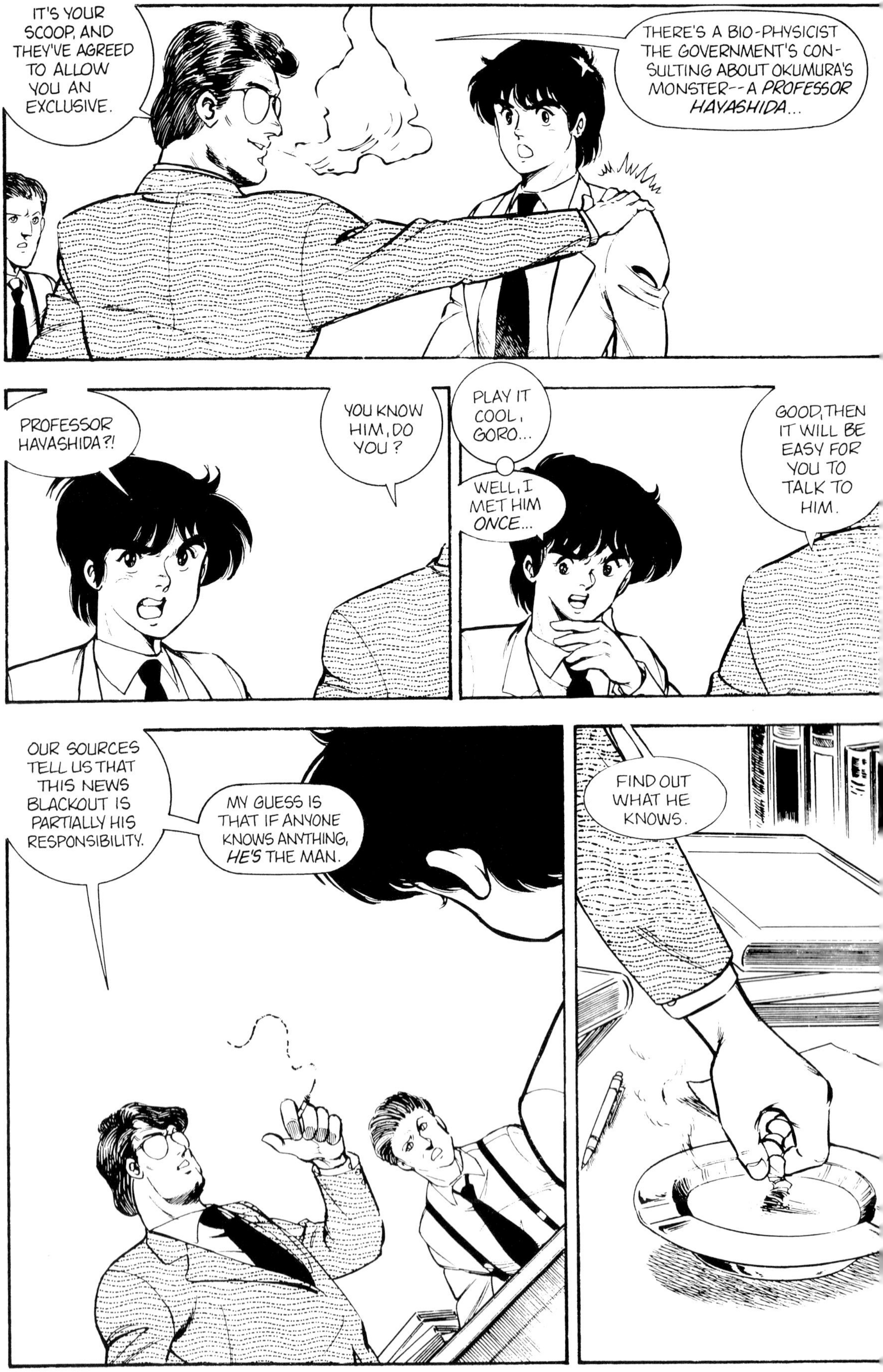
IT'S YOUR SCOOP, AND THEY'VE AGREED TO ALLOW YOU AN EXCLUSIVE.
THERE'S A BIO-PHYSICIST THE GOVERNMENT'S CON-SULTING ABOUT OKUMURA'S MONSTER--A *PROFESSOR HAYASHIDA*...
PROFESSOR HAYASHIDA?!
YOU KNOW HIM, DO YOU?
PLAY IT COOL, GORO...
WELL, I MET HIM *ONCE*...
GOOD, THEN IT WILL BE EASY FOR YOU TO TALK TO HIM.
OUR SOURCES TELL US THAT THIS NEWS BLACKOUT IS PARTIALLY HIS RESPONSIBILITY.
MY GUESS IS THAT IF ANYONE KNOWS ANYTHING, *HE'S* THE MAN.
FIND OUT WHAT HE KNOWS.

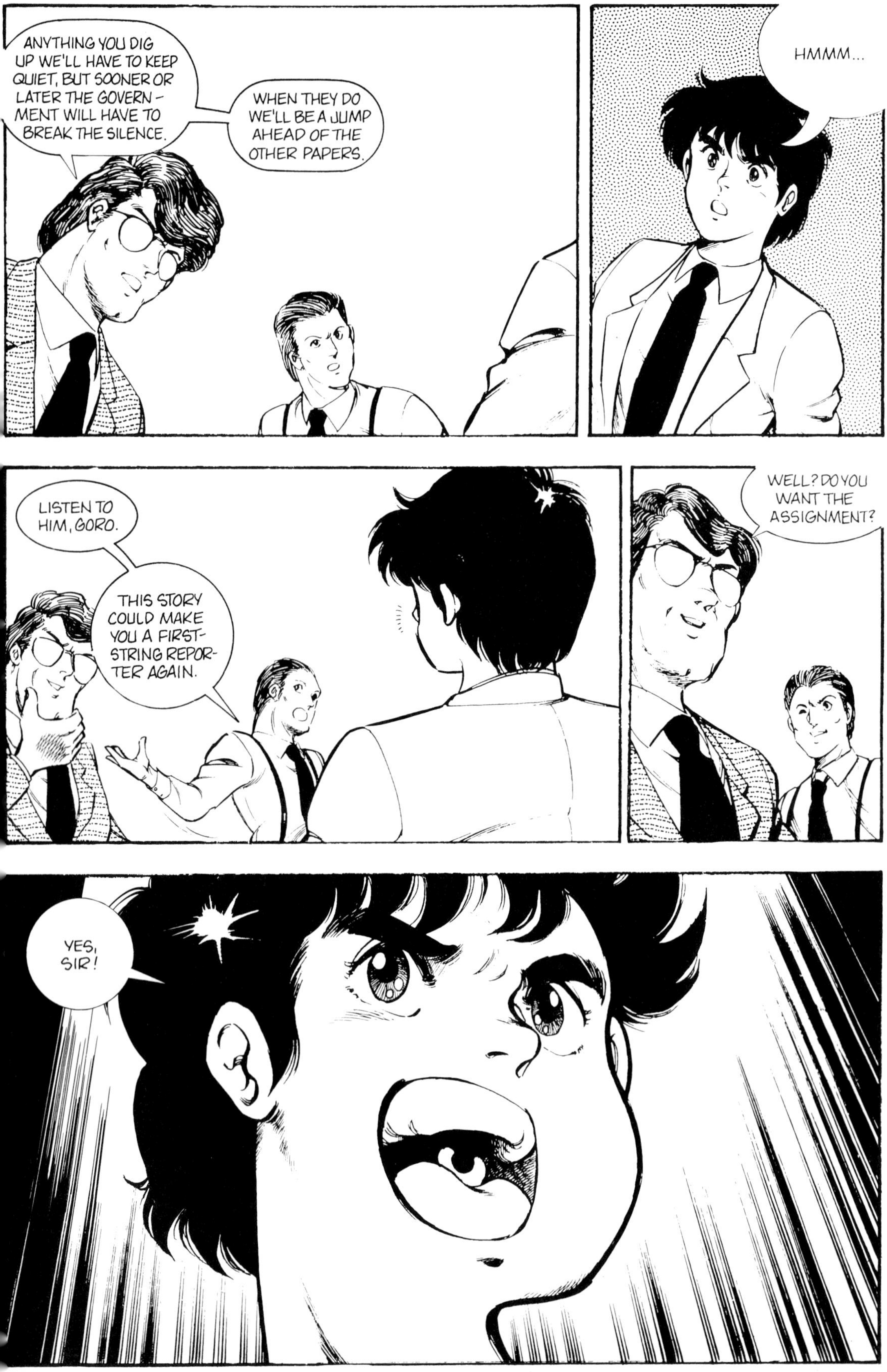
ANYTHING YOU DIG UP WE'LL HAVE TO KEEP QUIET, BUT SOONER OR LATER THE GOVERN-MENT WILL HAVE TO BREAK THE SILENCE.
WHEN THEY DO WE'LL BE A JUMP AHEAD OF THE OTHER PAPERS.
HMMM...
LISTEN TO HIM, GORO.
THIS STORY COULD MAKE YOU A FIRST-STRING REPORTER AGAIN.
WELL? DO YOU WANT THE ASSIGNMENT?
YES, SIR!

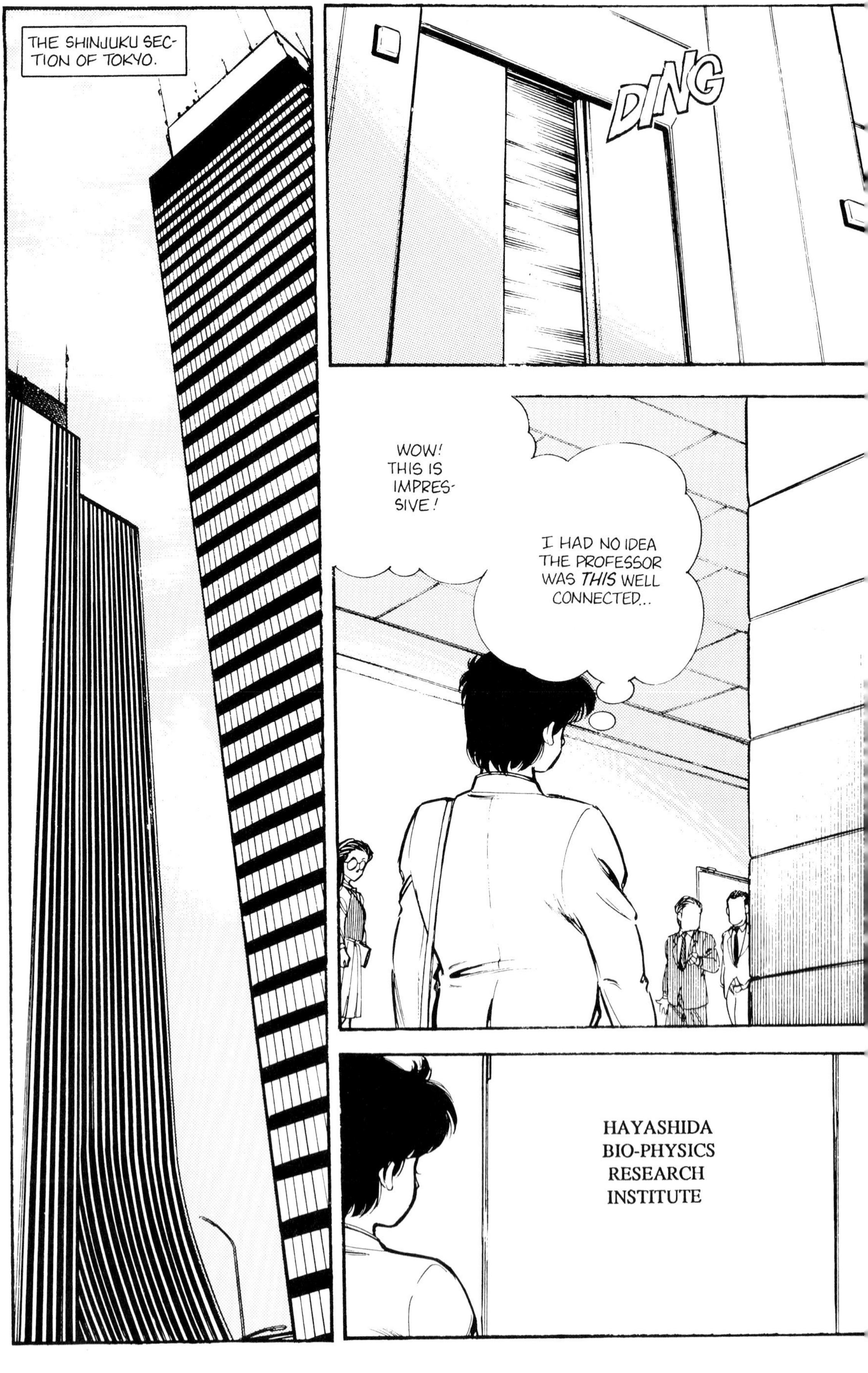
THE SHINJUKU SECTION OF TOKYO.
DING
WOW! THIS IS IMPRESSIVE!
I HAD NO IDEA THE PROFESSOR WAS THIS WELL CONNECTED...
HAYASHIDA BIO-PHYSICS RESEARCH INSTITUTE

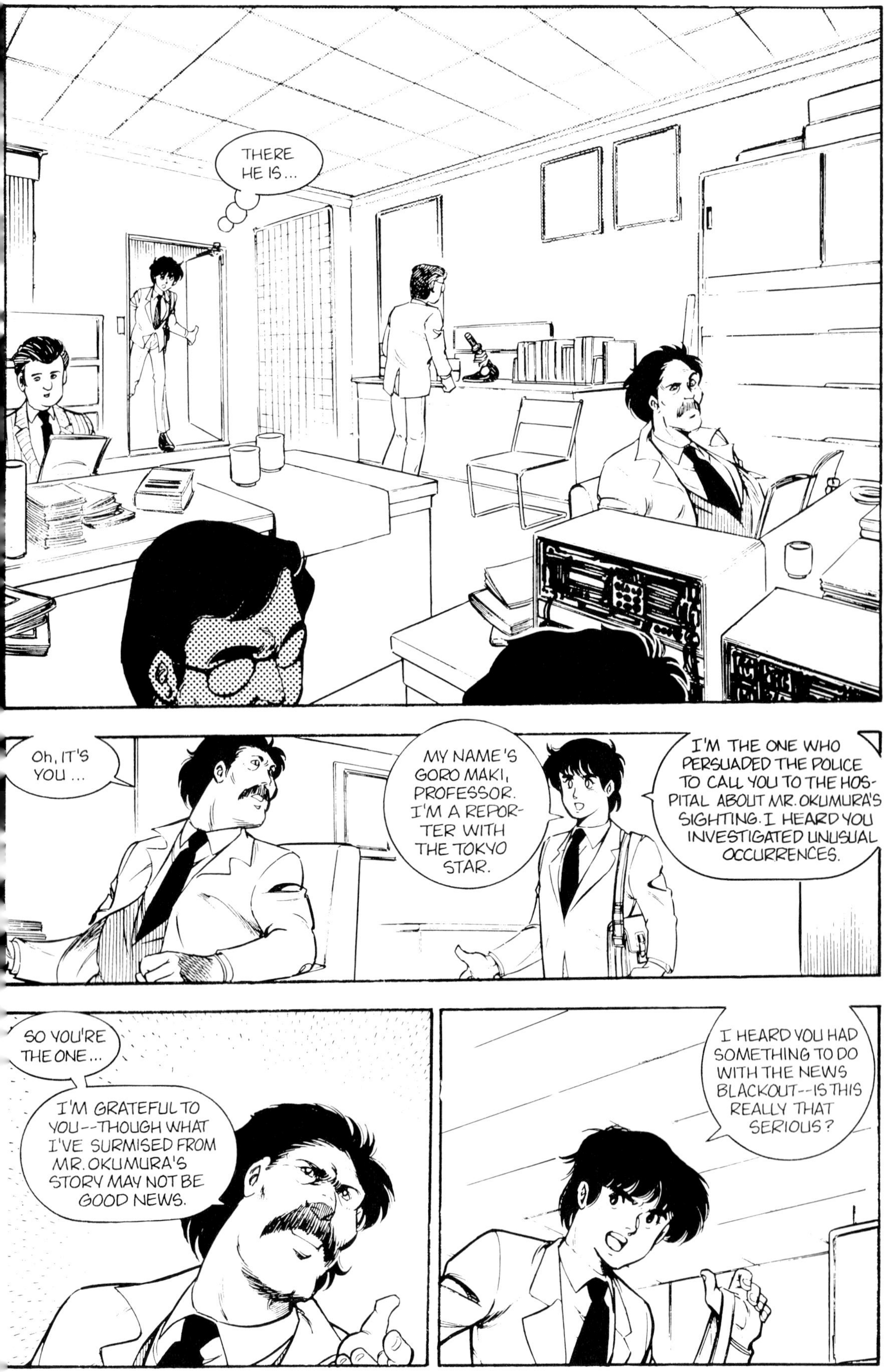
THERE HE IS...
Oh, IT'S YOU...
MY NAME'S GORO MAKI, PROFESSOR. I'M A REPORTER WITH THE TOKYO STAR.
I'M THE ONE WHO PERSUADED THE POLICE TO CALL YOU TO THE HOSPITAL ABOUT MR. OKUMURA'S SIGHTING. I HEARD YOU INVESTIGATED UNUSUAL OCCURRENCES.
SO YOU'RE THE ONE...
I'M GRATEFUL TO YOU--THOUGH WHAT I'VE SURMISED FROM MR. OKUMURA'S STORY MAY NOT BE GOOD NEWS.
I HEARD YOU HAD SOMETHING TO DO WITH THE NEWS BLACKOUT--IS THIS REALLY THAT SERIOUS?

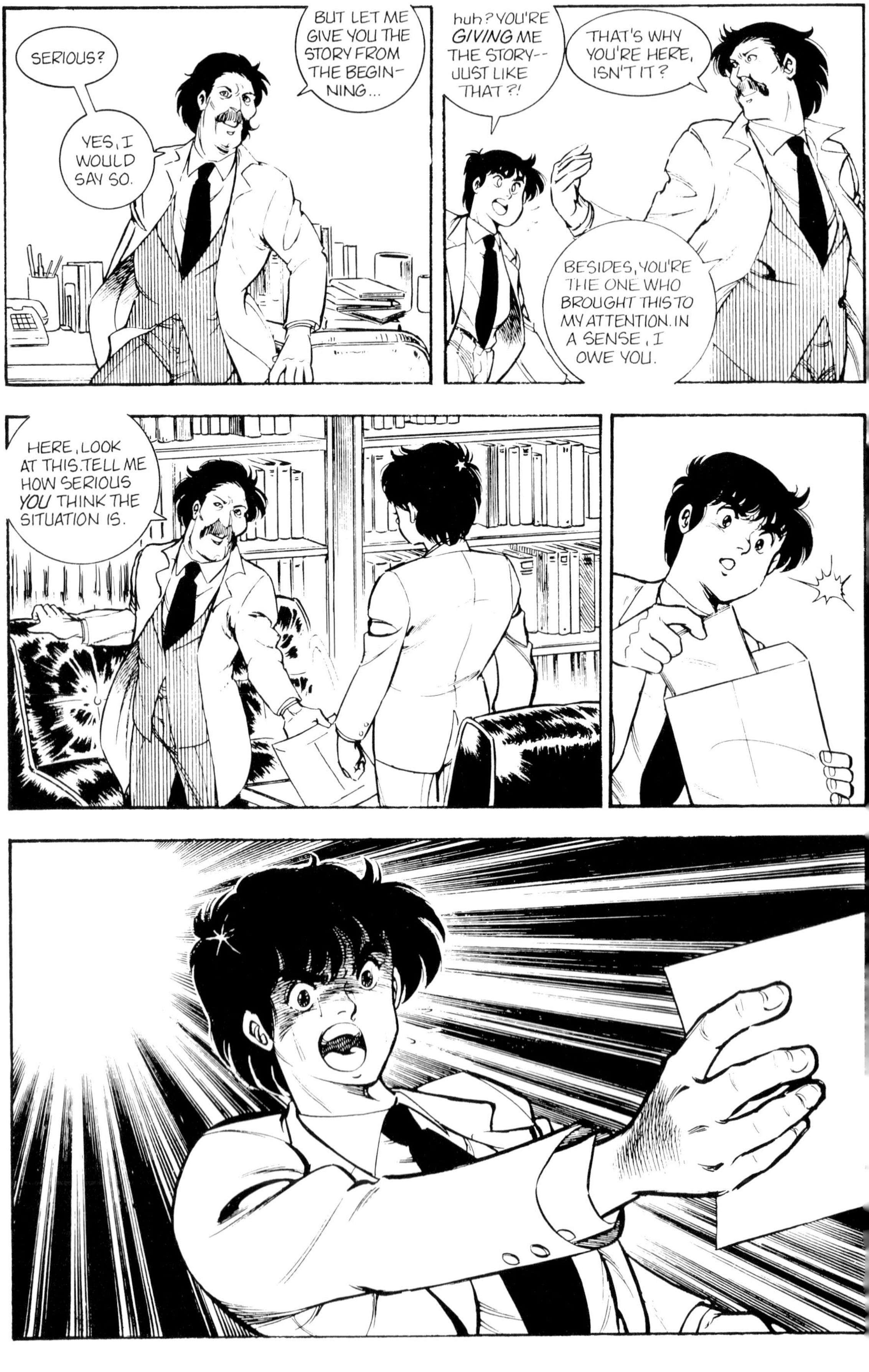
SERIOUS?
YES, I WOULD SAY SO.
BUT LET ME GIVE YOU THE STORY FROM THE BEGIN-NING...
huh? YOU'RE GIVING ME THE STORY-- JUST LIKE THAT?!
THAT'S WHY YOU'RE HERE, ISN'T IT?
BESIDES, YOU'RE THE ONE WHO BROUGHT THIS TO MY ATTENTION. IN A SENSE, I OWE YOU.
HERE, LOOK AT THIS. TELL ME HOW SERIOUS YOU THINK THE SITUATION IS.

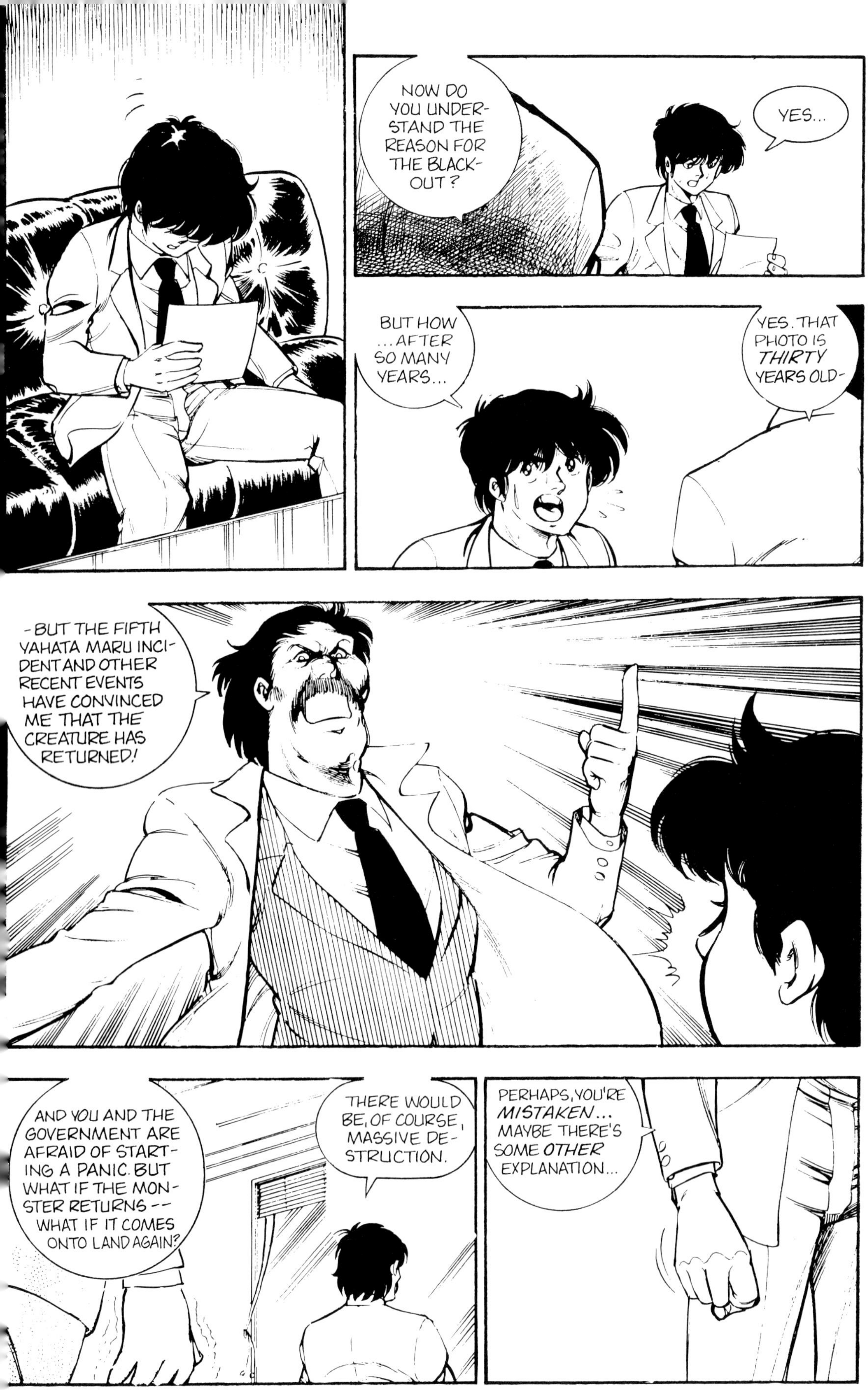
NOW DO YOU UNDERSTAND THE REASON FOR THE BLACKOUT?
YES...
BUT HOW ...AFTER SO MANY YEARS...
YES. THAT PHOTO IS THIRTY YEARS OLD-
-BUT THE FIFTH YAHATA MARU INCIDENT AND OTHER RECENT EVENTS HAVE CONVINCED ME THAT THE CREATURE HAS RETURNED!
AND YOU AND THE GOVERNMENT ARE AFRAID OF STARTING A PANIC. BUT WHAT IF THE MONSTER RETURNS -- WHAT IF IT COMES ONTO LAND AGAIN?
THERE WOULD BE, OF COURSE, MASSIVE DESTRUCTION.
PERHAPS, YOU'RE MISTAKEN... MAYBE THERE'S SOME OTHER EXPLANATION...

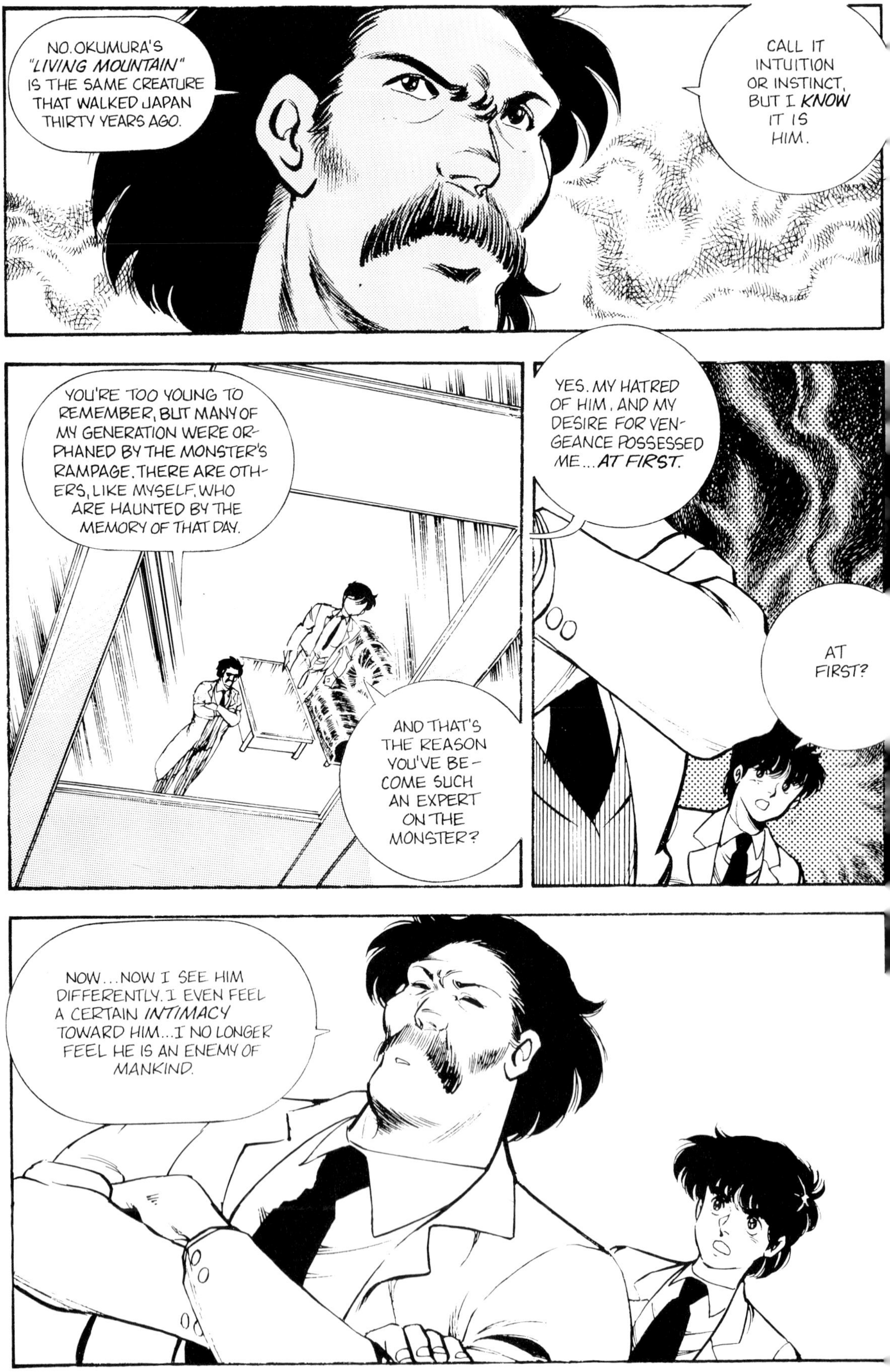

NO. OKUMURA'S "LIVING MOUNTAIN" IS THE SAME CREATURE THAT WALKED JAPAN THIRTY YEARS AGO.
CALL IT INTUITION OR INSTINCT, BUT I KNOW IT IS HIM.
YOU'RE TOO YOUNG TO REMEMBER, BUT MANY OF MY GENERATION WERE ORPHANED BY THE MONSTER'S RAMPAGE. THERE ARE OTHERS, LIKE MYSELF, WHO ARE HAUNTED BY THE MEMORY OF THAT DAY.
AND THAT'S THE REASON YOU'VE BECOME SUCH AN EXPERT ON THE MONSTER?
YES. MY HATRED OF HIM, AND MY DESIRE FOR VENGEANCE POSSESSED ME... AT FIRST.
AT FIRST?
NOW... NOW I SEE HIM DIFFERENTLY. I EVEN FEEL A CERTAIN INTIMACY TOWARD HIM... I NO LONGER FEEL HE IS AN ENEMY OF MANKIND.

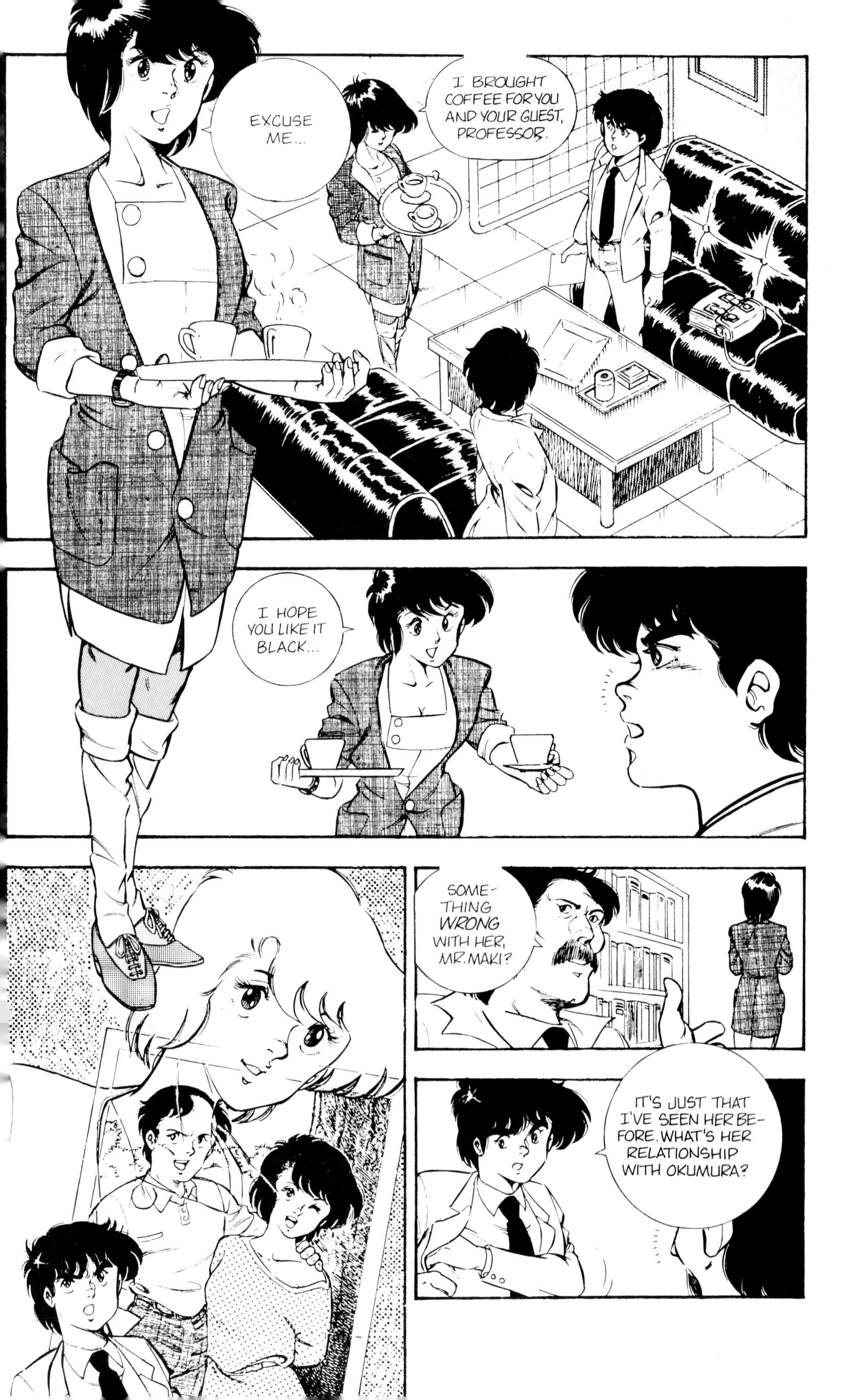
EXCUSE ME...
I BROUGHT COFFEE FOR YOU AND YOUR GUEST, PROFESSOR.
I HOPE YOU LIKE IT BLACK...
SOME-THING WRONG WITH HER, MR. MAKI?
IT'S JUST THAT I'VE SEEN HER BE-FORE. WHAT'S HER RELATIONSHIP WITH OKUMURA?

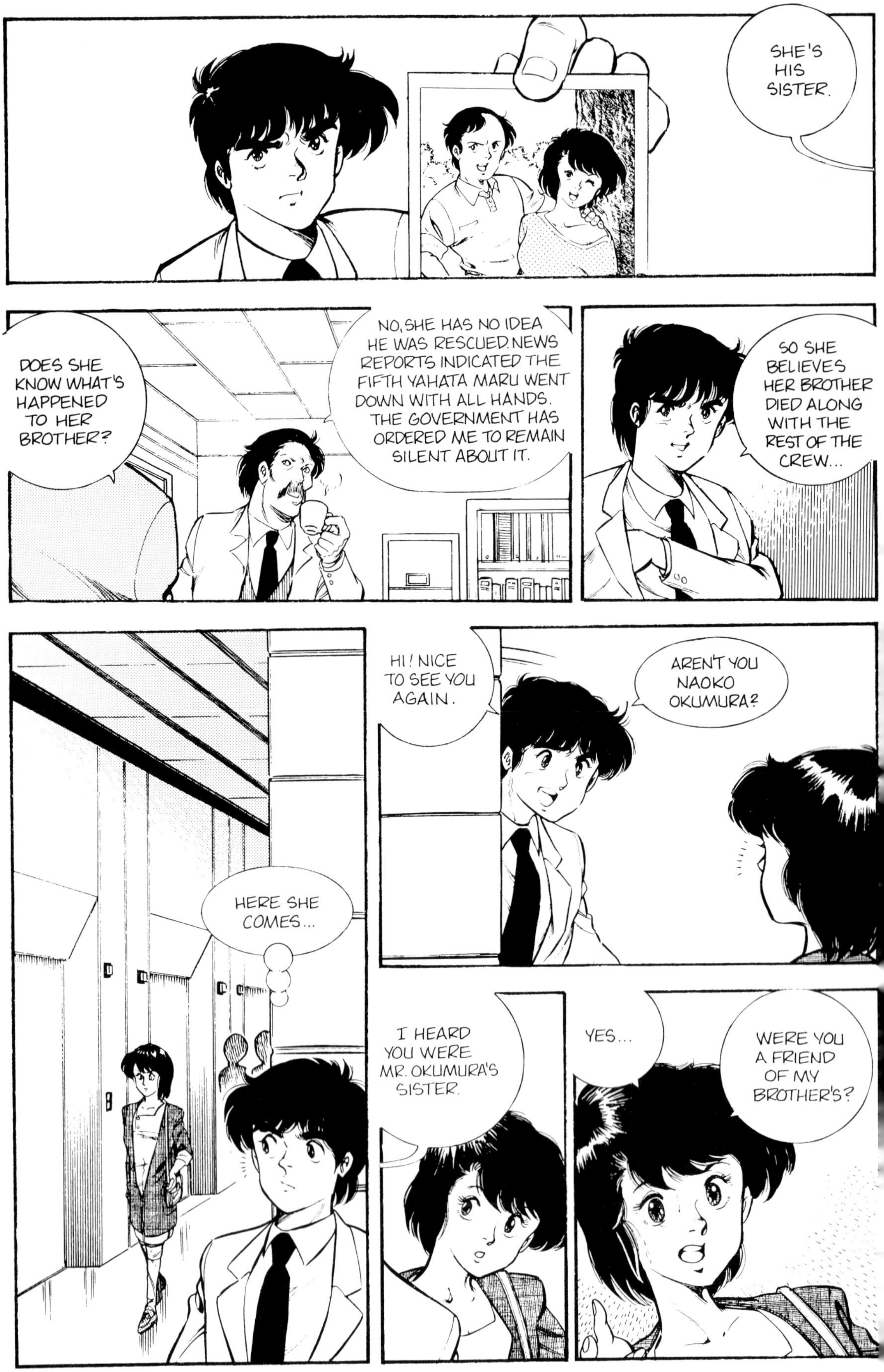
SHE'S HIS SISTER.
DOES SHE KNOW WHAT'S HAPPENED TO HER BROTHER?
NO, SHE HAS NO IDEA HE WAS RESCUED. NEWS REPORTS INDICATED THE FIFTH YAHATA MARU WENT DOWN WITH ALL HANDS. THE GOVERNMENT HAS ORDERED ME TO REMAIN SILENT ABOUT IT.
SO SHE BELIEVES HER BROTHER DIED ALONG WITH THE REST OF THE CREW...
HERE SHE COMES...
HI! NICE TO SEE YOU AGAIN.
AREN'T YOU NAOKO OKUMURA?
I HEARD YOU WERE MR. OKUMURA'S SISTER.
YES...
WERE YOU A FRIEND OF MY BROTHER'S?

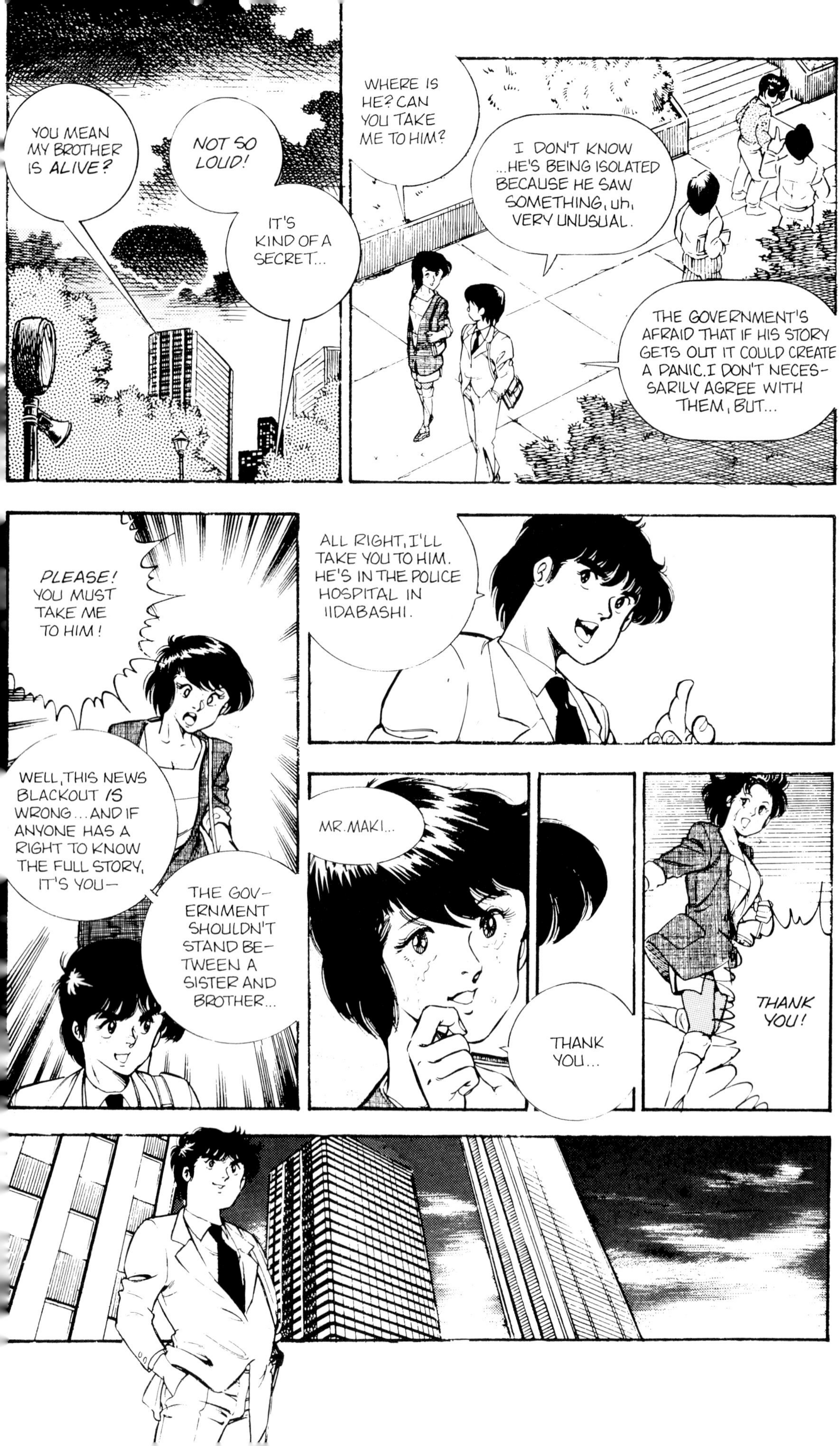
YOU MEAN MY BROTHER IS ALIVE?
NOT SO LOUD!
IT'S KIND OF A SECRET...
WHERE IS HE? CAN YOU TAKE ME TO HIM?
I DON'T KNOW ...HE'S BEING ISOLATED BECAUSE HE SAW SOMETHING, uh, VERY UNUSUAL.
THE GOVERNMENT'S AFRAID THAT IF HIS STORY GETS OUT IT COULD CREATE A PANIC. I DON'T NECES-SARILY AGREE WITH THEM, BUT...
PLEASE! YOU MUST TAKE ME TO HIM!
WELL, THIS NEWS BLACKOUT IS WRONG... AND IF ANYONE HAS A RIGHT TO KNOW THE FULL STORY, IT'S YOU—
THE GOV-ERNMENT SHOULDN'T STAND BE-TWEEN A SISTER AND BROTHER...
ALL RIGHT, I'LL TAKE YOU TO HIM. HE'S IN THE POLICE HOSPITAL IN IIDABASHI.
MR. MAKI...
THANK YOU...
THANK YOU!

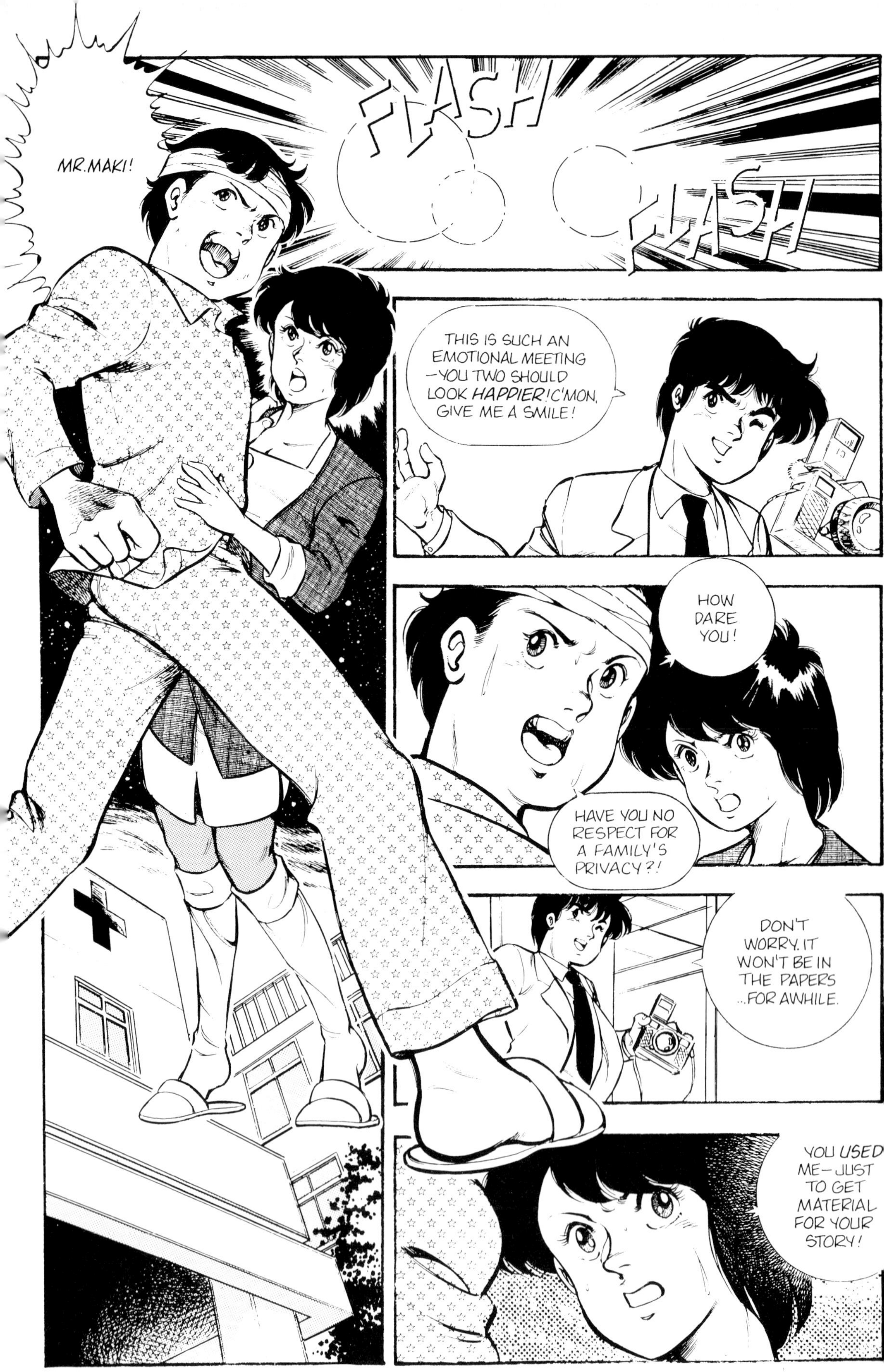
MR. MAKI!
FLASH
FLASH
THIS IS SUCH AN EMOTIONAL MEETING —YOU TWO SHOULD LOOK *HAPPIER*! C'MON, GIVE ME A SMILE!
HOW DARE YOU!
HAVE YOU NO RESPECT FOR A FAMILY'S PRIVACY?!
DON'T WORRY. IT WON'T BE IN THE PAPERS ...FOR AWHILE.
YOU *USED* ME— JUST TO GET MATERIAL FOR YOUR STORY!

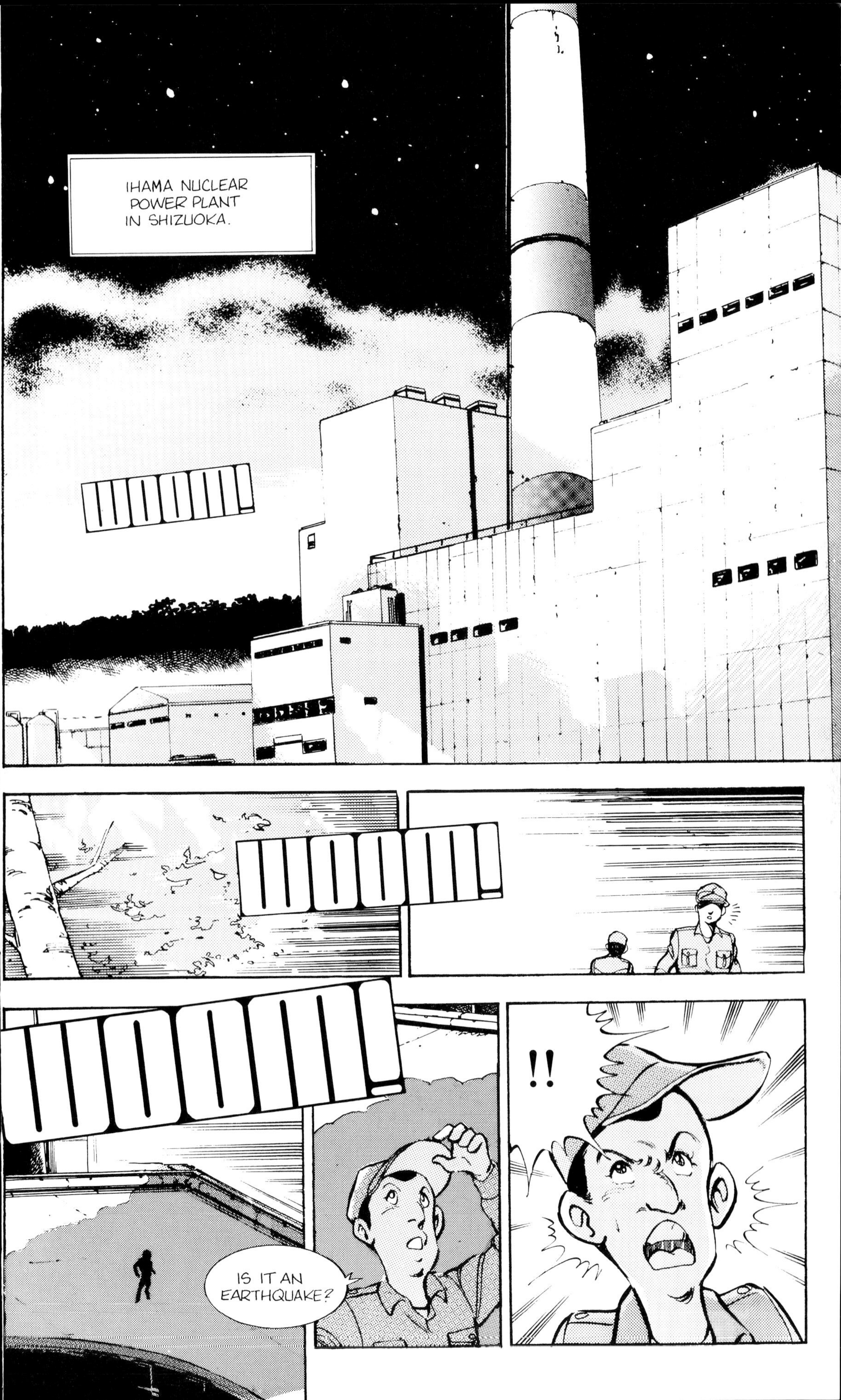
IHAMA NUCLEAR POWER PLANT IN SHIZUOKA.
WOOOM!
WOOOM!
WOOOM!
IS IT AN EARTHQUAKE?
!!

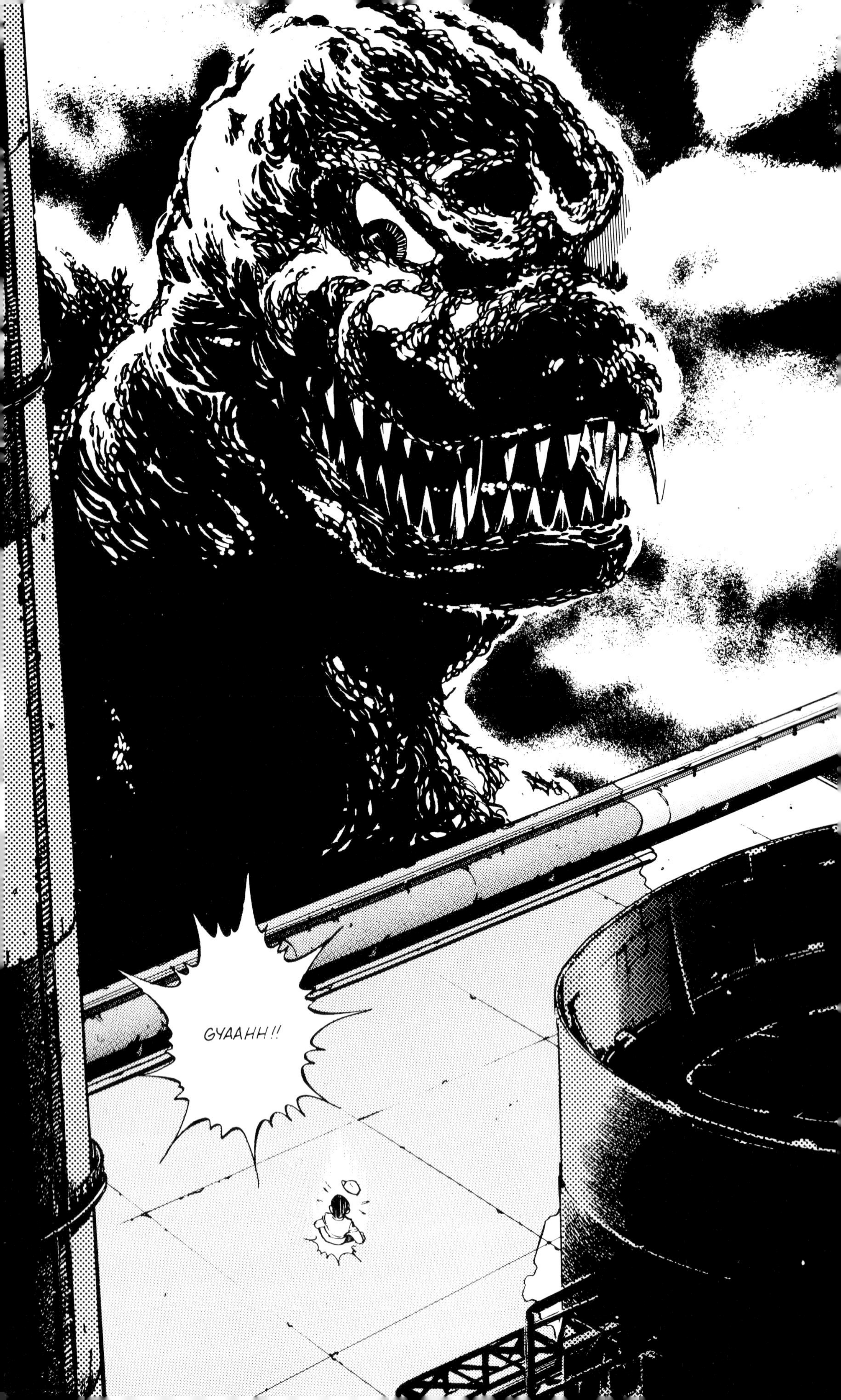
GYAAHH!!

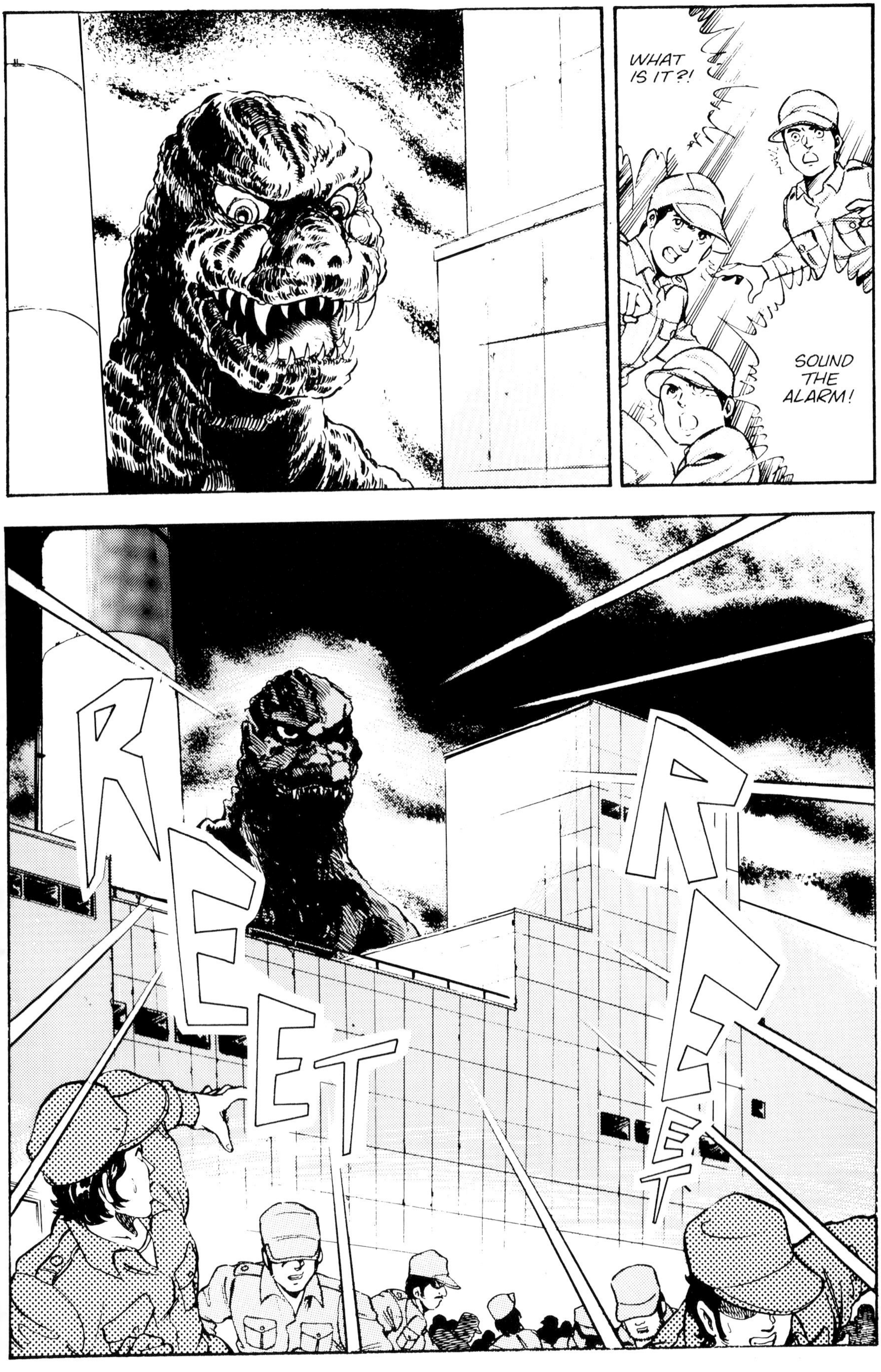
WHAT IS IT?!
SOUND THE ALARM!
REEET
REEET

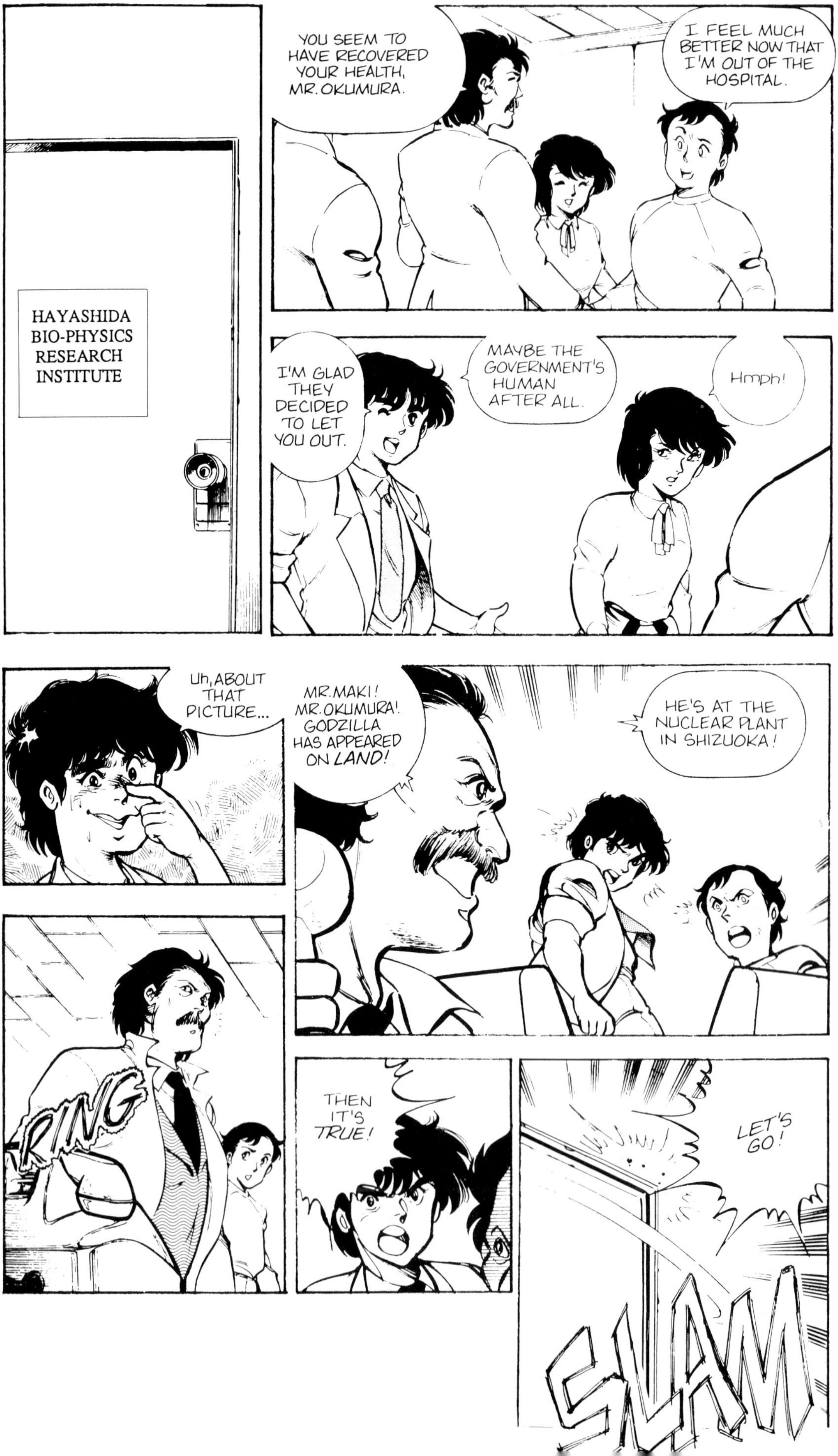
HAYASHIDA
BIO-PHYSICS
RESEARCH
INSTITUTE
YOU SEEM TO HAVE RECOVERED YOUR HEALTH, MR. OKUMURA.
I FEEL MUCH BETTER NOW THAT I'M OUT OF THE HOSPITAL.
I'M GLAD THEY DECIDED TO LET YOU OUT.
MAYBE THE GOVERNMENT'S HUMAN AFTER ALL.
Hmph!
Uh, ABOUT THAT PICTURE...
RING
MR. MAKI! MR. OKUMURA! GODZILLA HAS APPEARED ON LAND!
HE'S AT THE NUCLEAR PLANT IN SHIZUOKA!
THEN IT'S TRUE!
LET'S GO!
SLAM

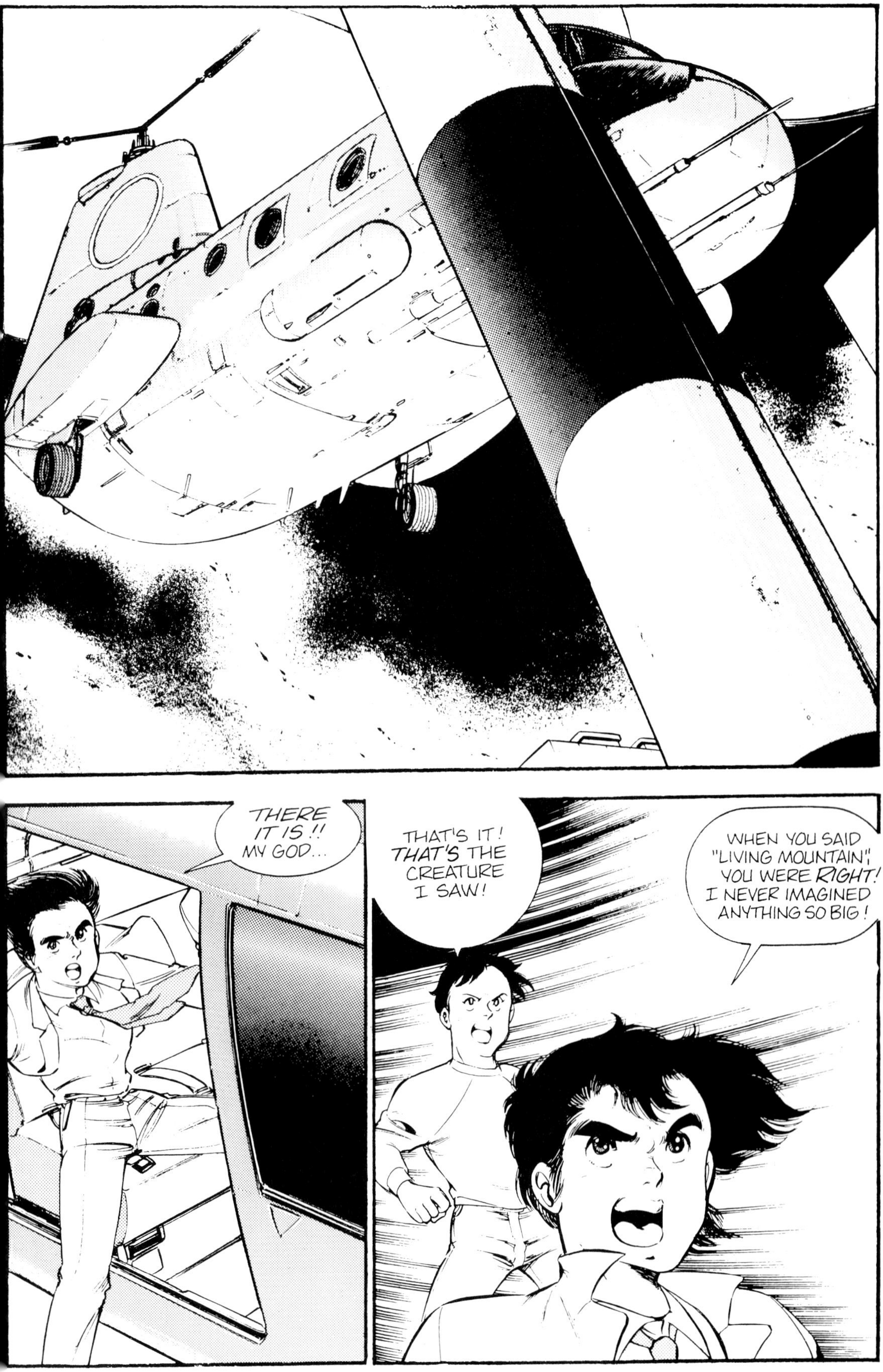
THERE IT IS !! MY GOD...
THAT'S IT! THAT'S THE CREATURE I SAW!
WHEN YOU SAID "LIVING MOUNTAIN", YOU WERE RIGHT! I NEVER IMAGINED ANYTHING SO BIG!

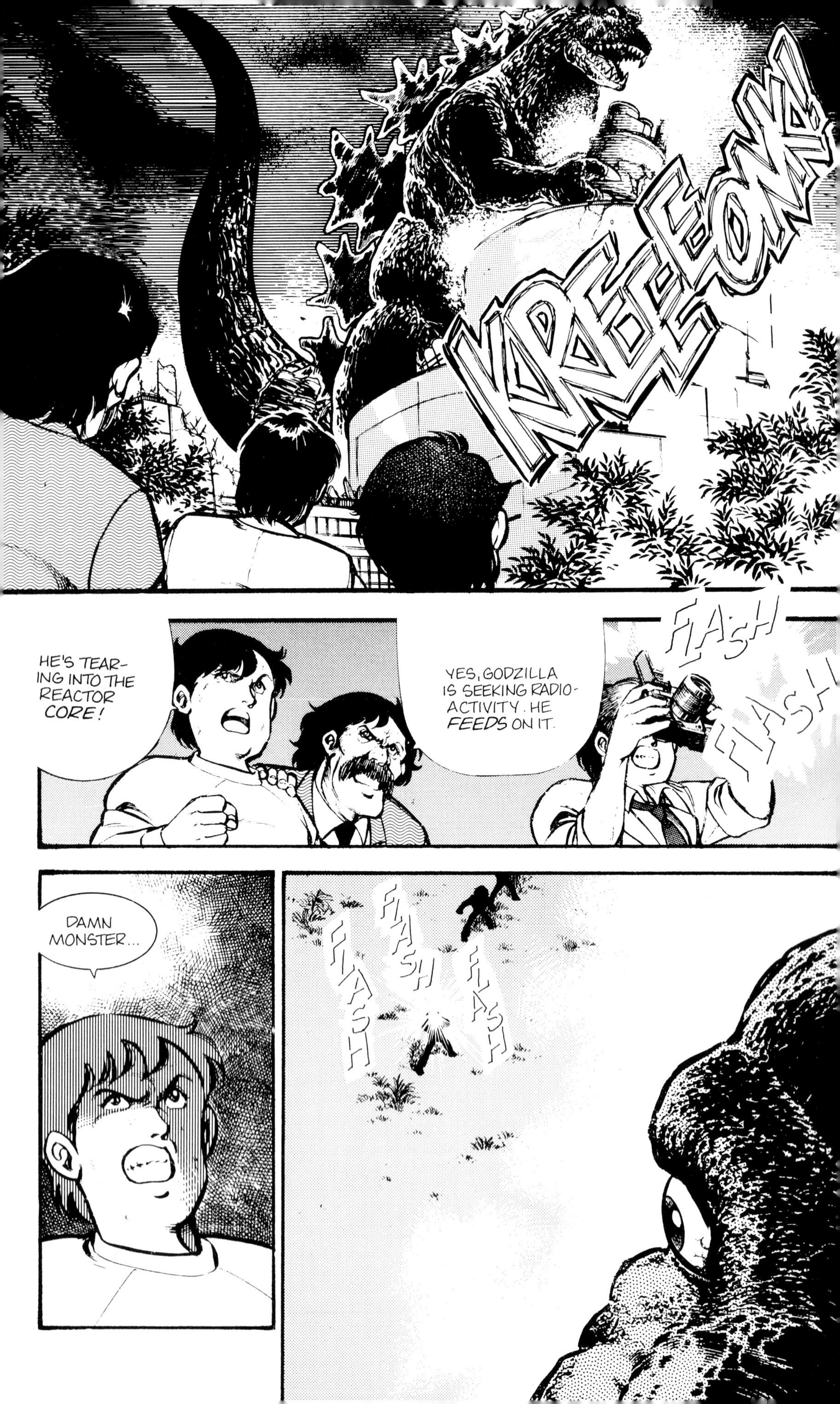

KREEEOW!
HE'S TEARING INTO THE REACTOR CORE!
YES, GODZILLA IS SEEKING RADIO-ACTIVITY. HE FEEDS ON IT.
FLASH
FLASH
DAMN MONSTER...
FLASH
FLASH
FLASH

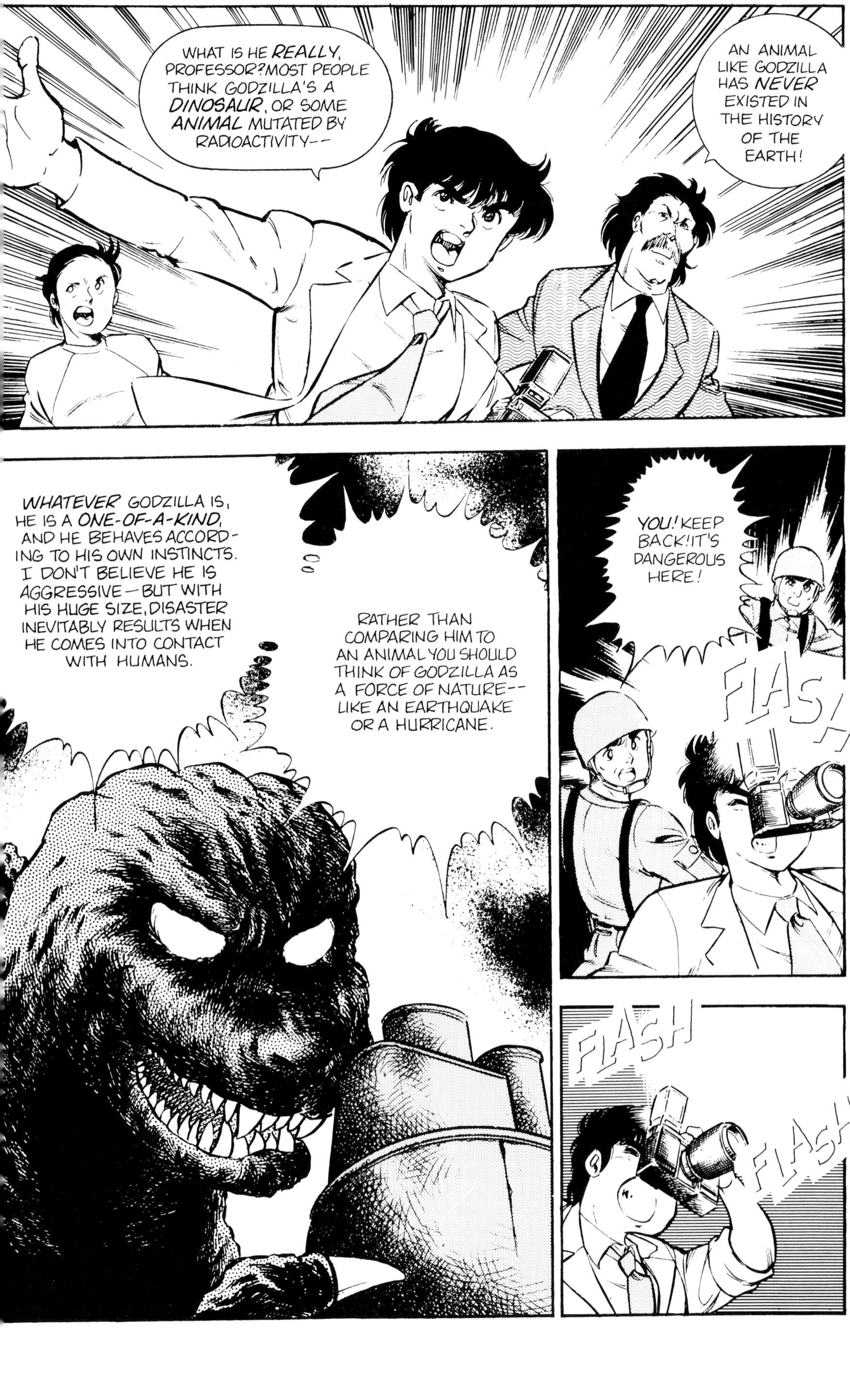
WHAT IS HE REALLY, PROFESSOR? MOST PEOPLE THINK GODZILLA'S A DINOSAUR, OR SOME ANIMAL MUTATED BY RADIOACTIVITY--
AN ANIMAL LIKE GODZILLA HAS NEVER EXISTED IN THE HISTORY OF THE EARTH!
WHATEVER GODZILLA IS, HE IS A ONE-OF-A-KIND, AND HE BEHAVES ACCORDING TO HIS OWN INSTINCTS. I DON'T BELIEVE HE IS AGGRESSIVE — BUT WITH HIS HUGE SIZE, DISASTER INEVITABLY RESULTS WHEN HE COMES INTO CONTACT WITH HUMANS.
RATHER THAN COMPARING HIM TO AN ANIMAL YOU SHOULD THINK OF GODZILLA AS A FORCE OF NATURE-- LIKE AN EARTHQUAKE OR A HURRICANE.
YOU! KEEP BACK! IT'S DANGEROUS HERE!
FLASH
FLASH
FLASH

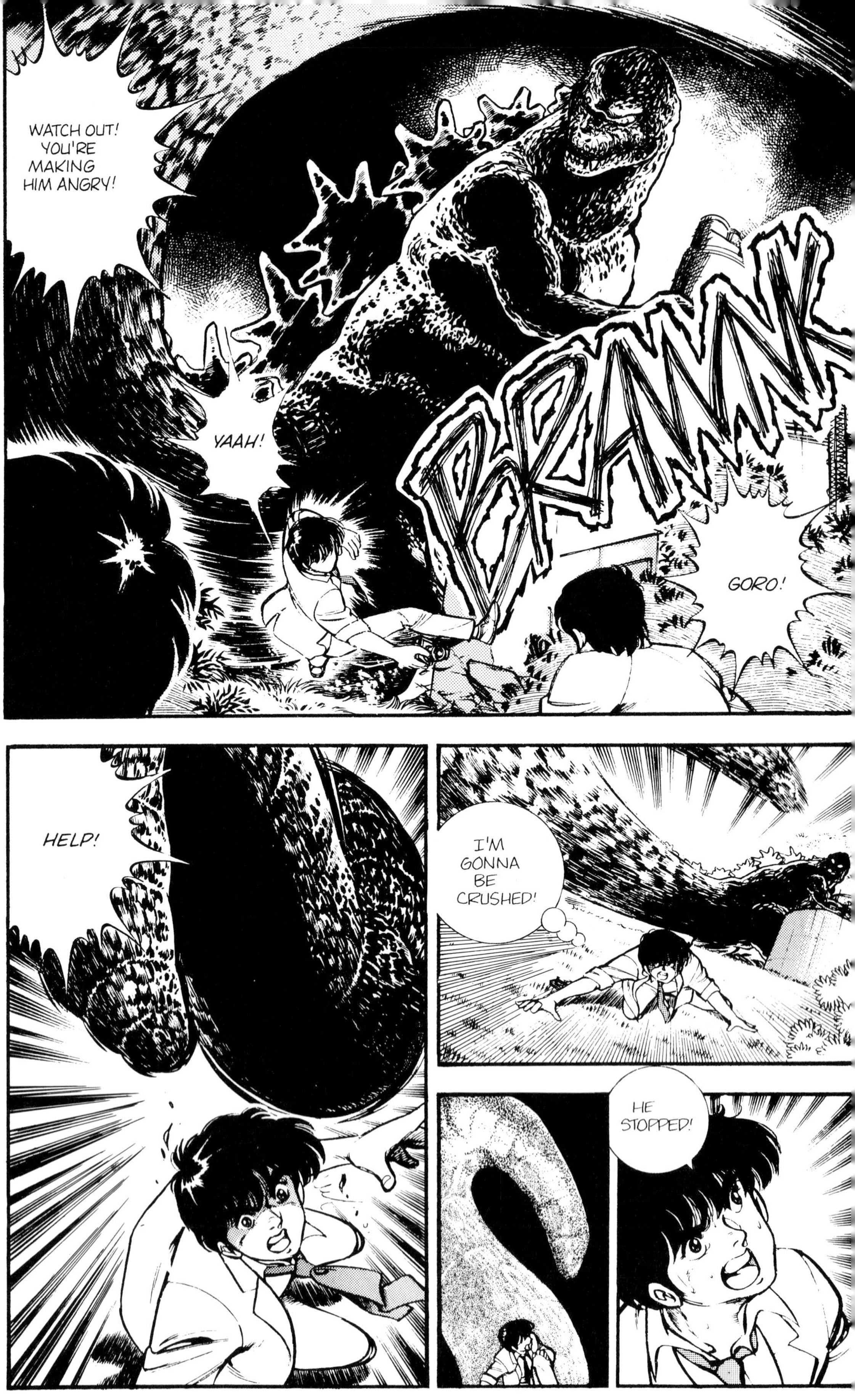
WATCH OUT! YOU'RE MAKING HIM ANGRY!
YAAH!
BRAAANK
GORO!
HELP!
I'M GONNA BE CRUSHED!
HE STOPPED!

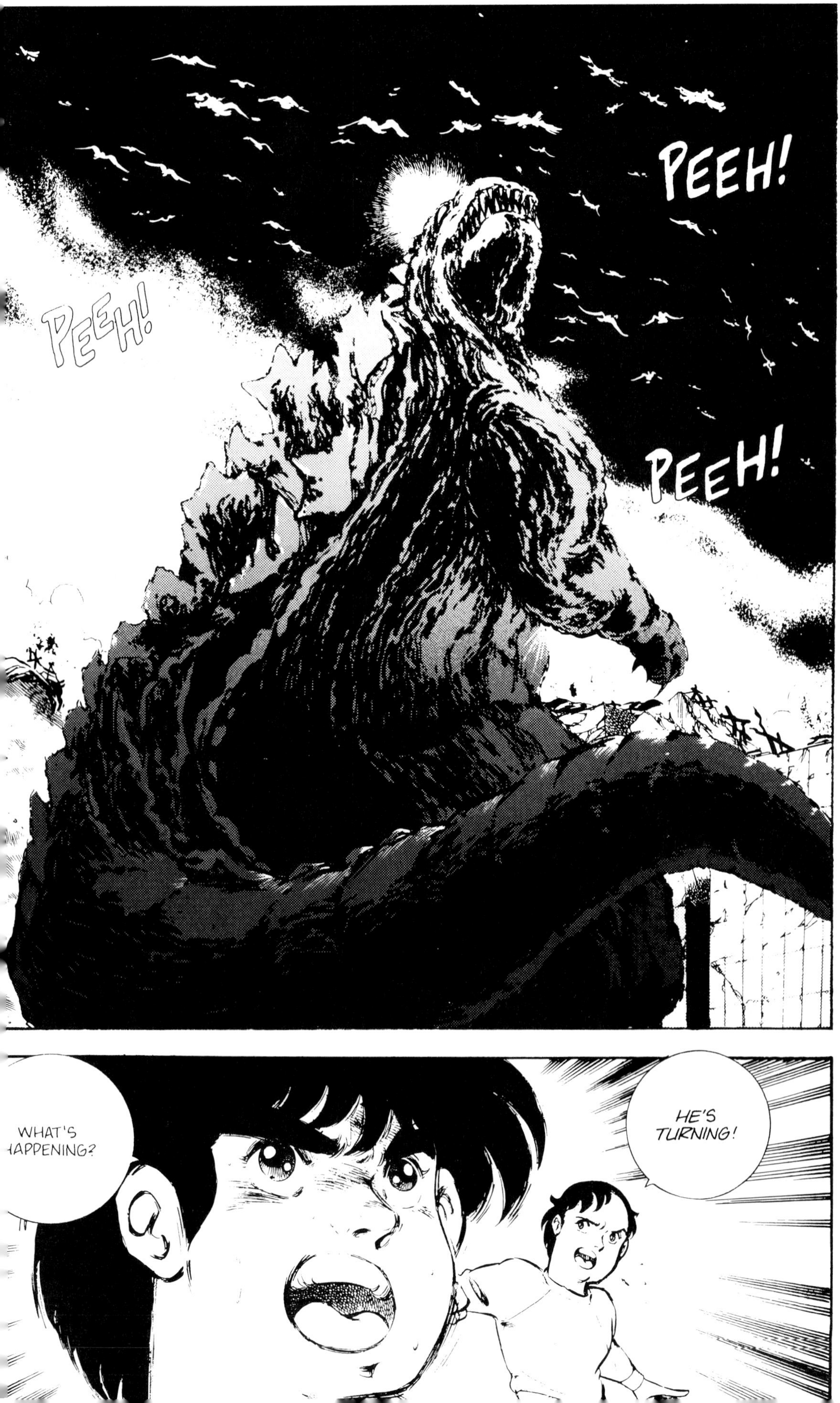
PEEH!
PEEH!
PEEH!
HE'S TURNING!
WHAT'S HAPPENING?

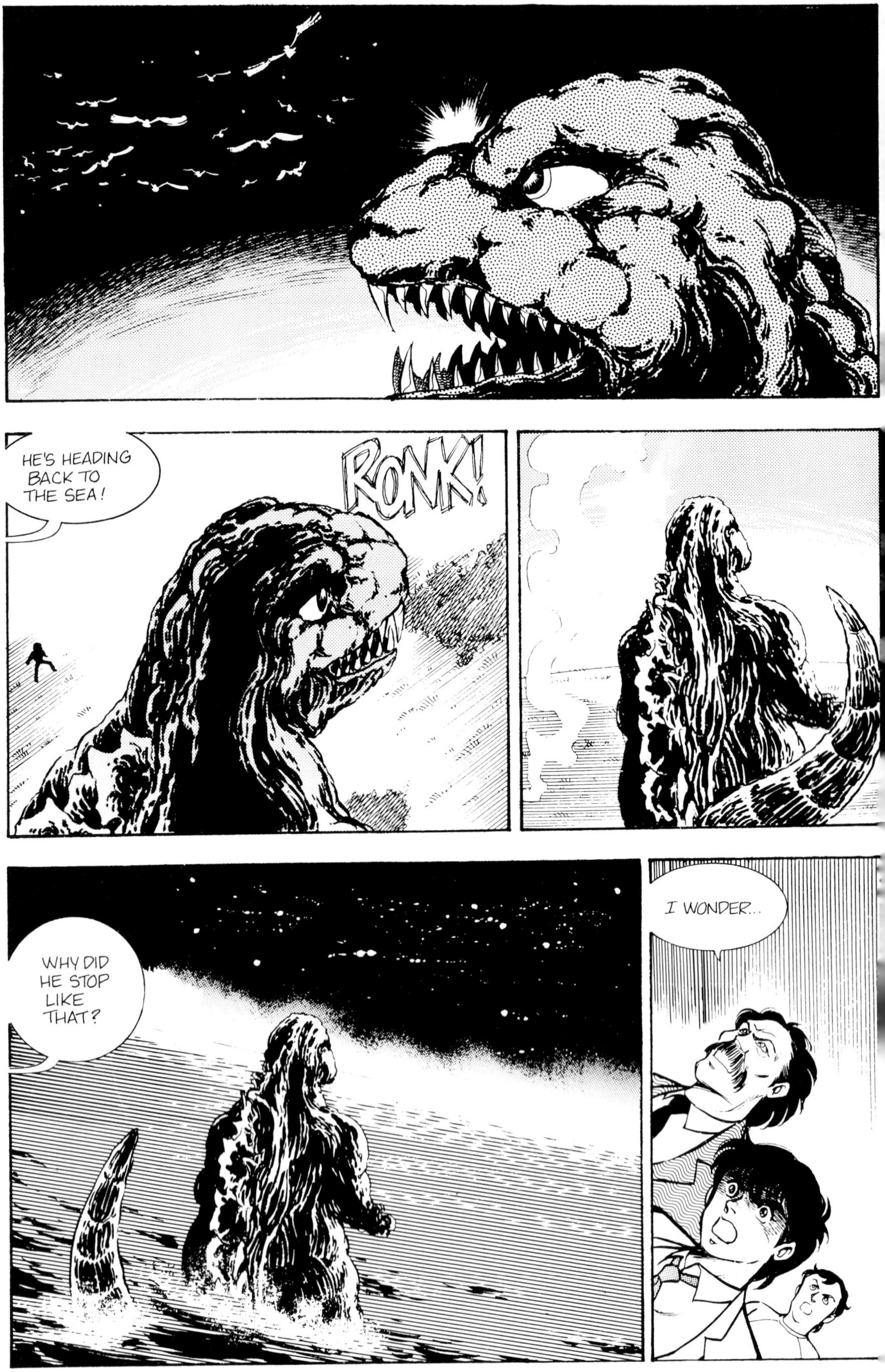
HE'S HEADING BACK TO THE SEA!
RONK!
WHY DID HE STOP LIKE THAT?
I WONDER...

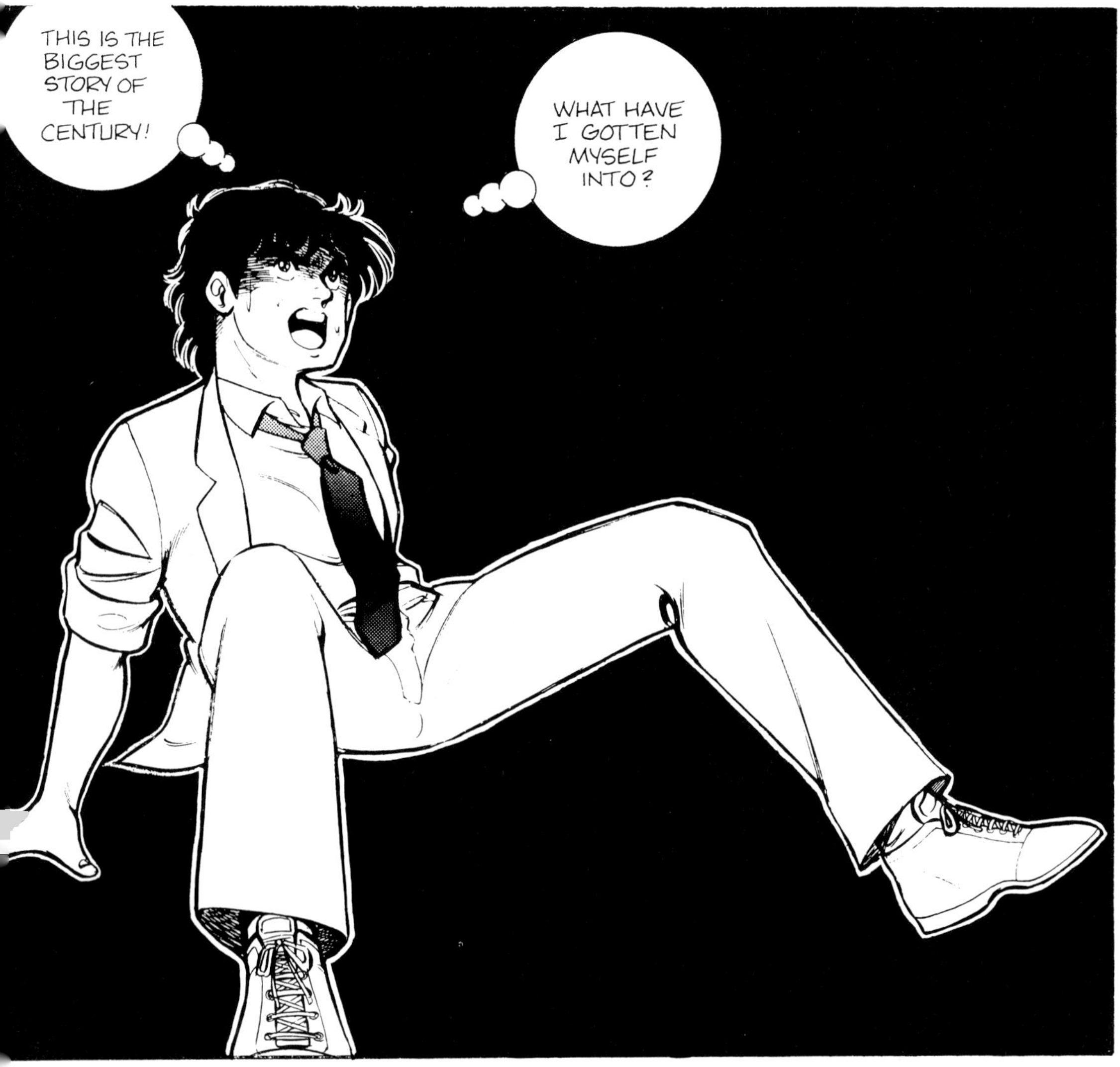
THIS IS THE BIGGEST STORY OF THE CENTURY!
WHAT HAVE I GOTTEN MYSELF INTO?

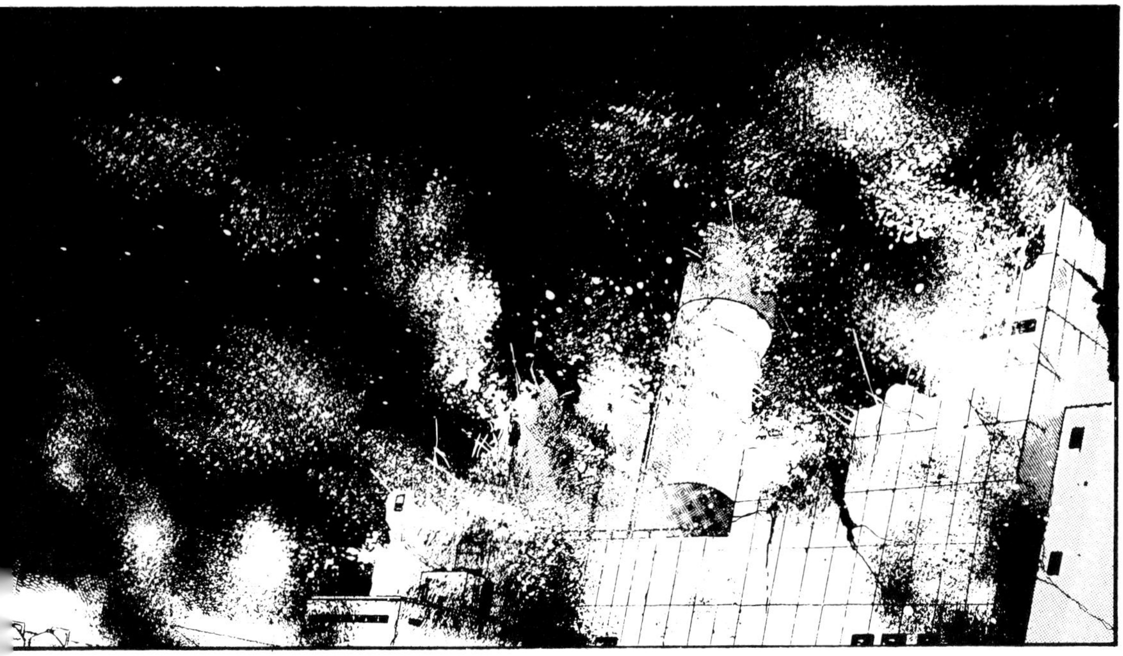

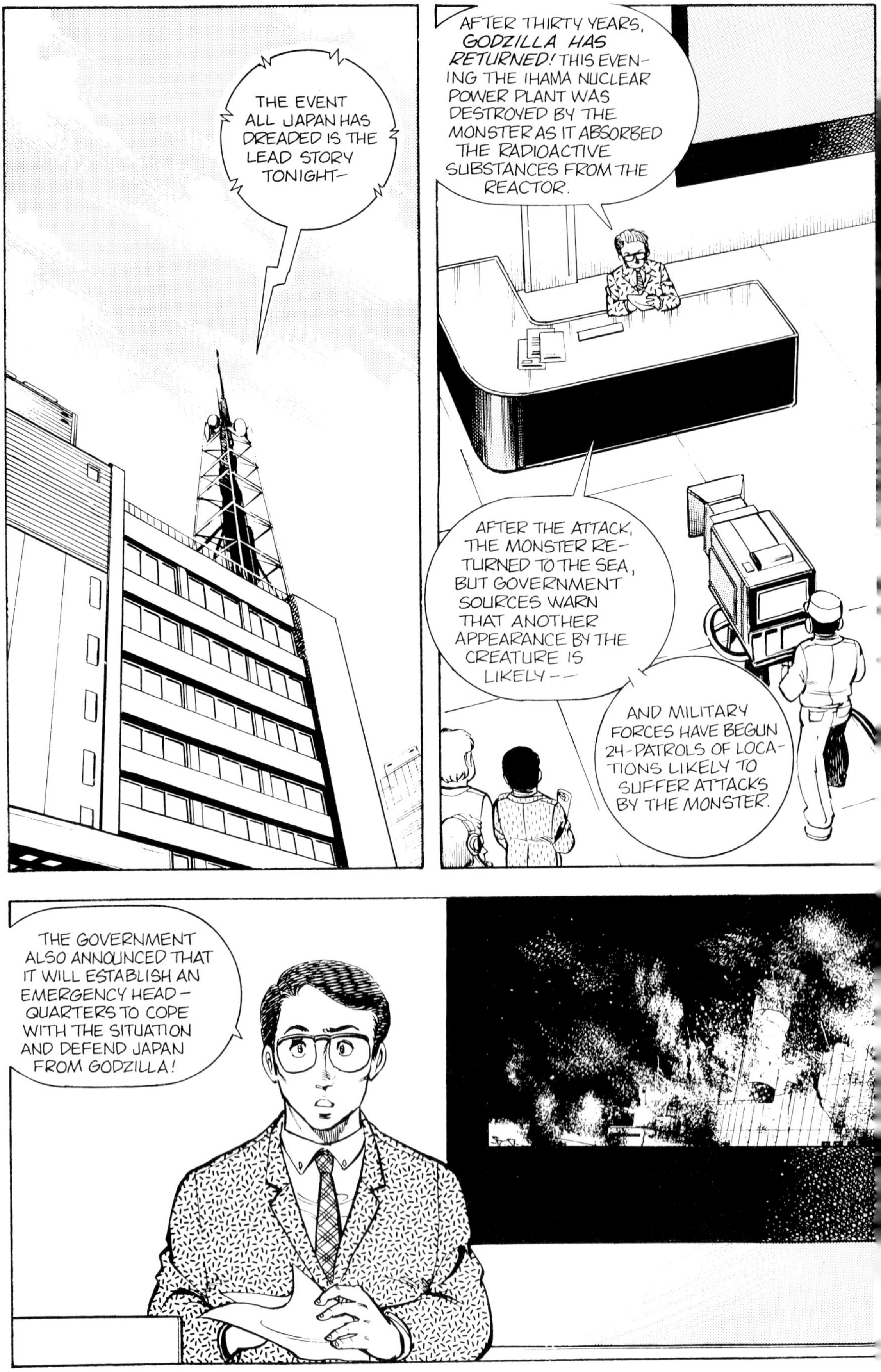
THE EVENT ALL JAPAN HAS DREADED IS THE LEAD STORY TONIGHT-
AFTER THIRTY YEARS, *GODZILLA HAS RETURNED!* THIS EVENING THE IHAMA NUCLEAR POWER PLANT WAS DESTROYED BY THE MONSTER AS IT ABSORBED THE RADIOACTIVE SUBSTANCES FROM THE REACTOR.
AFTER THE ATTACK, THE MONSTER RETURNED TO THE SEA, BUT GOVERNMENT SOURCES WARN THAT ANOTHER APPEARANCE BY THE CREATURE IS LIKELY--
AND MILITARY FORCES HAVE BEGUN 24-PATROLS OF LOCATIONS LIKELY TO SUFFER ATTACKS BY THE MONSTER.
THE GOVERNMENT ALSO ANNOUNCED THAT IT WILL ESTABLISH AN EMERGENCY HEADQUARTERS TO COPE WITH THE SITUATION AND DEFEND JAPAN FROM GODZILLA!

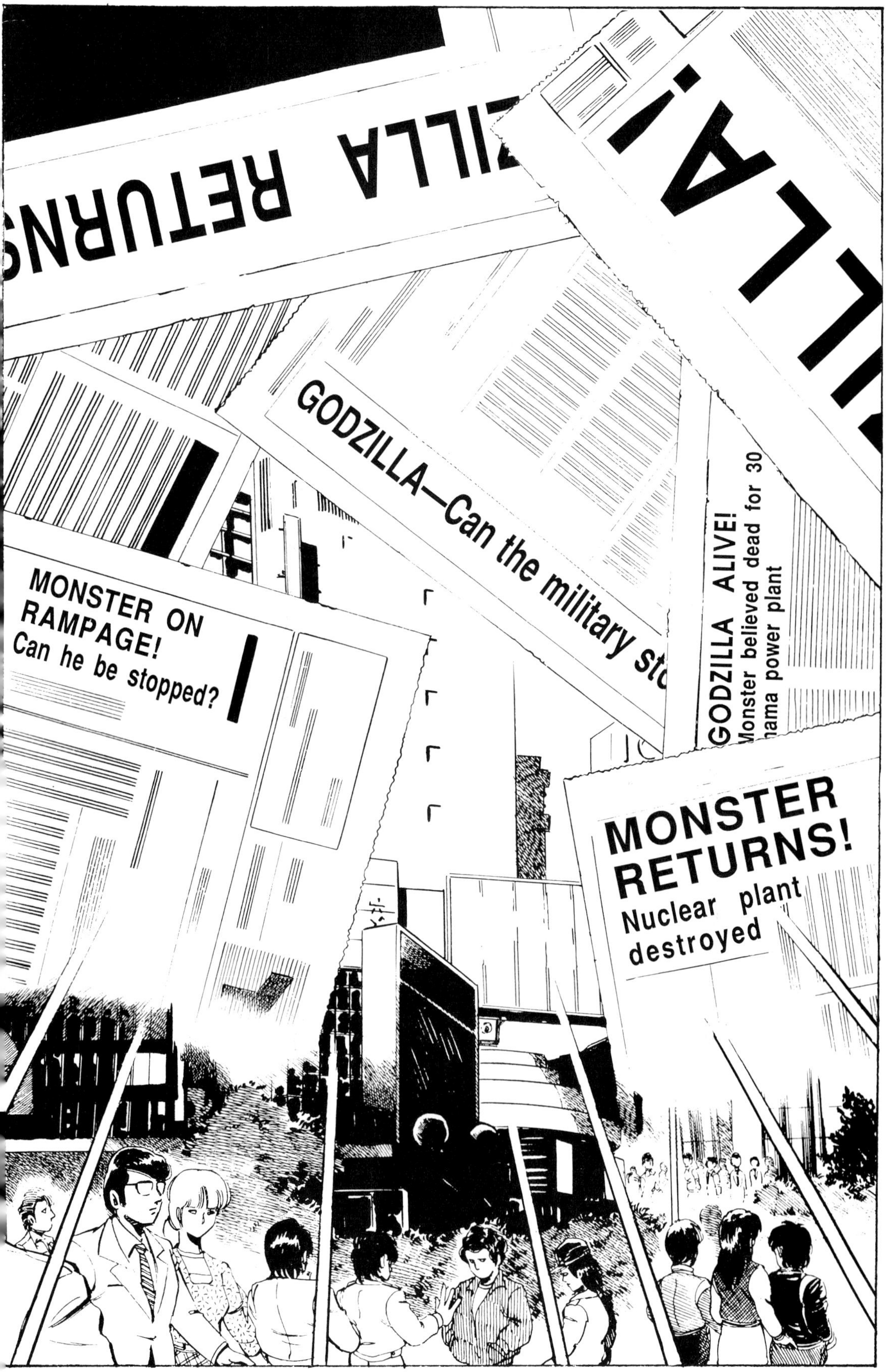

GODZILLA—Can the military
GODZILLA ALIVE!
Monster believed dead for 30
MONSTER ON RAMPAGE!
Can he be stopped?
MONSTER RETURNS!
Nuclear plant destroyed

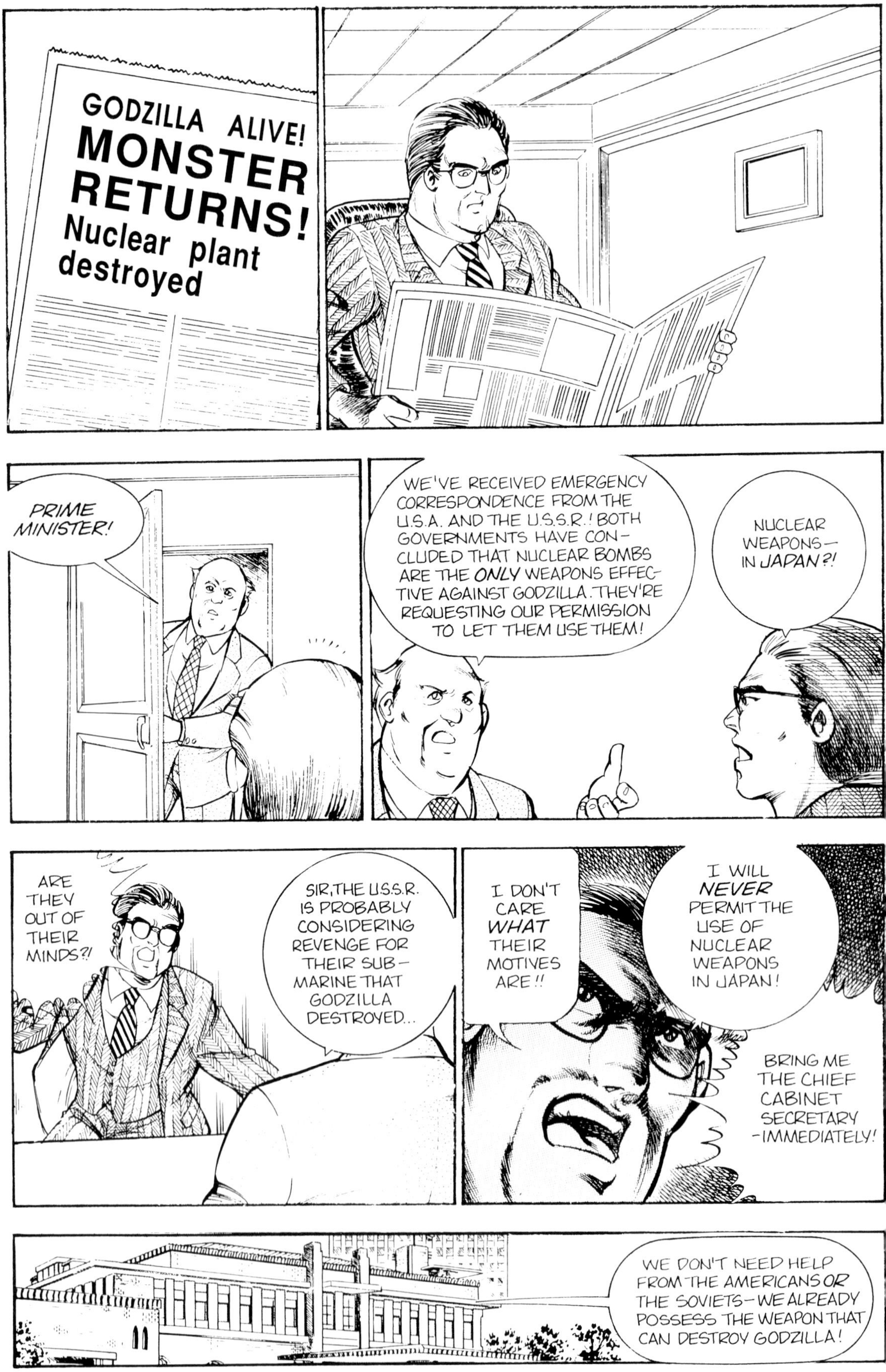
GODZILLA ALIVE! MONSTER RETURNS! Nuclear plant destroyed
PRIME MINISTER!
WE'VE RECEIVED EMERGENCY CORRESPONDENCE FROM THE U.S.A. AND THE U.S.S.R.! BOTH GOVERNMENTS HAVE CONCLUDED THAT NUCLEAR BOMBS ARE THE ONLY WEAPONS EFFECTIVE AGAINST GODZILLA. THEY'RE REQUESTING OUR PERMISSION TO LET THEM USE THEM!
NUCLEAR WEAPONS— IN JAPAN?!
ARE THEY OUT OF THEIR MINDS?!
SIR, THE U.S.S.R. IS PROBABLY CONSIDERING REVENGE FOR THEIR SUBMARINE THAT GODZILLA DESTROYED...
I DON'T CARE WHAT THEIR MOTIVES ARE!!
I WILL NEVER PERMIT THE USE OF NUCLEAR WEAPONS IN JAPAN!
BRING ME THE CHIEF CABINET SECRETARY -IMMEDIATELY!
WE DON'T NEED HELP FROM THE AMERICANS OR THE SOVIETS—WE ALREADY POSSESS THE WEAPON THAT CAN DESTROY GODZILLA!

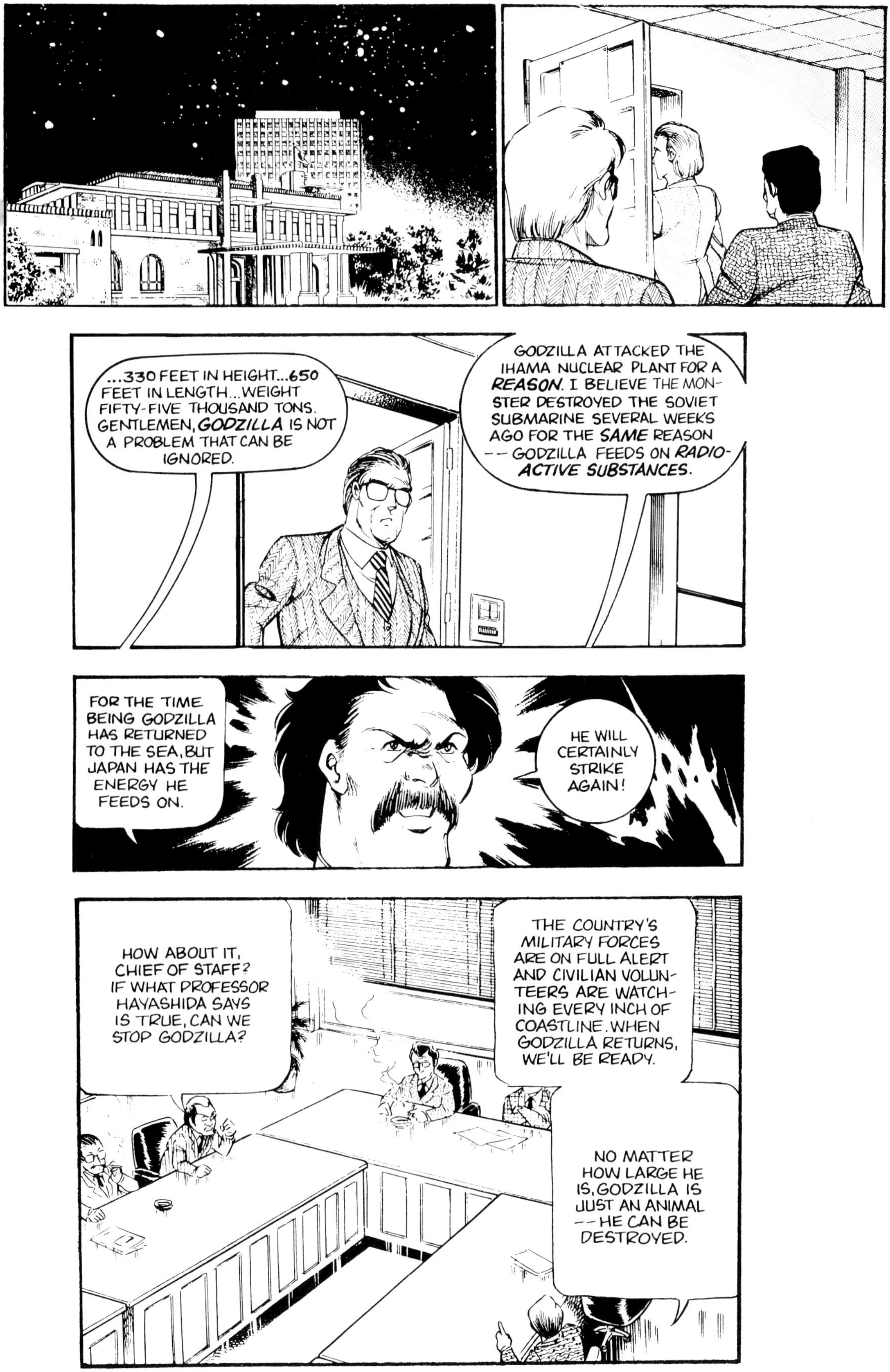
...330 FEET IN HEIGHT...650 FEET IN LENGTH...WEIGHT FIFTY-FIVE THOUSAND TONS. GENTLEMEN, GODZILLA IS NOT A PROBLEM THAT CAN BE IGNORED.
GODZILLA ATTACKED THE IHAMA NUCLEAR PLANT FOR A REASON. I BELIEVE THE MONSTER DESTROYED THE SOVIET SUBMARINE SEVERAL WEEKS AGO FOR THE SAME REASON -- GODZILLA FEEDS ON RADIOACTIVE SUBSTANCES.
FOR THE TIME BEING GODZILLA HAS RETURNED TO THE SEA, BUT JAPAN HAS THE ENERGY HE FEEDS ON.
HE WILL CERTAINLY STRIKE AGAIN!
HOW ABOUT IT, CHIEF OF STAFF? IF WHAT PROFESSOR HAYASHIDA SAYS IS TRUE, CAN WE STOP GODZILLA?
THE COUNTRY'S MILITARY FORCES ARE ON FULL ALERT AND CIVILIAN VOLUNTEERS ARE WATCHING EVERY INCH OF COASTLINE. WHEN GODZILLA RETURNS, WE'LL BE READY.
NO MATTER HOW LARGE HE IS, GODZILLA IS JUST AN ANIMAL -- HE CAN BE DESTROYED.

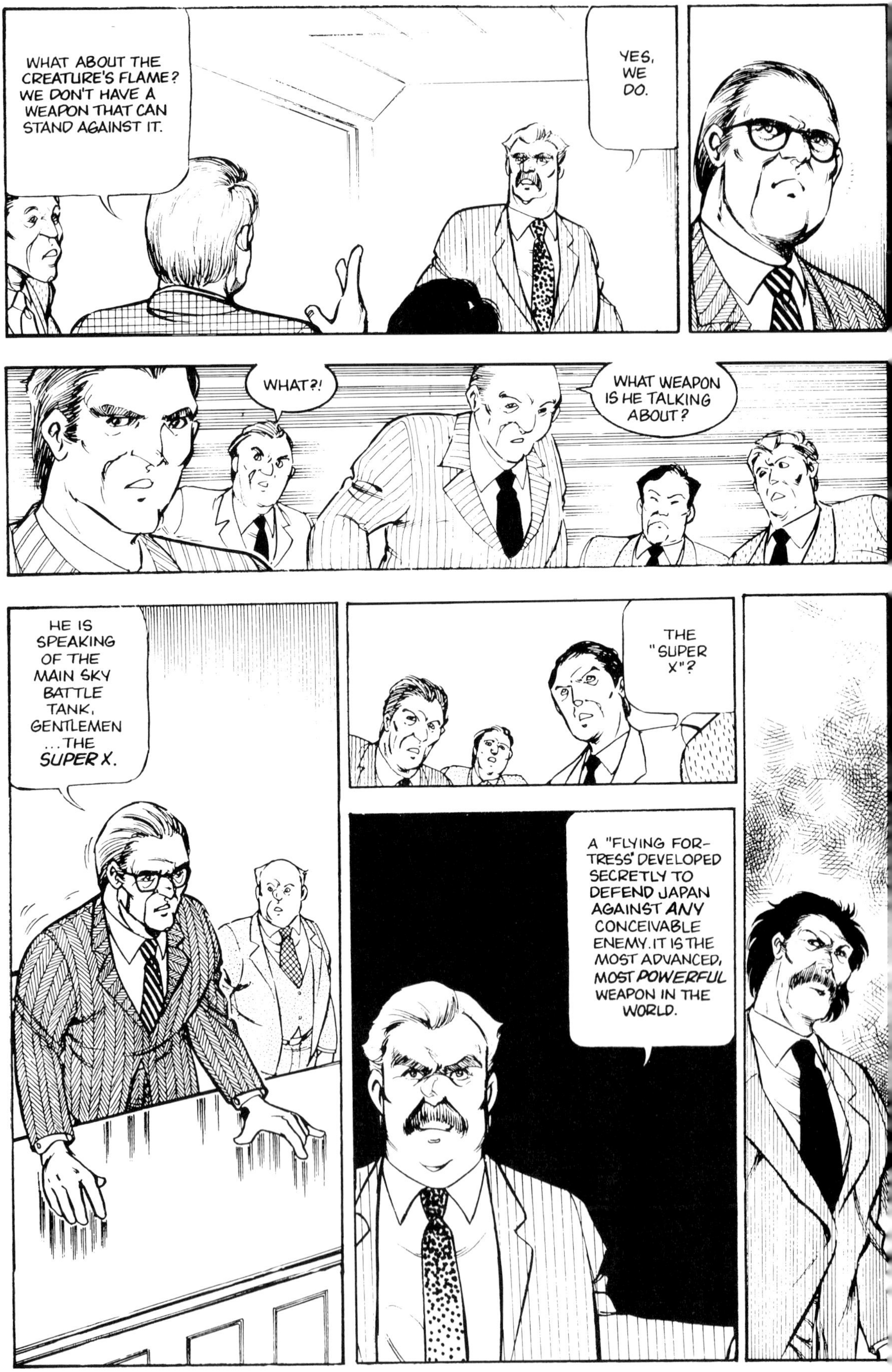

WHAT ABOUT THE CREATURE'S FLAME? WE DON'T HAVE A WEAPON THAT CAN STAND AGAINST IT.
YES, WE DO.
WHAT?!
WHAT WEAPON IS HE TALKING ABOUT?
HE IS SPEAKING OF THE MAIN SKY BATTLE TANK, GENTLEMEN ...THE SUPER X.
THE "SUPER X"?
A "FLYING FORTRESS" DEVELOPED SECRETLY TO DEFEND JAPAN AGAINST ANY CONCEIVABLE ENEMY. IT IS THE MOST ADVANCED, MOST POWERFUL WEAPON IN THE WORLD.

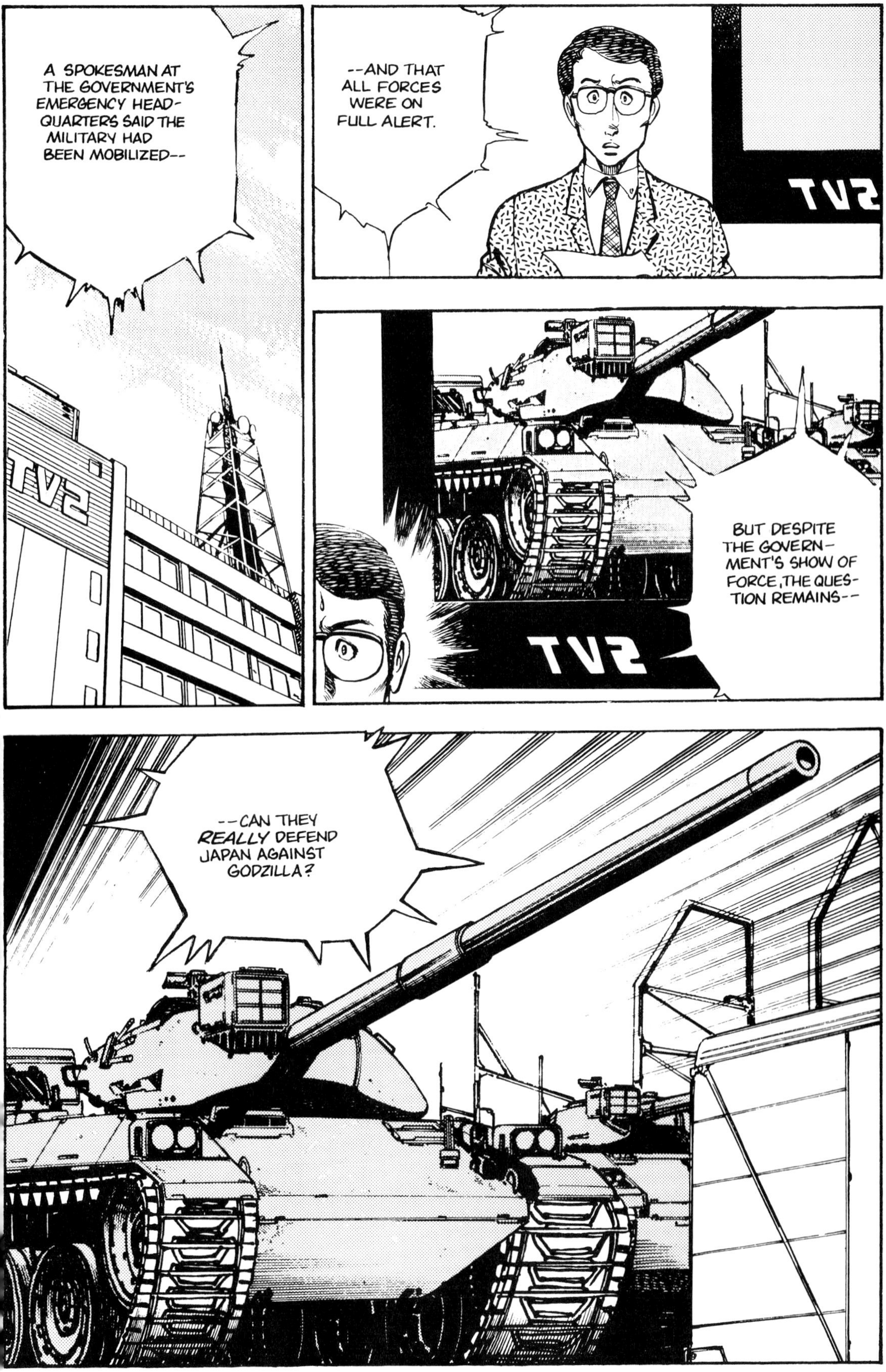
A SPOKESMAN AT THE GOVERNMENT'S EMERGENCY HEAD-QUARTERS SAID THE MILITARY HAD BEEN MOBILIZED--
TV2
--AND THAT ALL FORCES WERE ON FULL ALERT.
TV2
BUT DESPITE THE GOVERN-MENT'S SHOW OF FORCE, THE QUES-TION REMAINS--
TV2
--CAN THEY *REALLY* DEFEND JAPAN AGAINST GODZILLA?

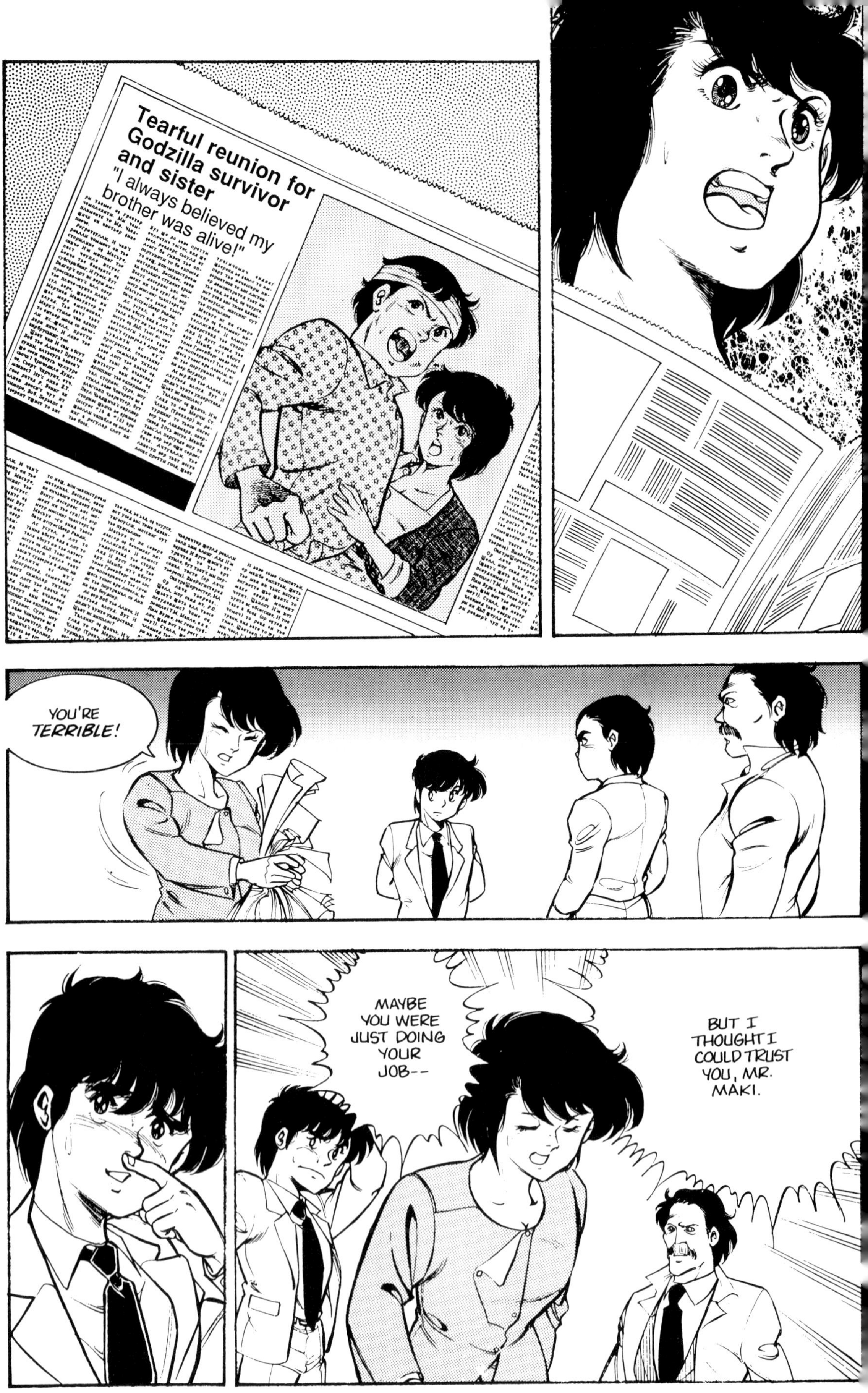
Tearful reunion for Godzilla survivor and sister
"I always believed my brother was alive!"
YOU'RE TERRIBLE!
MAYBE YOU WERE JUST DOING YOUR JOB--
BUT I THOUGHT I COULD TRUST YOU, MR. MAKI.

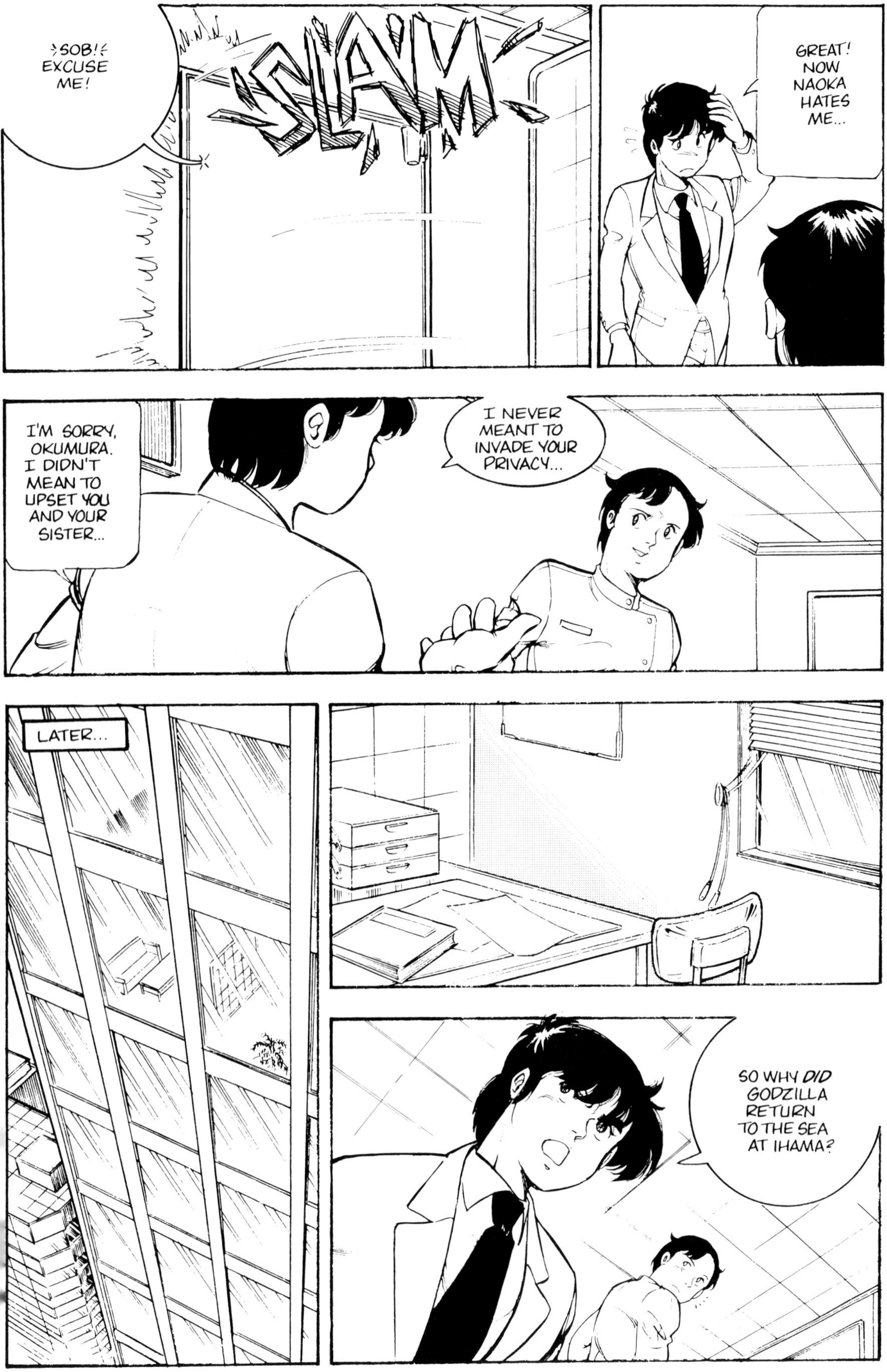

SOB! EXCUSE ME!
SLAM
GREAT! NOW NAOKA HATES ME...
I'M SORRY, OKUMURA. I DIDN'T MEAN TO UPSET YOU AND YOUR SISTER...
I NEVER MEANT TO INVADE YOUR PRIVACY...
LATER...
SO WHY *DID* GODZILLA RETURN TO THE SEA AT IHAMA?

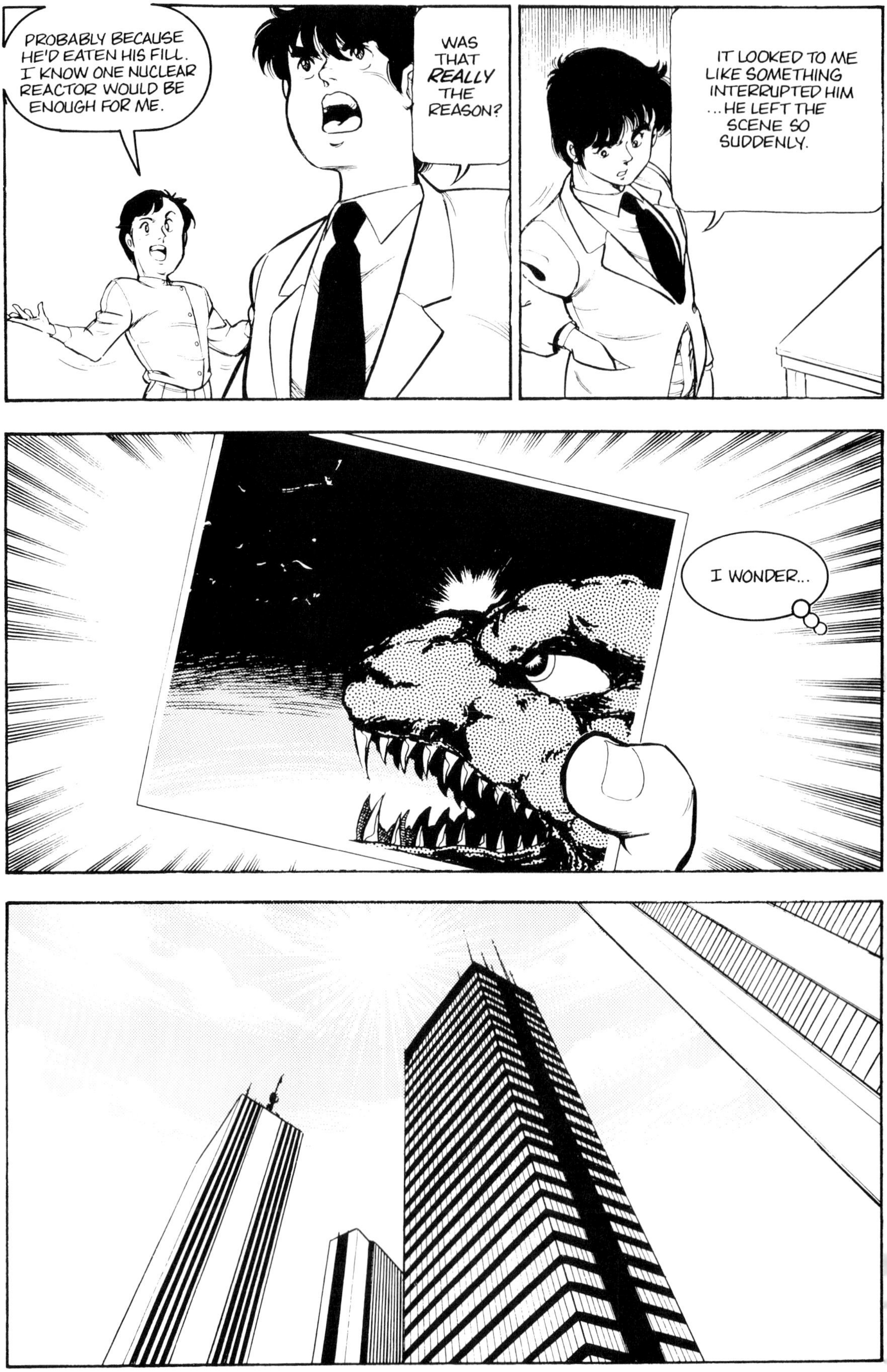
PROBABLY BECAUSE HE'D EATEN HIS FILL. I KNOW ONE NUCLEAR REACTOR WOULD BE ENOUGH FOR ME.
WAS THAT REALLY THE REASON?
IT LOOKED TO ME LIKE SOMETHING INTERRUPTED HIM ...HE LEFT THE SCENE SO SUDDENLY.
I WONDER...

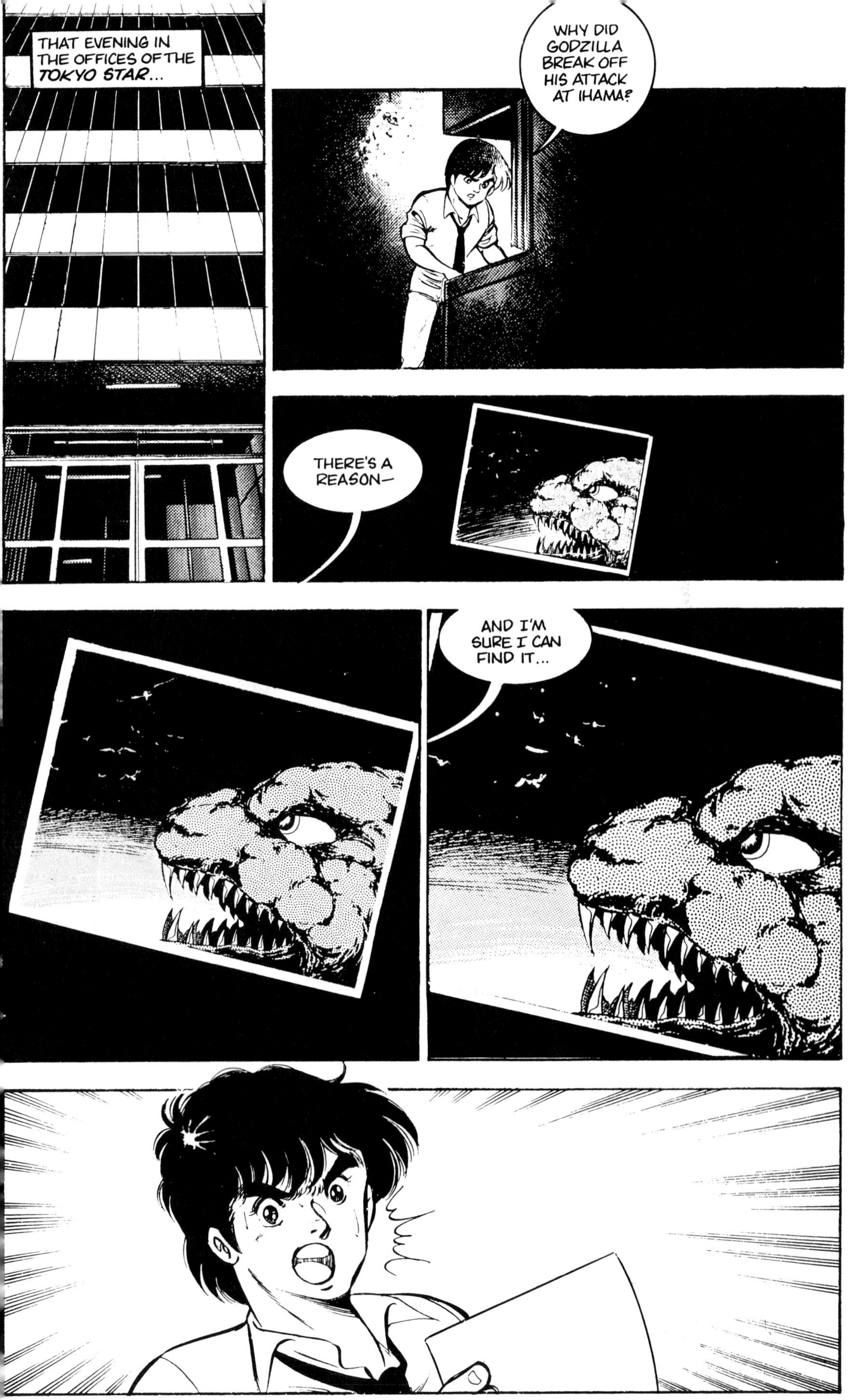
THAT EVENING IN THE OFFICES OF THE *TOKYO STAR*...
WHY DID GODZILLA BREAK OFF HIS ATTACK AT IHAMA?
THERE'S A REASON—
AND I'M SURE I CAN FIND IT...

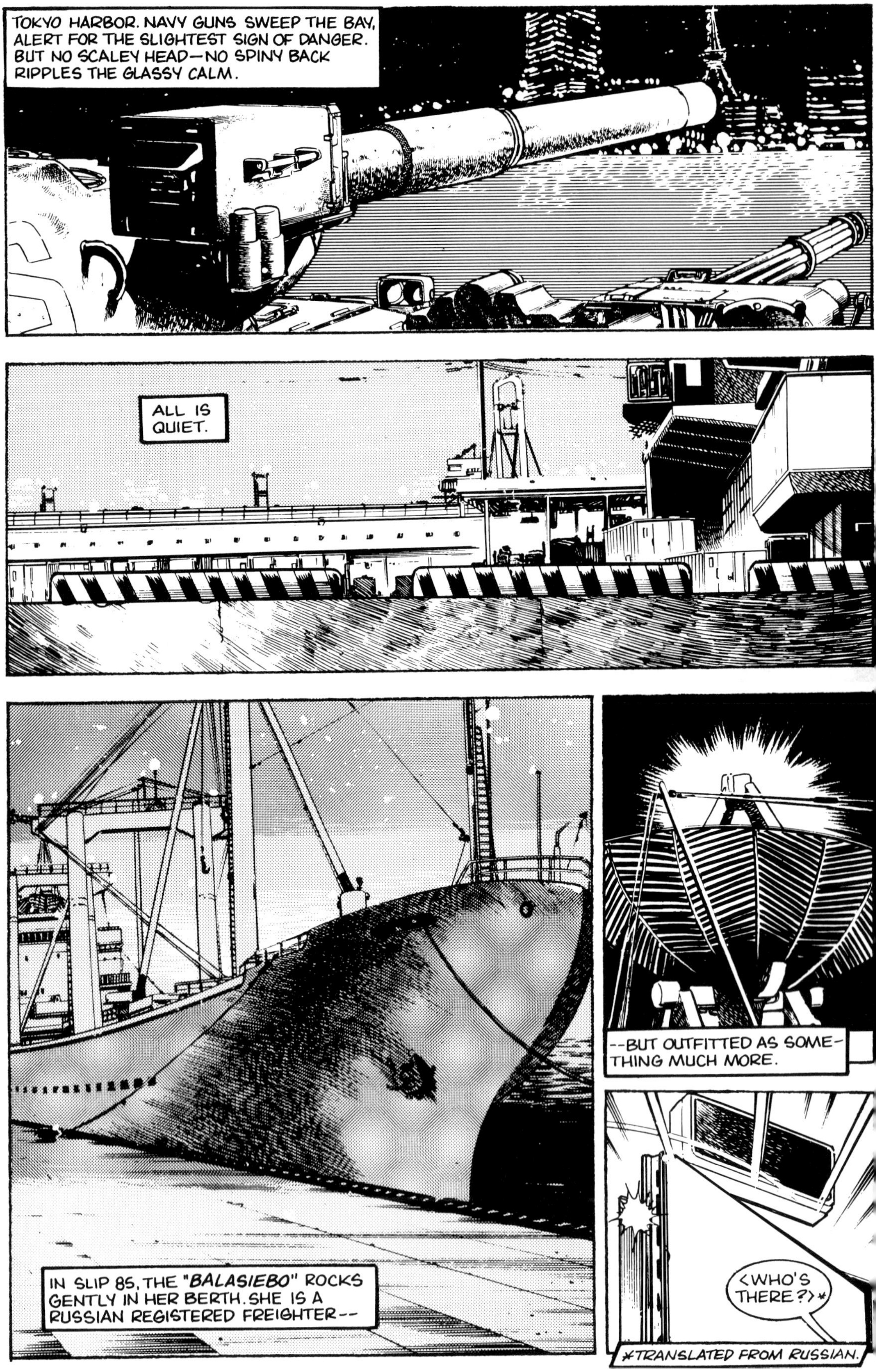
TOKYO HARBOR. NAVY GUNS SWEEP THE BAY, ALERT FOR THE SLIGHTEST SIGN OF DANGER. BUT NO SCALEY HEAD—NO SPINY BACK RIPPLES THE GLASSY CALM.
ALL IS QUIET.
IN SLIP 85, THE "BALASIEBO" ROCKS GENTLY IN HER BERTH. SHE IS A RUSSIAN REGISTERED FREIGHTER--
--BUT OUTFITTED AS SOMETHING MUCH MORE.
<WHO'S THERE?>*
*TRANSLATED FROM RUSSIAN.

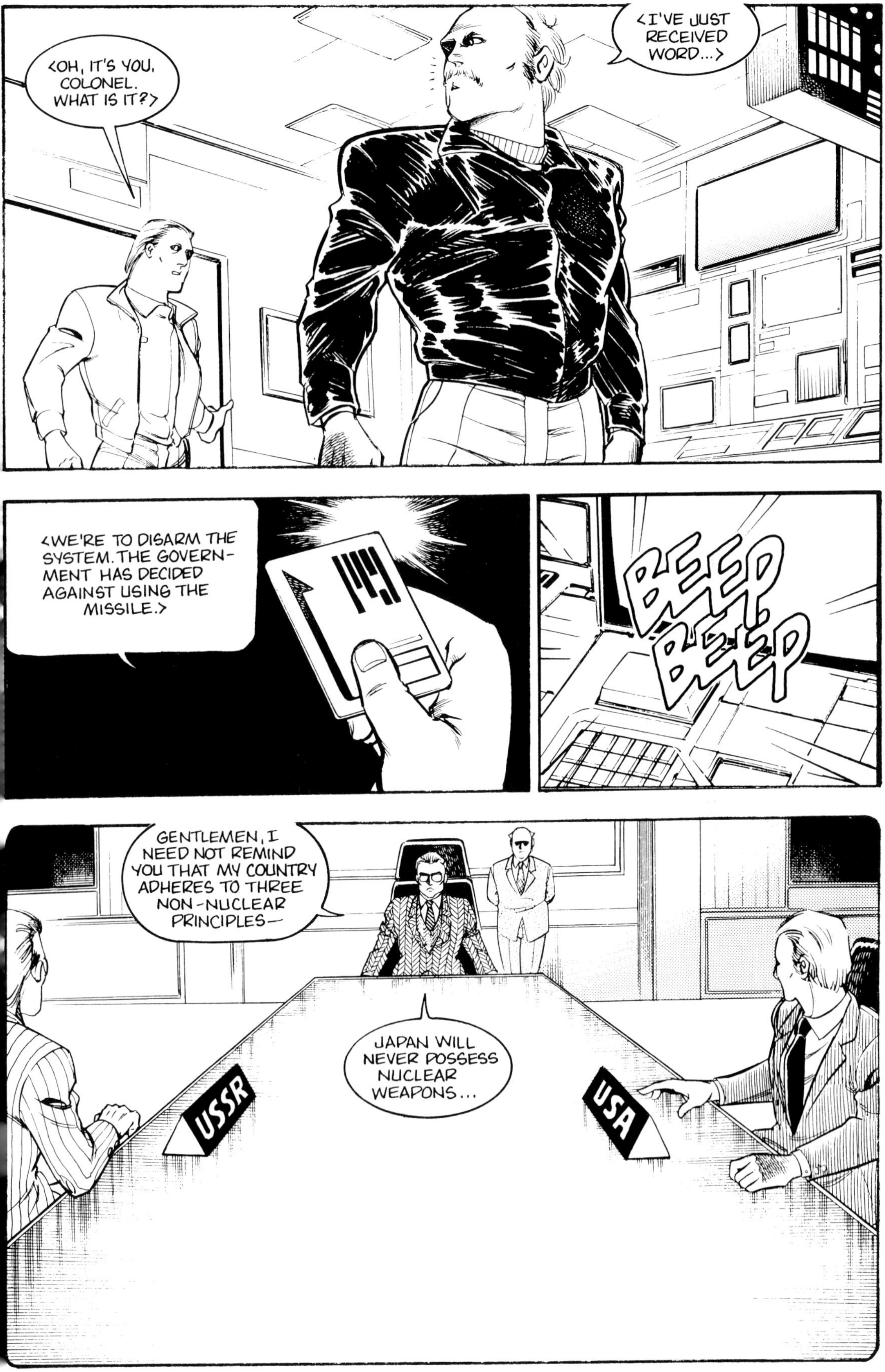
<OH, IT'S YOU, COLONEL. WHAT IS IT?>
<I'VE JUST RECEIVED WORD...>
<WE'RE TO DISARM THE SYSTEM. THE GOVERNMENT HAS DECIDED AGAINST USING THE MISSILE.>
BEEP BEEP
GENTLEMEN, I NEED NOT REMIND YOU THAT MY COUNTRY ADHERES TO THREE NON-NUCLEAR PRINCIPLES—
USSR
USA
JAPAN WILL NEVER POSSESS NUCLEAR WEAPONS...

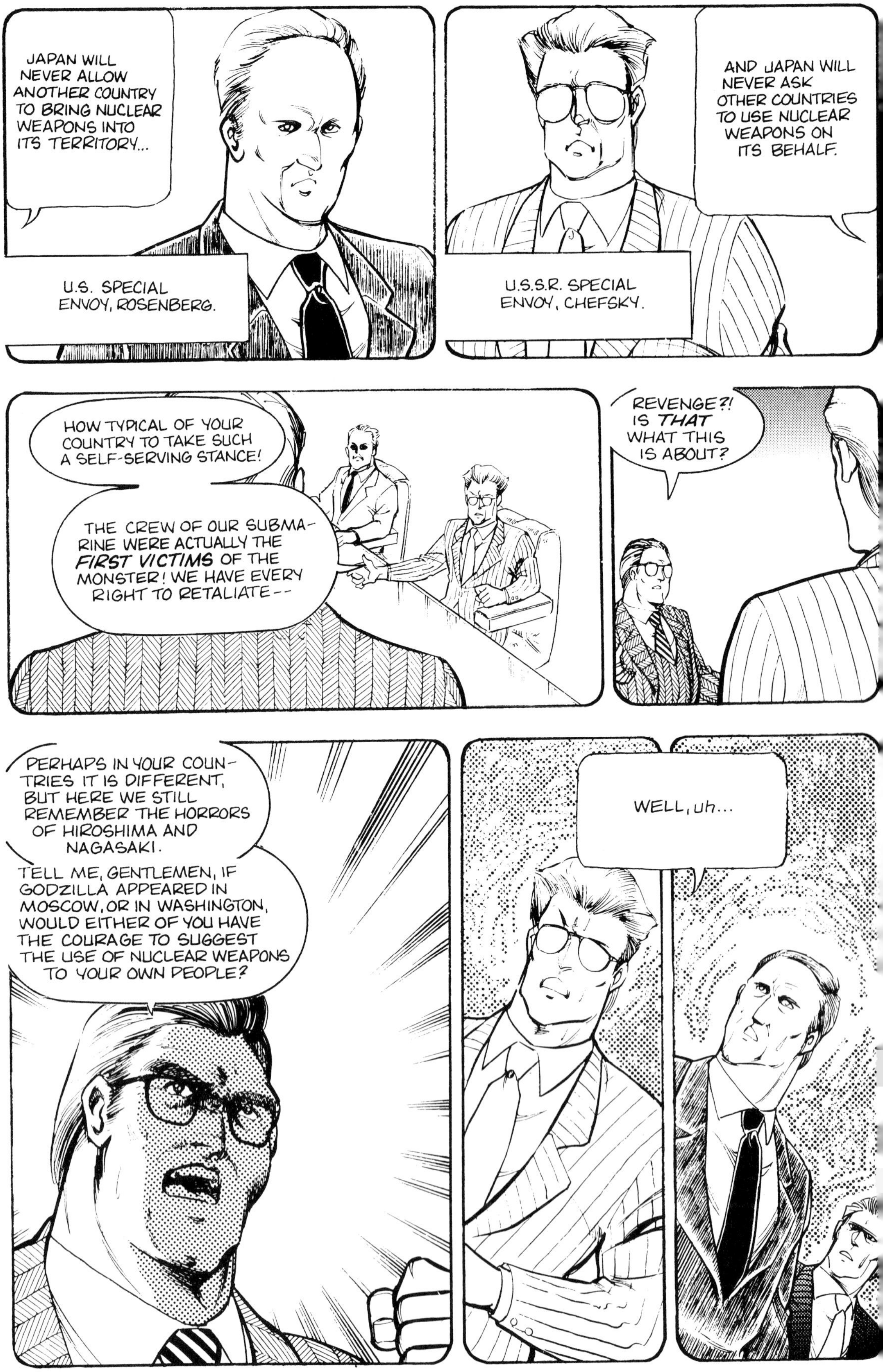
JAPAN WILL NEVER ALLOW ANOTHER COUNTRY TO BRING NUCLEAR WEAPONS INTO ITS TERRITORY...
U.S. SPECIAL ENVOY, ROSENBERG.
AND JAPAN WILL NEVER ASK OTHER COUNTRIES TO USE NUCLEAR WEAPONS ON ITS BEHALF.
U.S.S.R. SPECIAL ENVOY, CHEFSKY.
HOW TYPICAL OF YOUR COUNTRY TO TAKE SUCH A SELF-SERVING STANCE!
THE CREW OF OUR SUBMARINE WERE ACTUALLY THE *FIRST VICTIMS* OF THE MONSTER! WE HAVE EVERY RIGHT TO RETALIATE--
REVENGE?! IS *THAT* WHAT THIS IS ABOUT?
PERHAPS IN YOUR COUNTRIES IT IS DIFFERENT, BUT HERE WE STILL REMEMBER THE HORRORS OF HIROSHIMA AND NAGASAKI.
TELL ME, GENTLEMEN, IF GODZILLA APPEARED IN MOSCOW, OR IN WASHINGTON, WOULD EITHER OF YOU HAVE THE COURAGE TO SUGGEST THE USE OF NUCLEAR WEAPONS TO YOUR OWN PEOPLE?
WELL, uh...

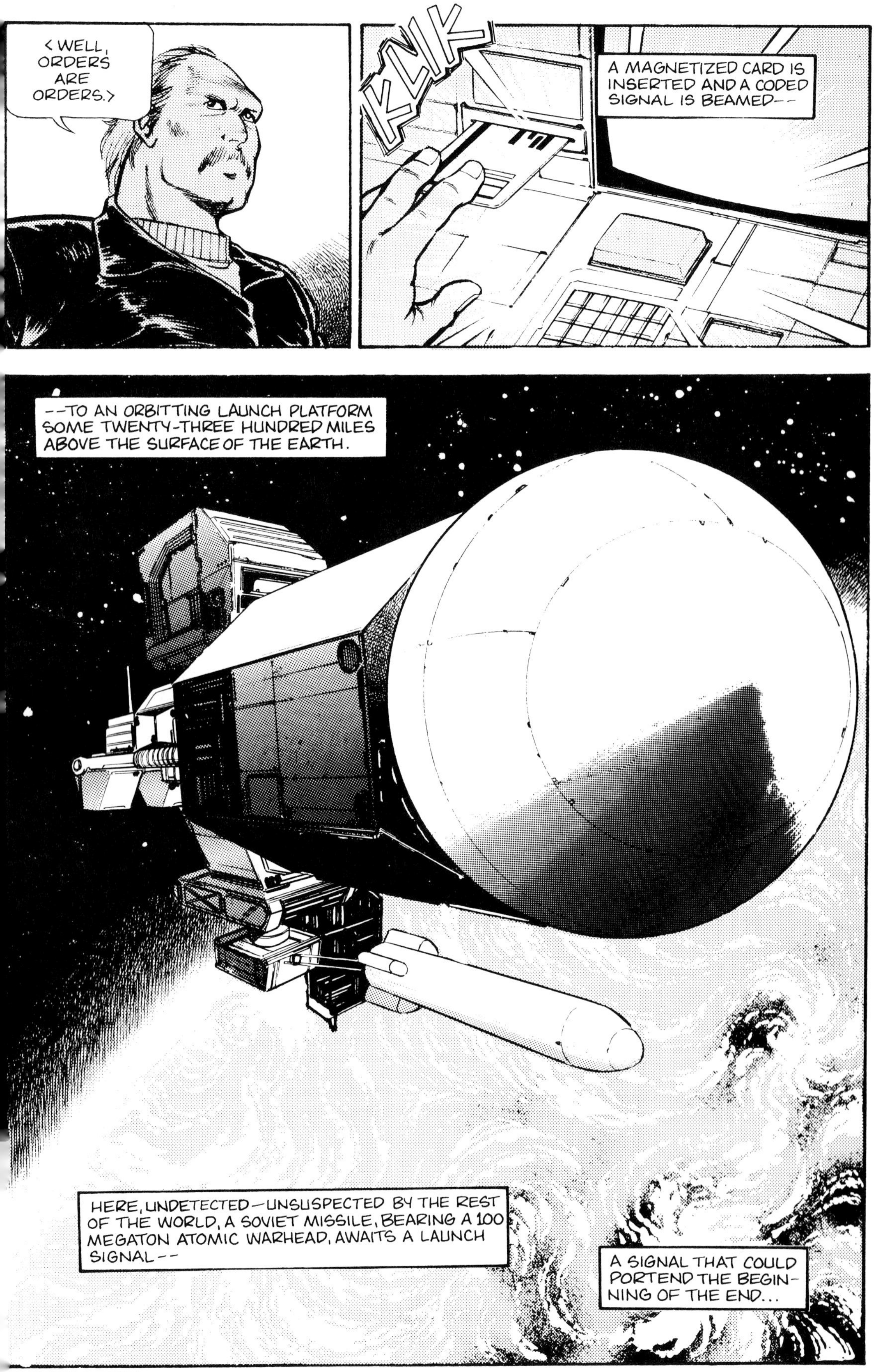
<WELL, ORDERS ARE ORDERS.>
KLIK
A MAGNETIZED CARD IS INSERTED AND A CODED SIGNAL IS BEAMED--
--TO AN ORBITTING LAUNCH PLATFORM SOME TWENTY-THREE HUNDRED MILES ABOVE THE SURFACE OF THE EARTH.
HERE, UNDETECTED—UNSUSPECTED BY THE REST OF THE WORLD, A SOVIET MISSILE, BEARING A 100 MEGATON ATOMIC WARHEAD, AWAITS A LAUNCH SIGNAL--
A SIGNAL THAT COULD PORTEND THE BEGIN-NING OF THE END...

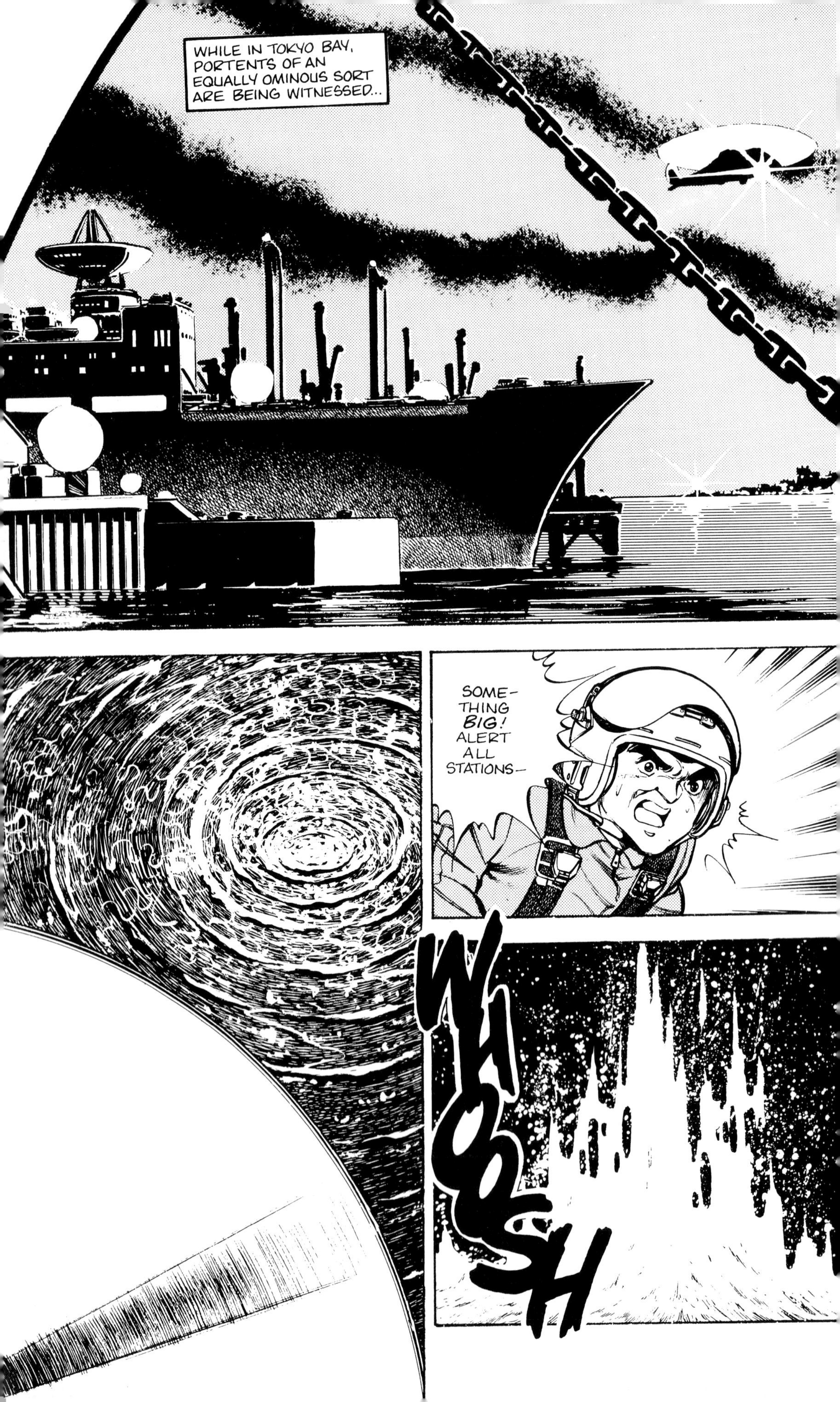
WHILE IN TOKYO BAY, PORTENTS OF AN EQUALLY OMINOUS SORT ARE BEING WITNESSED...
SOME-THING BIG! ALERT ALL STATIONS-
WHOOOSH

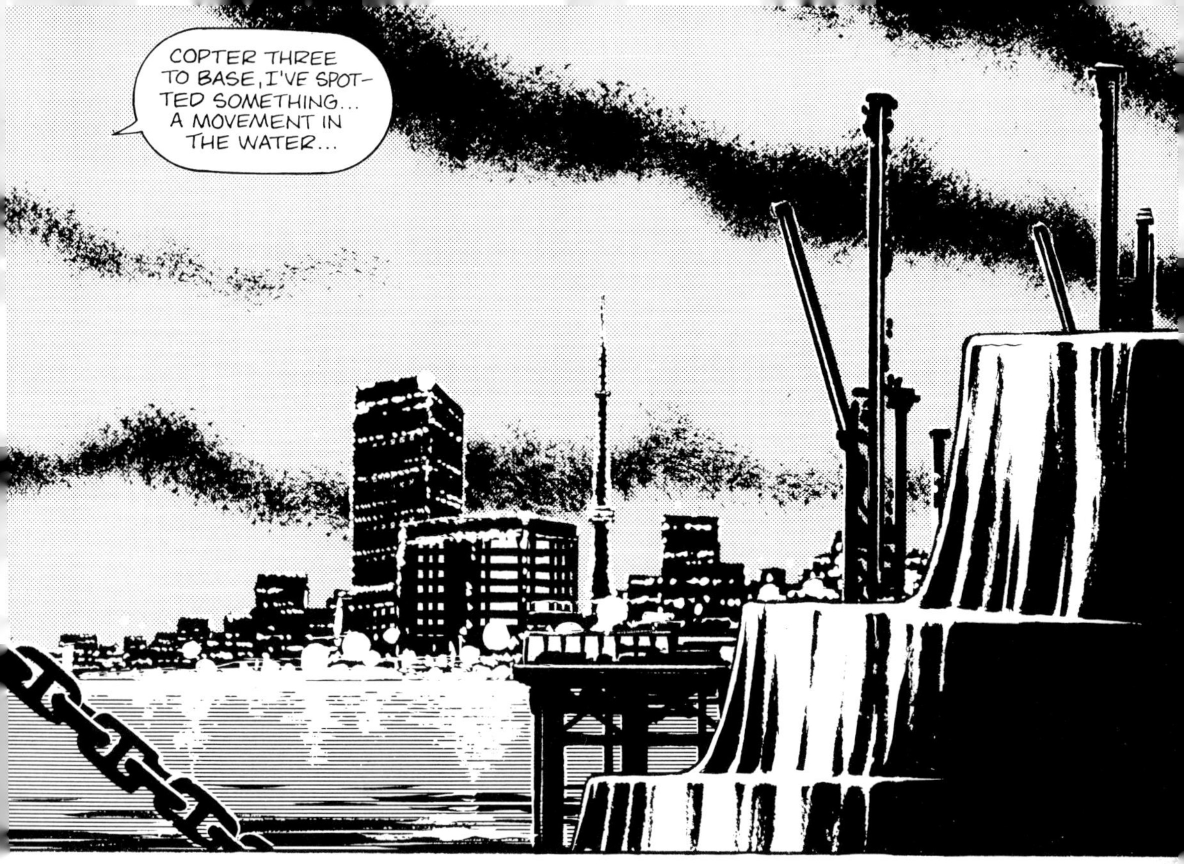
COPTER THREE TO BASE, I'VE SPOTTED SOMETHING... A MOVEMENT IN THE WATER...

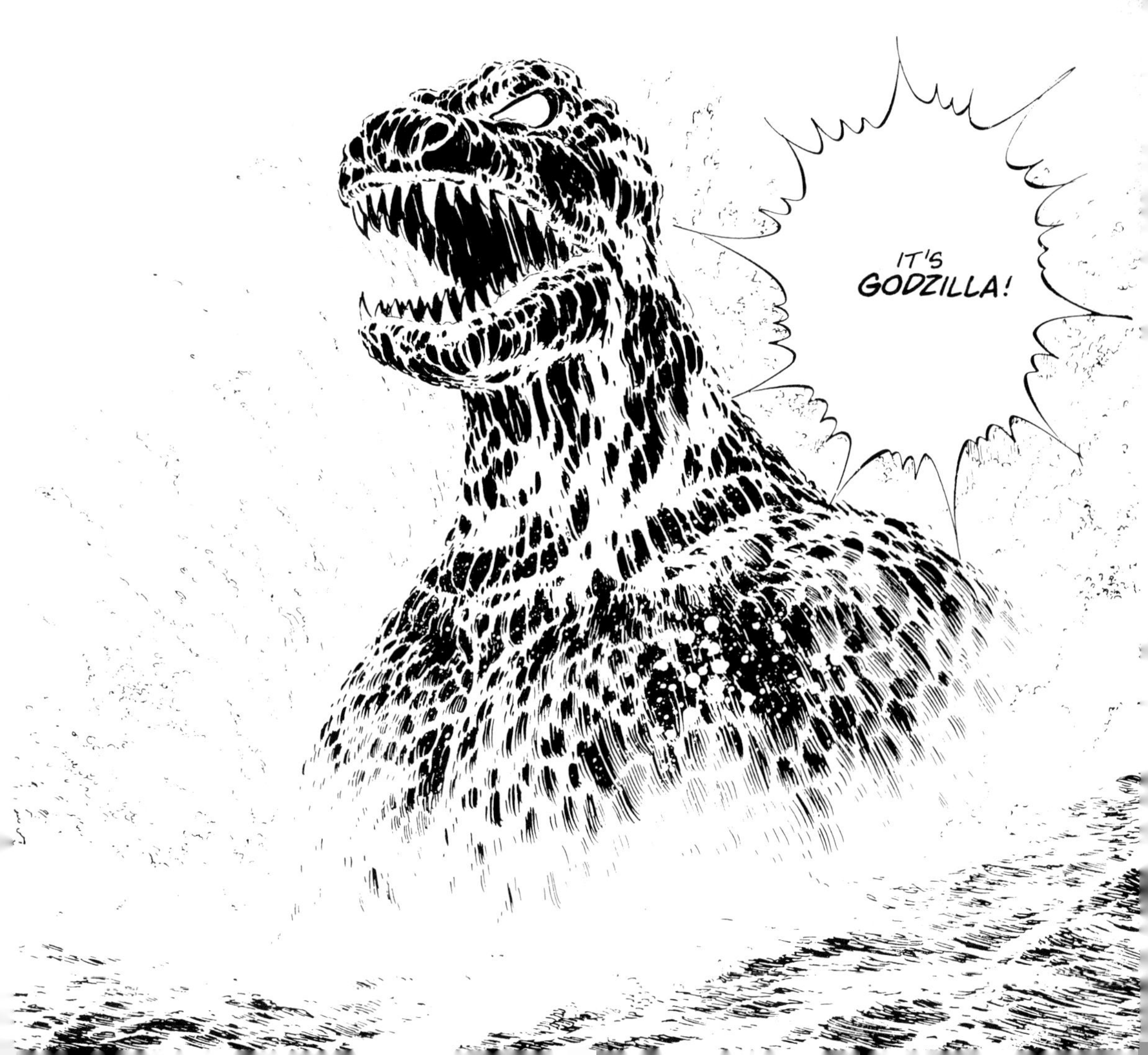
IT'S GODZILLA!

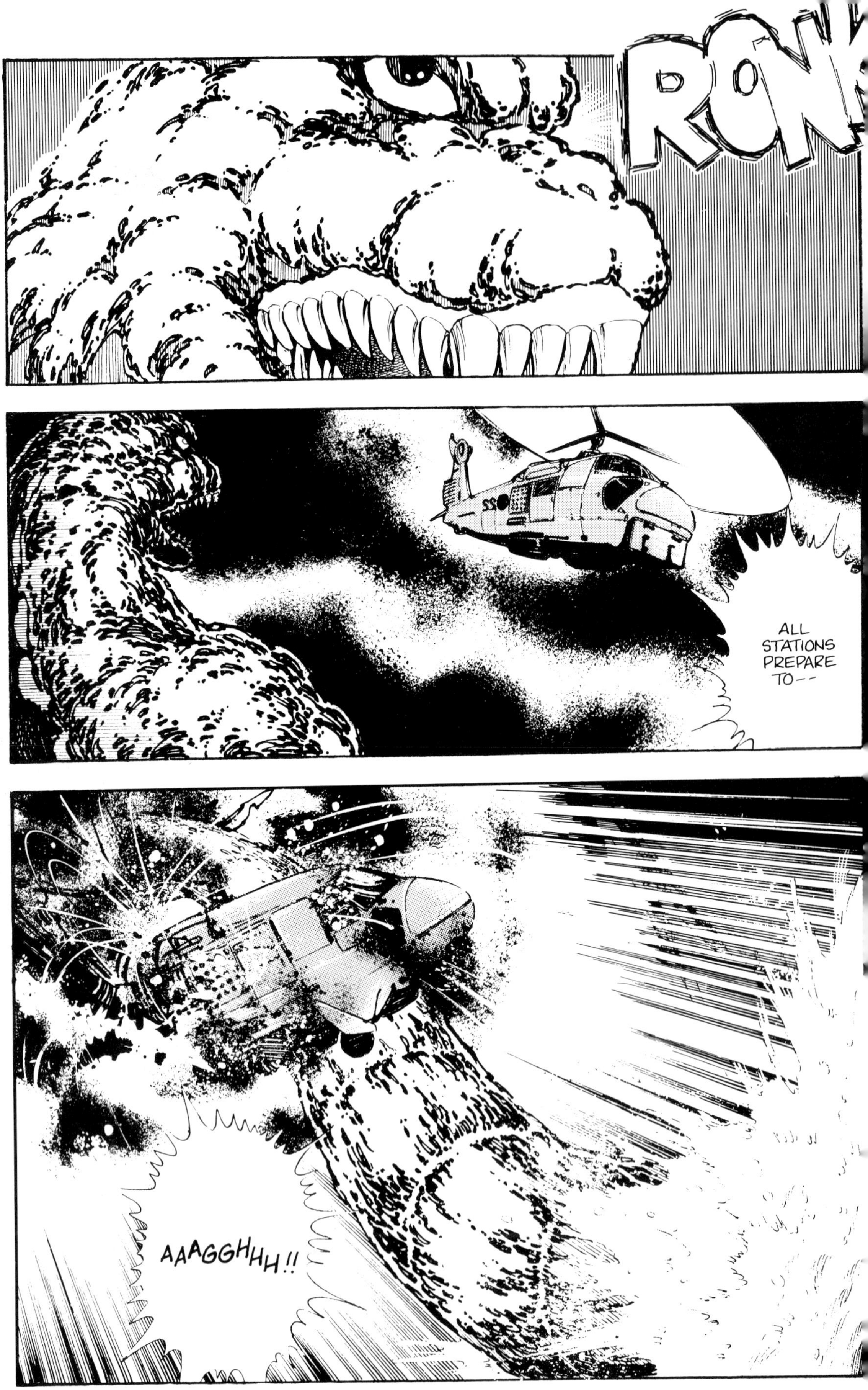
RON
ALL STATIONS PREPARE TO--
AAAGGHHH!!

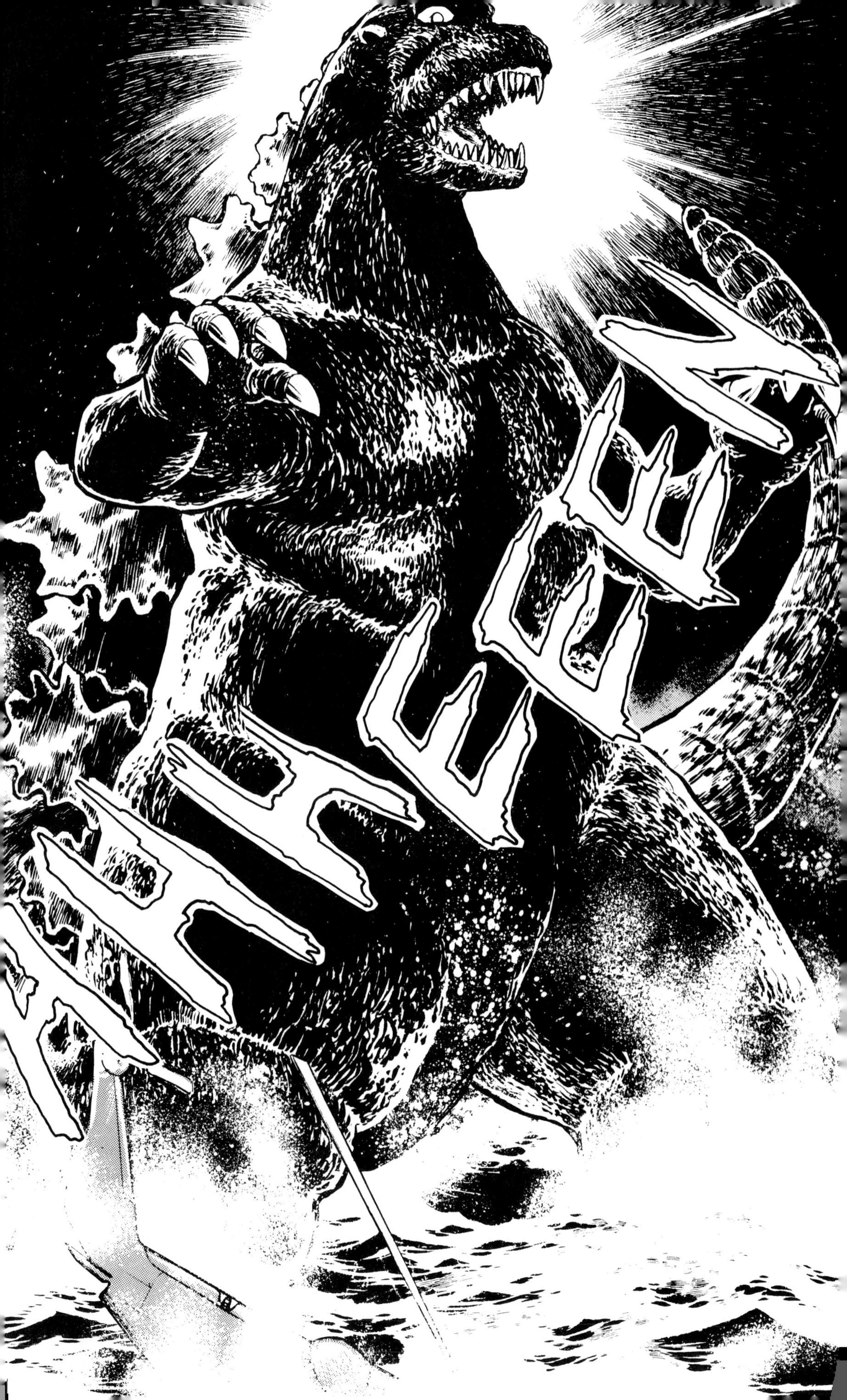

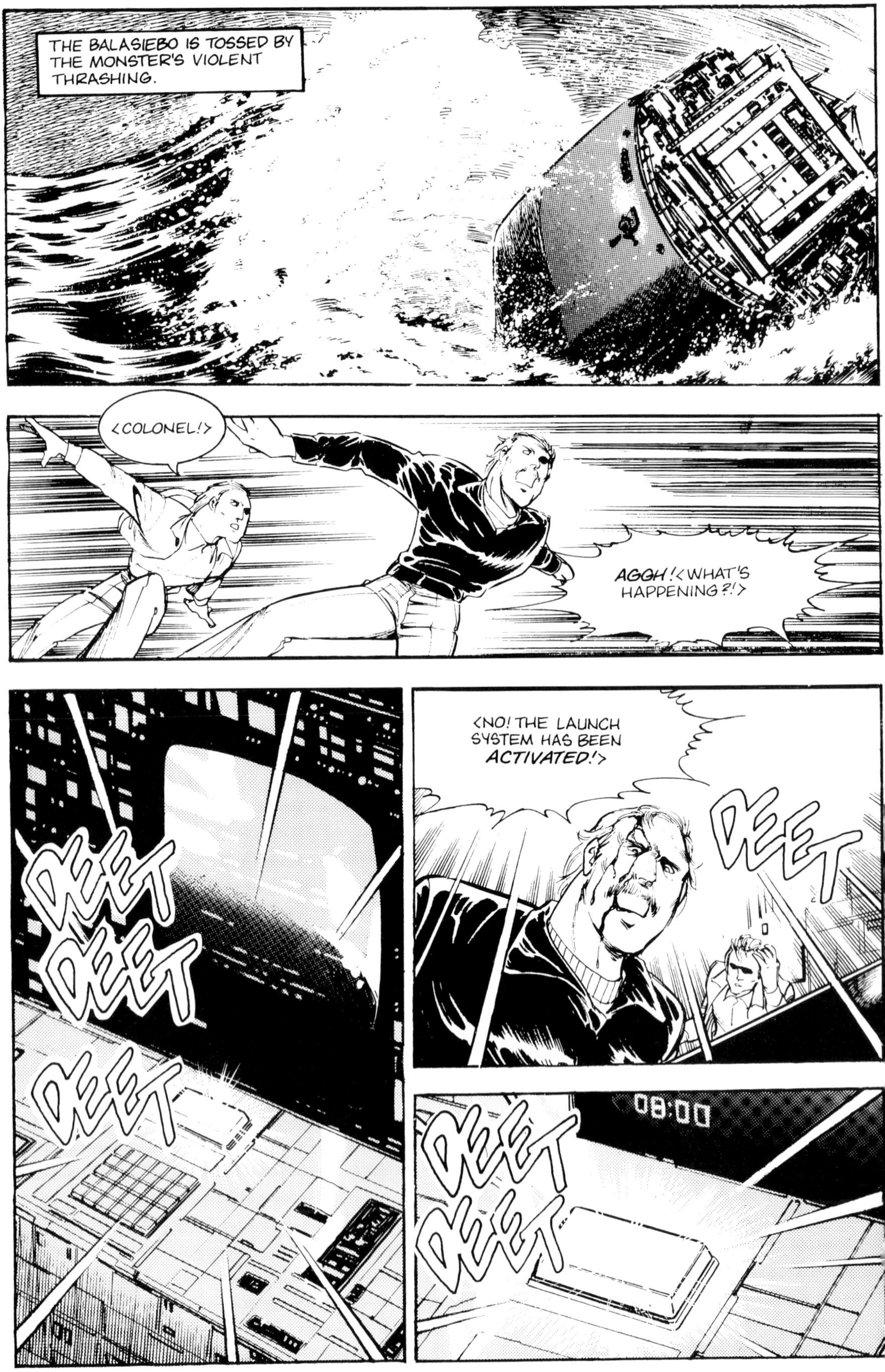
THE BALASIEBO IS TOSSED BY THE MONSTER'S VIOLENT THRASHING.
<COLONEL!>
AGGH! <WHAT'S HAPPENING?!>
DEET
DEET
DEET
<NO! THE LAUNCH SYSTEM HAS BEEN ACTIVATED!>
DEET
08:00
DEET
DEET

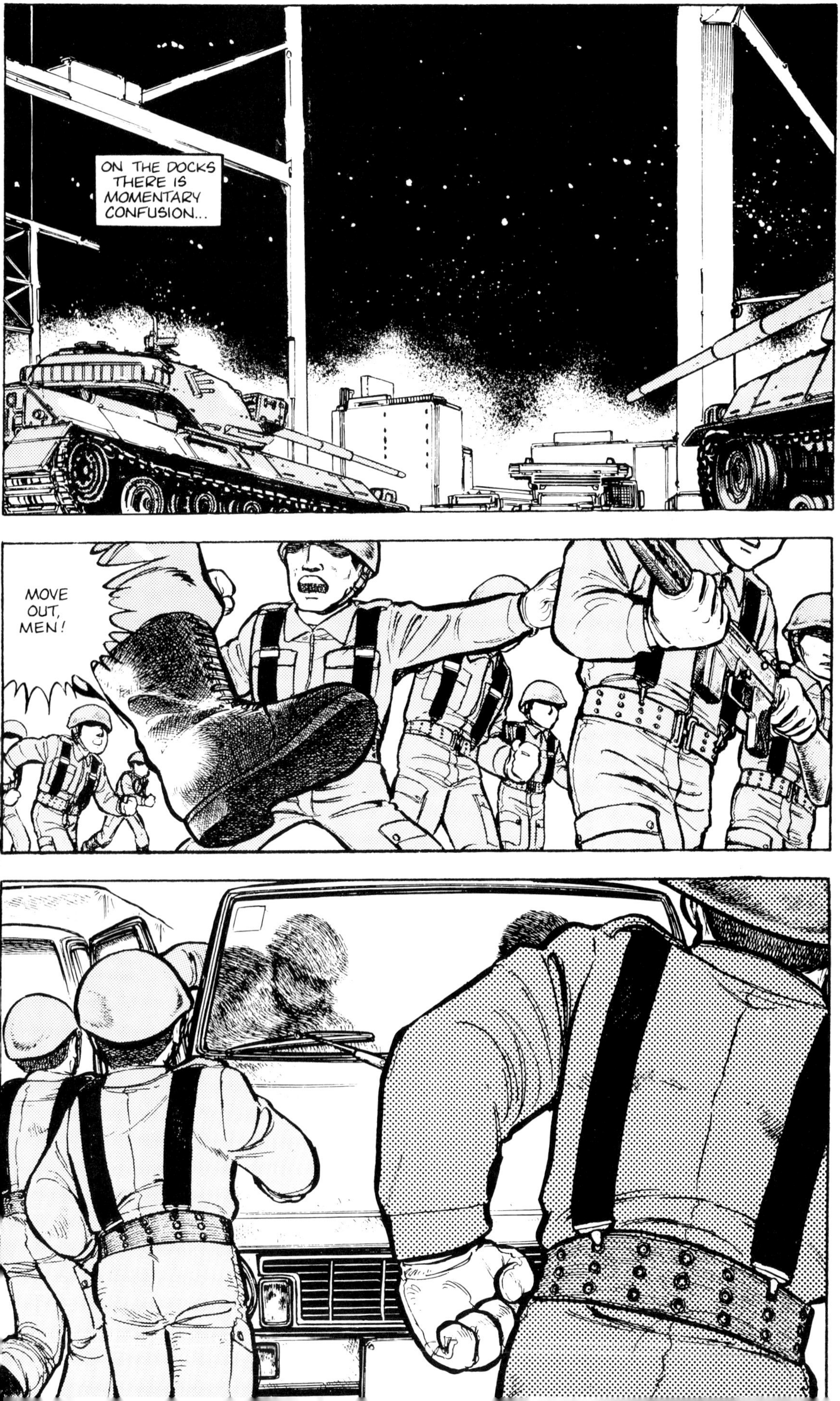
ON THE DOCKS THERE IS MOMENTARY CONFUSION...
MOVE OUT, MEN!

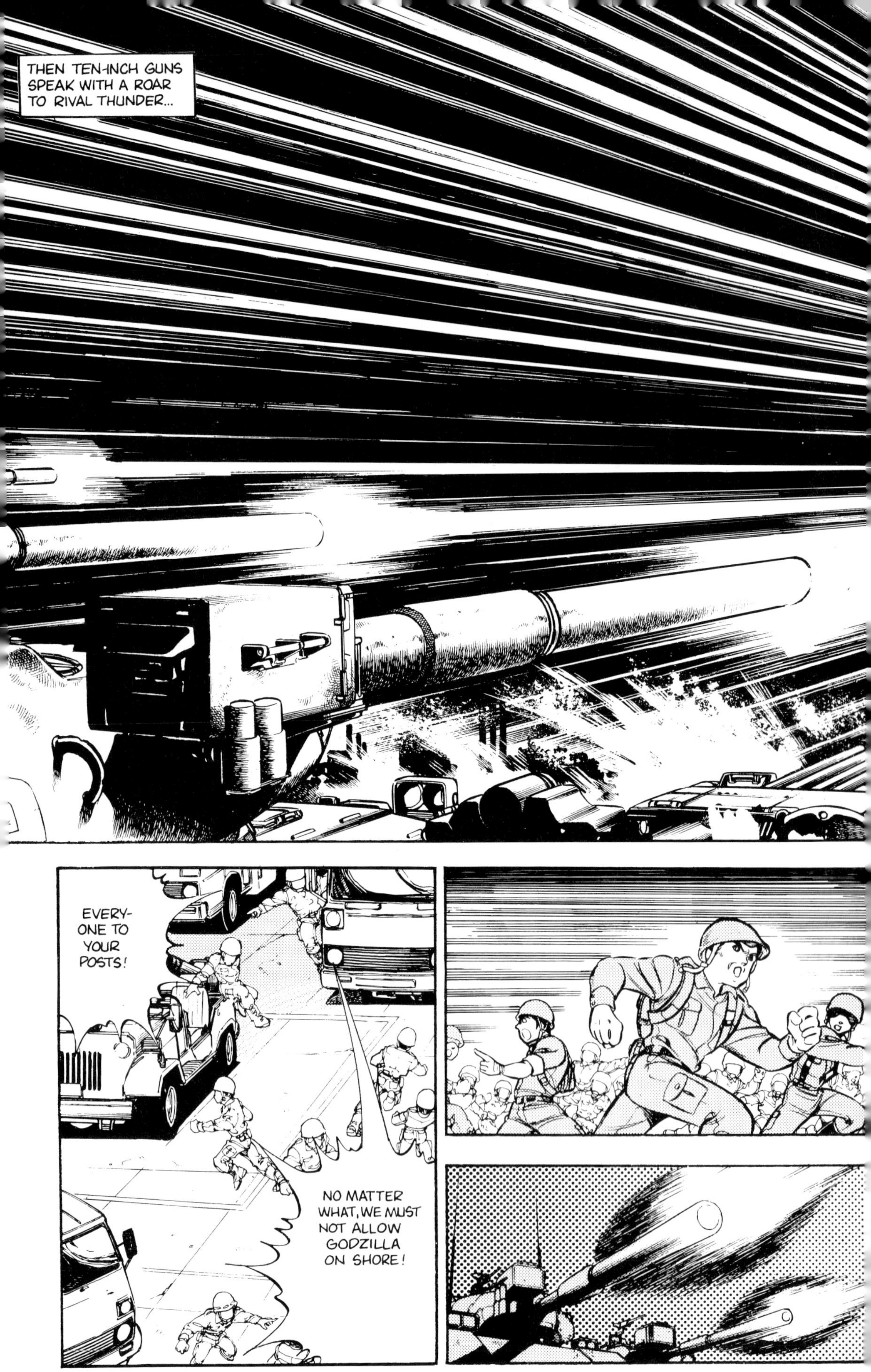
THEN TEN-INCH GUNS SPEAK WITH A ROAR TO RIVAL THUNDER...
EVERY-ONE TO YOUR POSTS!
NO MATTER WHAT, WE MUST NOT ALLOW GODZILLA ON SHORE!

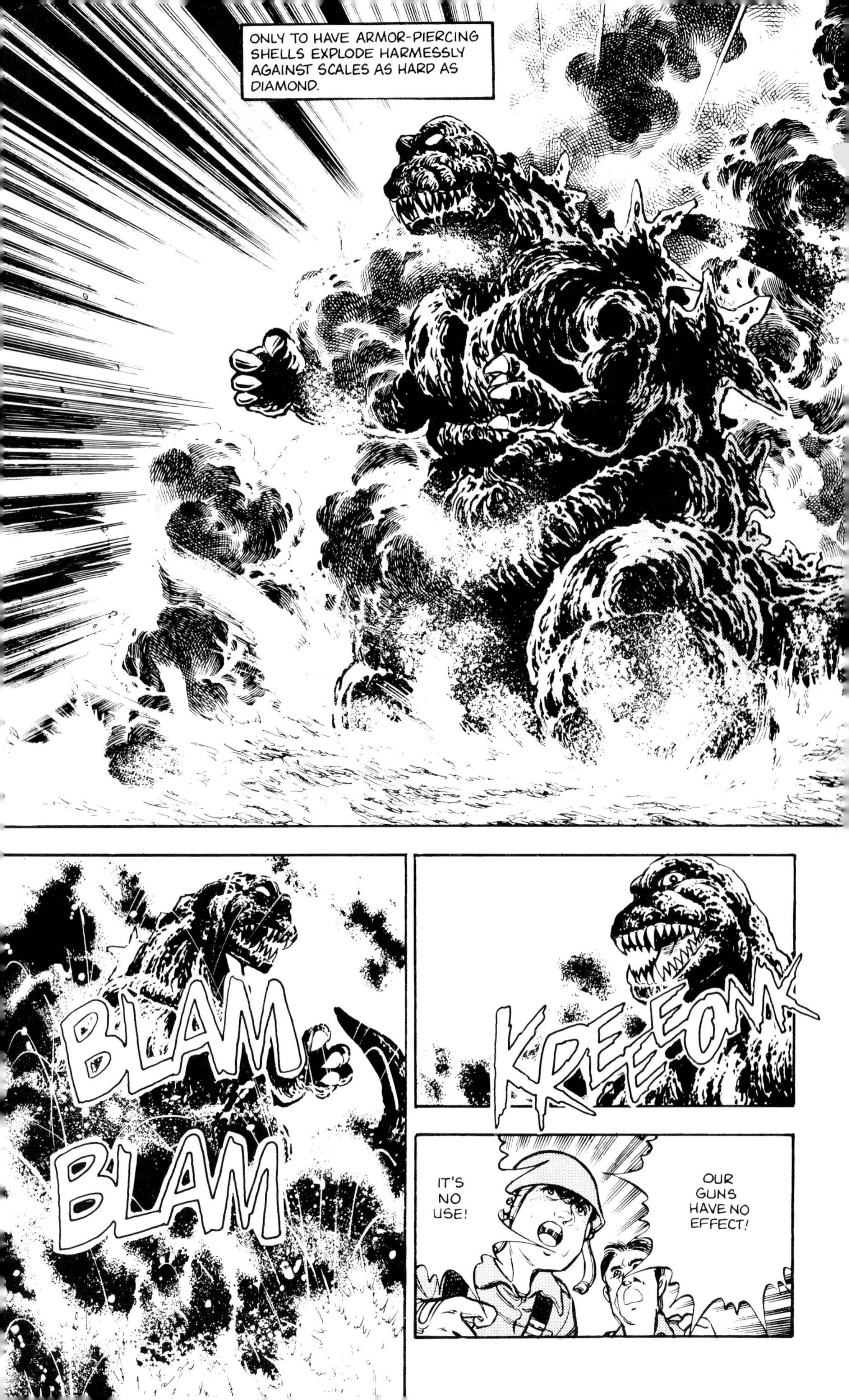
ONLY TO HAVE ARMOR-PIERCING SHELLS EXPLODE HARMESSLY AGAINST SCALES AS HARD AS DIAMOND.
BLAM
BLAM
KREEEONK
IT'S NO USE!
OUR GUNS HAVE NO EFFECT!

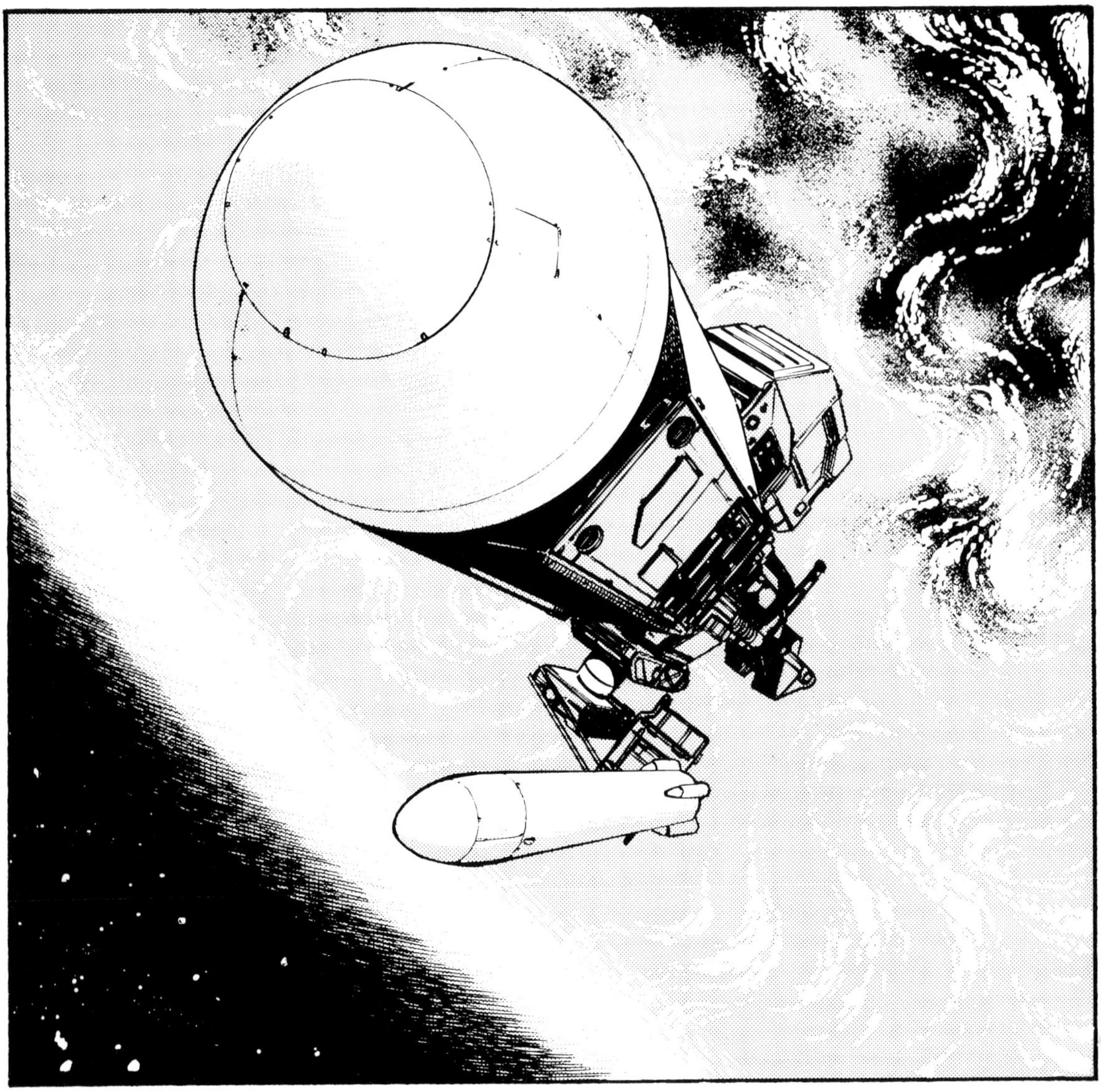
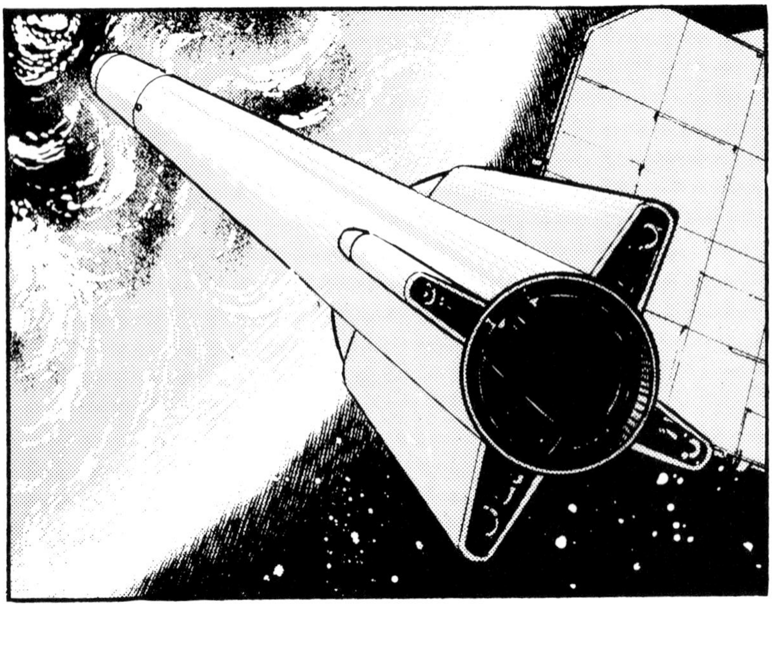
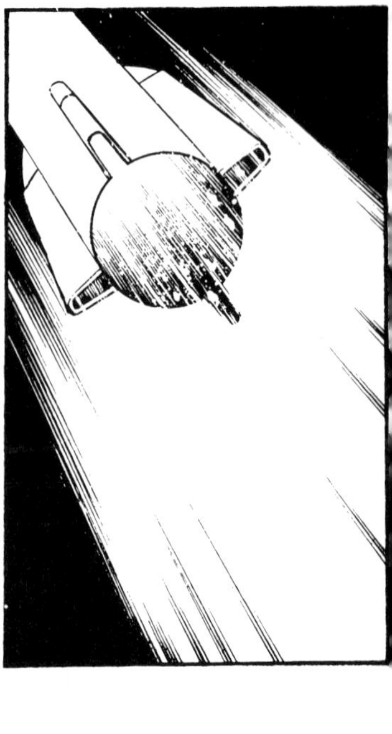

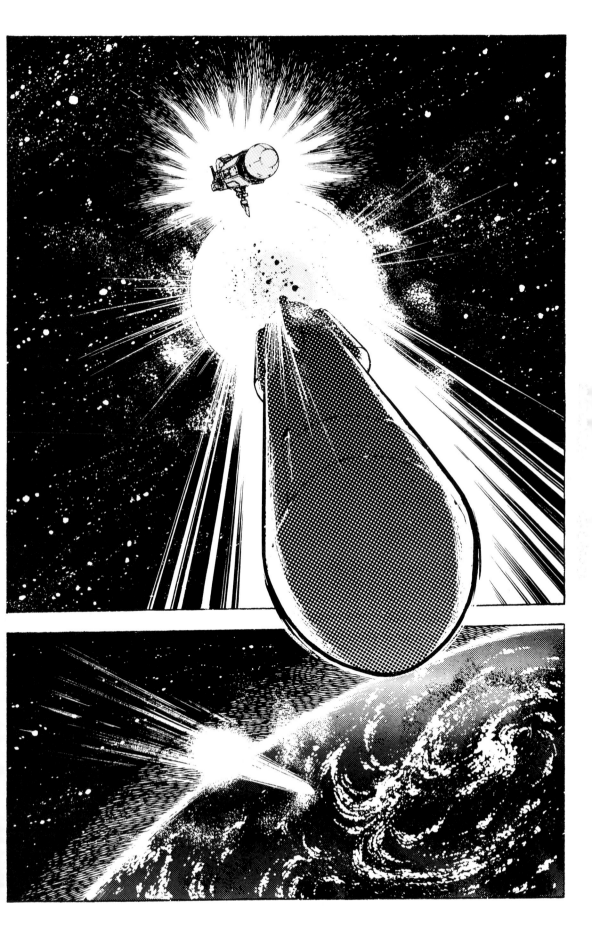

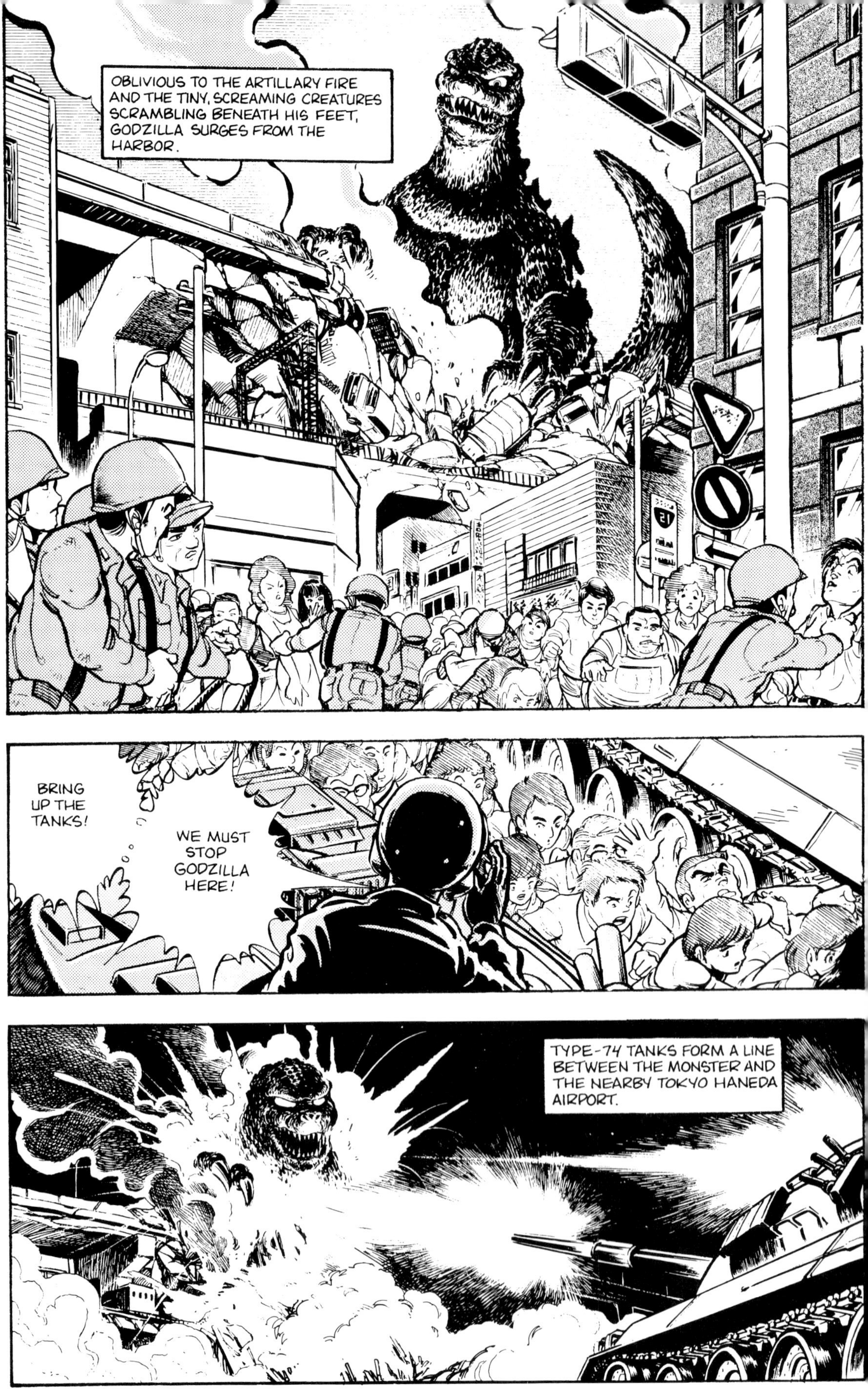
OBLIVIOUS TO THE ARTILLARY FIRE AND THE TINY, SCREAMING CREATURES SCRAMBLING BENEATH HIS FEET, GODZILLA SURGES FROM THE HARBOR.
BRING UP THE TANKS!
WE MUST STOP GODZILLA HERE!
TYPE-74 TANKS FORM A LINE BETWEEN THE MONSTER AND THE NEARBY TOKYO HANEDA AIRPORT.

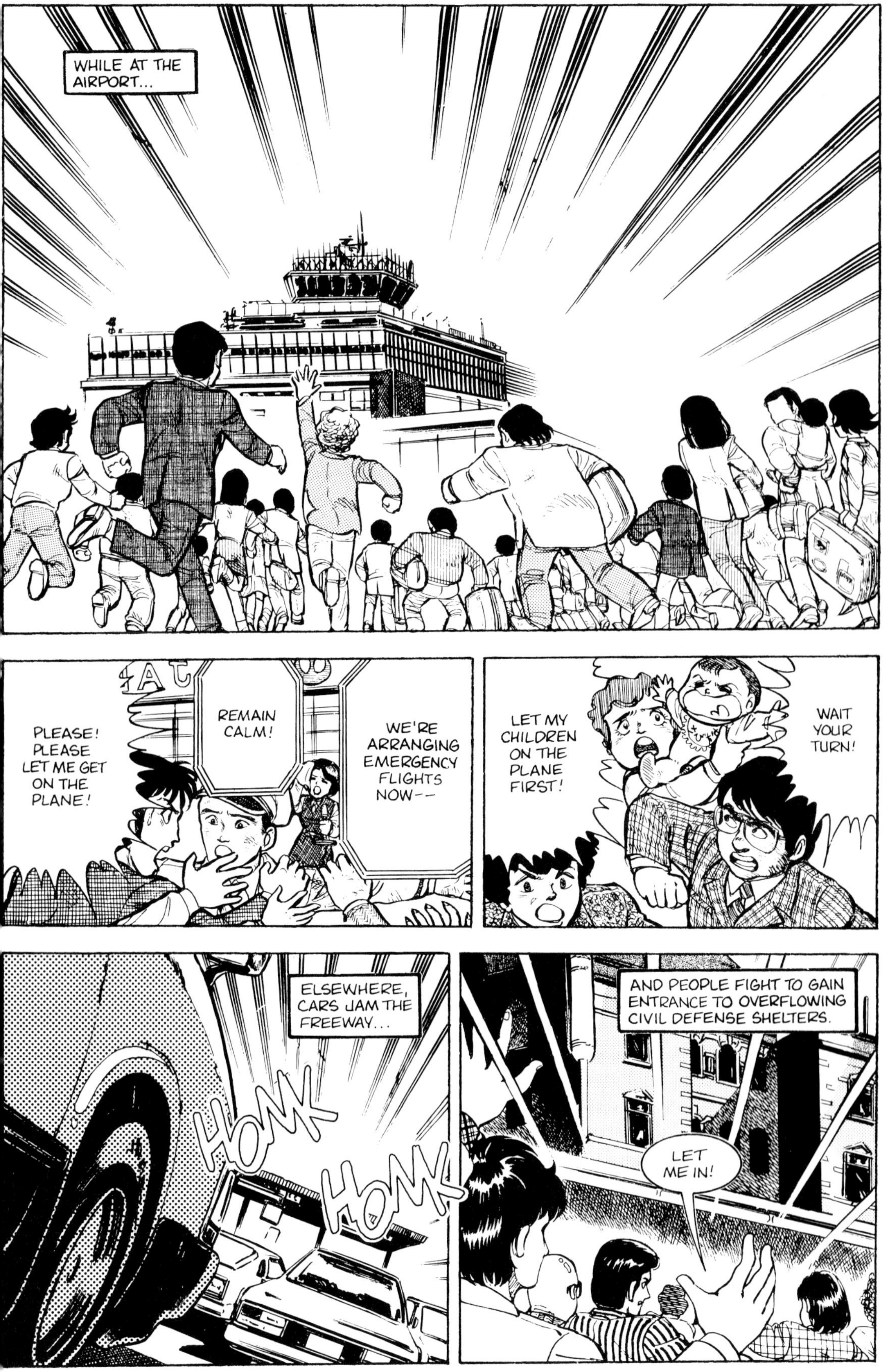
WHILE AT THE AIRPORT...
PLEASE! PLEASE LET ME GET ON THE PLANE!
REMAIN CALM!
WE'RE ARRANGING EMERGENCY FLIGHTS NOW--
LET MY CHILDREN ON THE PLANE FIRST!
WAIT YOUR TURN!
ELSEWHERE, CARS JAM THE FREEWAY...
HONK
HONK
AND PEOPLE FIGHT TO GAIN ENTRANCE TO OVERFLOWING CIVIL DEFENSE SHELTERS.
LET ME IN!

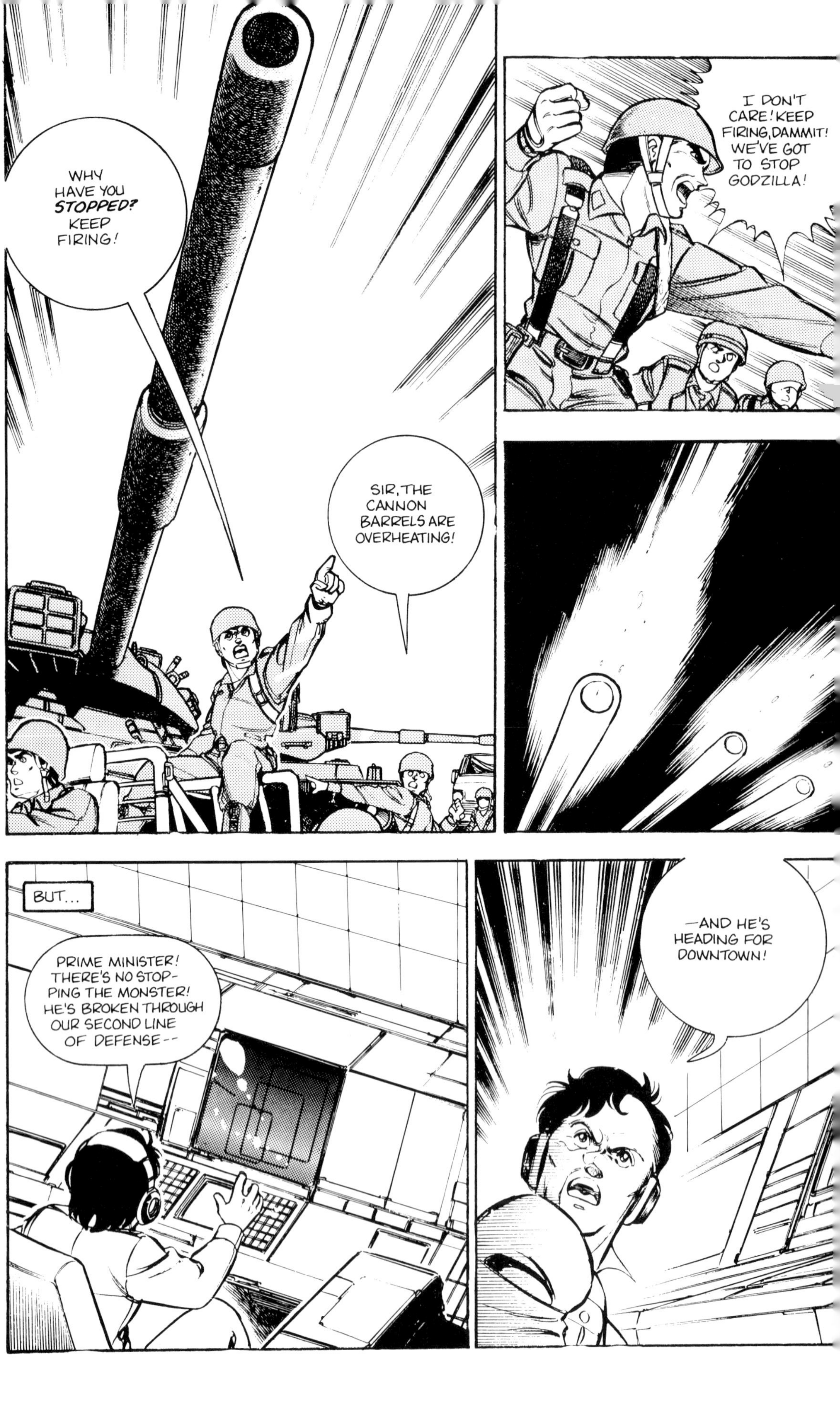
WHY HAVE YOU STOPPED? KEEP FIRING!
SIR, THE CANNON BARRELS ARE OVERHEATING!
I DON'T CARE! KEEP FIRING, DAMMIT! WE'VE GOT TO STOP GODZILLA!
BUT...
PRIME MINISTER! THERE'S NO STOP-PING THE MONSTER! HE'S BROKEN THROUGH OUR SECOND LINE OF DEFENSE--
—AND HE'S HEADING FOR DOWNTOWN!

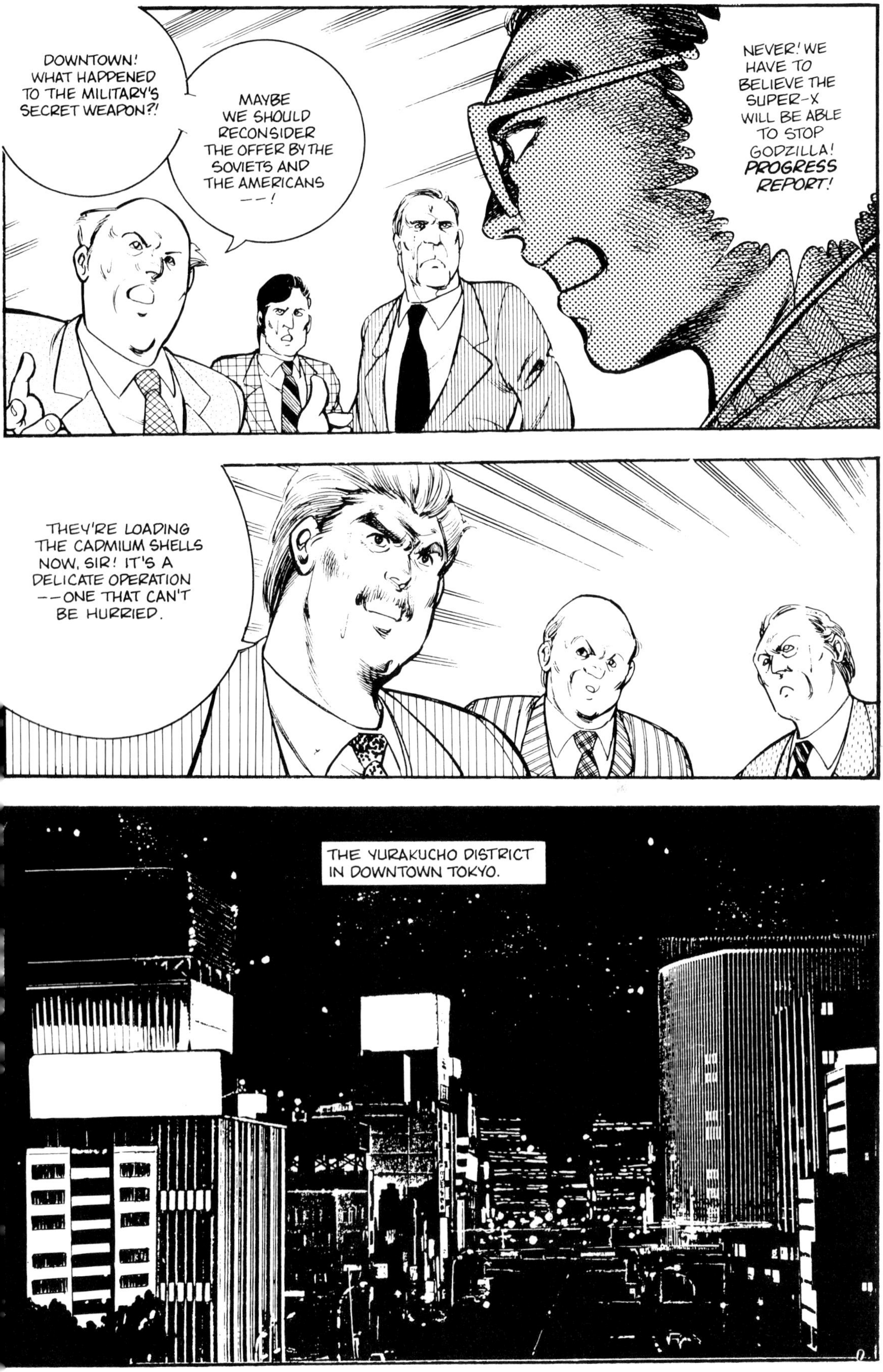
DOWNTOWN! WHAT HAPPENED TO THE MILITARY'S SECRET WEAPON?!
MAYBE WE SHOULD RECONSIDER THE OFFER BY THE SOVIETS AND THE AMERICANS --!
NEVER! WE HAVE TO BELIEVE THE SUPER-X WILL BE ABLE TO STOP GODZILLA! PROGRESS REPORT!
THEY'RE LOADING THE CADMIUM SHELLS NOW, SIR! IT'S A DELICATE OPERATION --ONE THAT CAN'T BE HURRIED.
THE YURAKUCHO DISTRICT IN DOWNTOWN TOKYO.

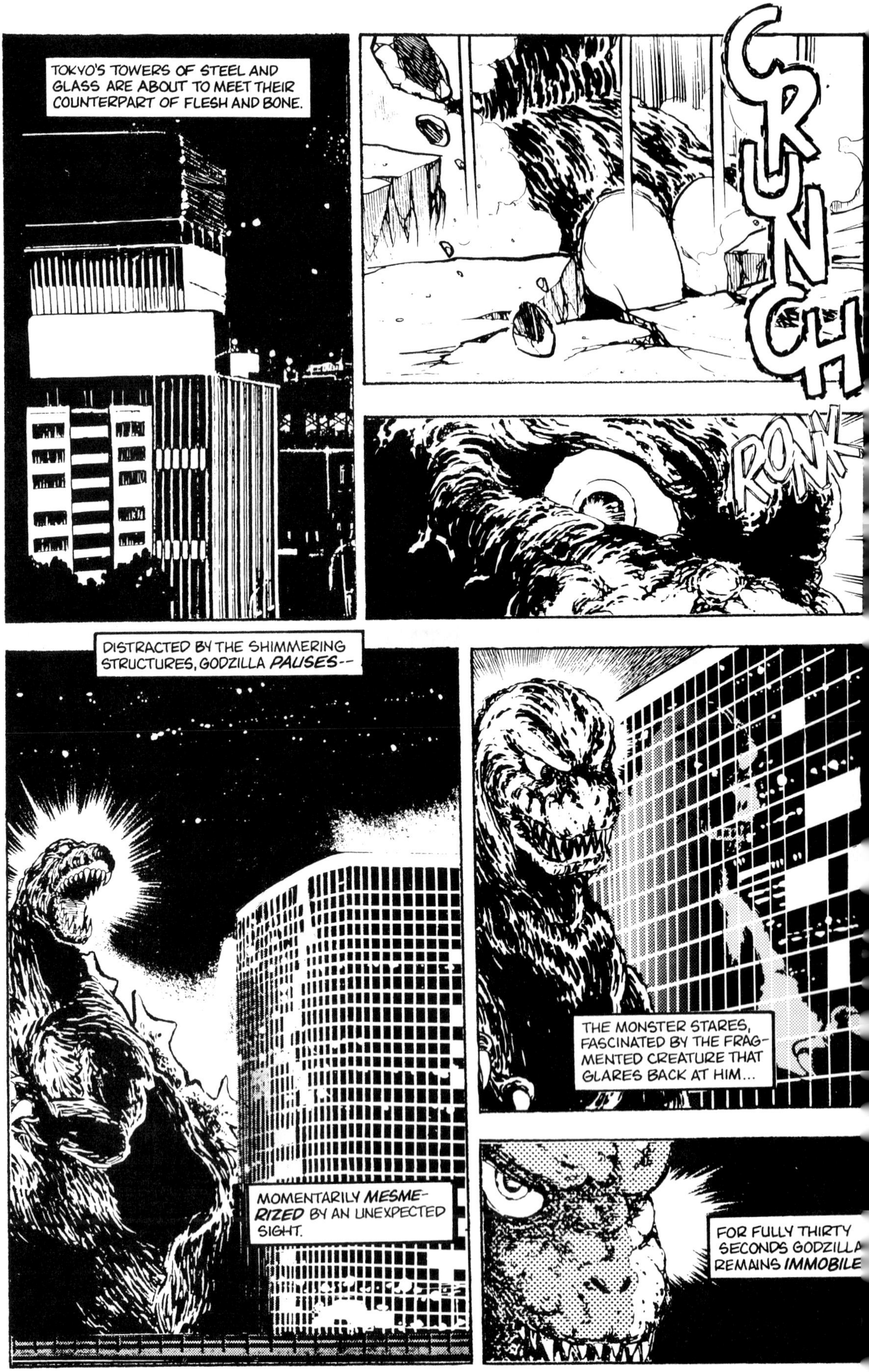
TOKYO'S TOWERS OF STEEL AND GLASS ARE ABOUT TO MEET THEIR COUNTERPART OF FLESH AND BONE.
CRUNCH
RONK
DISTRACTED BY THE SHIMMERING STRUCTURES, GODZILLA PAUSES--
MOMENTARILY MESMERIZED BY AN UNEXPECTED SIGHT.
THE MONSTER STARES, FASCINATED BY THE FRAGMENTED CREATURE THAT GLARES BACK AT HIM...
FOR FULLY THIRTY SECONDS GODZILLA REMAINS IMMOBILE

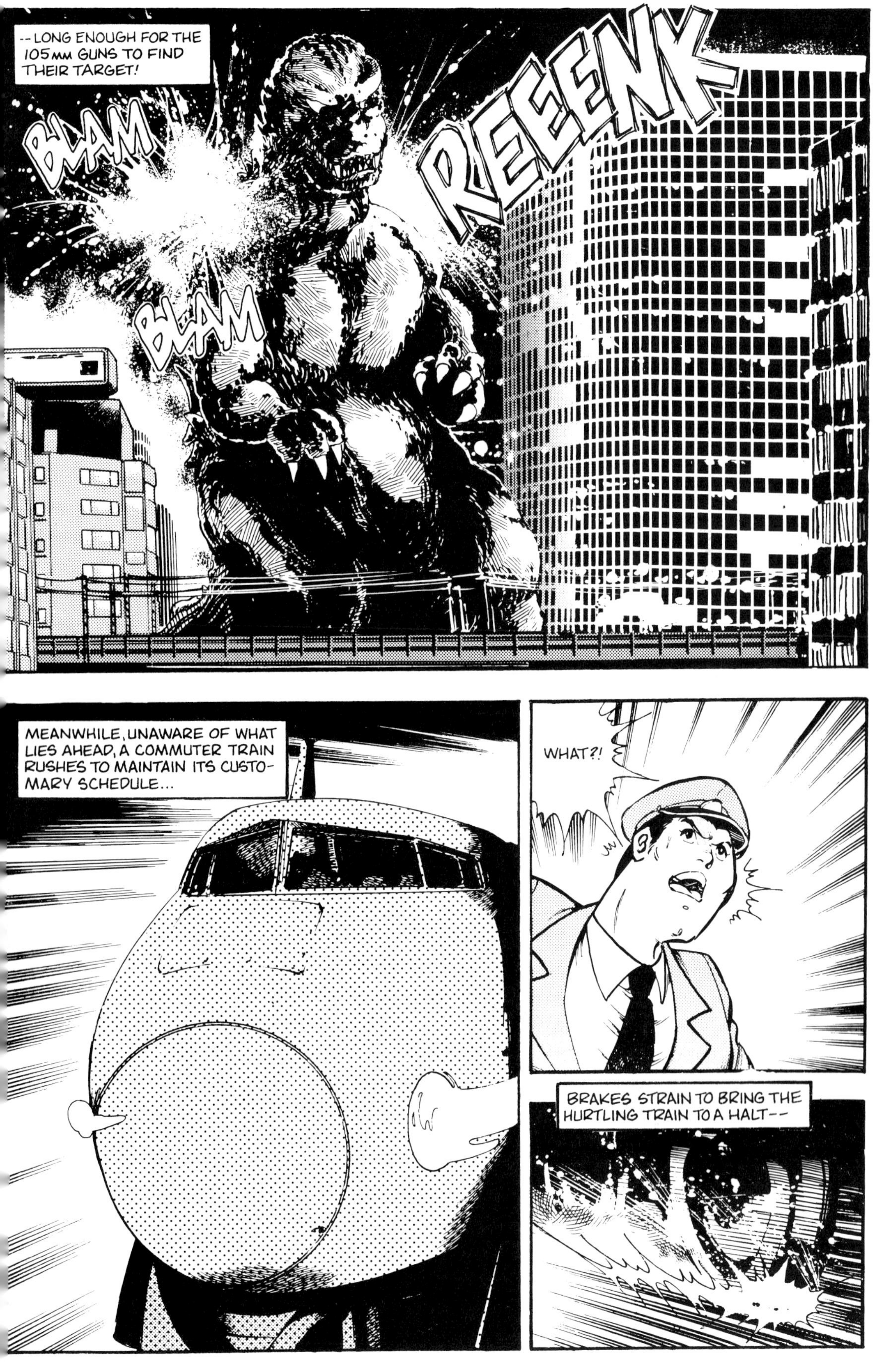
--LONG ENOUGH FOR THE 105MM GUNS TO FIND THEIR TARGET!
BLAM
BLAM
REEENK
MEANWHILE, UNAWARE OF WHAT LIES AHEAD, A COMMUTER TRAIN RUSHES TO MAINTAIN ITS CUSTOMARY SCHEDULE...
WHAT?!
BRAKES STRAIN TO BRING THE HURTLING TRAIN TO A HALT--

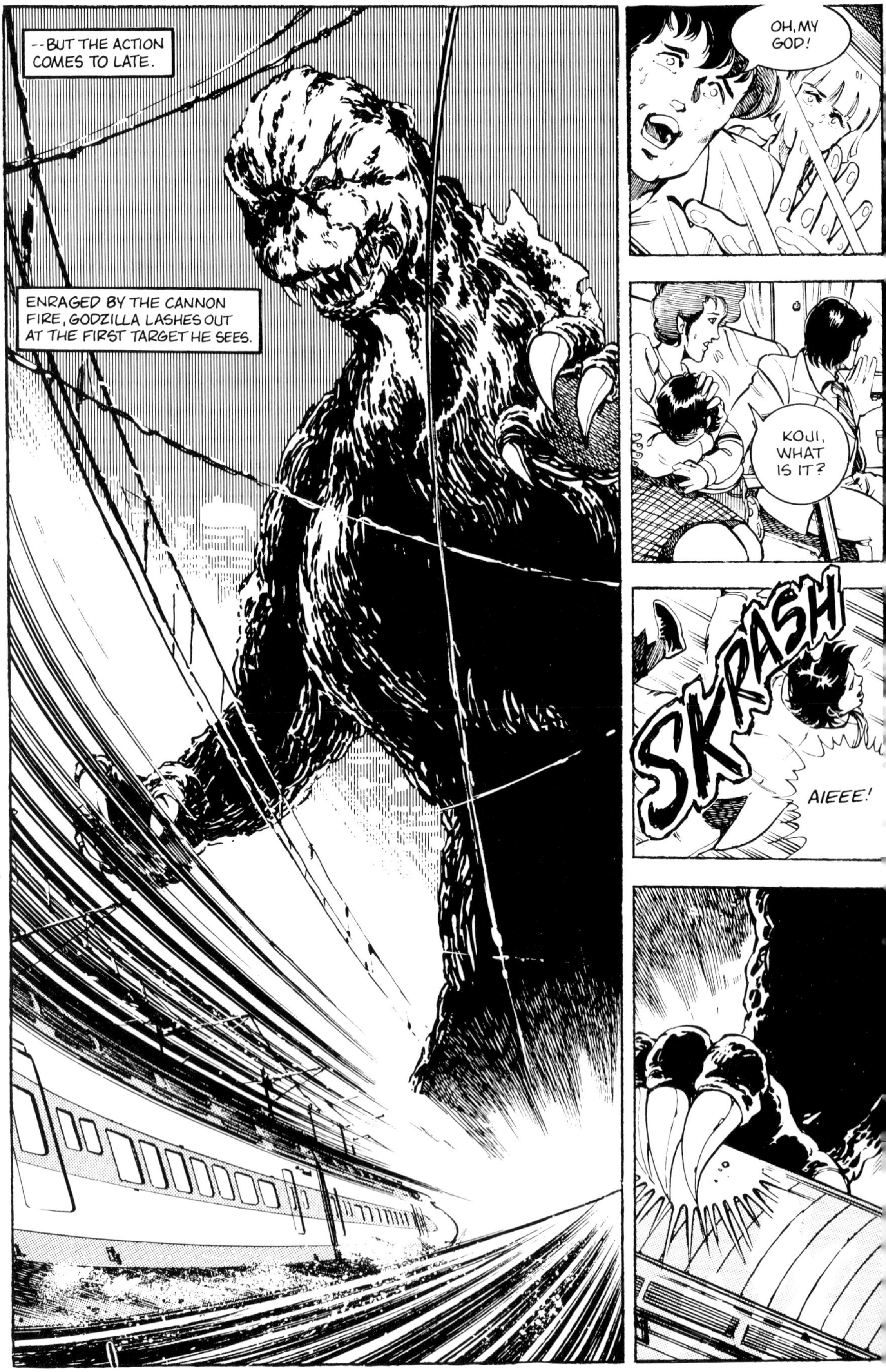
--BUT THE ACTION COMES TO LATE.
ENRAGED BY THE CANNON FIRE, GODZILLA LASHES OUT AT THE FIRST TARGET HE SEES.
OH, MY GOD!
KOJI, WHAT IS IT?
SKRASH
AIEEE!

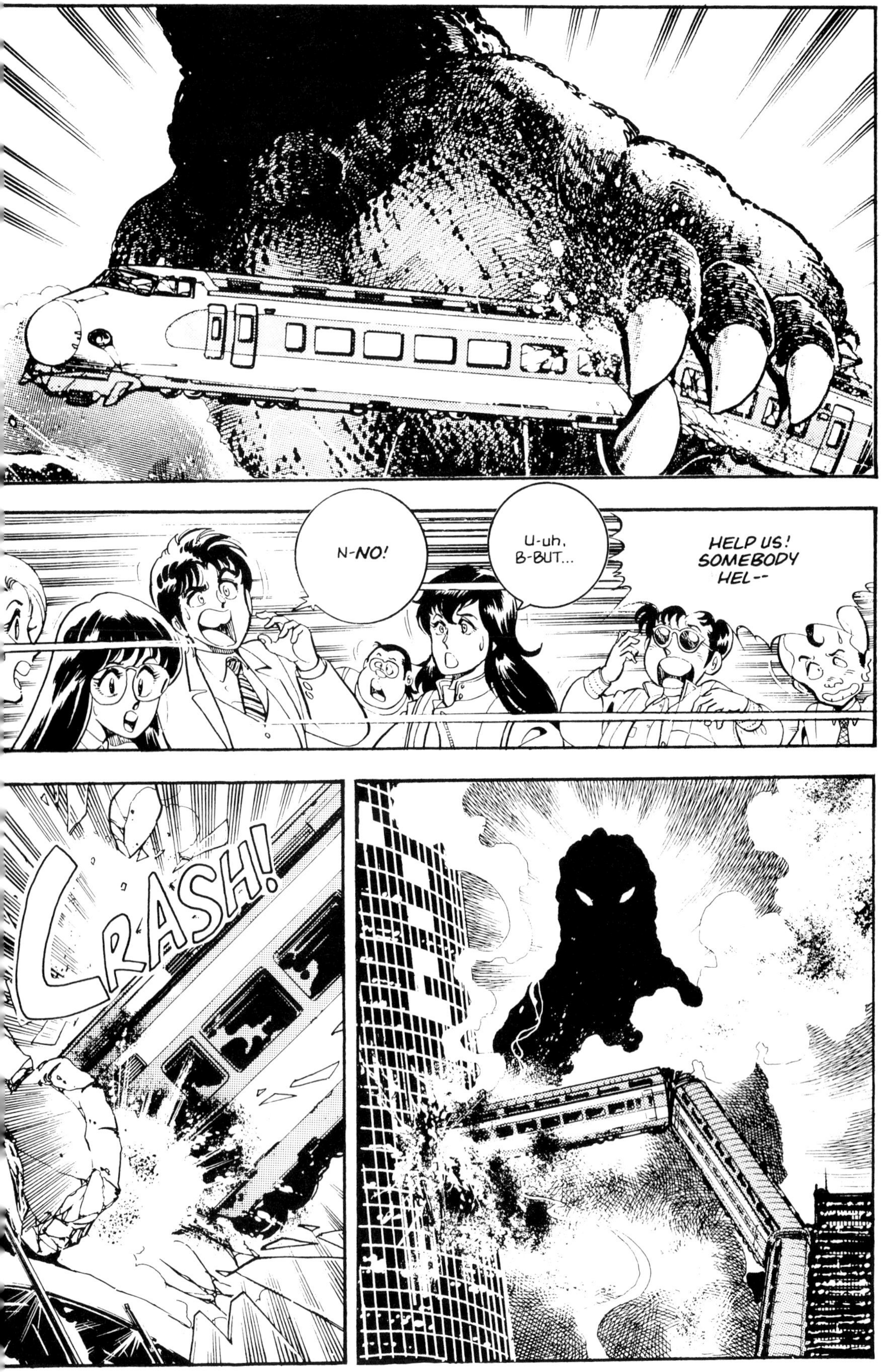
N-NO!
U-uh, B-BUT...
HELP US! SOMEBODY HEL--
CRASH!

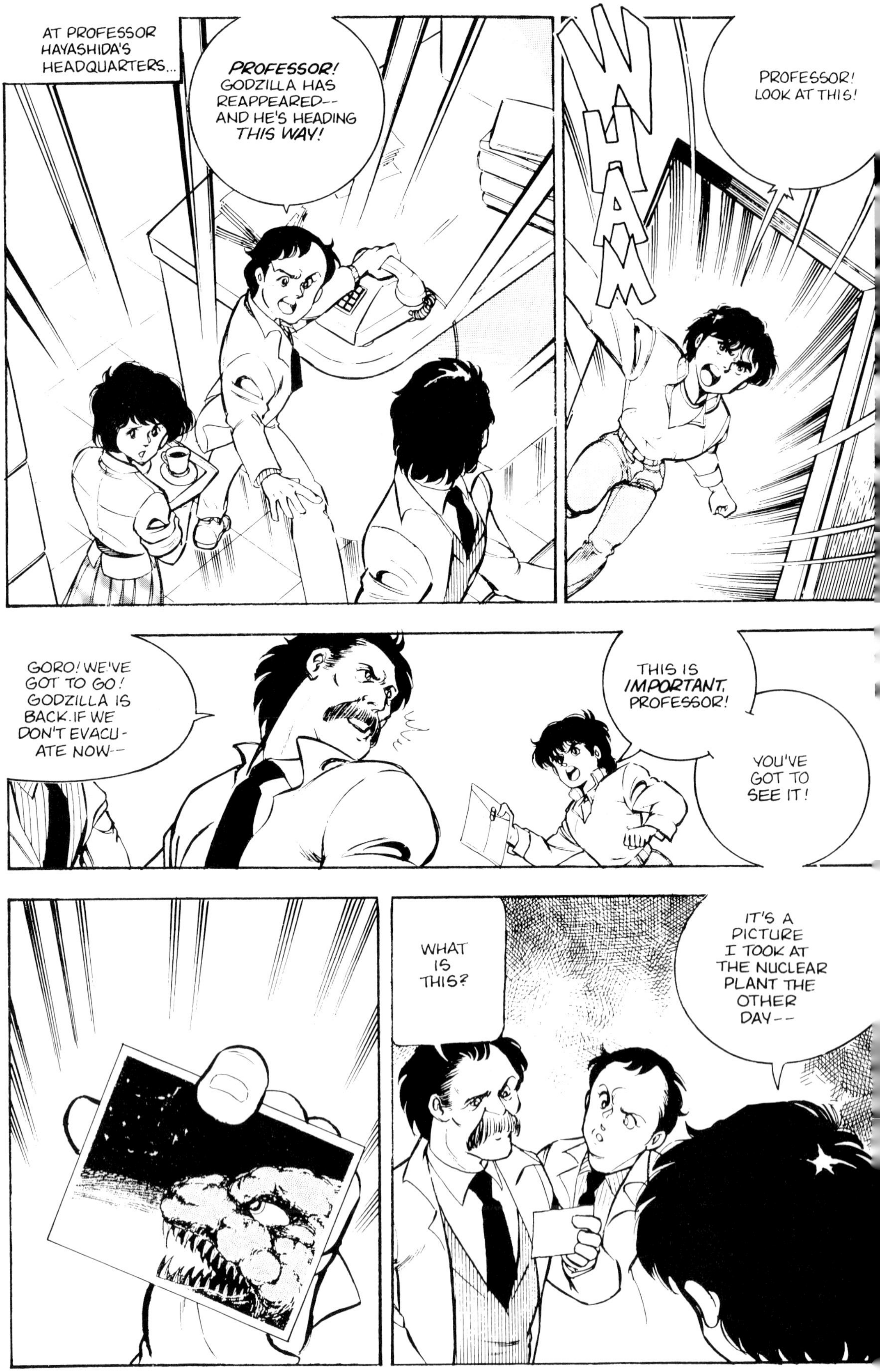
AT PROFESSOR HAYASHIDA'S HEADQUARTERS...
PROFESSOR! GODZILLA HAS REAPPEARED-- AND HE'S HEADING THIS WAY!
WHAM
PROFESSOR! LOOK AT THIS!
GORO! WE'VE GOT TO GO! GODZILLA IS BACK. IF WE DON'T EVACU-ATE NOW--
THIS IS IMPORTANT, PROFESSOR!
YOU'VE GOT TO SEE IT!
WHAT IS THIS?
IT'S A PICTURE I TOOK AT THE NUCLEAR PLANT THE OTHER DAY--

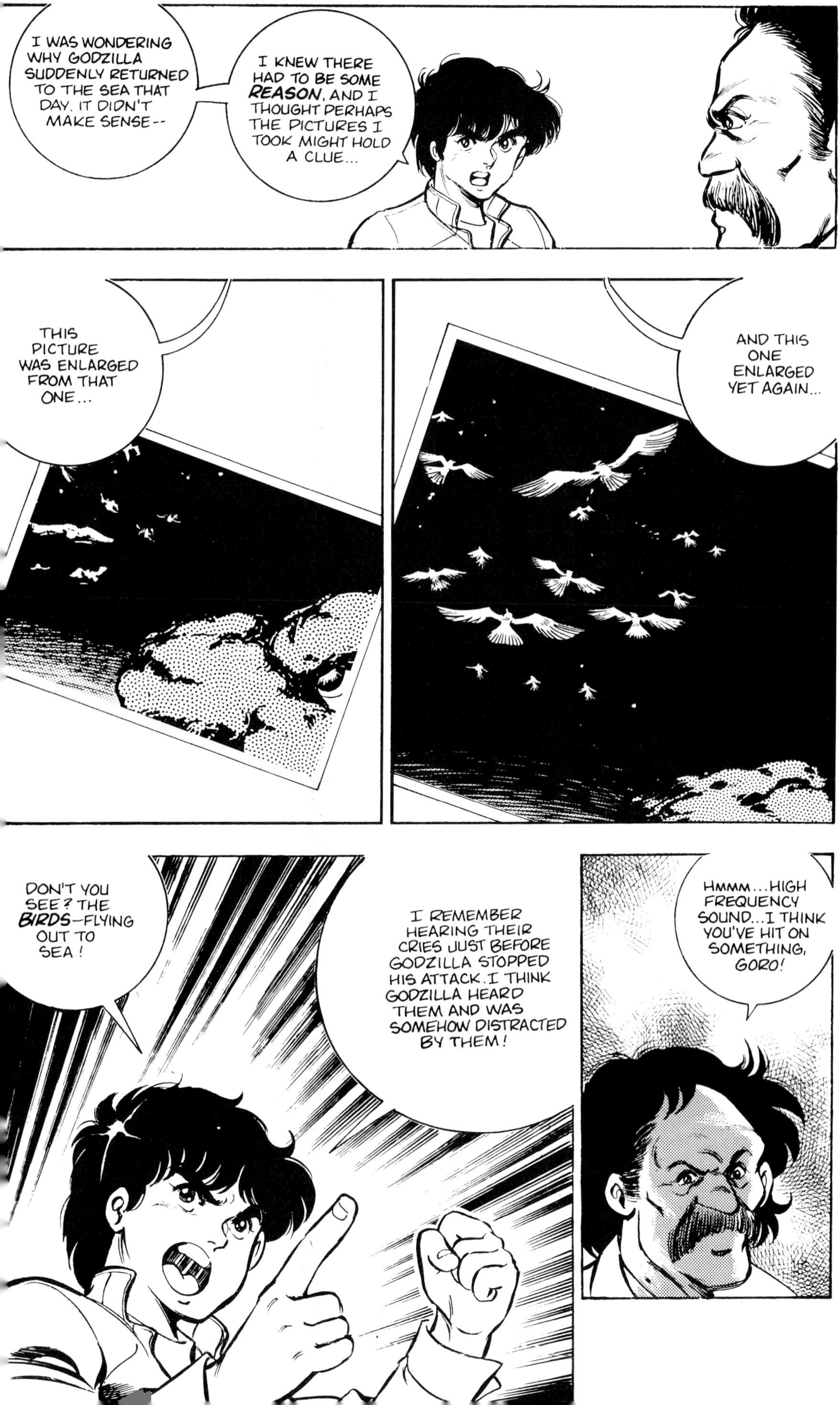
I WAS WONDERING WHY GODZILLA SUDDENLY RETURNED TO THE SEA THAT DAY. IT DIDN'T MAKE SENSE--
I KNEW THERE HAD TO BE SOME REASON, AND I THOUGHT PERHAPS THE PICTURES I TOOK MIGHT HOLD A CLUE...
THIS PICTURE WAS ENLARGED FROM THAT ONE...
AND THIS ONE ENLARGED YET AGAIN...
DON'T YOU SEE? THE BIRDS—FLYING OUT TO SEA!
I REMEMBER HEARING THEIR CRIES JUST BEFORE GODZILLA STOPPED HIS ATTACK. I THINK GODZILLA HEARD THEM AND WAS SOMEHOW DISTRACTED BY THEM!
HMMM...HIGH FREQUENCY SOUND...I THINK YOU'VE HIT ON SOMETHING, GORO!

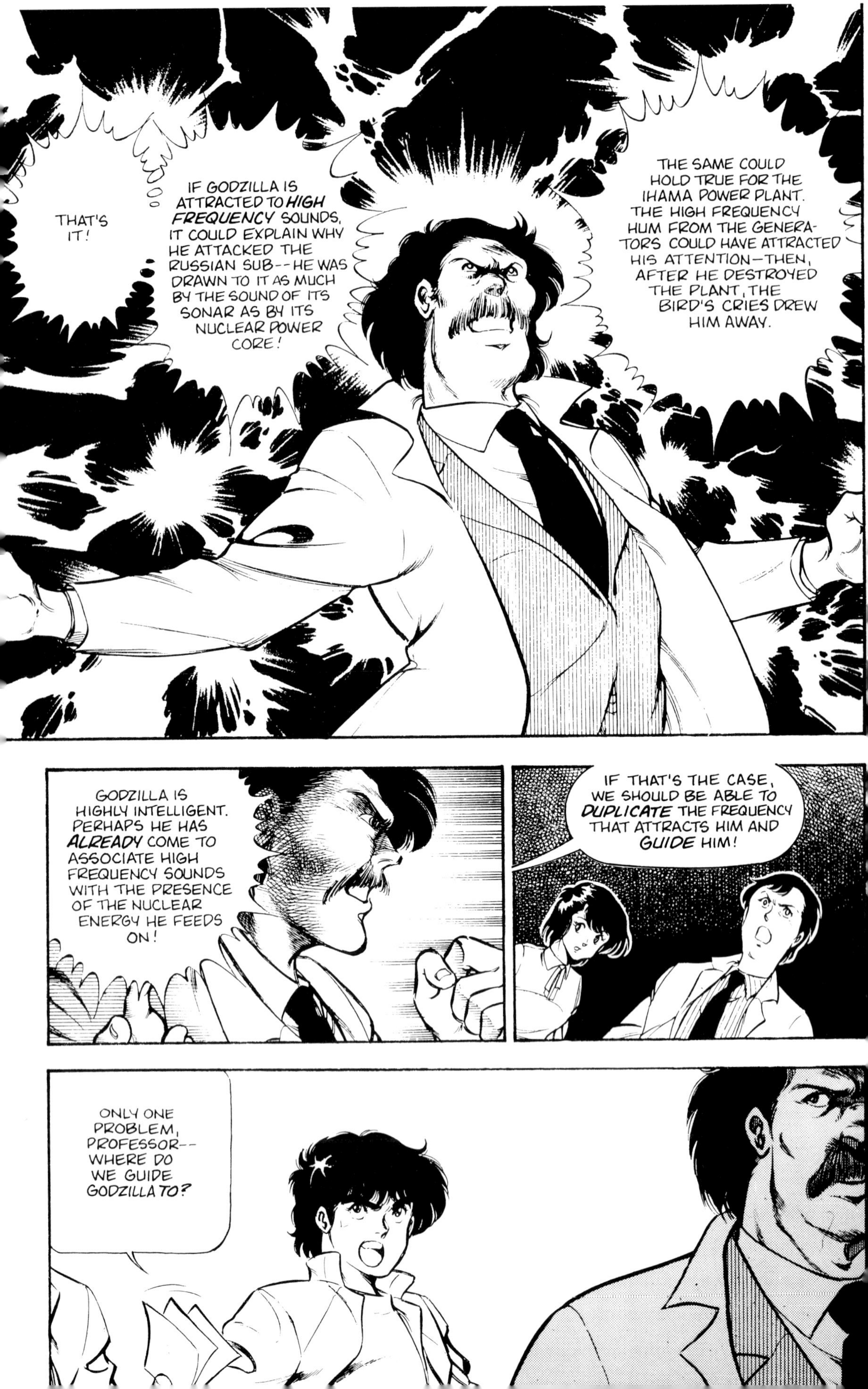
THAT'S IT!
IF GODZILLA IS ATTRACTED TO HIGH FREQUENCY SOUNDS, IT COULD EXPLAIN WHY HE ATTACKED THE RUSSIAN SUB--HE WAS DRAWN TO IT AS MUCH BY THE SOUND OF ITS SONAR AS BY ITS NUCLEAR POWER CORE!
THE SAME COULD HOLD TRUE FOR THE IHAMA POWER PLANT. THE HIGH FREQUENCY HUM FROM THE GENERATORS COULD HAVE ATTRACTED HIS ATTENTION—THEN, AFTER HE DESTROYED THE PLANT, THE BIRD'S CRIES DREW HIM AWAY.
GODZILLA IS HIGHLY INTELLIGENT. PERHAPS HE HAS ALREADY COME TO ASSOCIATE HIGH FREQUENCY SOUNDS WITH THE PRESENCE OF THE NUCLEAR ENERGY HE FEEDS ON!
IF THAT'S THE CASE, WE SHOULD BE ABLE TO DUPLICATE THE FREQUENCY THAT ATTRACTS HIM AND GUIDE HIM!
ONLY ONE PROBLEM, PROFESSOR--WHERE DO WE GUIDE GODZILLA TO?

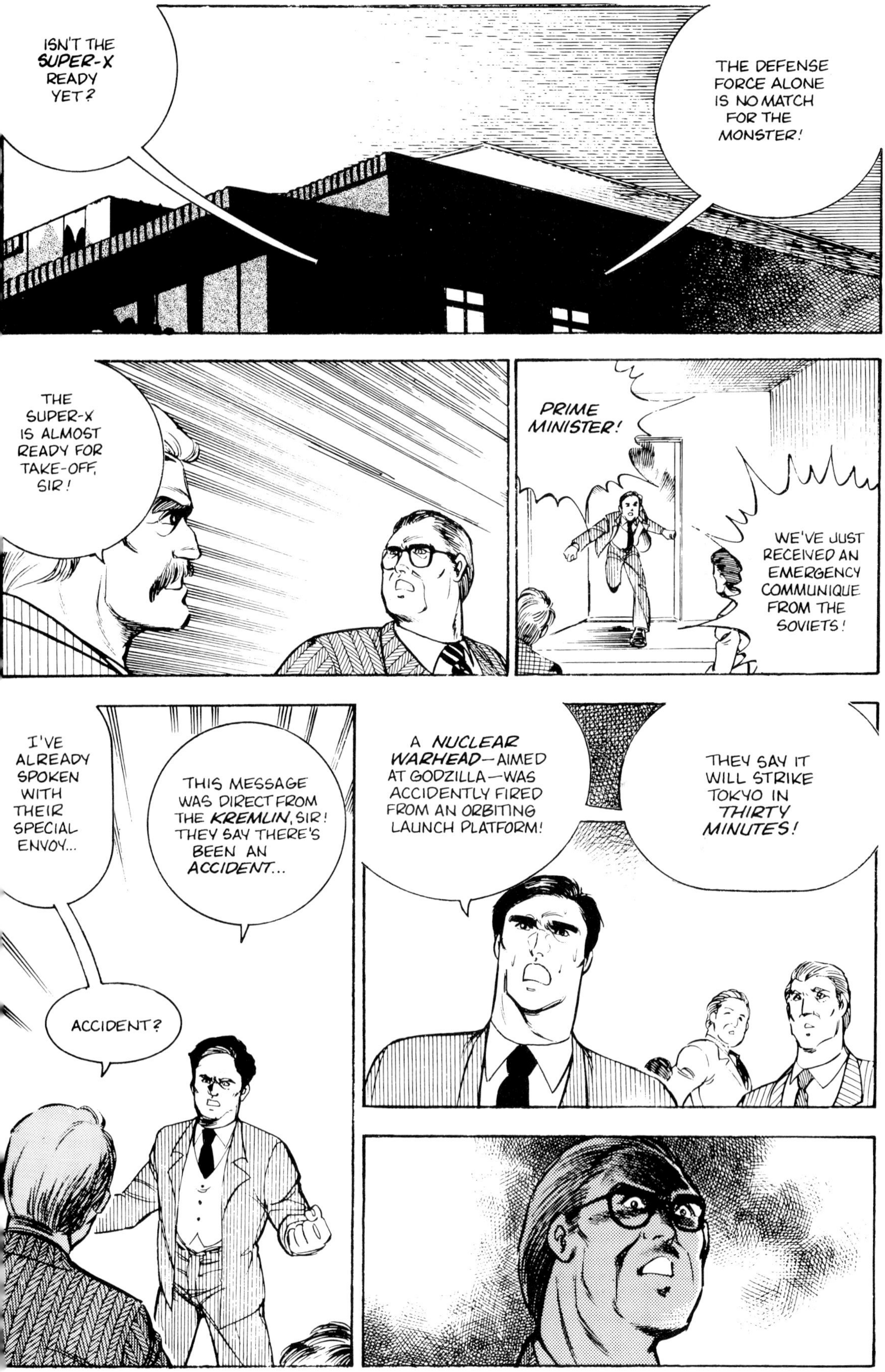
ISN'T THE SUPER-X READY YET?
THE DEFENSE FORCE ALONE IS NO MATCH FOR THE MONSTER!
THE SUPER-X IS ALMOST READY FOR TAKE-OFF, SIR!
PRIME MINISTER!
WE'VE JUST RECEIVED AN EMERGENCY COMMUNIQUE FROM THE SOVIETS!
I'VE ALREADY SPOKEN WITH THEIR SPECIAL ENVOY...
THIS MESSAGE WAS DIRECT FROM THE KREMLIN, SIR! THEY SAY THERE'S BEEN AN ACCIDENT...
ACCIDENT?
A NUCLEAR WARHEAD—AIMED AT GODZILLA—WAS ACCIDENTLY FIRED FROM AN ORBITING LAUNCH PLATFORM!
THEY SAY IT WILL STRIKE TOKYO IN THIRTY MINUTES!

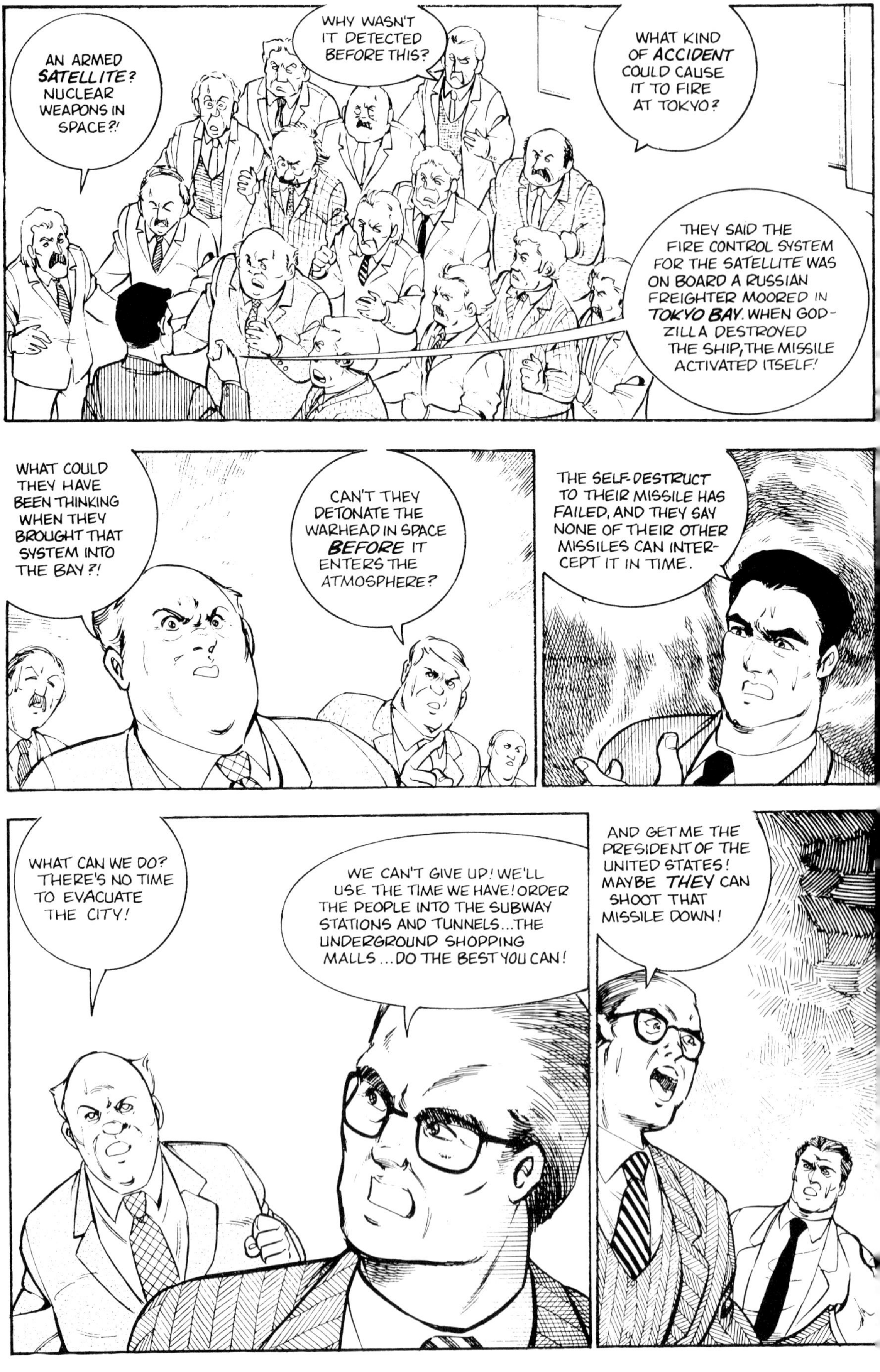

AN ARMED SATELLITE? NUCLEAR WEAPONS IN SPACE?!
WHY WASN'T IT DETECTED BEFORE THIS?
WHAT KIND OF ACCIDENT COULD CAUSE IT TO FIRE AT TOKYO?
THEY SAID THE FIRE CONTROL SYSTEM FOR THE SATELLITE WAS ON BOARD A RUSSIAN FREIGHTER MOORED IN TOKYO BAY. WHEN GOD-ZILLA DESTROYED THE SHIP, THE MISSILE ACTIVATED ITSELF!
WHAT COULD THEY HAVE BEEN THINKING WHEN THEY BROUGHT THAT SYSTEM INTO THE BAY?!
CAN'T THEY DETONATE THE WARHEAD IN SPACE BEFORE IT ENTERS THE ATMOSPHERE?
THE SELF-DESTRUCT TO THEIR MISSILE HAS FAILED, AND THEY SAY NONE OF THEIR OTHER MISSILES CAN INTER-CEPT IT IN TIME.
WHAT CAN WE DO? THERE'S NO TIME TO EVACUATE THE CITY!
WE CAN'T GIVE UP! WE'LL USE THE TIME WE HAVE! ORDER THE PEOPLE INTO THE SUBWAY STATIONS AND TUNNELS...THE UNDERGROUND SHOPPING MALLS...DO THE BEST YOU CAN!
AND GET ME THE PRESIDENT OF THE UNITED STATES! MAYBE THEY CAN SHOOT THAT MISSILE DOWN!

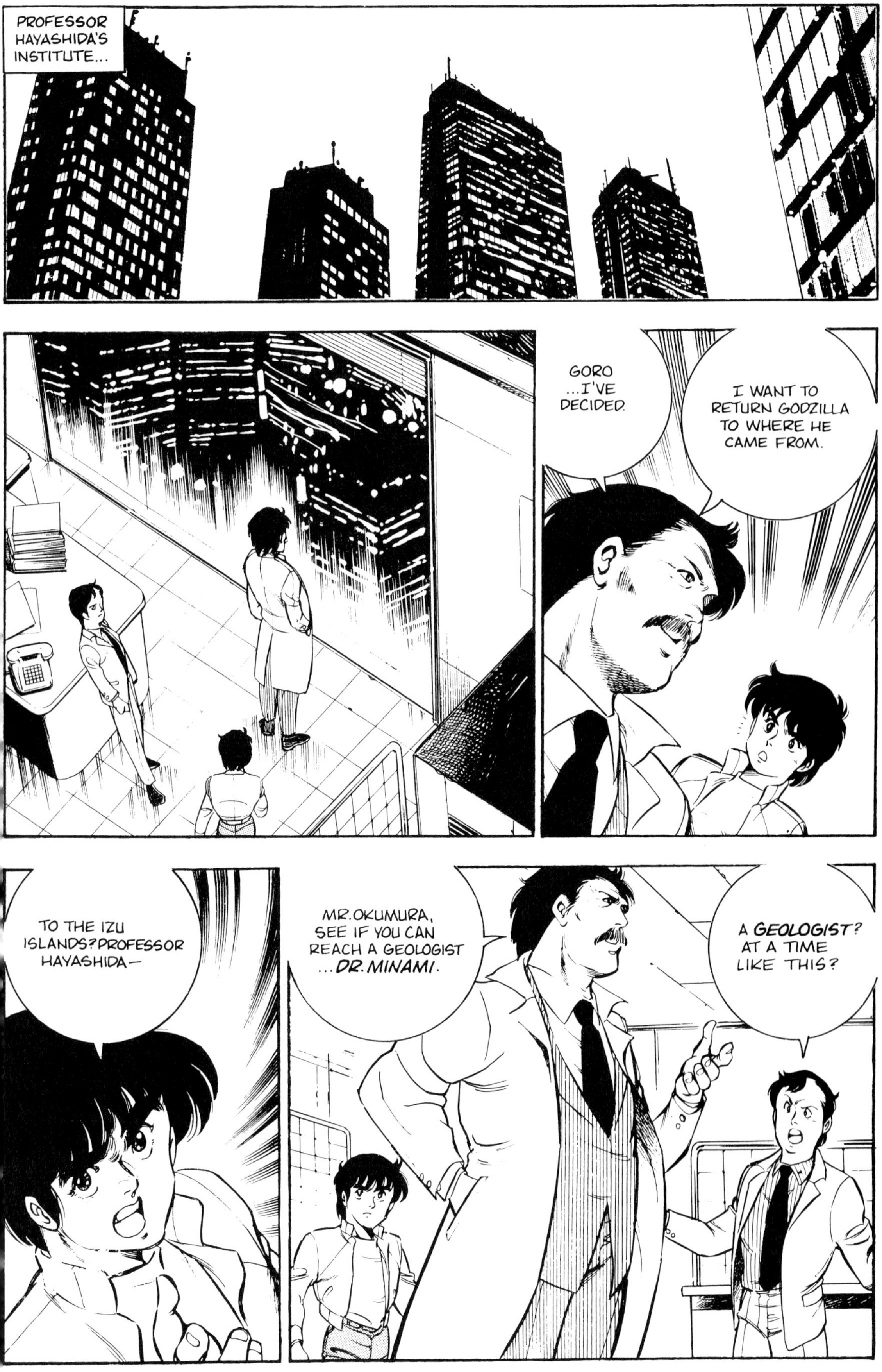
PROFESSOR HAYASHIDA'S INSTITUTE...
GORO ...I'VE DECIDED.
I WANT TO RETURN GODZILLA TO WHERE HE CAME FROM.
TO THE IZU ISLANDS? PROFESSOR HAYASHIDA—
MR. OKUMURA, SEE IF YOU CAN REACH A GEOLOGIST ...DR. MINAMI.
A GEOLOGIST? AT A TIME LIKE THIS?

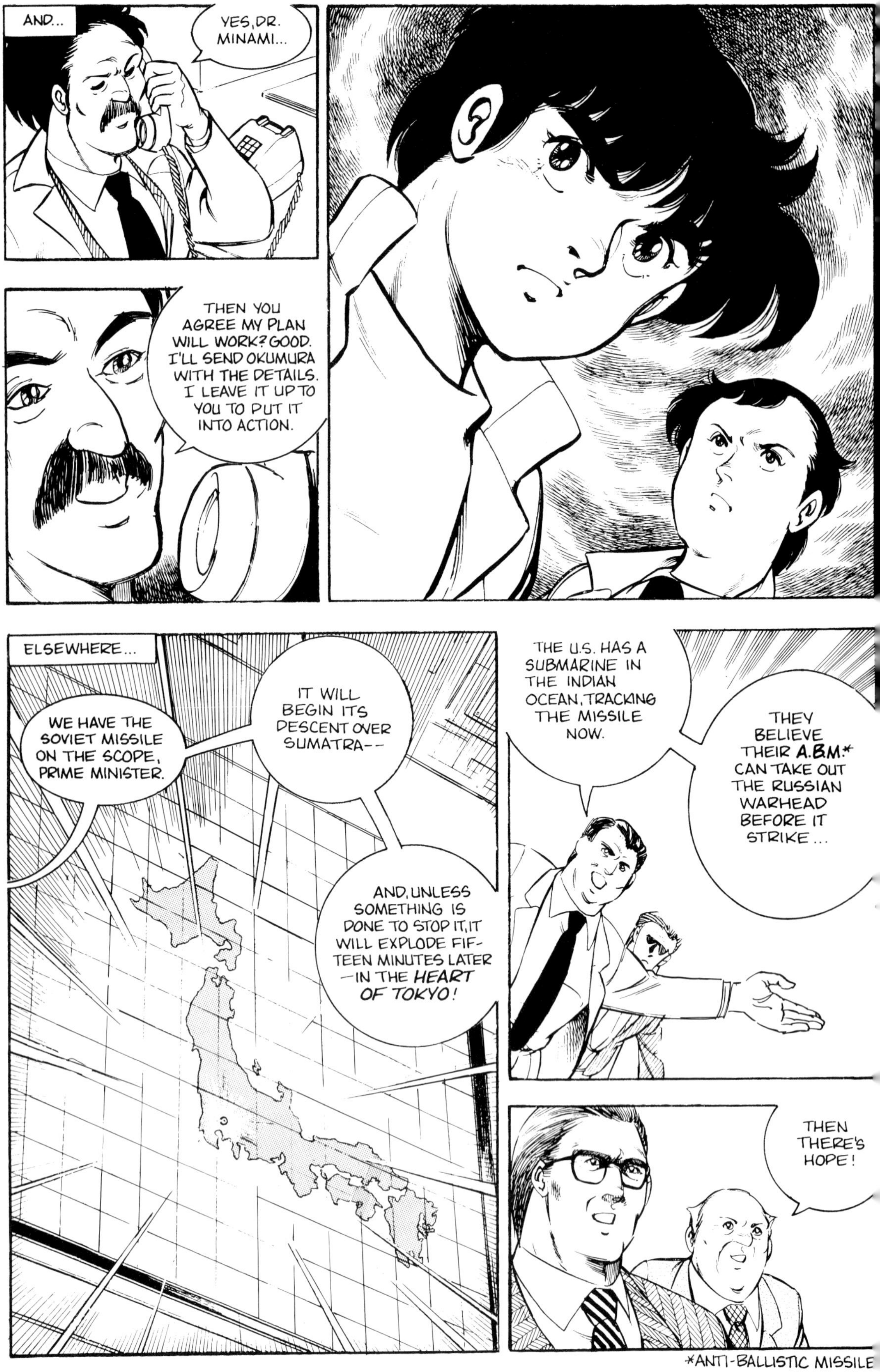
AND...
YES, DR. MINAMI...
THEN YOU AGREE MY PLAN WILL WORK? GOOD. I'LL SEND OKUMURA WITH THE DETAILS. I LEAVE IT UP TO YOU TO PUT IT INTO ACTION.
ELSEWHERE...
WE HAVE THE SOVIET MISSILE ON THE SCOPE, PRIME MINISTER.
IT WILL BEGIN ITS DESCENT OVER SUMATRA--
AND, UNLESS SOMETHING IS DONE TO STOP IT, IT WILL EXPLODE FIFTEEN MINUTES LATER --IN THE HEART OF TOKYO!
THE U.S. HAS A SUBMARINE IN THE INDIAN OCEAN, TRACKING THE MISSILE NOW.
THEY BELIEVE THEIR A.B.M.* CAN TAKE OUT THE RUSSIAN WARHEAD BEFORE IT STRIKE...
THEN THERE'S HOPE!

*ANTI-BALLISTIC MISSILE

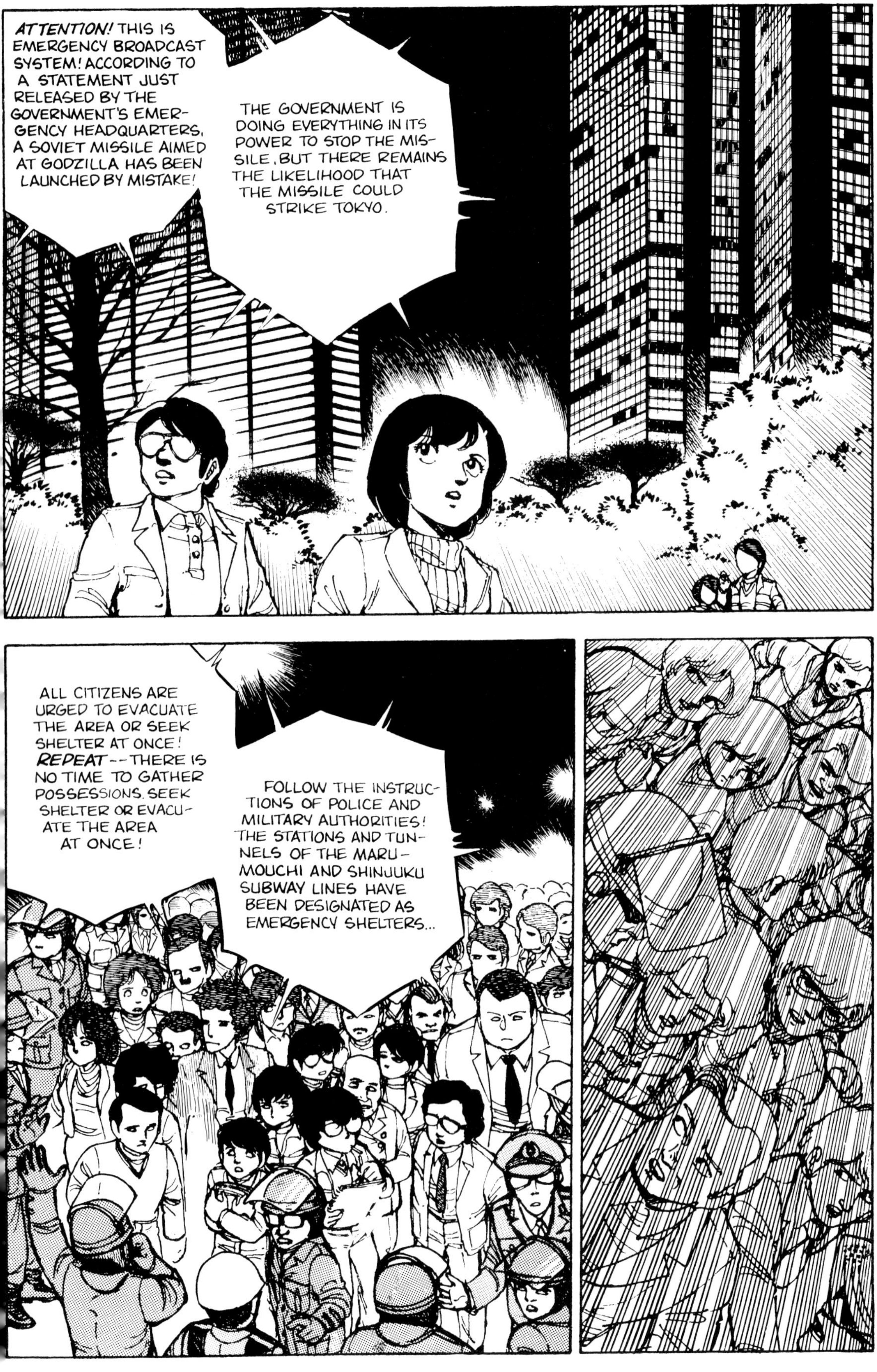
ATTENTION! THIS IS EMERGENCY BROADCAST SYSTEM! ACCORDING TO A STATEMENT JUST RELEASED BY THE GOVERNMENT'S EMERGENCY HEADQUARTERS, A SOVIET MISSILE AIMED AT GODZILLA HAS BEEN LAUNCHED BY MISTAKE!
THE GOVERNMENT IS DOING EVERYTHING IN ITS POWER TO STOP THE MISSILE, BUT THERE REMAINS THE LIKELIHOOD THAT THE MISSILE COULD STRIKE TOKYO.
ALL CITIZENS ARE URGED TO EVACUATE THE AREA OR SEEK SHELTER AT ONCE! REPEAT--THERE IS NO TIME TO GATHER POSSESSIONS. SEEK SHELTER OR EVACUATE THE AREA AT ONCE!
FOLLOW THE INSTRUCTIONS OF POLICE AND MILITARY AUTHORITIES! THE STATIONS AND TUNNELS OF THE MARUMOUCHI AND SHINJUKU SUBWAY LINES HAVE BEEN DESIGNATED AS EMERGENCY SHELTERS...

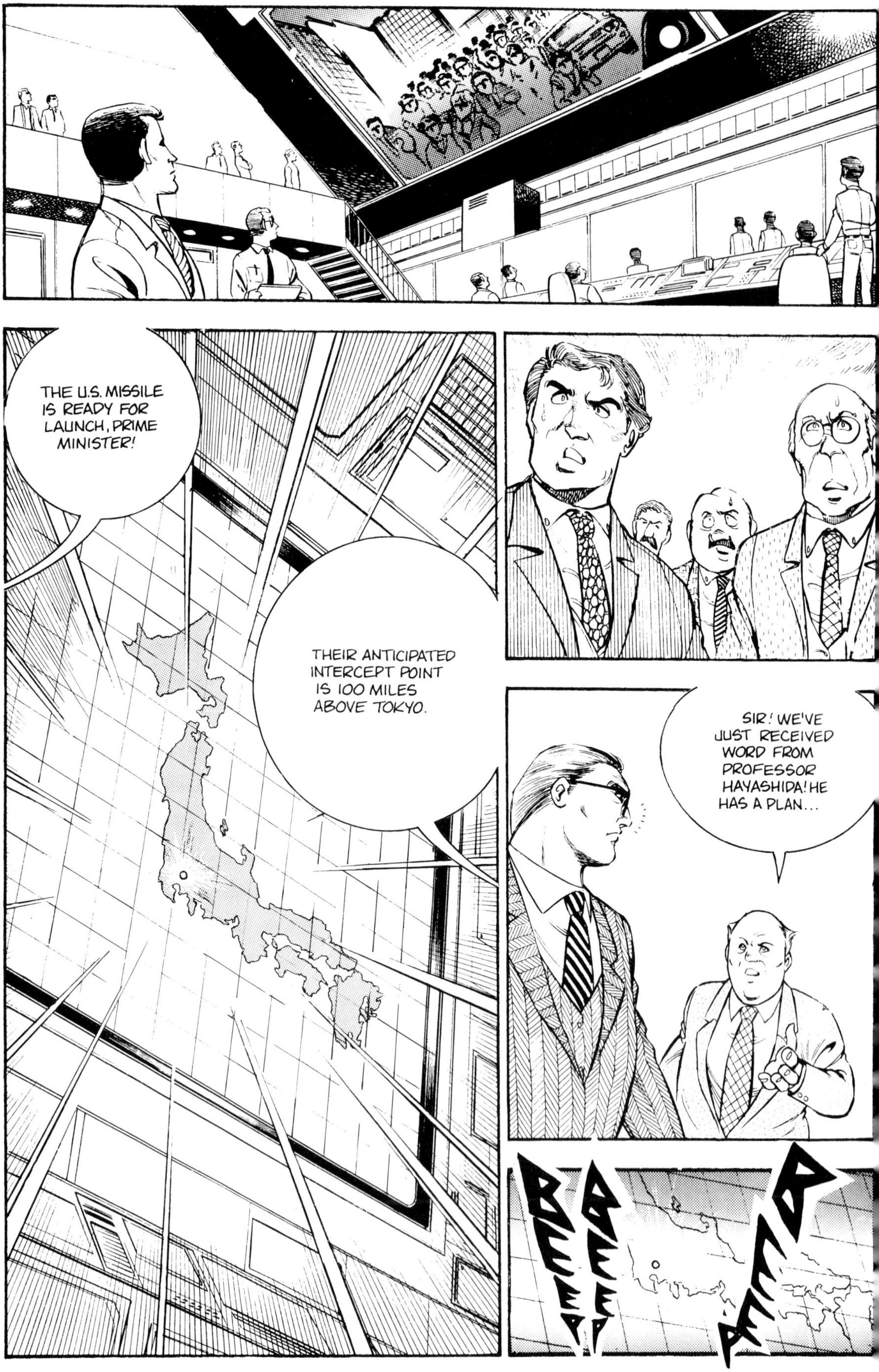
THE U.S. MISSILE IS READY FOR LAUNCH, PRIME MINISTER!
THEIR ANTICIPATED INTERCEPT POINT IS 100 MILES ABOVE TOKYO.
SIR! WE'VE JUST RECEIVED WORD FROM PROFESSOR HAYASHIDA! HE HAS A PLAN...
BEEEP
BEEEP
RRRR

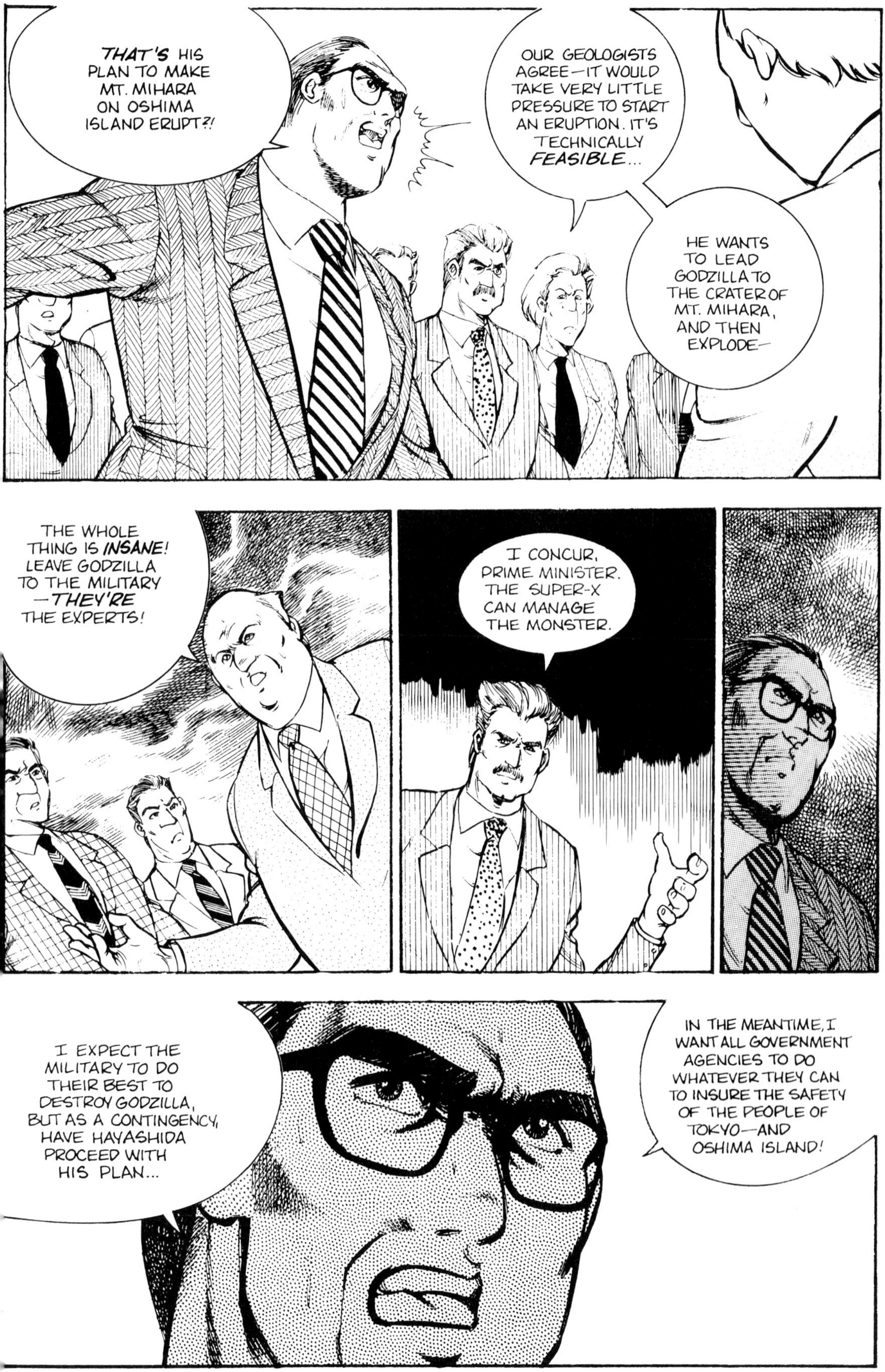
THAT'S HIS PLAN TO MAKE MT. MIHARA ON OSHIMA ISLAND ERUPT?!
OUR GEOLOGISTS AGREE—IT WOULD TAKE VERY LITTLE PRESSURE TO START AN ERUPTION. IT'S TECHNICALLY FEASIBLE...
HE WANTS TO LEAD GODZILLA TO THE CRATER OF MT. MIHARA, AND THEN EXPLODE—
THE WHOLE THING IS INSANE! LEAVE GODZILLA TO THE MILITARY —THEY'RE THE EXPERTS!
I CONCUR, PRIME MINISTER. THE SUPER-X CAN MANAGE THE MONSTER.
I EXPECT THE MILITARY TO DO THEIR BEST TO DESTROY GODZILLA, BUT AS A CONTINGENCY, HAVE HAYASHIDA PROCEED WITH HIS PLAN...
IN THE MEANTIME, I WANT ALL GOVERNMENT AGENCIES TO DO WHATEVER THEY CAN TO INSURE THE SAFETY OF THE PEOPLE OF TOKYO—AND OSHIMA ISLAND!

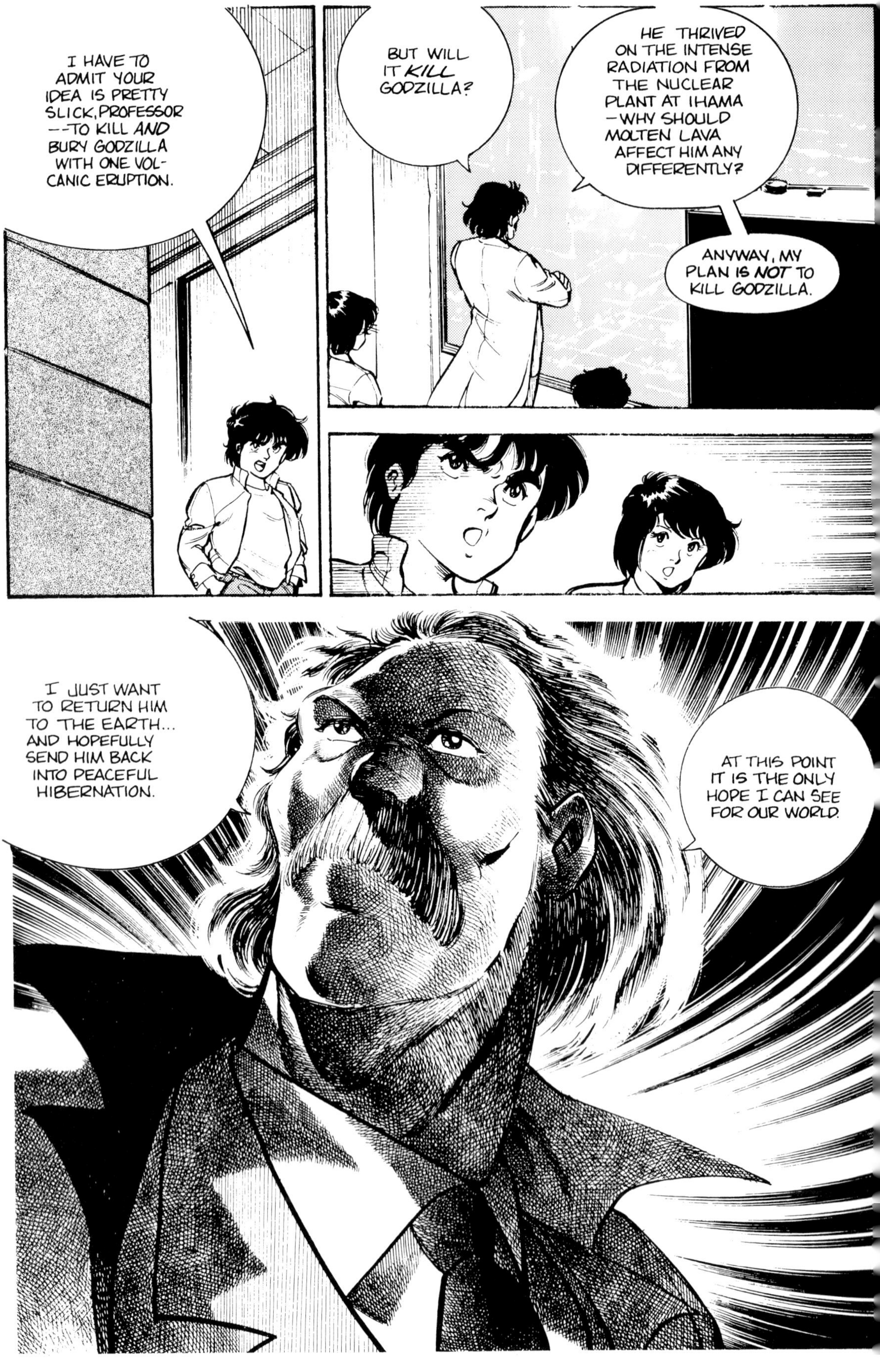
I HAVE TO ADMIT YOUR IDEA IS PRETTY SLICK, PROFESSOR --TO KILL *AND* BURY GODZILLA WITH ONE VOLCANIC ERUPTION.
BUT WILL IT *KILL* GODZILLA?
HE THRIVED ON THE INTENSE RADIATION FROM THE NUCLEAR PLANT AT IHAMA -WHY SHOULD MOLTEN LAVA AFFECT HIM ANY DIFFERENTLY?
ANYWAY, MY PLAN IS *NOT* TO KILL GODZILLA.
I JUST WANT TO RETURN HIM TO THE EARTH... AND HOPEFULLY SEND HIM BACK INTO PEACEFUL HIBERNATION.
AT THIS POINT IT IS THE ONLY HOPE I CAN SEE FOR OUR WORLD.

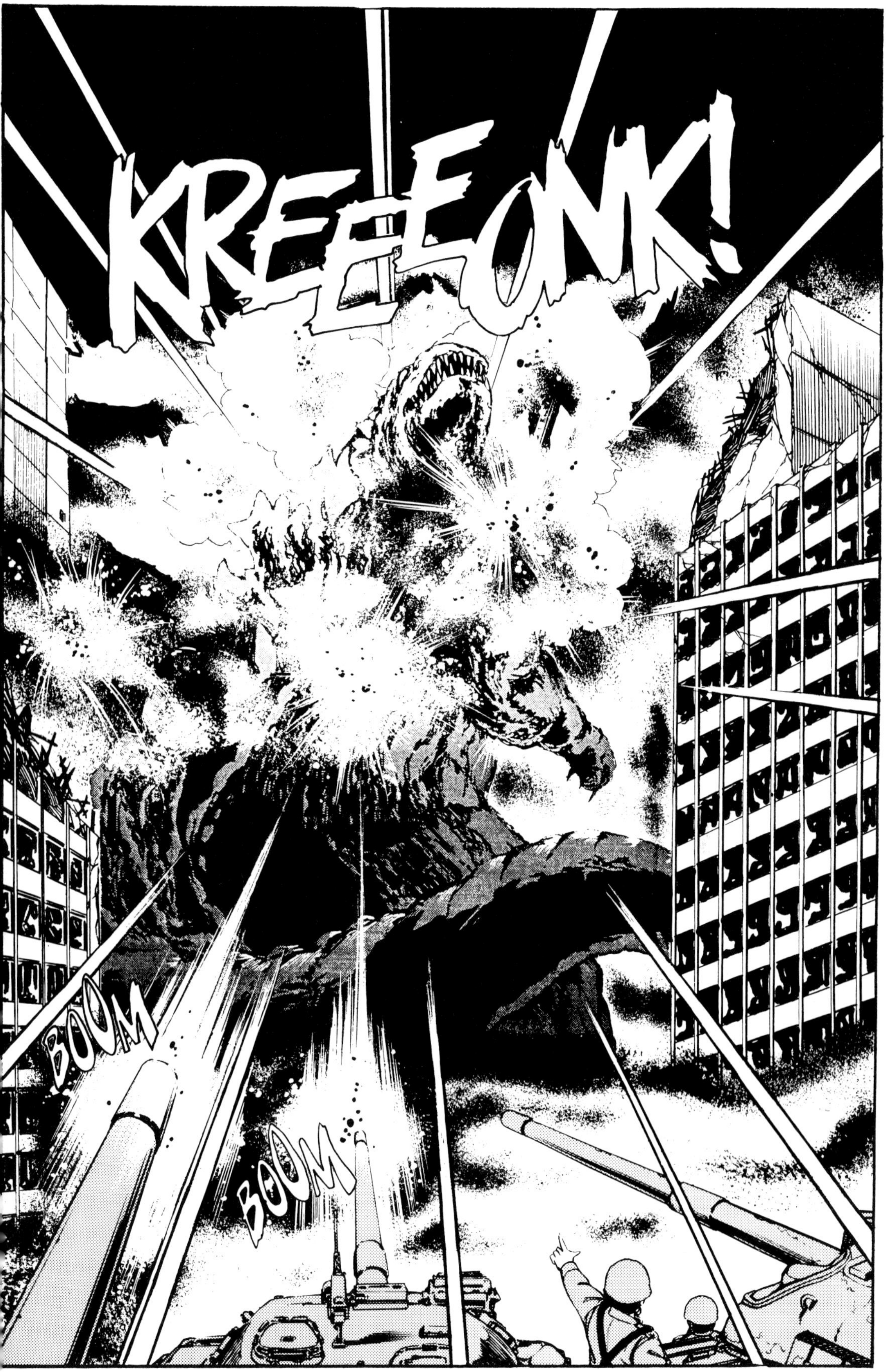
KREEONK!
BOOM
BOOM

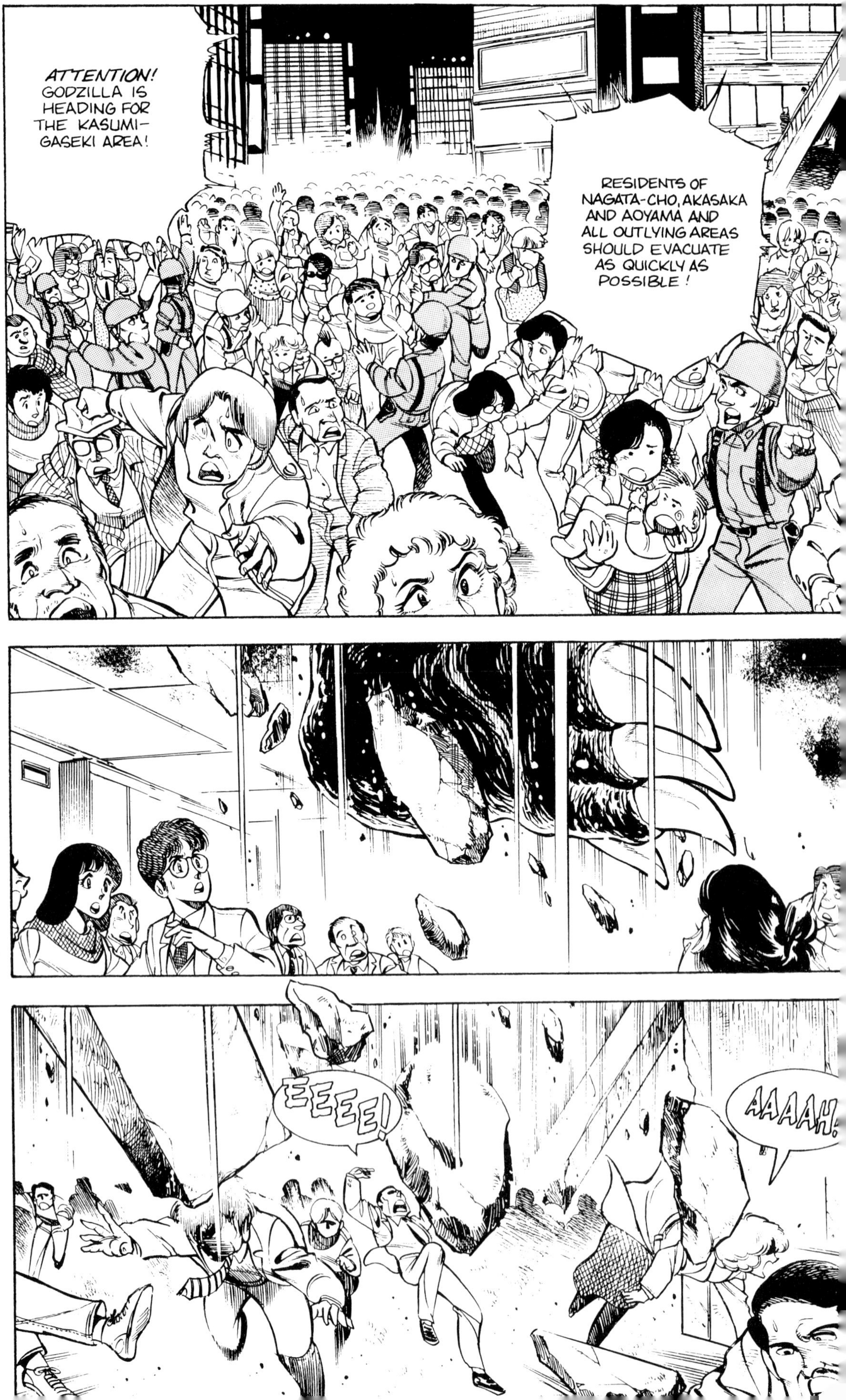

ATTENTION! GODZILLA IS HEADING FOR THE KASUMI-GASEKI AREA!
RESIDENTS OF NAGATA-CHO, AKASAKA AND AOYAMA AND ALL OUTLYING AREAS SHOULD EVACUATE AS QUICKLY AS POSSIBLE!
EEEEE!
AAAAH!

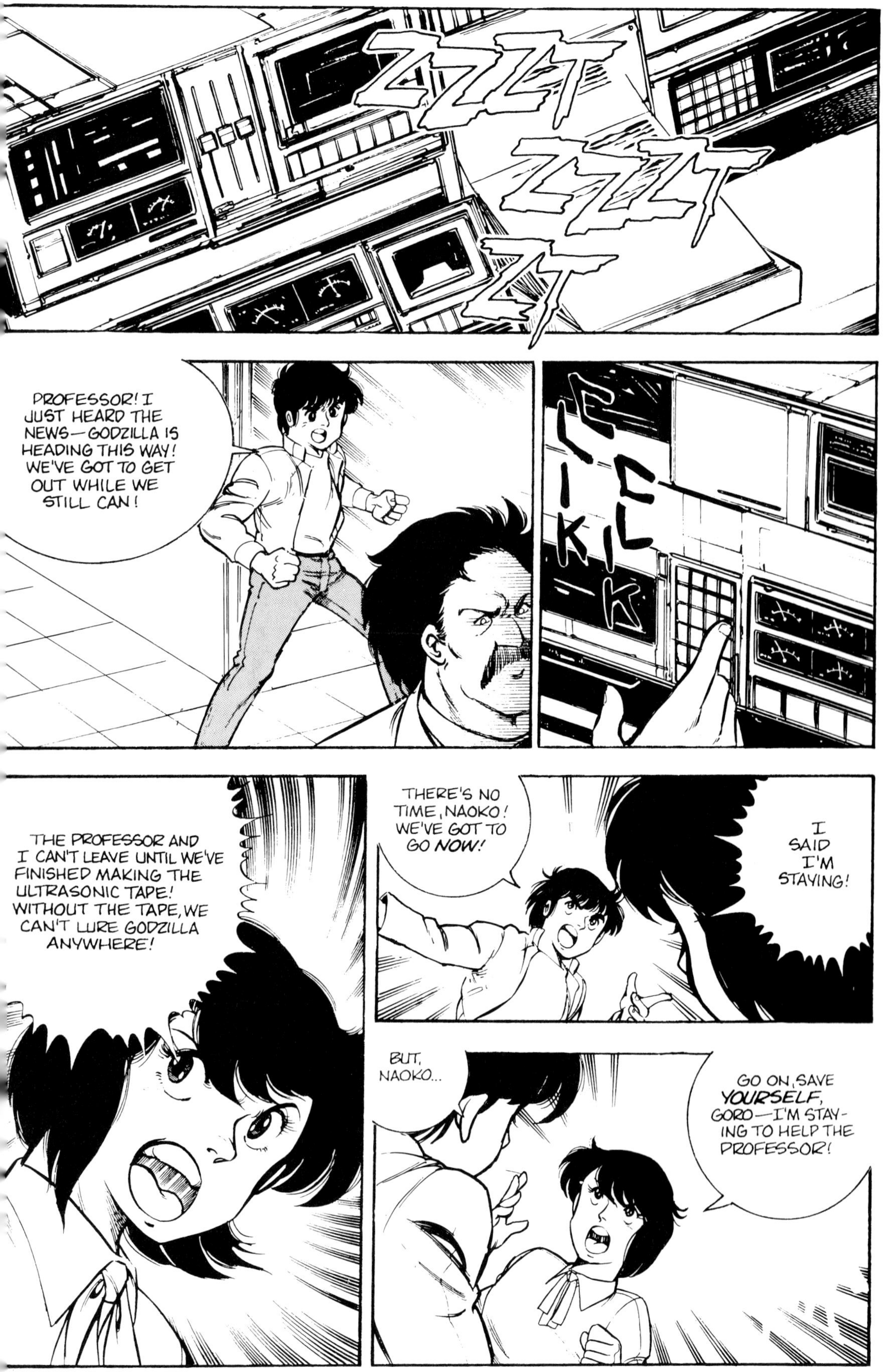
ZZZZT
ZZZZT
ZT
PROFESSOR! I JUST HEARD THE NEWS—GODZILLA IS HEADING THIS WAY! WE'VE GOT TO GET OUT WHILE WE STILL CAN!
CLICK
CLICK
THE PROFESSOR AND I CAN'T LEAVE UNTIL WE'VE FINISHED MAKING THE ULTRASONIC TAPE! WITHOUT THE TAPE, WE CAN'T LURE GODZILLA ANYWHERE!
THERE'S NO TIME, NAOKO! WE'VE GOT TO GO *NOW!*
I SAID I'M STAYING!
BUT, NAOKO...
GO ON, SAVE ***YOURSELF***, GORO—I'M STAYING TO HELP THE PROFESSOR!

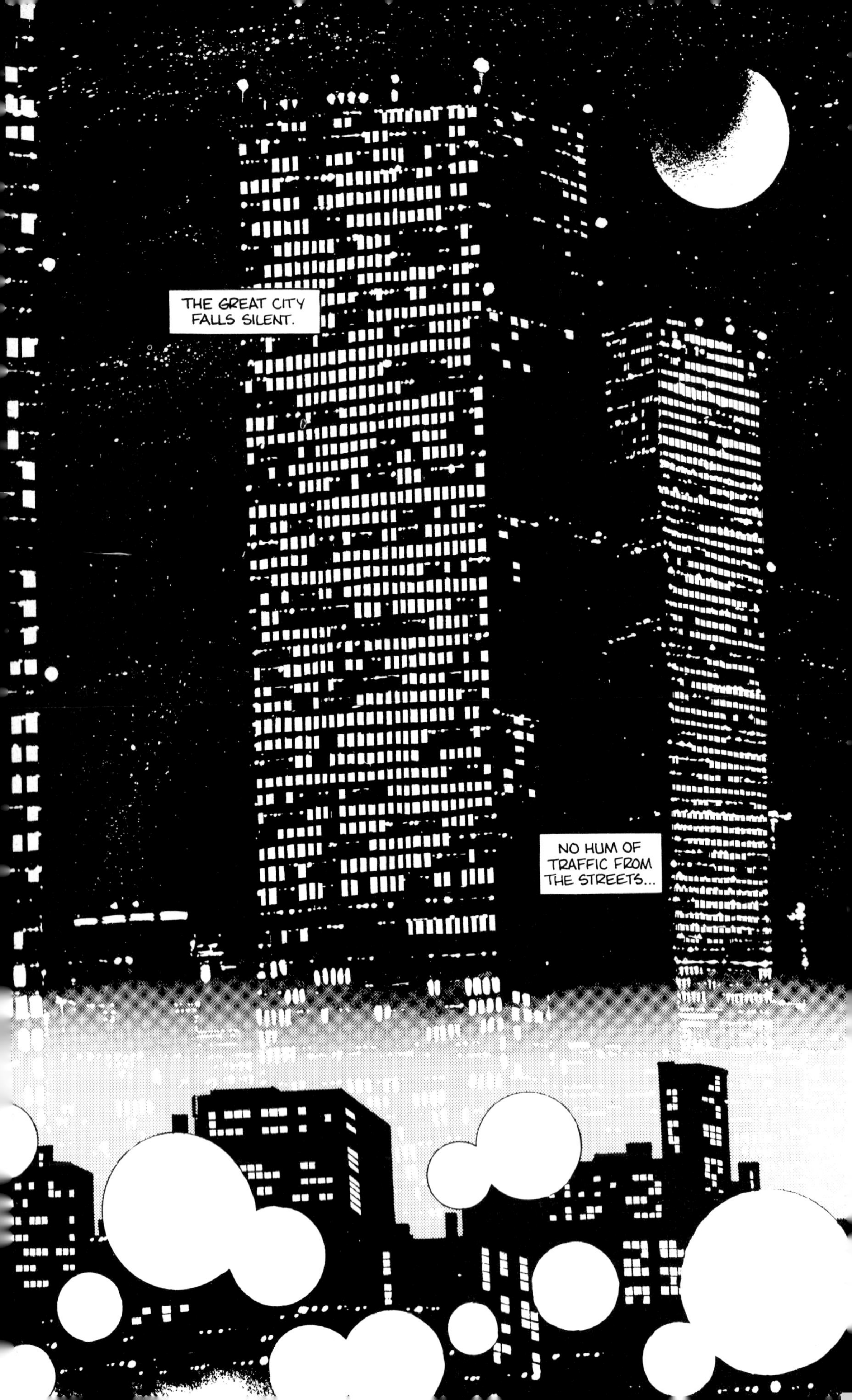
THE GREAT CITY FALLS SILENT.
NO HUM OF TRAFFIC FROM THE STREETS...

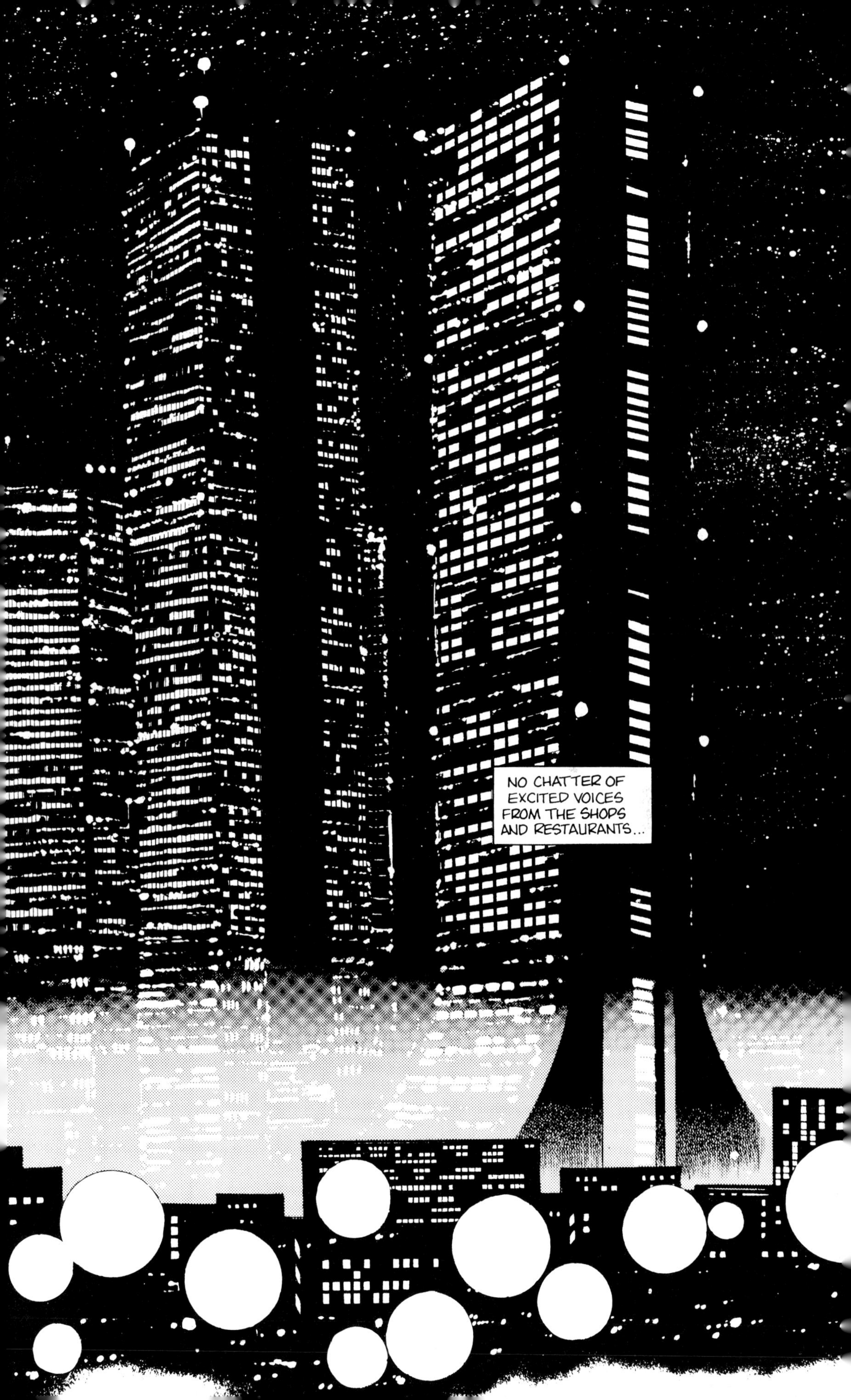
NO CHATTER OF EXCITED VOICES FROM THE SHOPS AND RESTAURANTS...

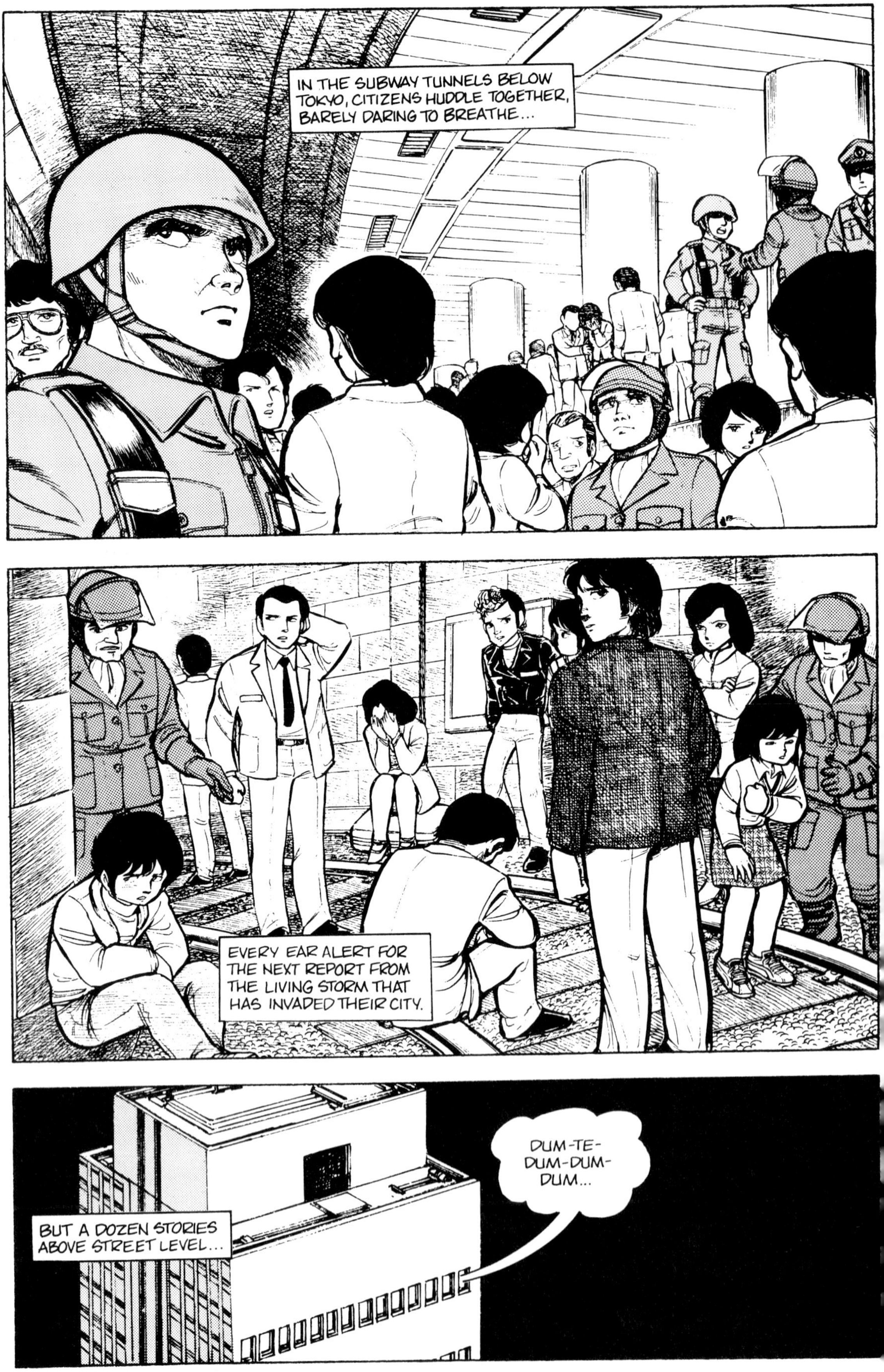
IN THE SUBWAY TUNNELS BELOW TOKYO, CITIZENS HUDDLE TOGETHER, BARELY DARING TO BREATHE...
EVERY EAR ALERT FOR THE NEXT REPORT FROM THE LIVING STORM THAT HAS INVADED THEIR CITY.
BUT A DOZEN STORIES ABOVE STREET LEVEL...
DUM-TE-DUM-DUM-DUM...

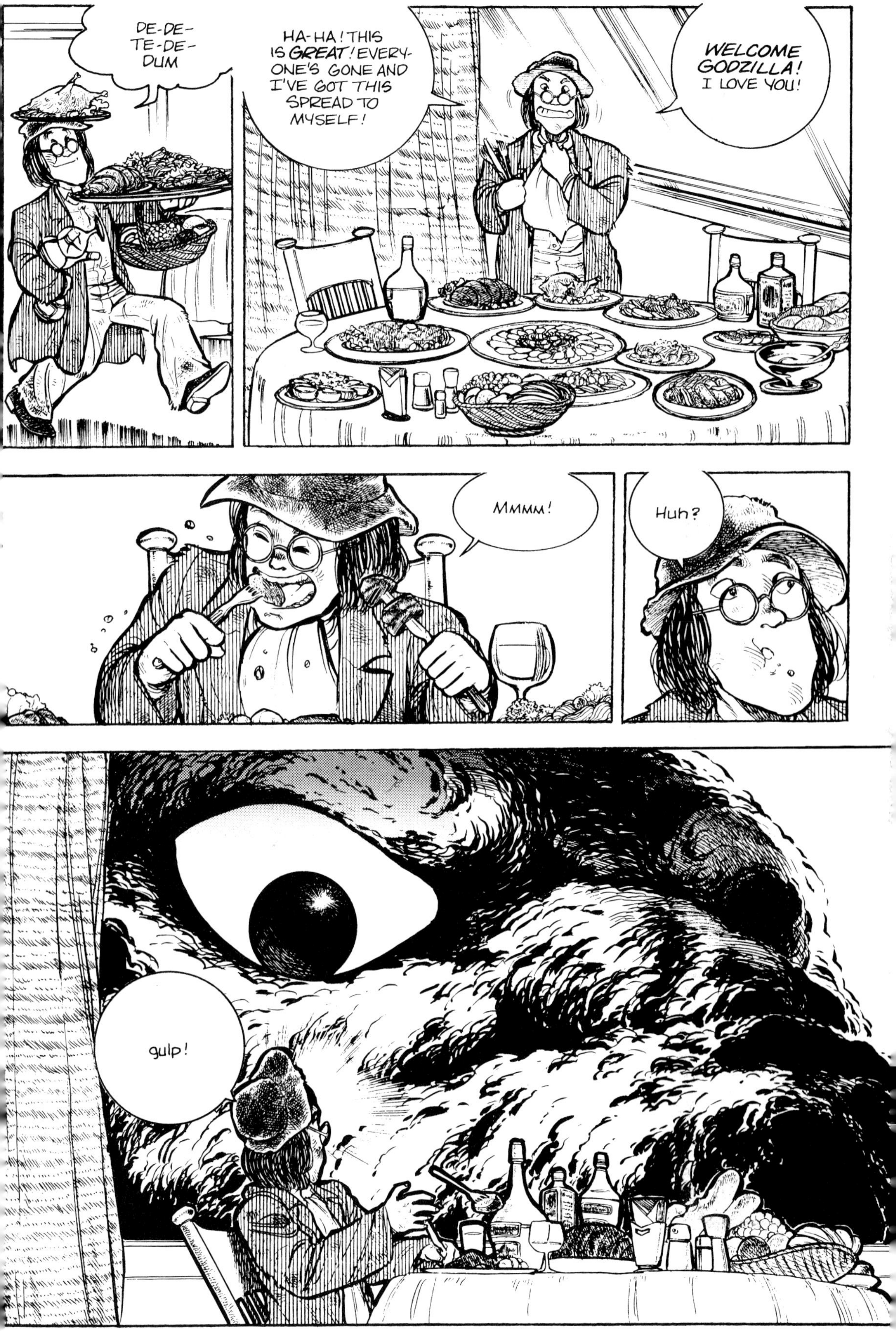
DE-DE-TE-DE-DUM
HA-HA! THIS IS GREAT! EVERYONE'S GONE AND I'VE GOT THIS SPREAD TO MYSELF!
WELCOME GODZILLA! I LOVE YOU!
MMMM!
Huh?
gulp!

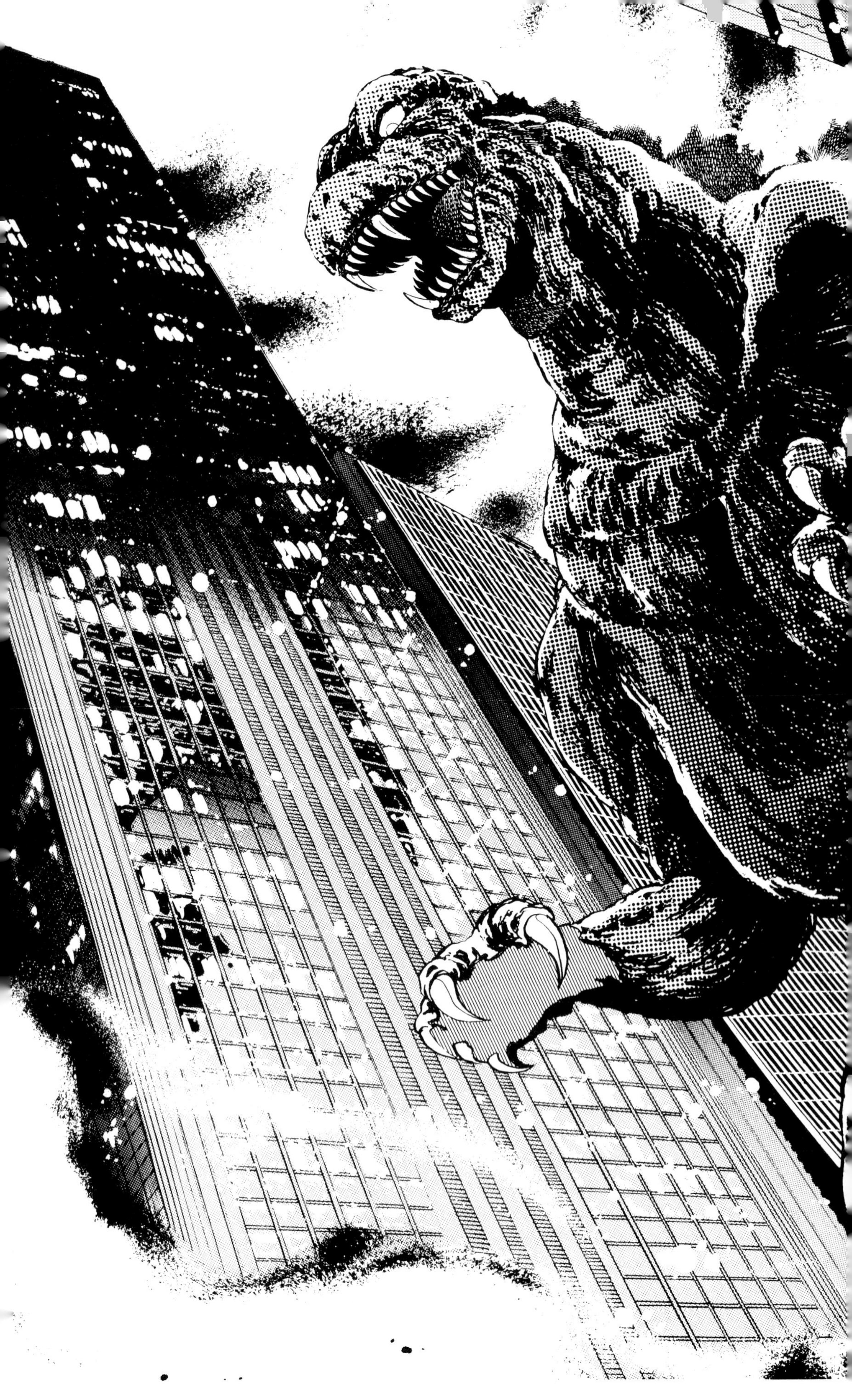

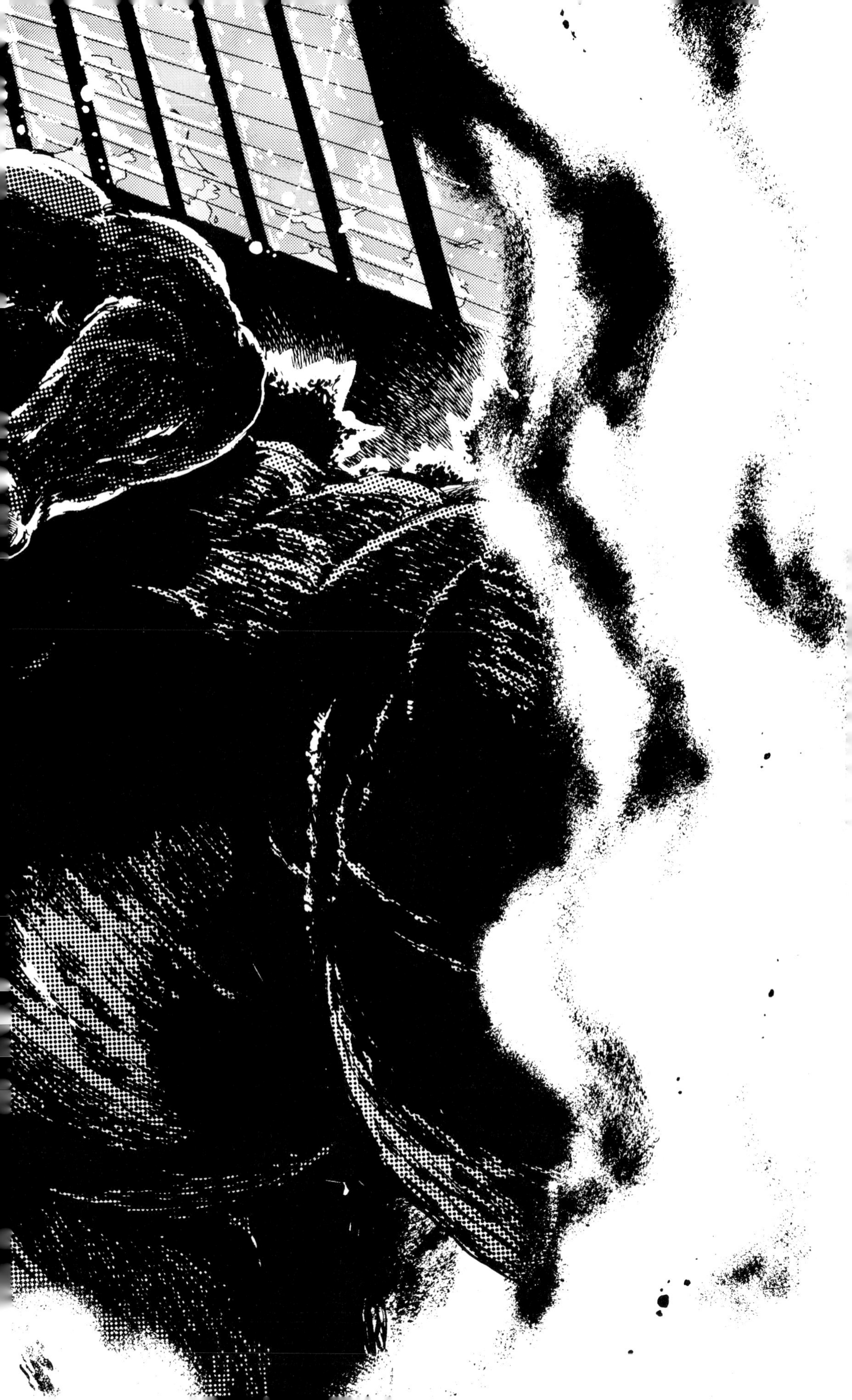

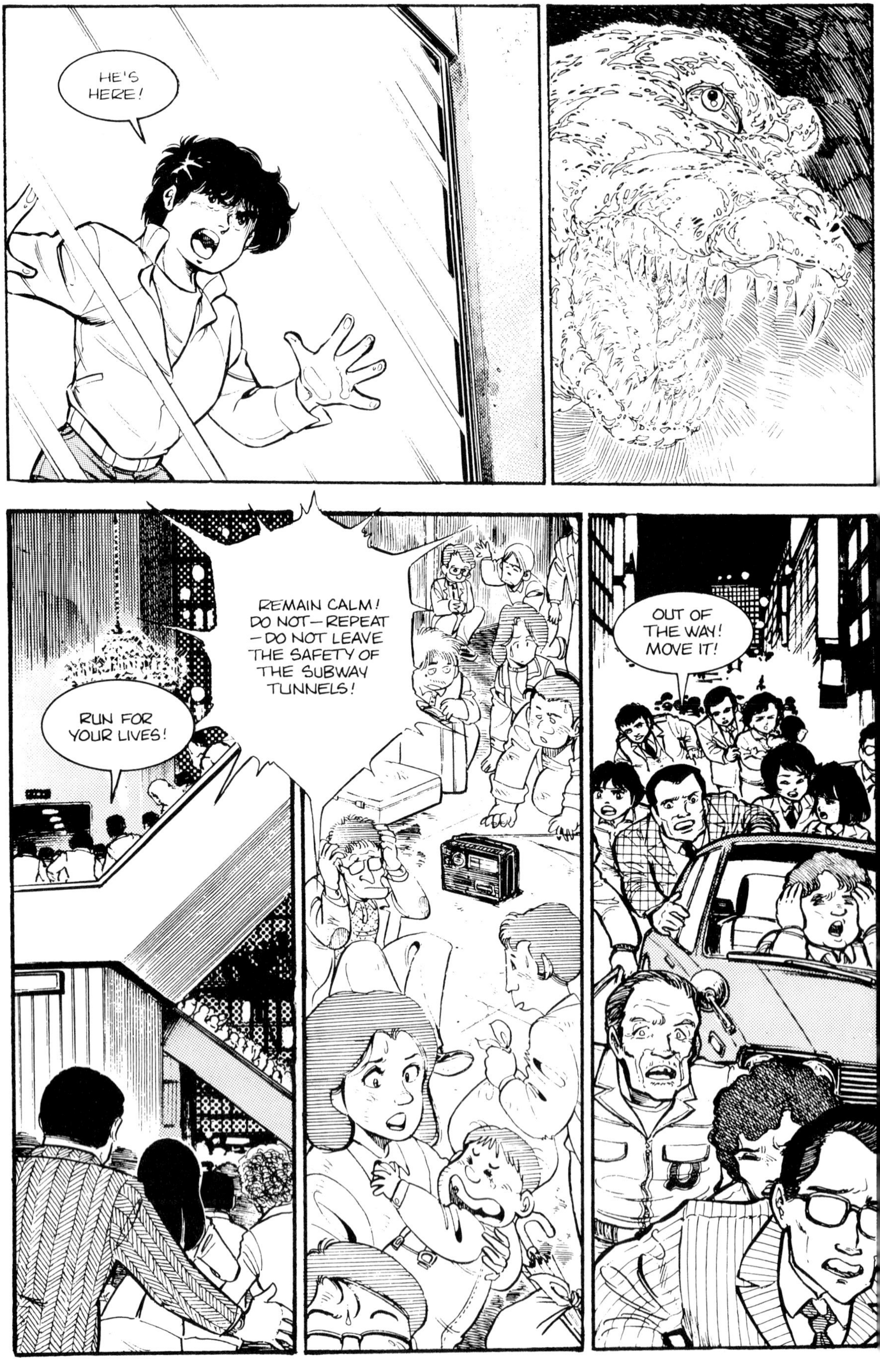
HE'S HERE!
REMAIN CALM! DO NOT—REPEAT—DO NOT LEAVE THE SAFETY OF THE SUBWAY TUNNELS!
RUN FOR YOUR LIVES!
OUT OF THE WAY! MOVE IT!

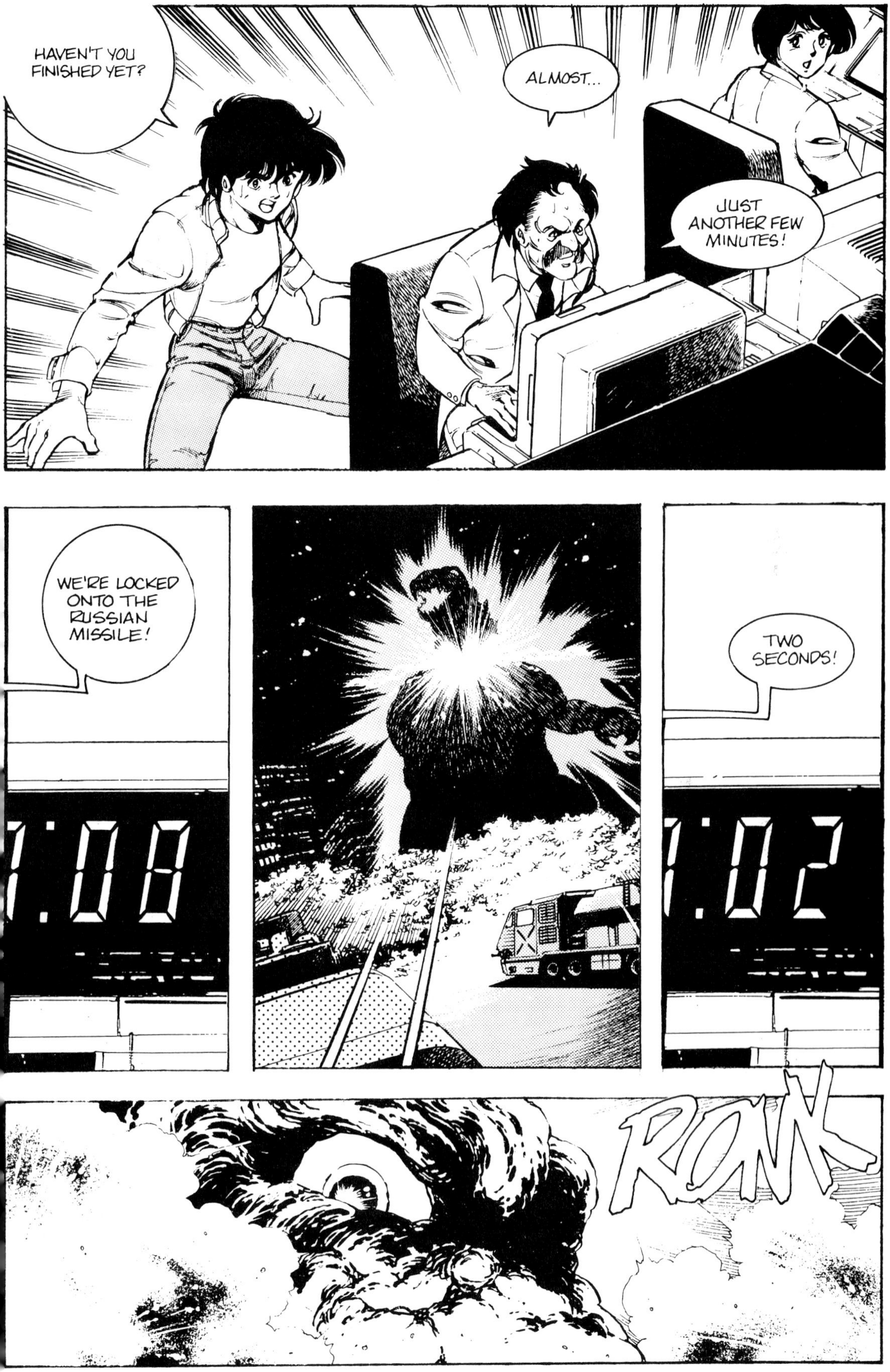
HAVEN'T YOU FINISHED YET?
ALMOST...
JUST ANOTHER FEW MINUTES!
WE'RE LOCKED ONTO THE RUSSIAN MISSILE!
TWO SECONDS!
RONK

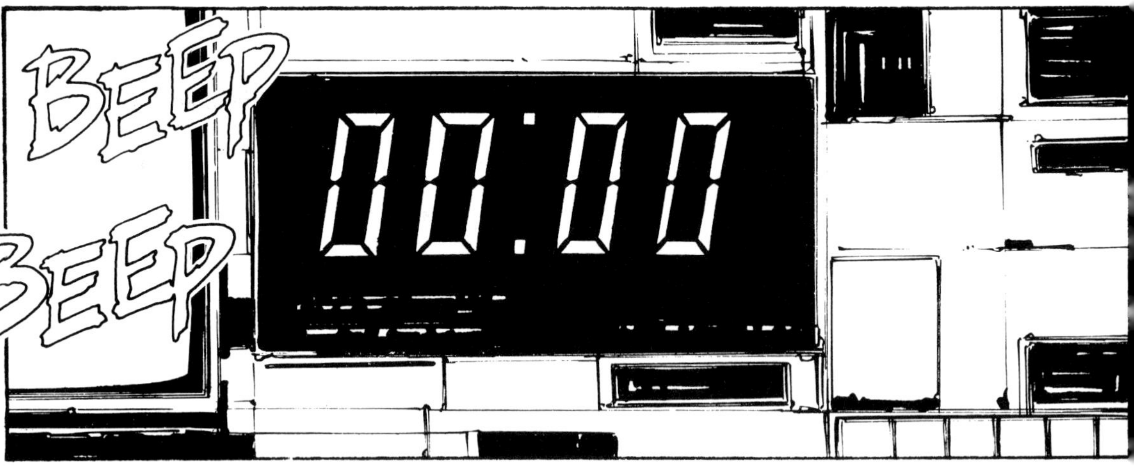
BEEP
BEEP
00:00

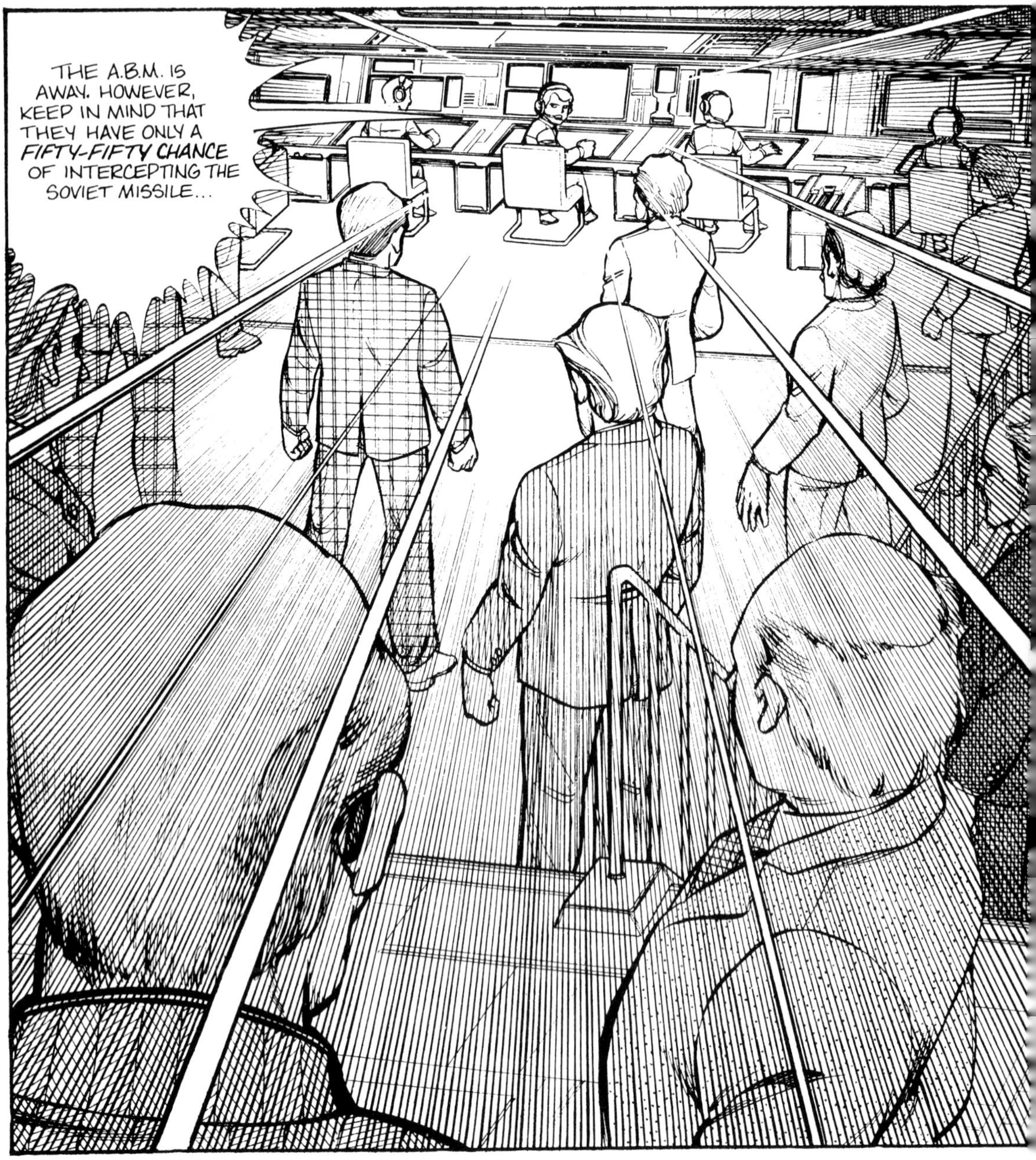
THE A.B.M. IS AWAY. HOWEVER, KEEP IN MIND THAT THEY HAVE ONLY A FIFTY-FIFTY CHANCE OF INTERCEPTING THE SOVIET MISSILE...

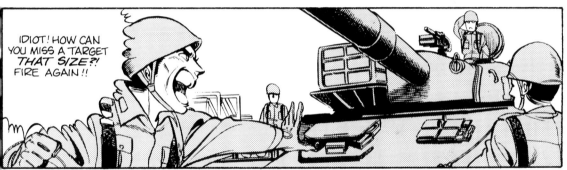

IDIOT! HOW CAN YOU MISS A TARGET *THAT SIZE*?! FIRE AGAIN!!

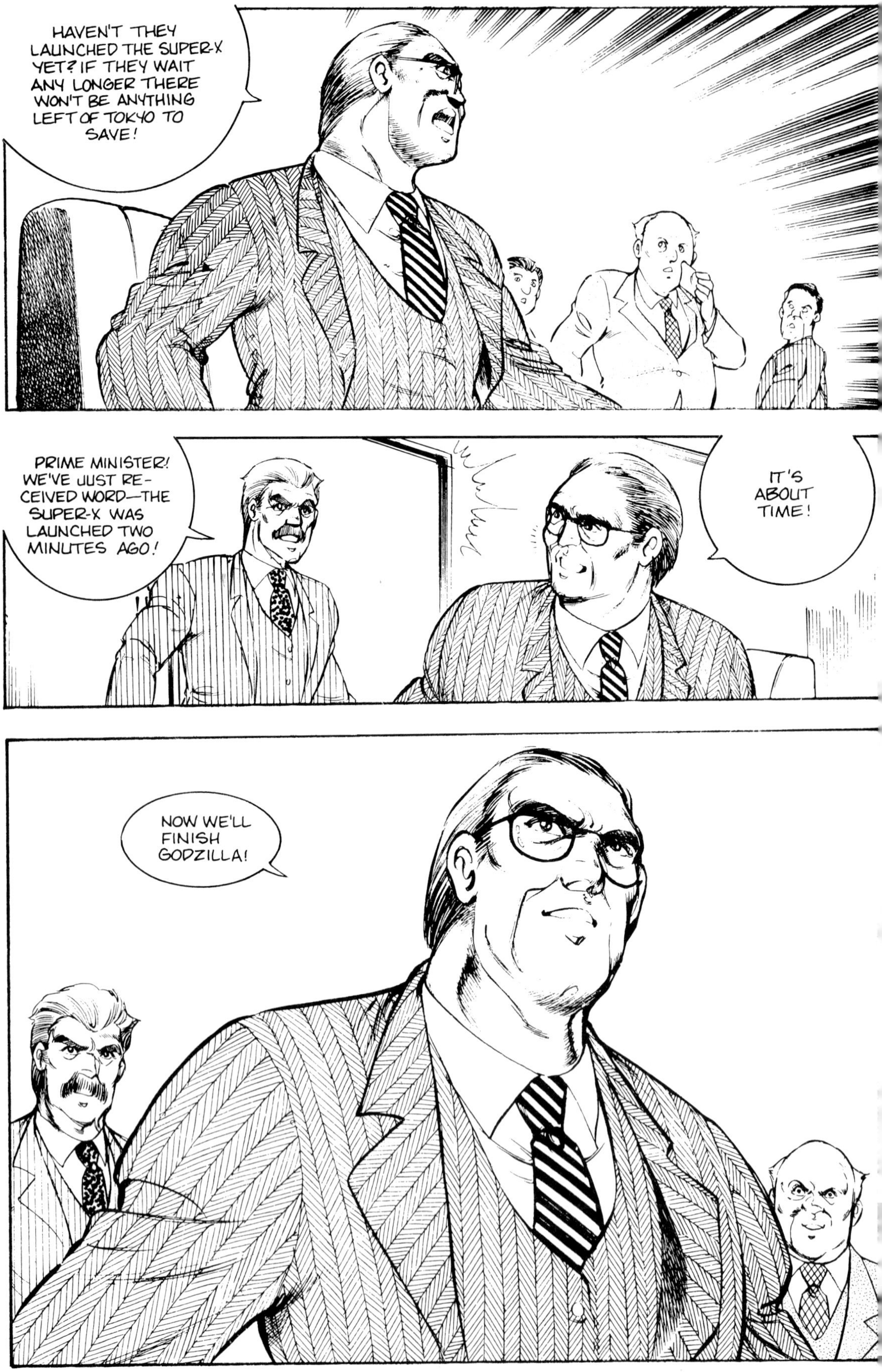
HAVEN'T THEY LAUNCHED THE SUPER-X YET? IF THEY WAIT ANY LONGER THERE WON'T BE ANYTHING LEFT OF TOKYO TO SAVE!
PRIME MINISTER! WE'VE JUST RE-CEIVED WORD—THE SUPER-X WAS LAUNCHED TWO MINUTES AGO!
IT'S ABOUT TIME!
NOW WE'LL FINISH GODZILLA!

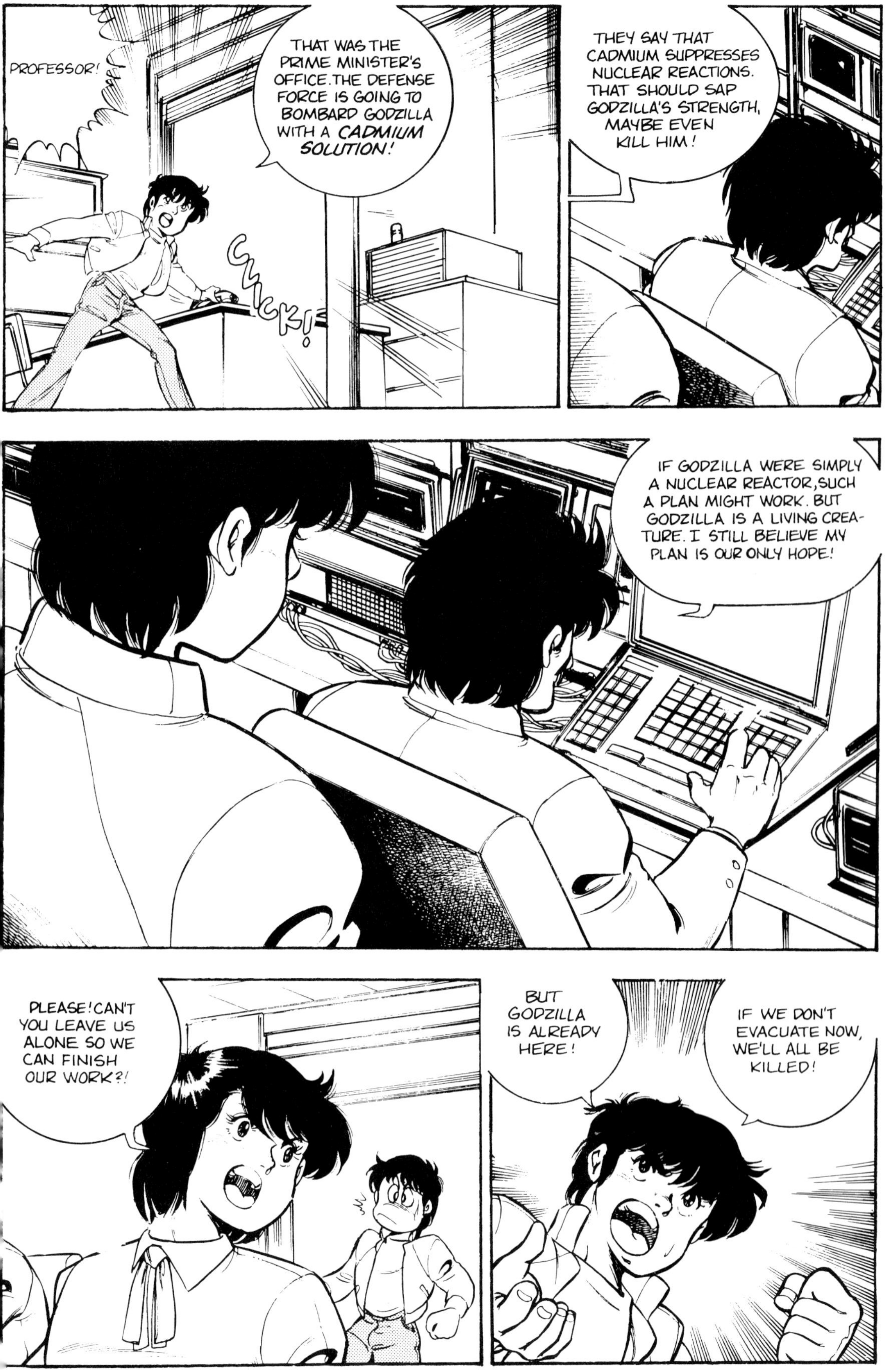
PROFESSOR!
THAT WAS THE PRIME MINISTER'S OFFICE. THE DEFENSE FORCE IS GOING TO BOMBARD GODZILLA WITH A CADMIUM SOLUTION!
CLICK!
THEY SAY THAT CADMIUM SUPPRESSES NUCLEAR REACTIONS. THAT SHOULD SAP GODZILLA'S STRENGTH, MAYBE EVEN KILL HIM!
IF GODZILLA WERE SIMPLY A NUCLEAR REACTOR, SUCH A PLAN MIGHT WORK. BUT GODZILLA IS A LIVING CREATURE. I STILL BELIEVE MY PLAN IS OUR ONLY HOPE!
PLEASE! CAN'T YOU LEAVE US ALONE SO WE CAN FINISH OUR WORK?!
BUT GODZILLA IS ALREADY HERE!
IF WE DON'T EVACUATE NOW, WE'LL ALL BE KILLED!

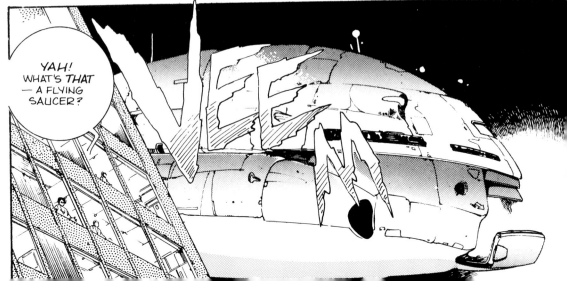

YAH! WHAT'S *THAT* — A FLYING SAUCER?

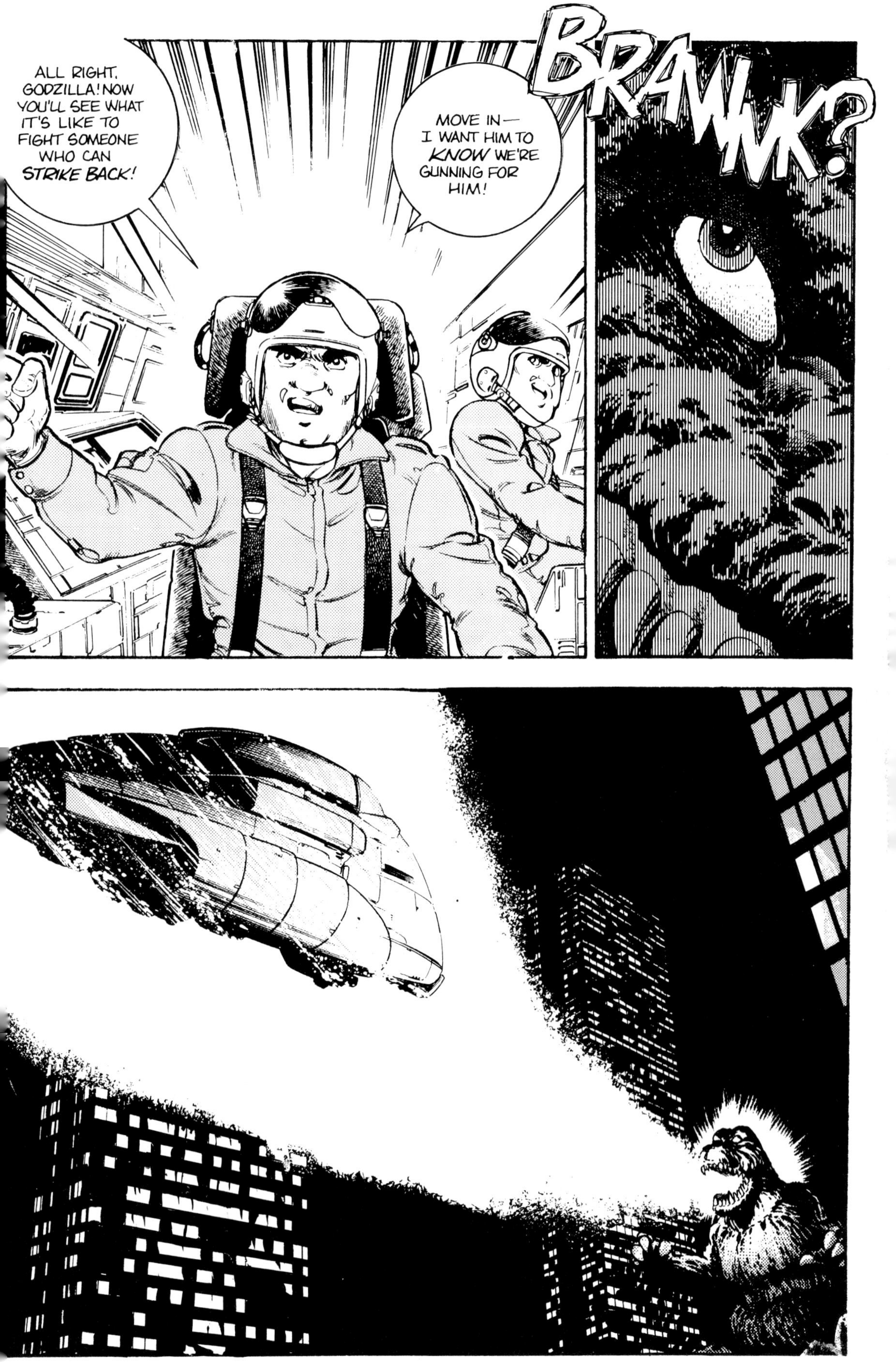
ALL RIGHT, GODZILLA! NOW YOU'LL SEE WHAT IT'S LIKE TO FIGHT SOMEONE WHO CAN STRIKE BACK!
MOVE IN— I WANT HIM TO KNOW WE'RE GUNNING FOR HIM!
BRAWNK?

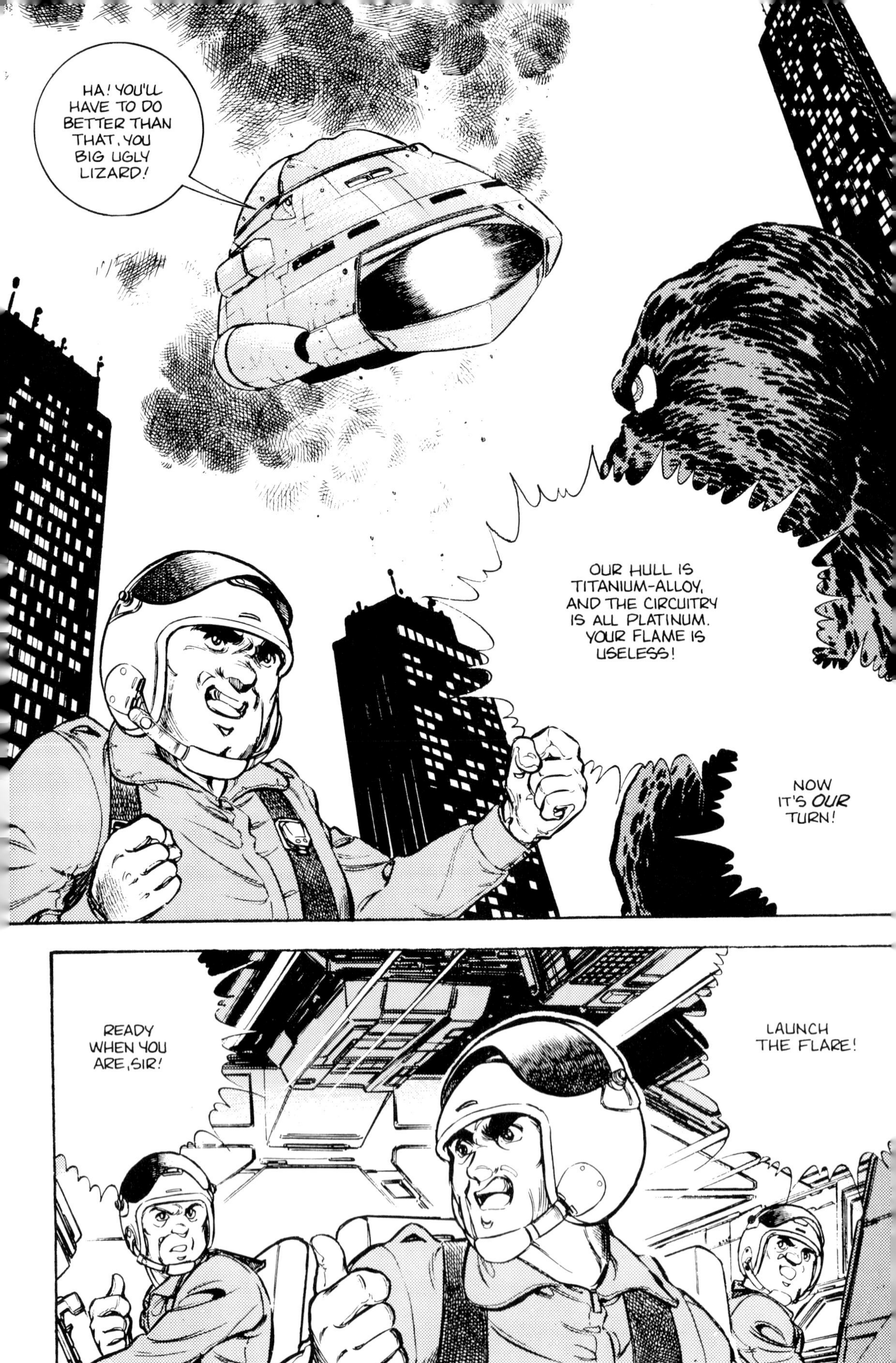
HA! YOU'LL HAVE TO DO BETTER THAN THAT, YOU BIG UGLY LIZARD!
OUR HULL IS TITANIUM-ALLOY, AND THE CIRCUITRY IS ALL PLATINUM. YOUR FLAME IS USELESS!
NOW IT'S *OUR* TURN!
LAUNCH THE FLARE!
READY WHEN YOU ARE, SIR!

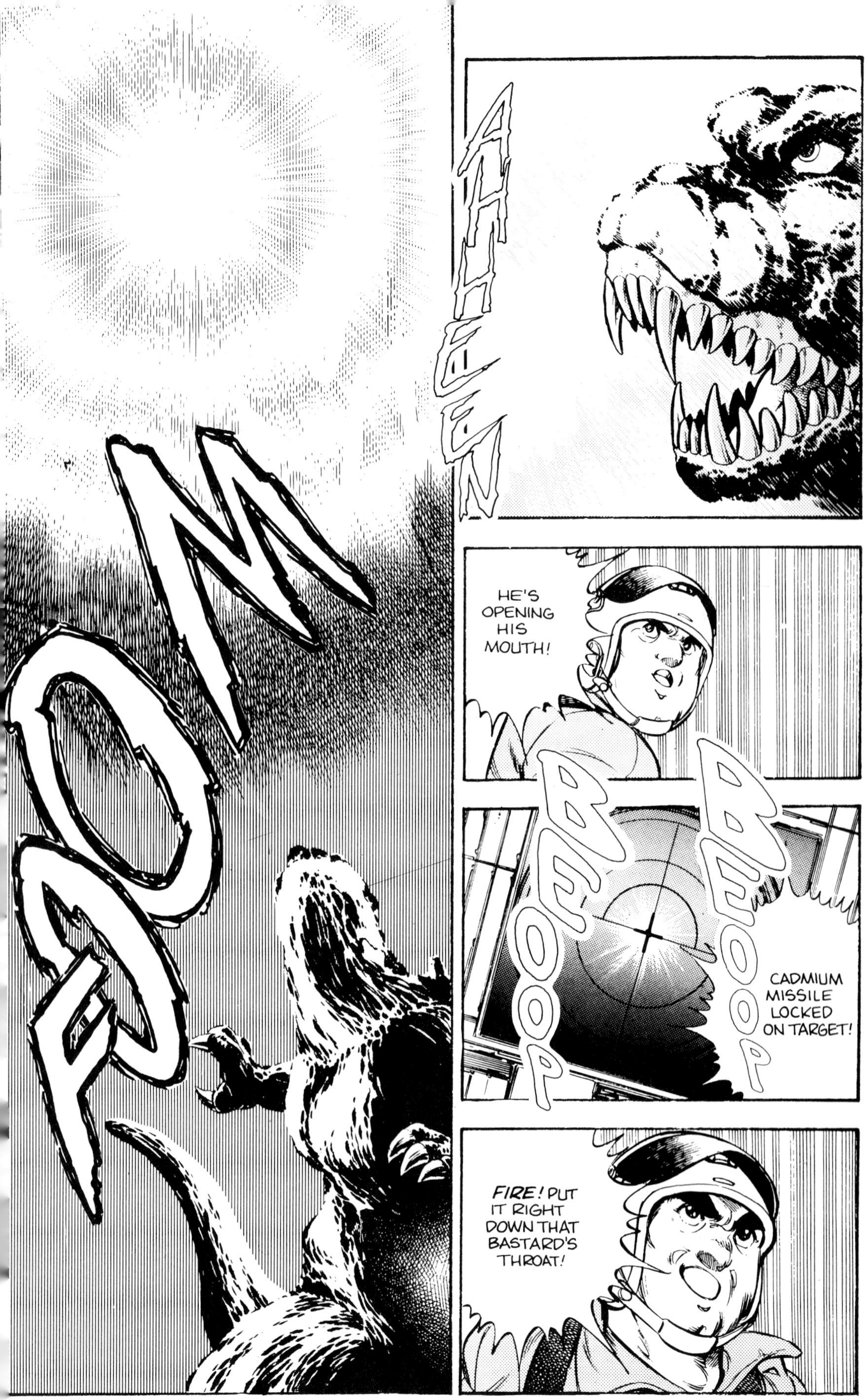
HE'S OPENING HIS MOUTH!
BEEOOP
BEEOOP
CADMIUM MISSILE LOCKED ON TARGET!
FIRE! PUT IT RIGHT DOWN THAT BASTARD'S THROAT!

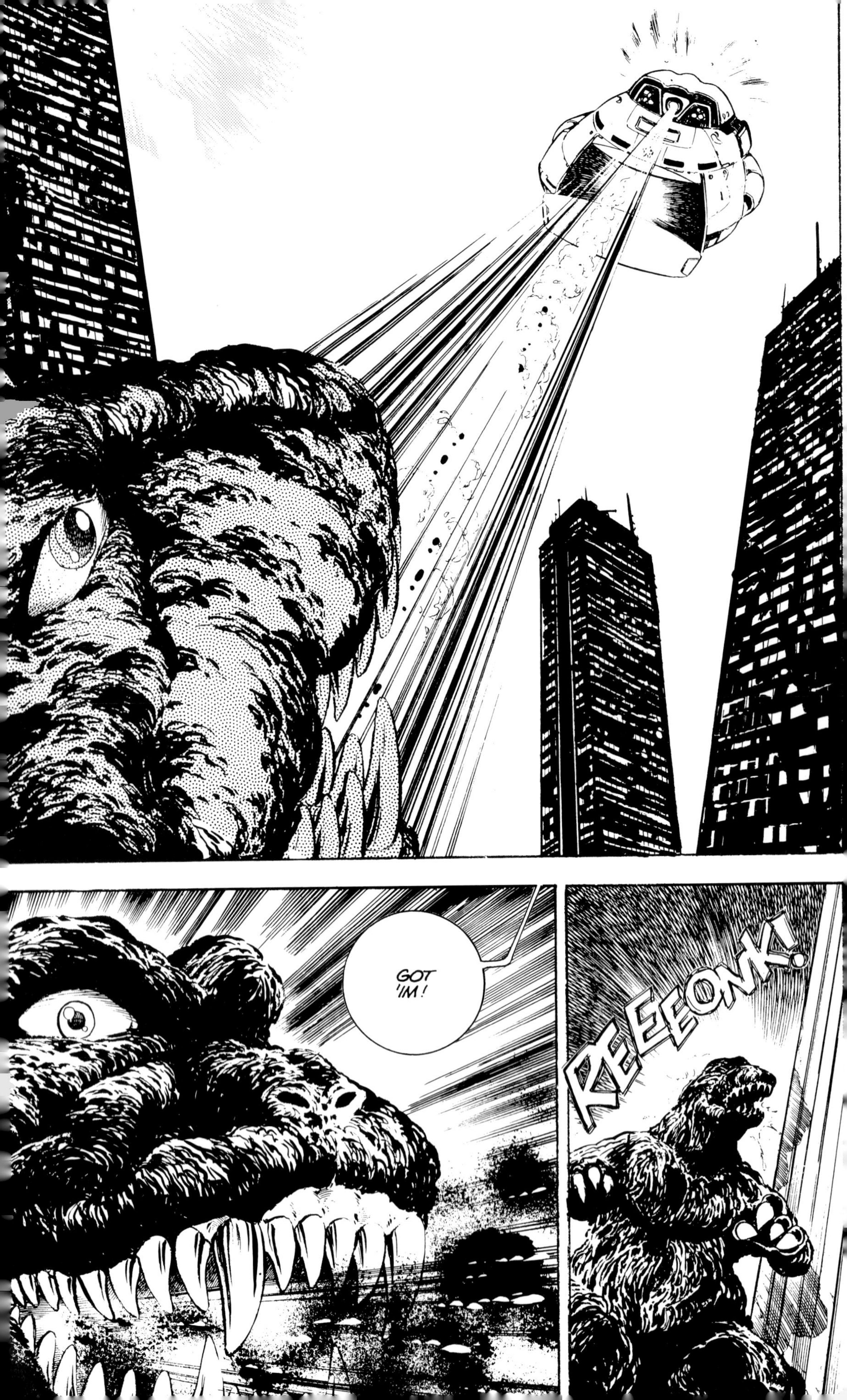
GOT 'IM!
REEEONK!

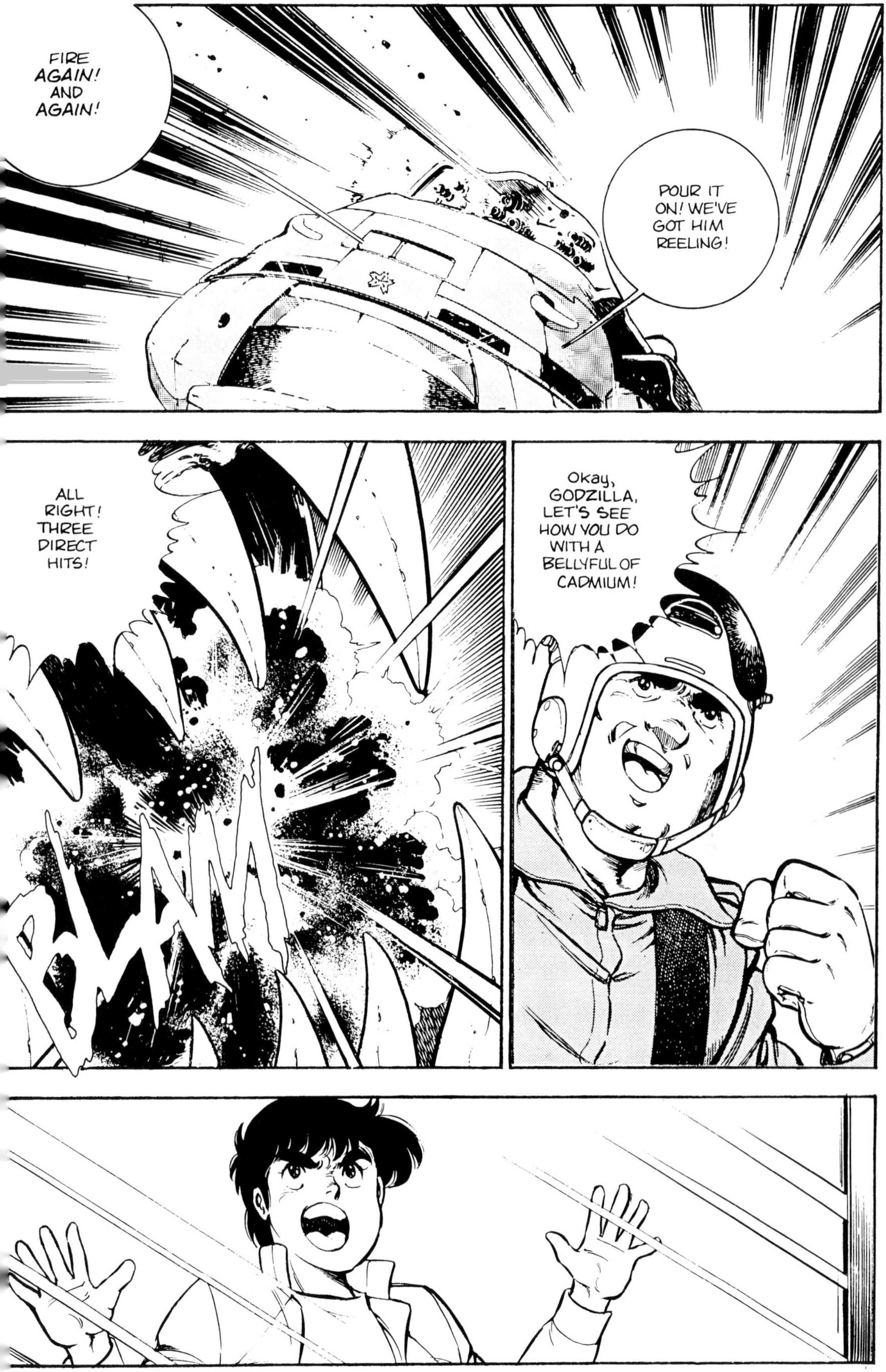
FIRE AGAIN! AND AGAIN!
POUR IT ON! WE'VE GOT HIM REELING!
ALL RIGHT! THREE DIRECT HITS!
BLAM
Okay, GODZILLA, LET'S SEE HOW YOU DO WITH A BELLYFUL OF CADMIUM!

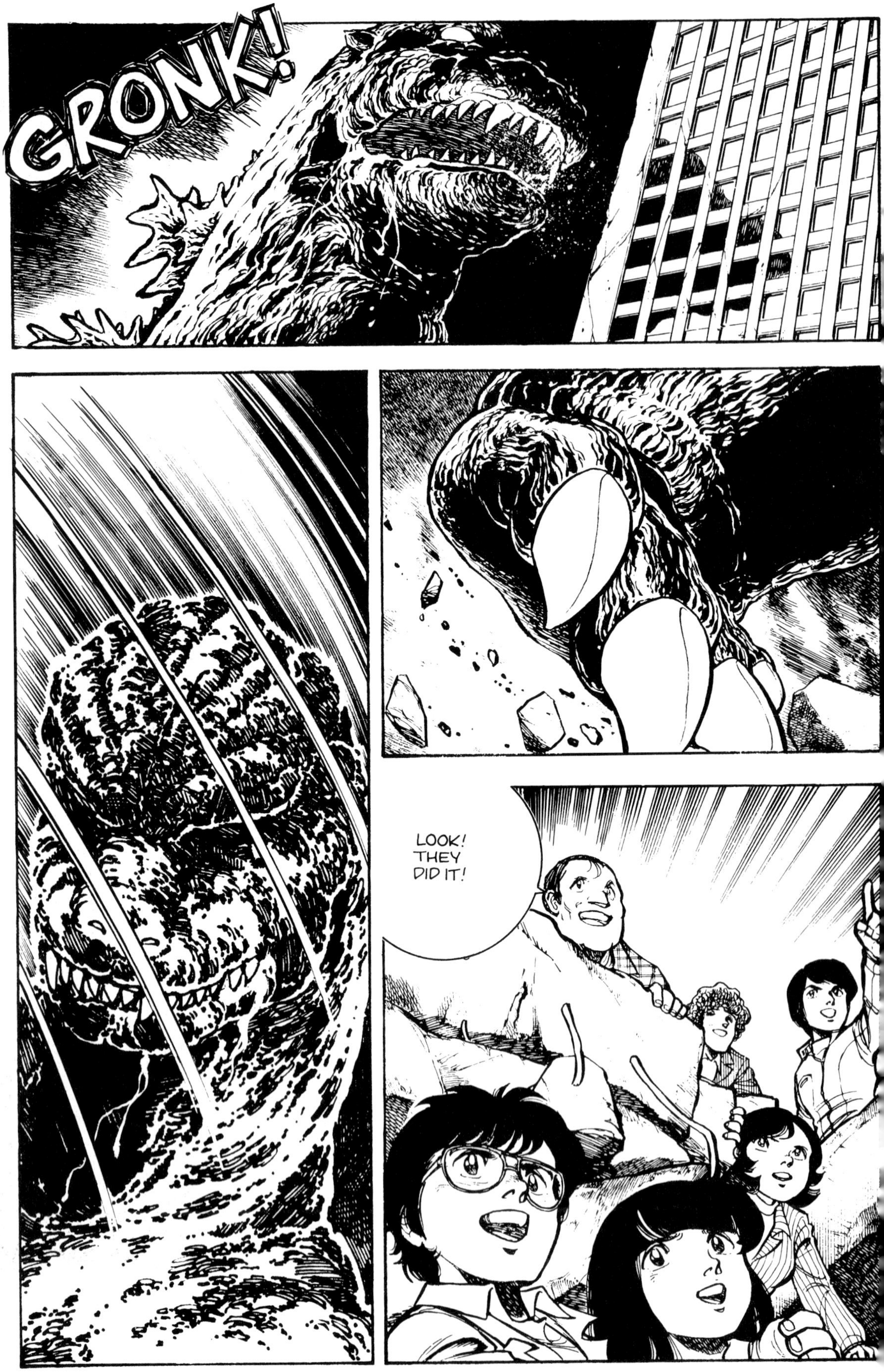
GRONK!
LOOK! THEY DID IT!

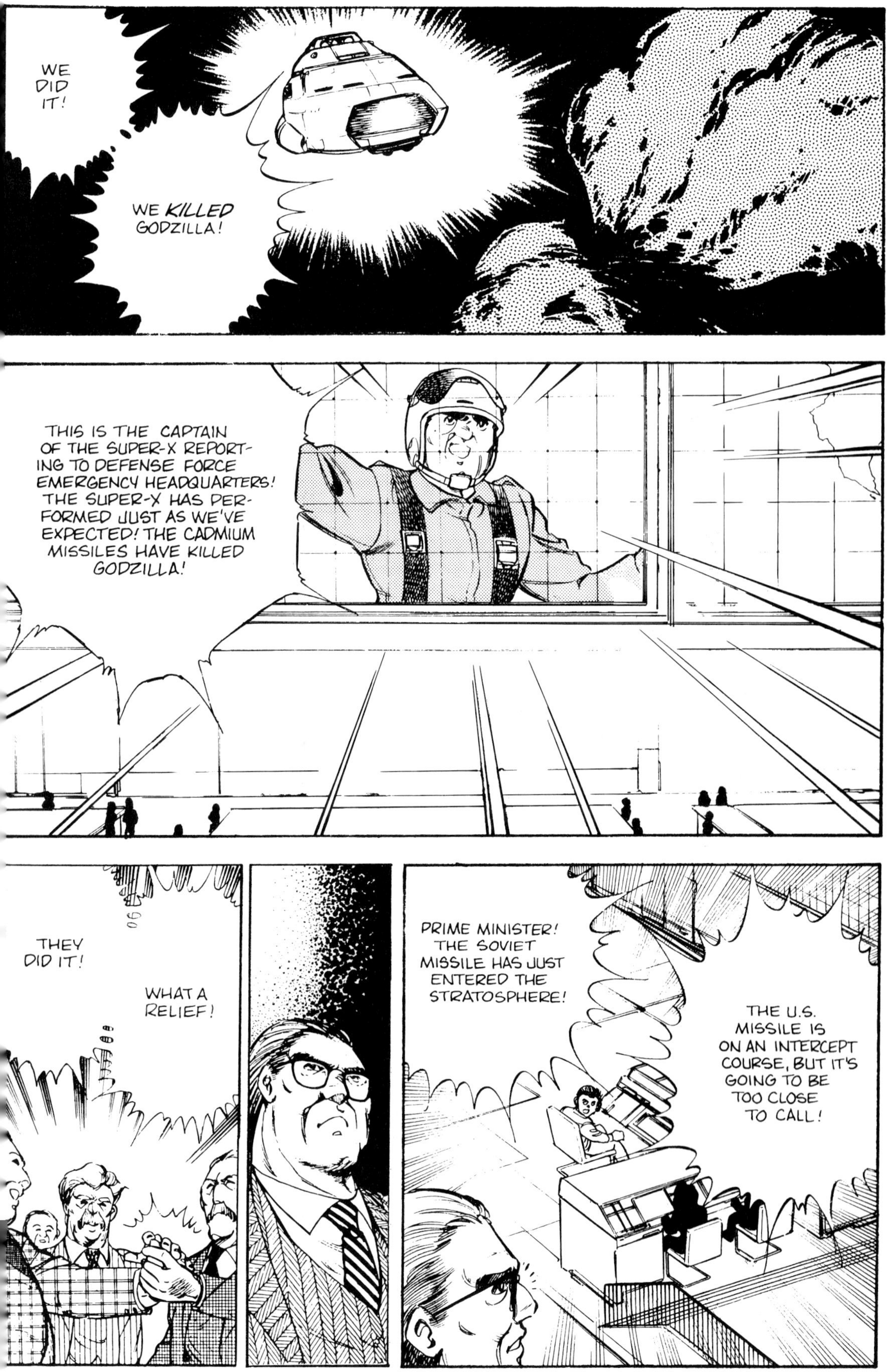
WE DID IT!
WE KILLED GODZILLA!
THIS IS THE CAPTAIN OF THE SUPER-X REPORTING TO DEFENSE FORCE EMERGENCY HEADQUARTERS! THE SUPER-X HAS PERFORMED JUST AS WE'VE EXPECTED! THE CADMIUM MISSILES HAVE KILLED GODZILLA!
THEY DID IT!
WHAT A RELIEF!
PRIME MINISTER! THE SOVIET MISSILE HAS JUST ENTERED THE STRATOSPHERE!
THE U.S. MISSILE IS ON AN INTERCEPT COURSE, BUT IT'S GOING TO BE TOO CLOSE TO CALL!

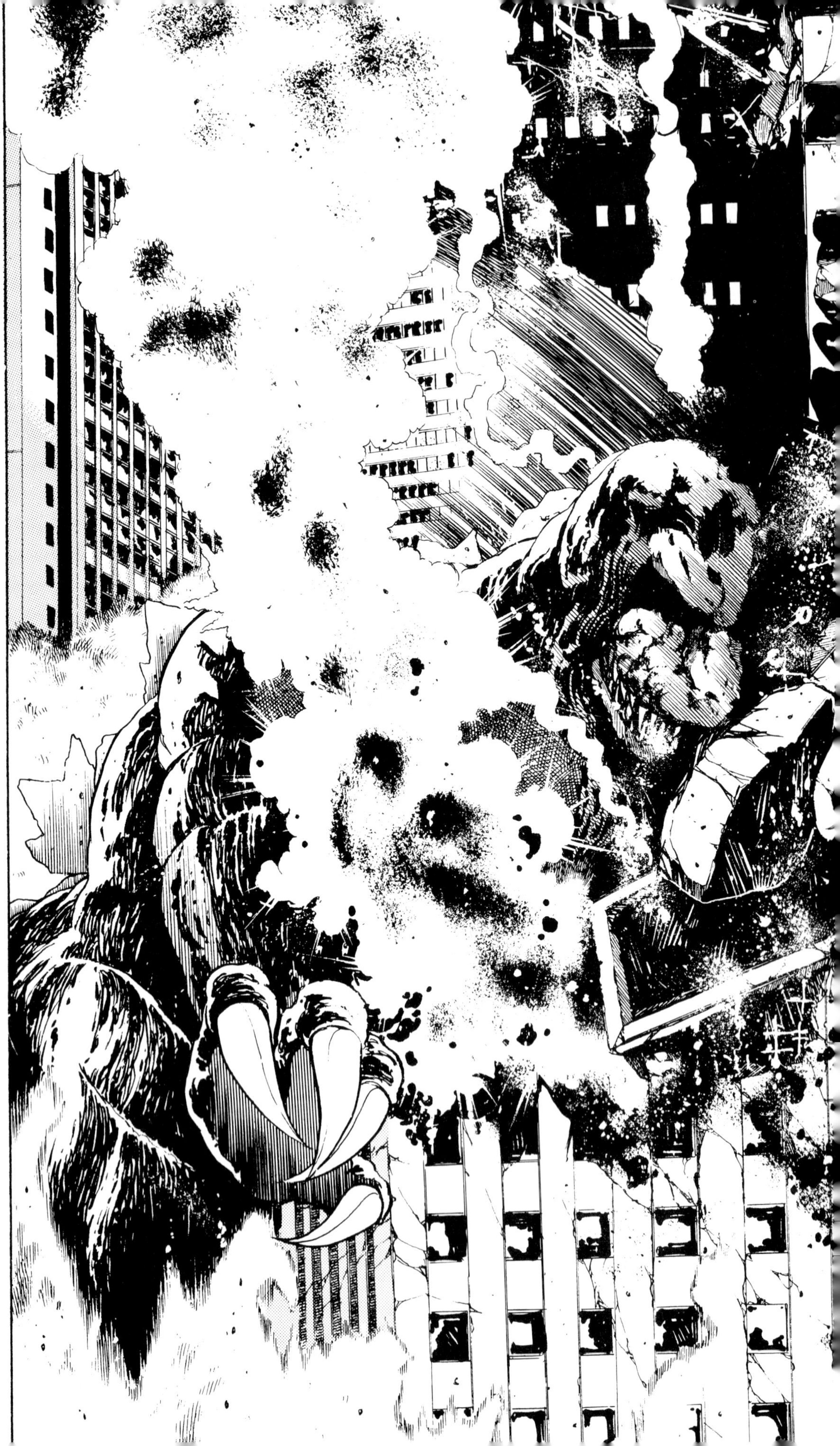

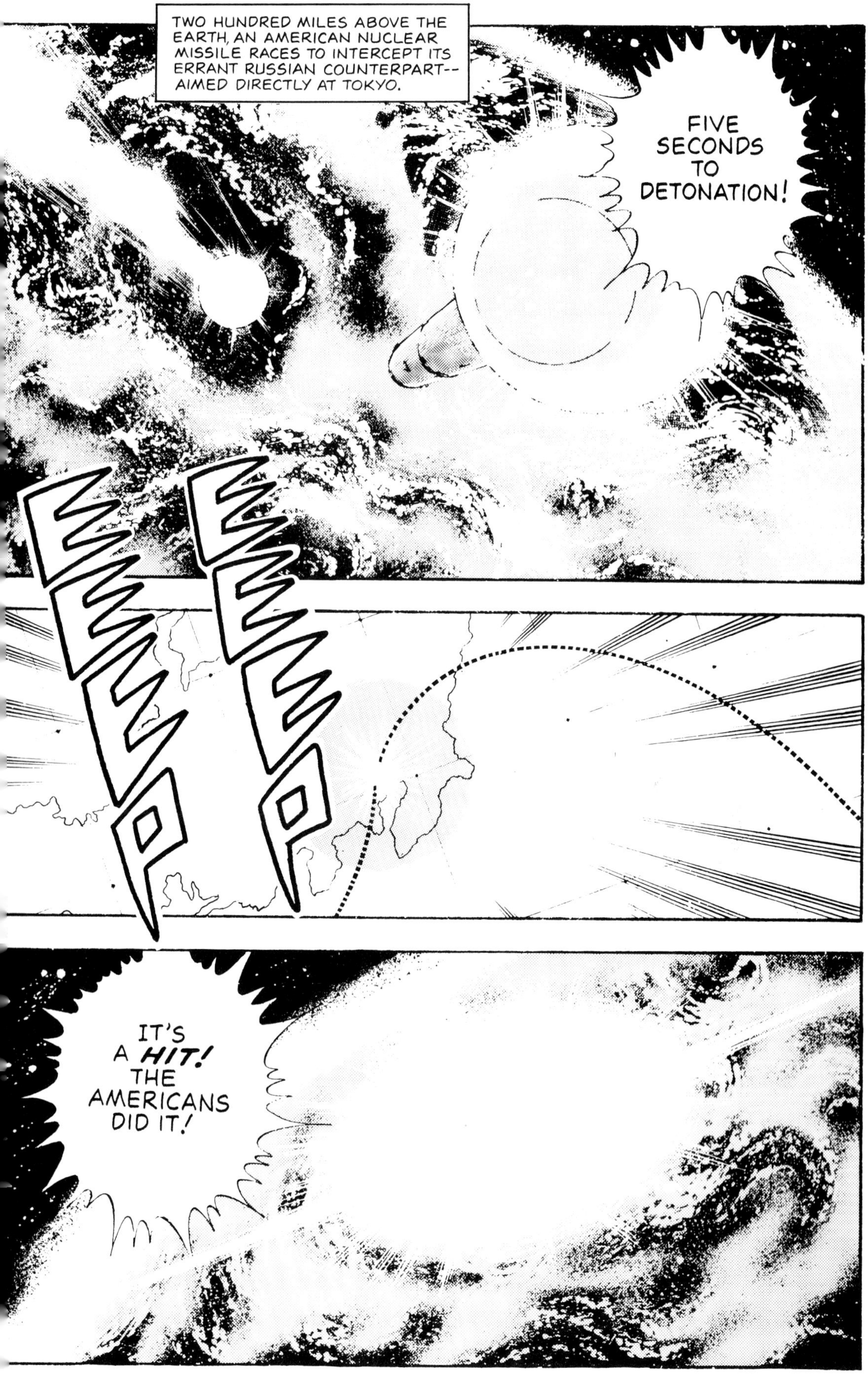
TWO HUNDRED MILES ABOVE THE EARTH, AN AMERICAN NUCLEAR MISSILE RACES TO INTERCEPT ITS ERRANT RUSSIAN COUNTERPART-- AIMED DIRECTLY AT TOKYO.
FIVE SECONDS TO DETONATION!
EEEEP EEEEP
IT'S A HIT! THE AMERICANS DID IT!

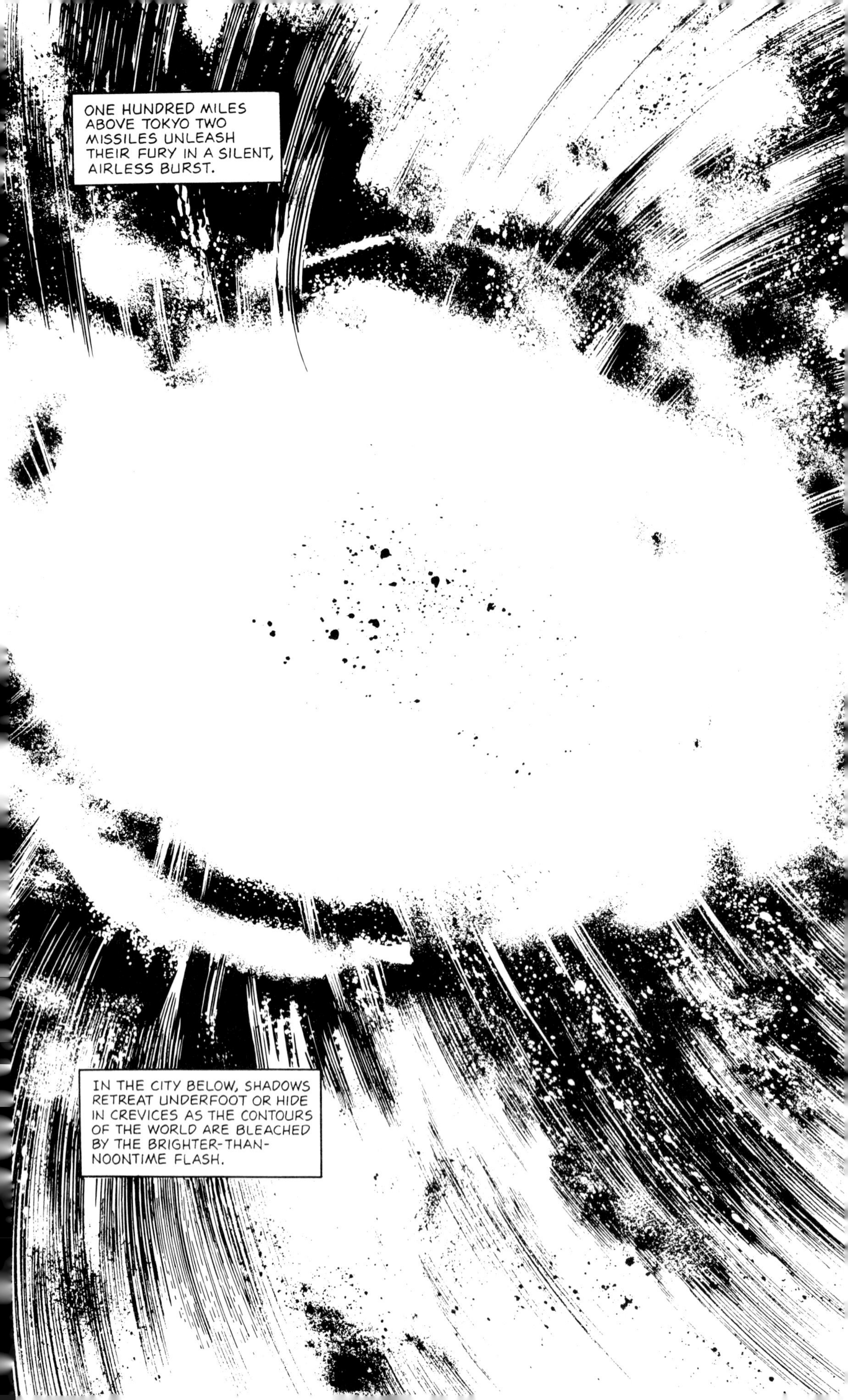
ONE HUNDRED MILES ABOVE TOKYO TWO MISSILES UNLEASH THEIR FURY IN A SILENT, AIRLESS BURST.
IN THE CITY BELOW, SHADOWS RETREAT UNDERFOOT OR HIDE IN CREVICES AS THE CONTOURS OF THE WORLD ARE BLEACHED BY THE BRIGHTER-THAN-NOONTIME FLASH.

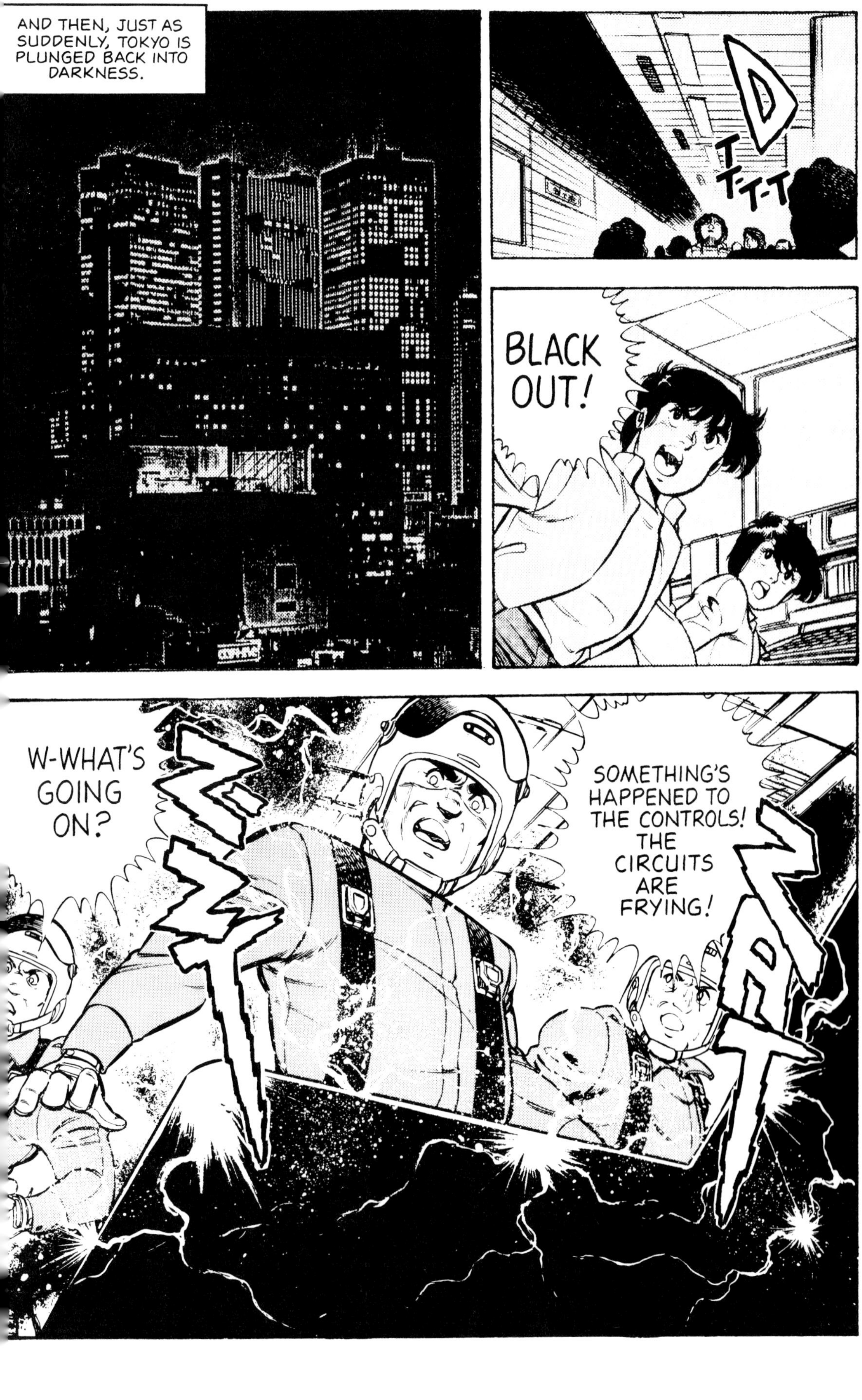
AND THEN, JUST AS SUDDENLY, TOKYO IS PLUNGED BACK INTO DARKNESS.
DT-T-T-T
BLACK OUT!
W-WHAT'S GOING ON?
ZZZT
SOMETHING'S HAPPENED TO THE CONTROLS! THE CIRCUITS ARE FRYING!
ZAPT

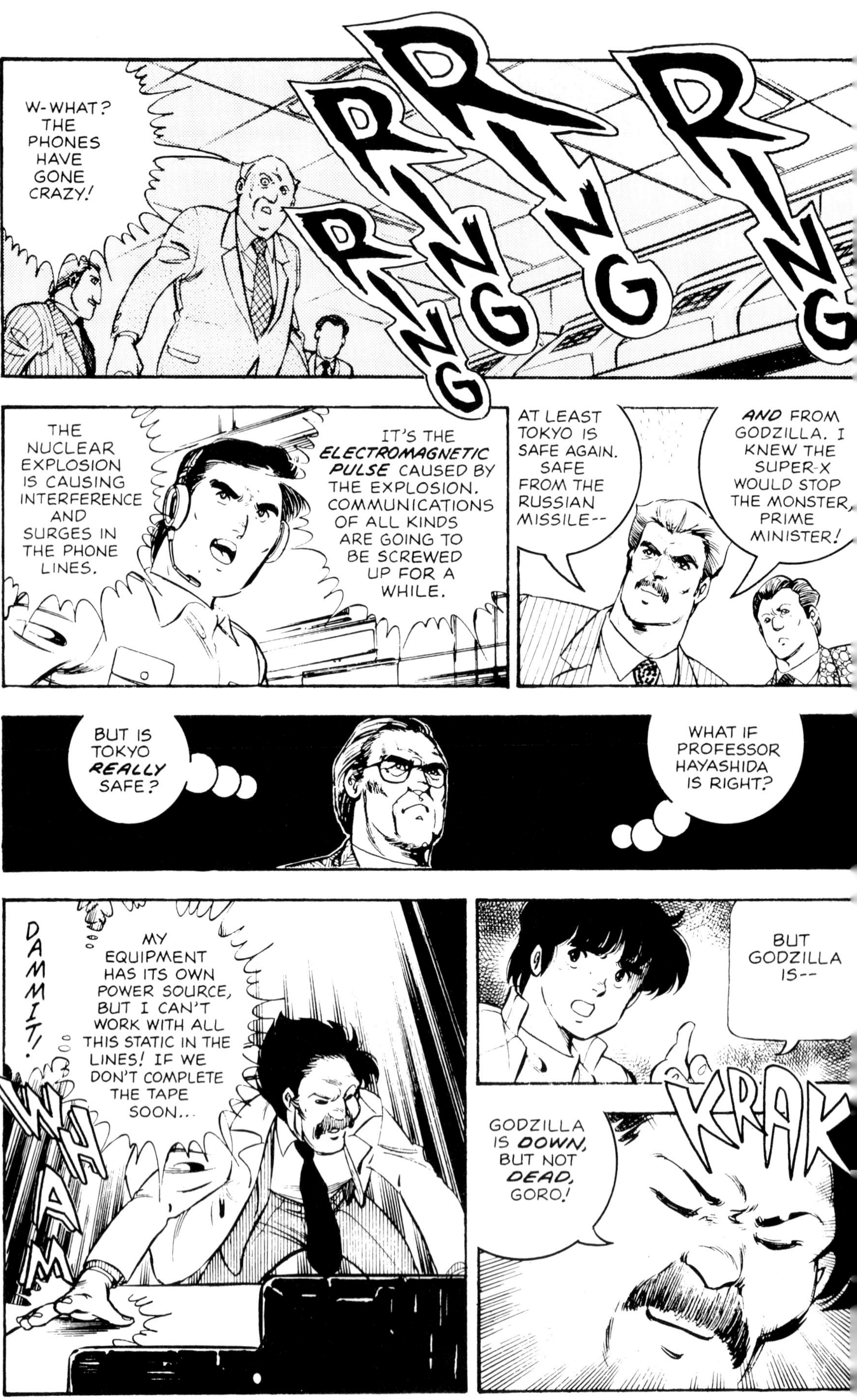
W-WHAT? THE PHONES HAVE GONE CRAZY!
RRING RRING RING RING
THE NUCLEAR EXPLOSION IS CAUSING INTERFERENCE AND SURGES IN THE PHONE LINES.
IT'S THE ELECTROMAGNETIC PULSE CAUSED BY THE EXPLOSION. COMMUNICATIONS OF ALL KINDS ARE GOING TO BE SCREWED UP FOR A WHILE.
AT LEAST TOKYO IS SAFE AGAIN. SAFE FROM THE RUSSIAN MISSILE--
AND FROM GODZILLA. I KNEW THE SUPER-X WOULD STOP THE MONSTER, PRIME MINISTER!
BUT IS TOKYO REALLY SAFE?
WHAT IF PROFESSOR HAYASHIDA IS RIGHT?
DAMMIT!
MY EQUIPMENT HAS ITS OWN POWER SOURCE, BUT I CAN'T WORK WITH ALL THIS STATIC IN THE LINES! IF WE DON'T COMPLETE THE TAPE SOON...
WHAM
BUT GODZILLA IS--
KRAK
GODZILLA IS DOWN, BUT NOT DEAD, GORO!

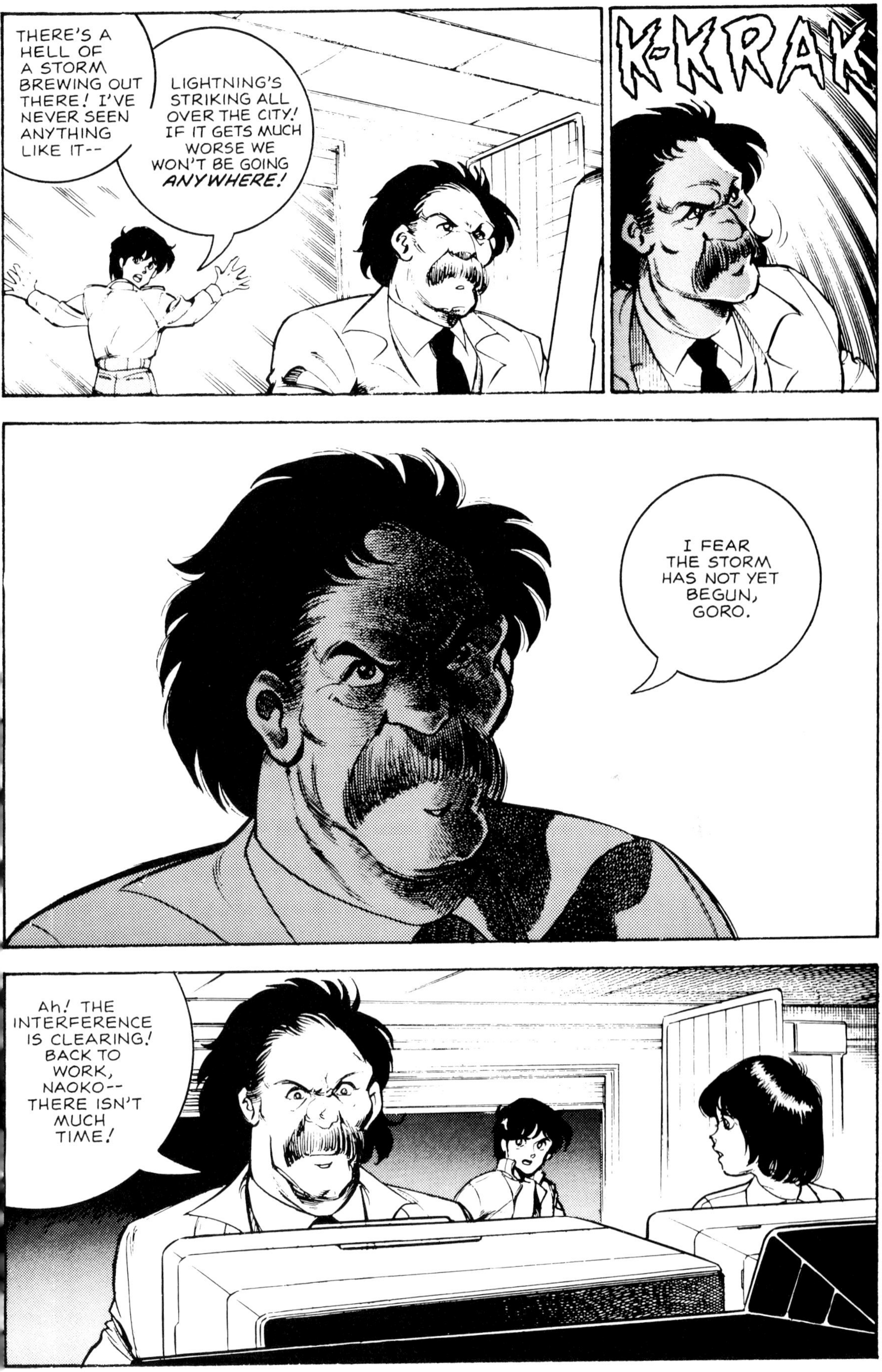
THERE'S A HELL OF A STORM BREWING OUT THERE! I'VE NEVER SEEN ANYTHING LIKE IT--
LIGHTNING'S STRIKING ALL OVER THE CITY! IF IT GETS MUCH WORSE WE WON'T BE GOING *ANYWHERE!*
K-KRAK
I FEAR THE STORM HAS NOT YET BEGUN, GORO.
Ah! THE INTERFERENCE IS CLEARING! BACK TO WORK, NAOKO-- THERE ISN'T MUCH TIME!

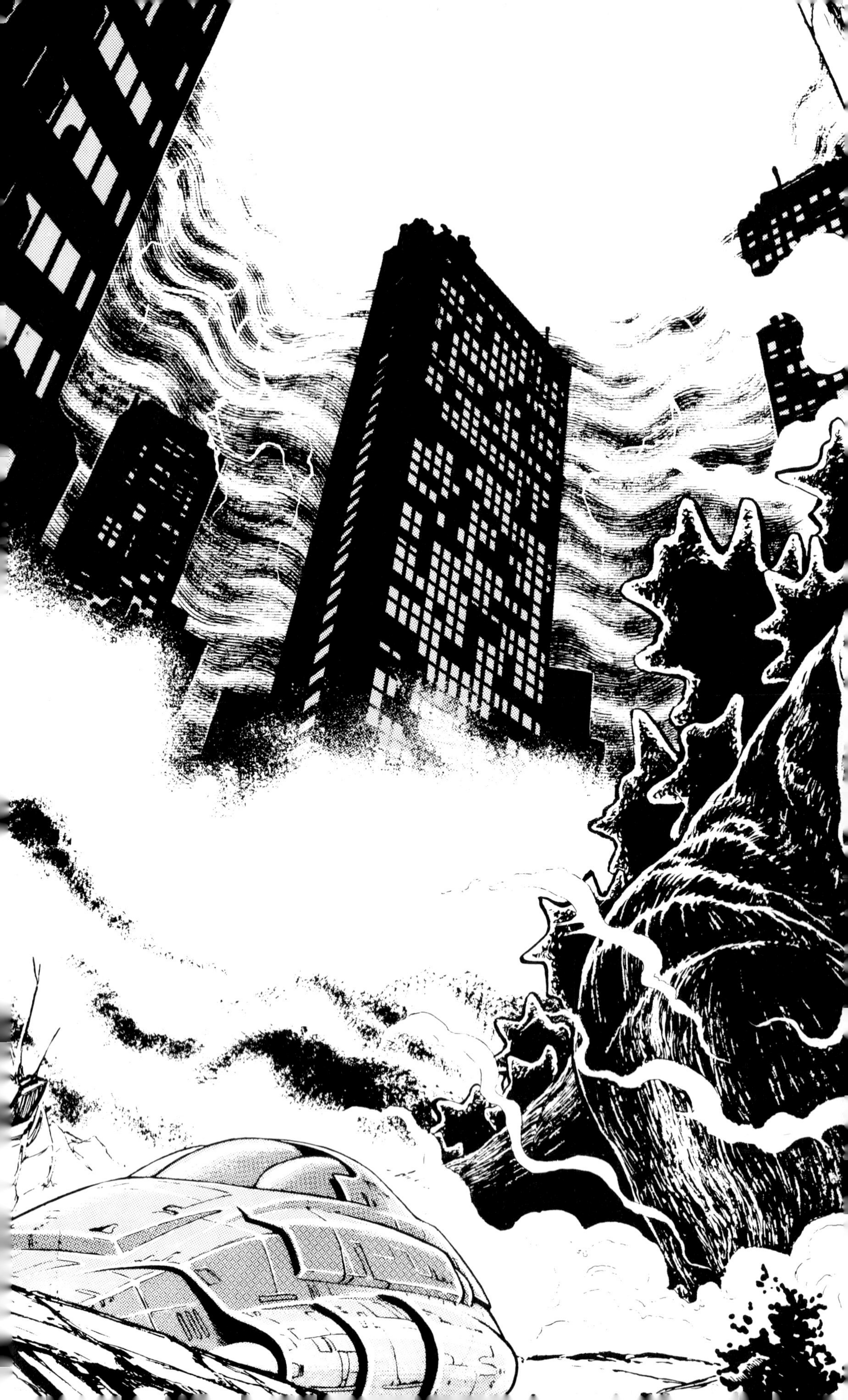

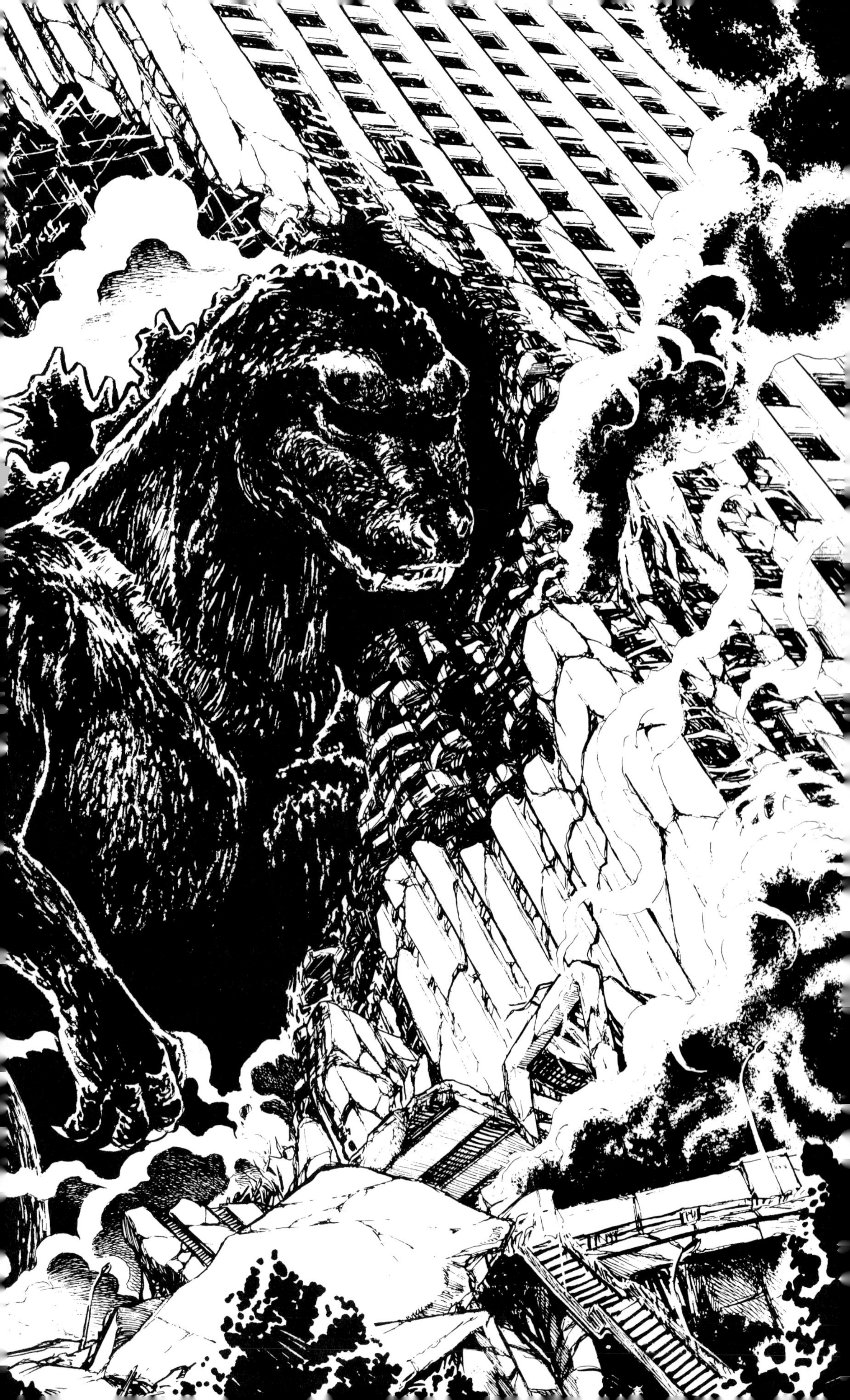

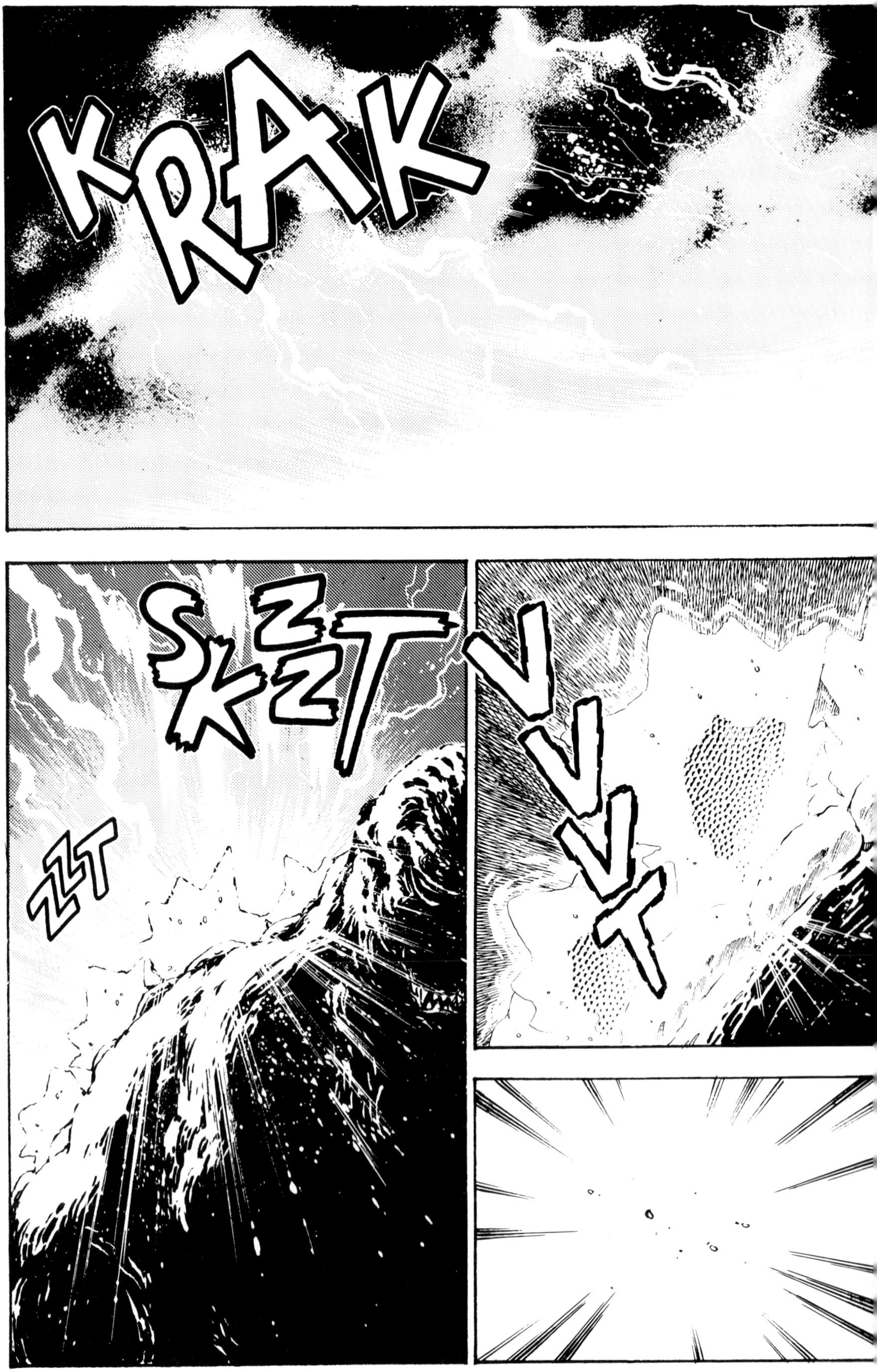
KRAK
SKZZT
ZZT
VVVVT

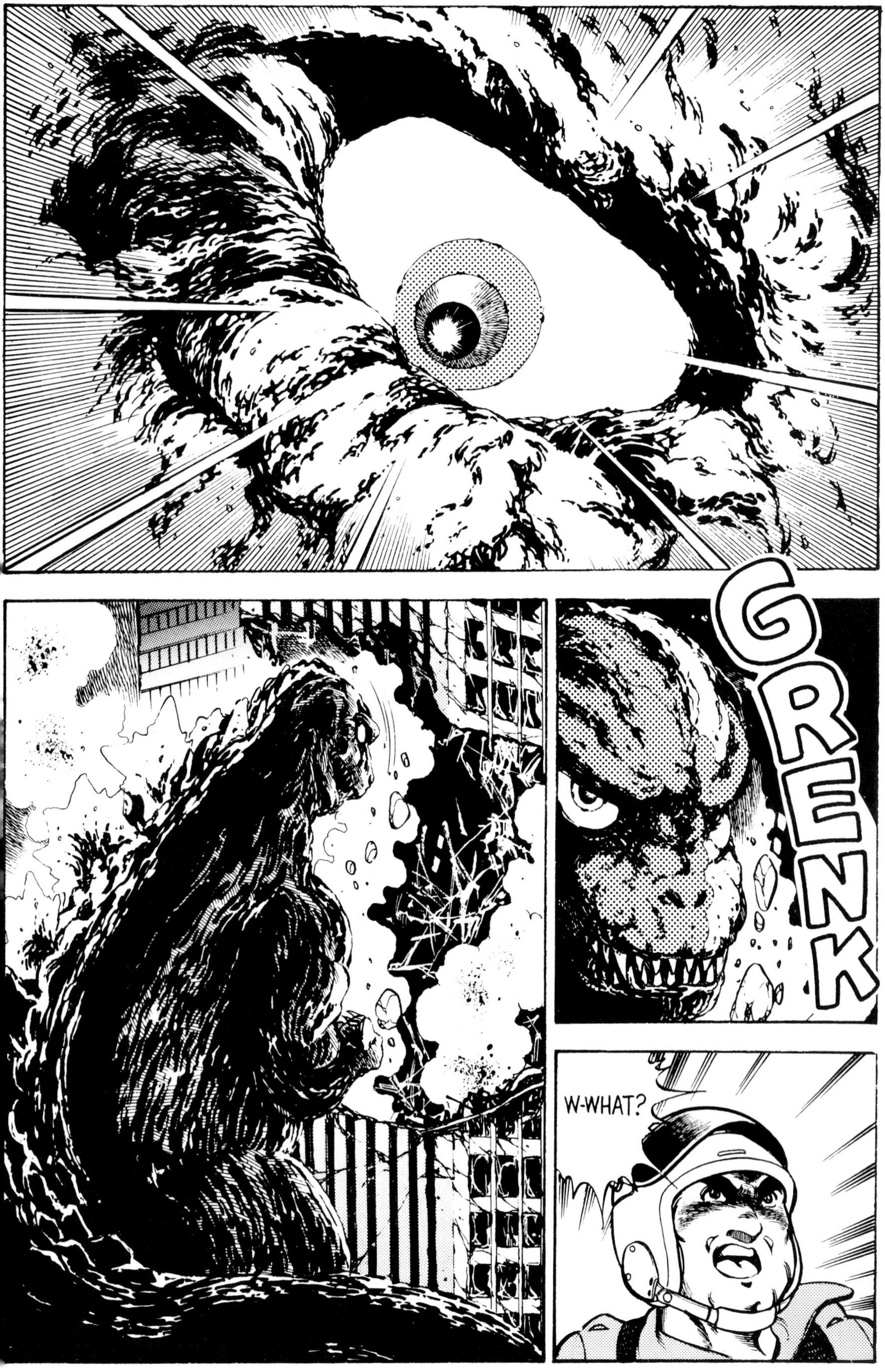
GRENK
W-WHAT?

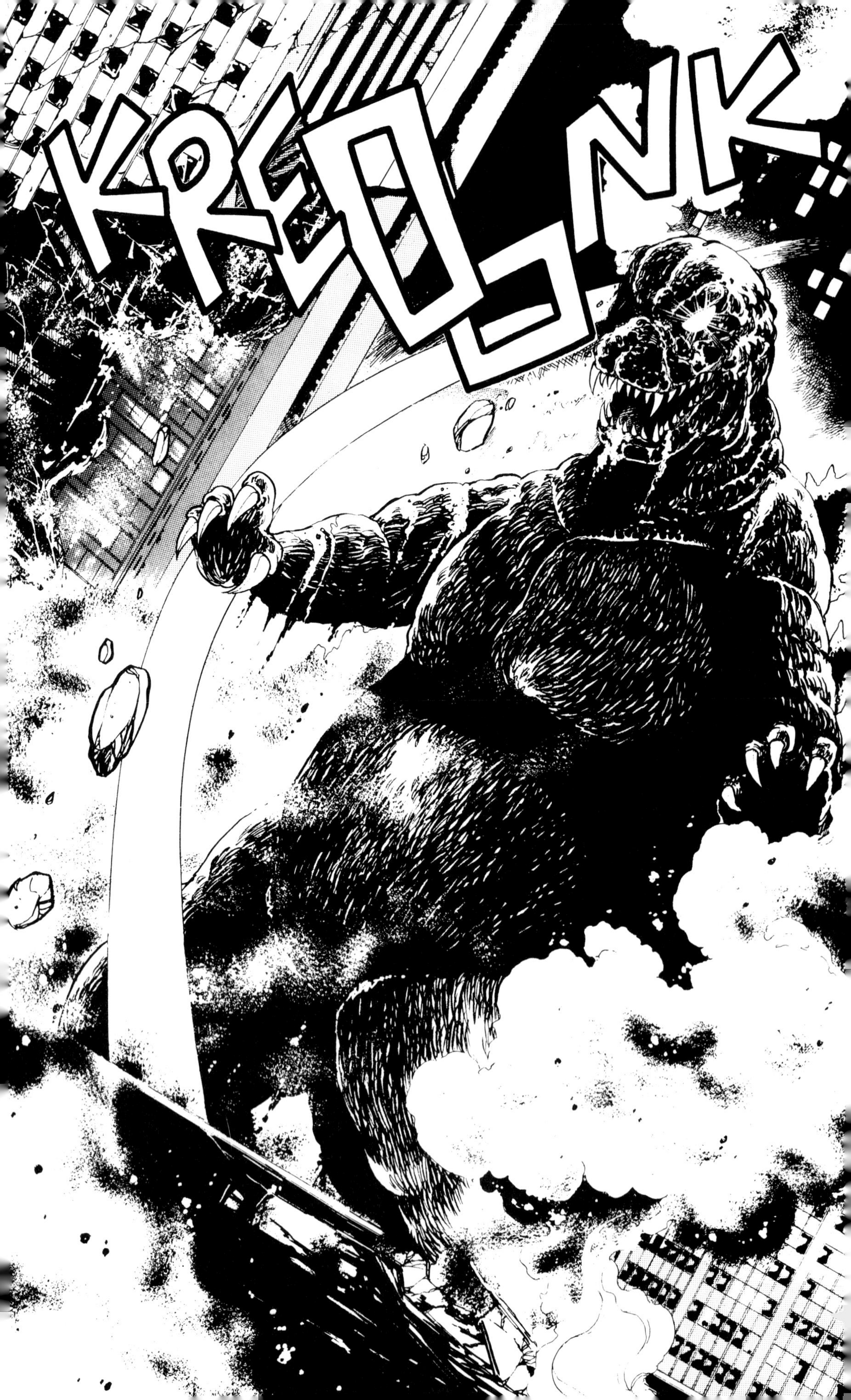
KREDUNK

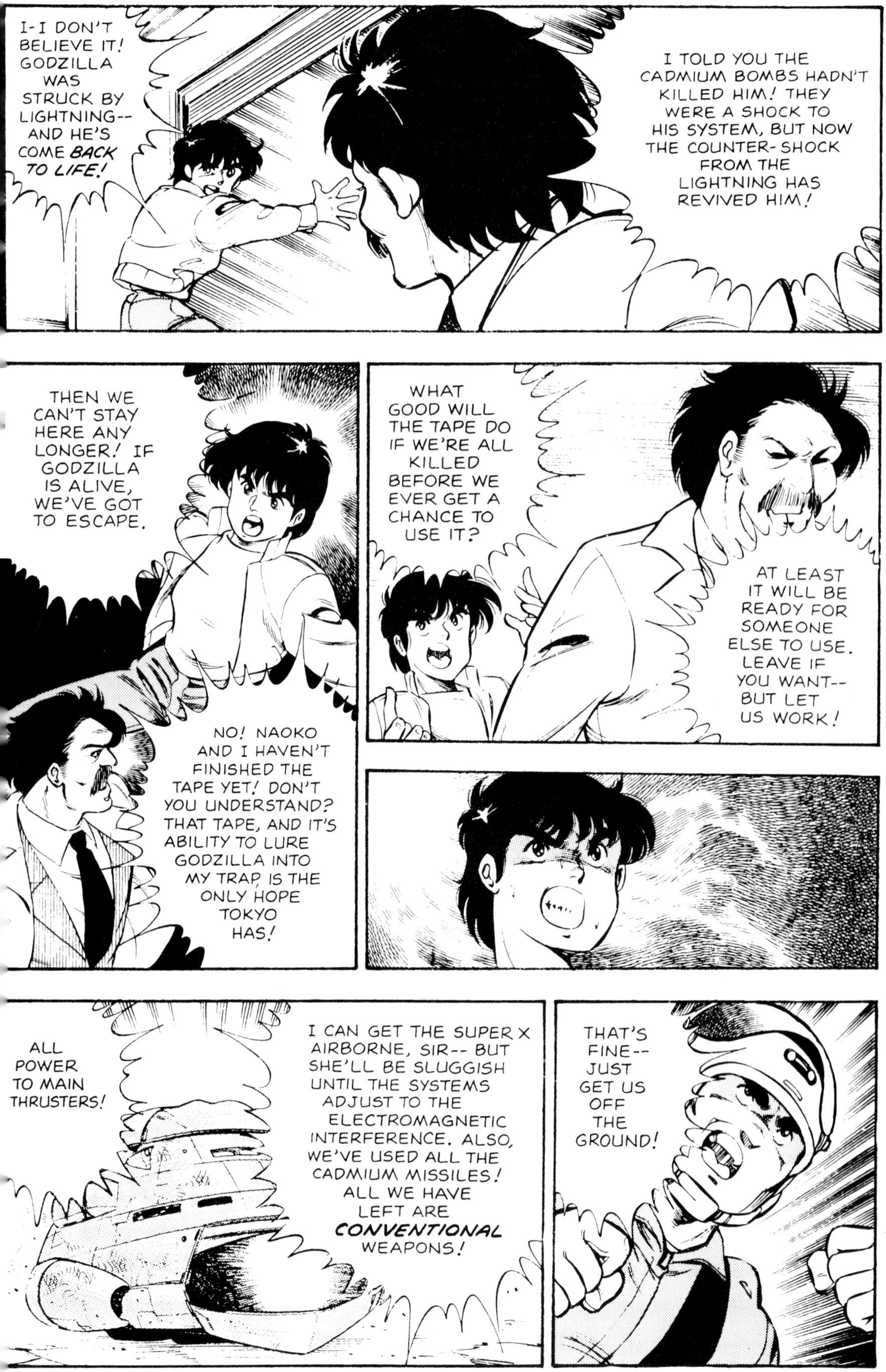
I-I DON'T BELIEVE IT! GODZILLA WAS STRUCK BY LIGHTNING-- AND HE'S COME *BACK TO LIFE!*
I TOLD YOU THE CADMIUM BOMBS HADN'T KILLED HIM! THEY WERE A SHOCK TO HIS SYSTEM, BUT NOW THE COUNTER-SHOCK FROM THE LIGHTNING HAS REVIVED HIM!
THEN WE CAN'T STAY HERE ANY LONGER! IF GODZILLA IS ALIVE, WE'VE GOT TO ESCAPE.
NO! NAOKO AND I HAVEN'T FINISHED THE TAPE YET! DON'T YOU UNDERSTAND? THAT TAPE, AND IT'S ABILITY TO LURE GODZILLA INTO MY TRAP, IS THE ONLY HOPE TOKYO HAS!
WHAT GOOD WILL THE TAPE DO IF WE'RE ALL KILLED BEFORE WE EVER GET A CHANCE TO USE IT?
AT LEAST IT WILL BE READY FOR SOMEONE ELSE TO USE. LEAVE IF YOU WANT-- BUT LET US WORK!
ALL POWER TO MAIN THRUSTERS!
I CAN GET THE SUPER X AIRBORNE, SIR-- BUT SHE'LL BE SLUGGISH UNTIL THE SYSTEMS ADJUST TO THE ELECTROMAGNETIC INTERFERENCE. ALSO, WE'VE USED ALL THE CADMIUM MISSILES! ALL WE HAVE LEFT ARE *CONVENTIONAL* WEAPONS!
THAT'S FINE-- JUST GET US OFF THE GROUND!

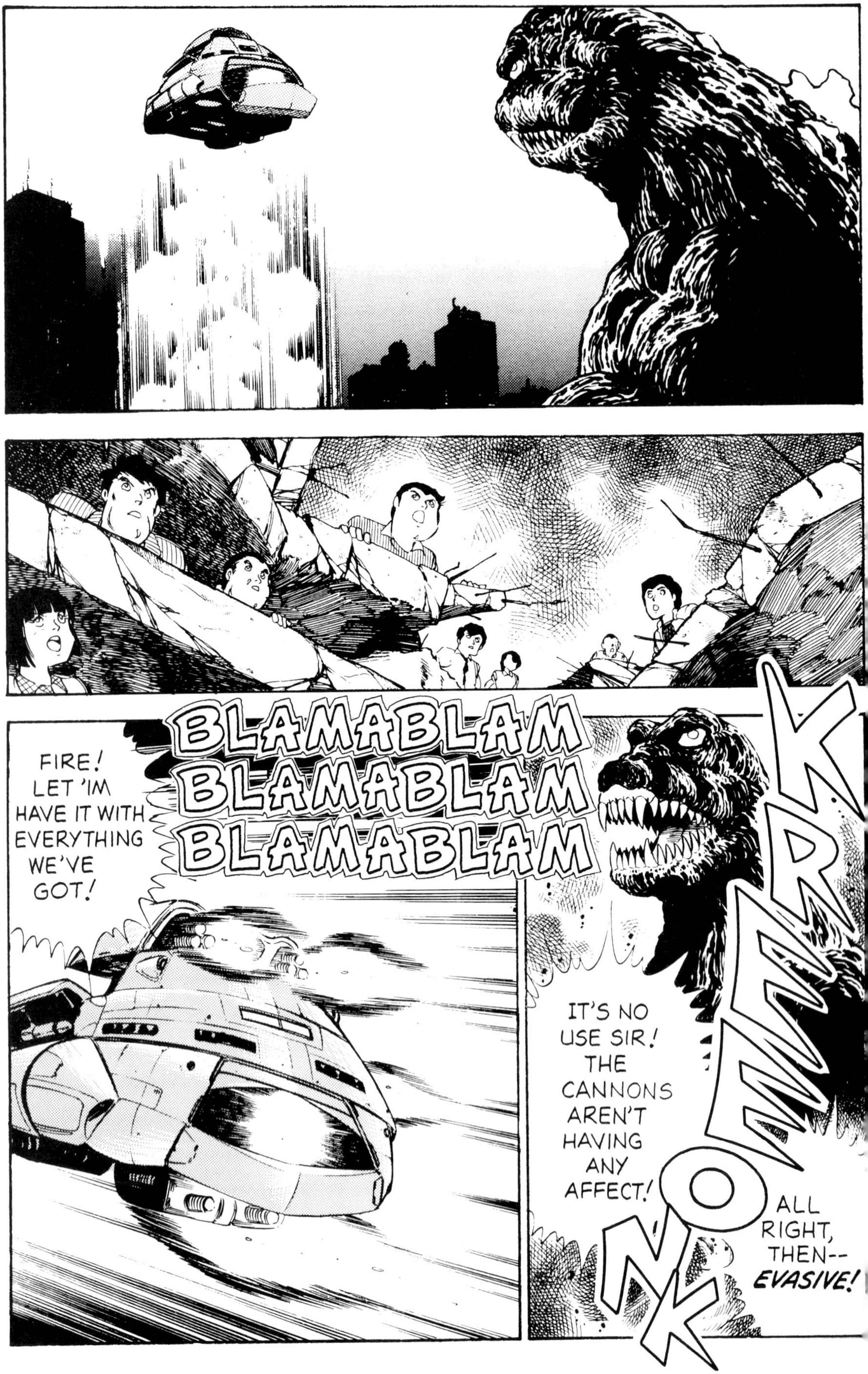
BLAMABLAM
BLAMABLAM
BLAMABLAM
FIRE! LET 'IM HAVE IT WITH EVERYTHING WE'VE GOT!
KRAAAAW
ONK
IT'S NO USE SIR! THE CANNONS AREN'T HAVING ANY AFFECT!
ALL RIGHT, THEN-- EVASIVE!

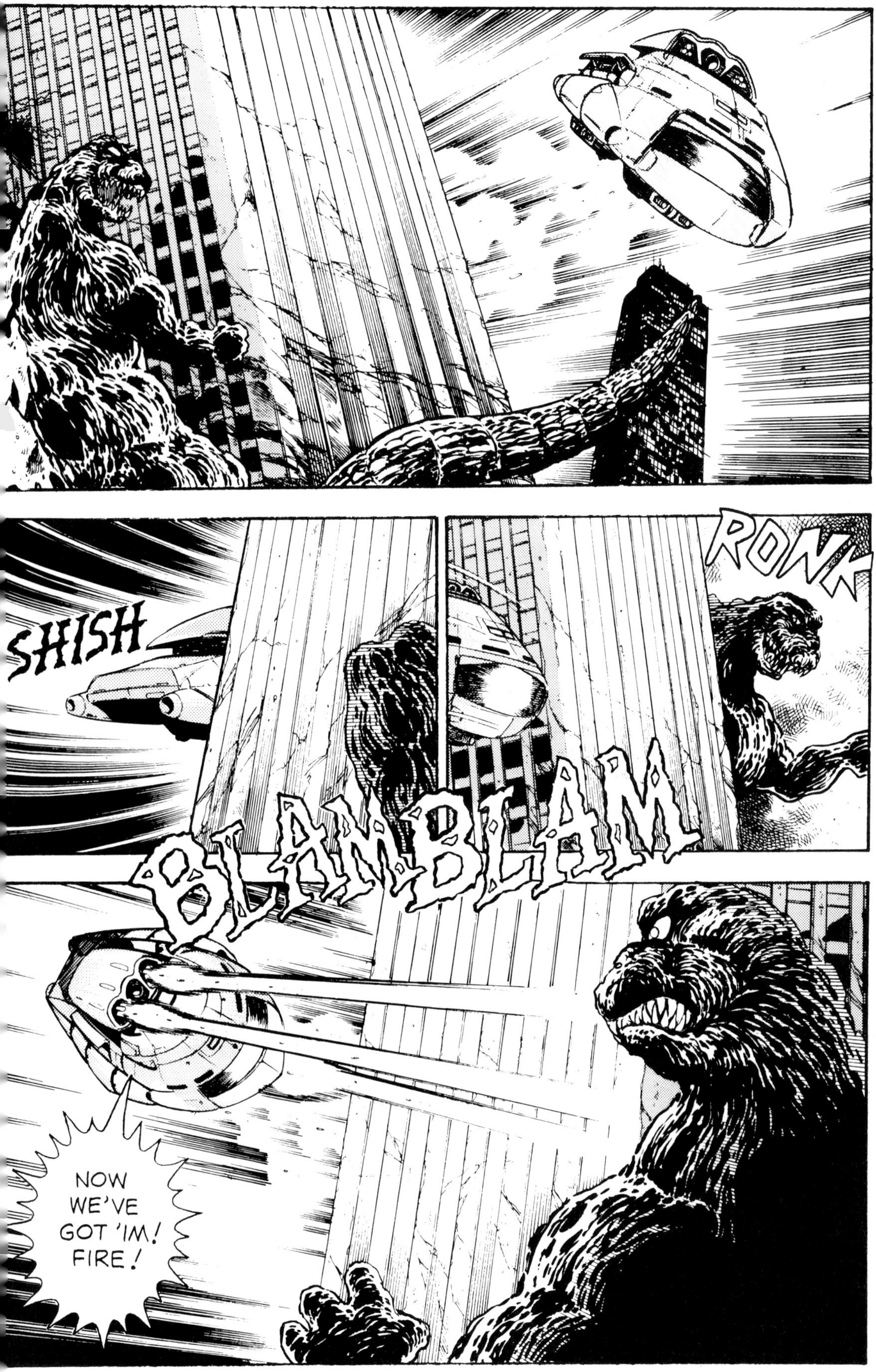
SHISH
RONK
BLAMBLAM
NOW WE'VE GOT 'IM! FIRE!

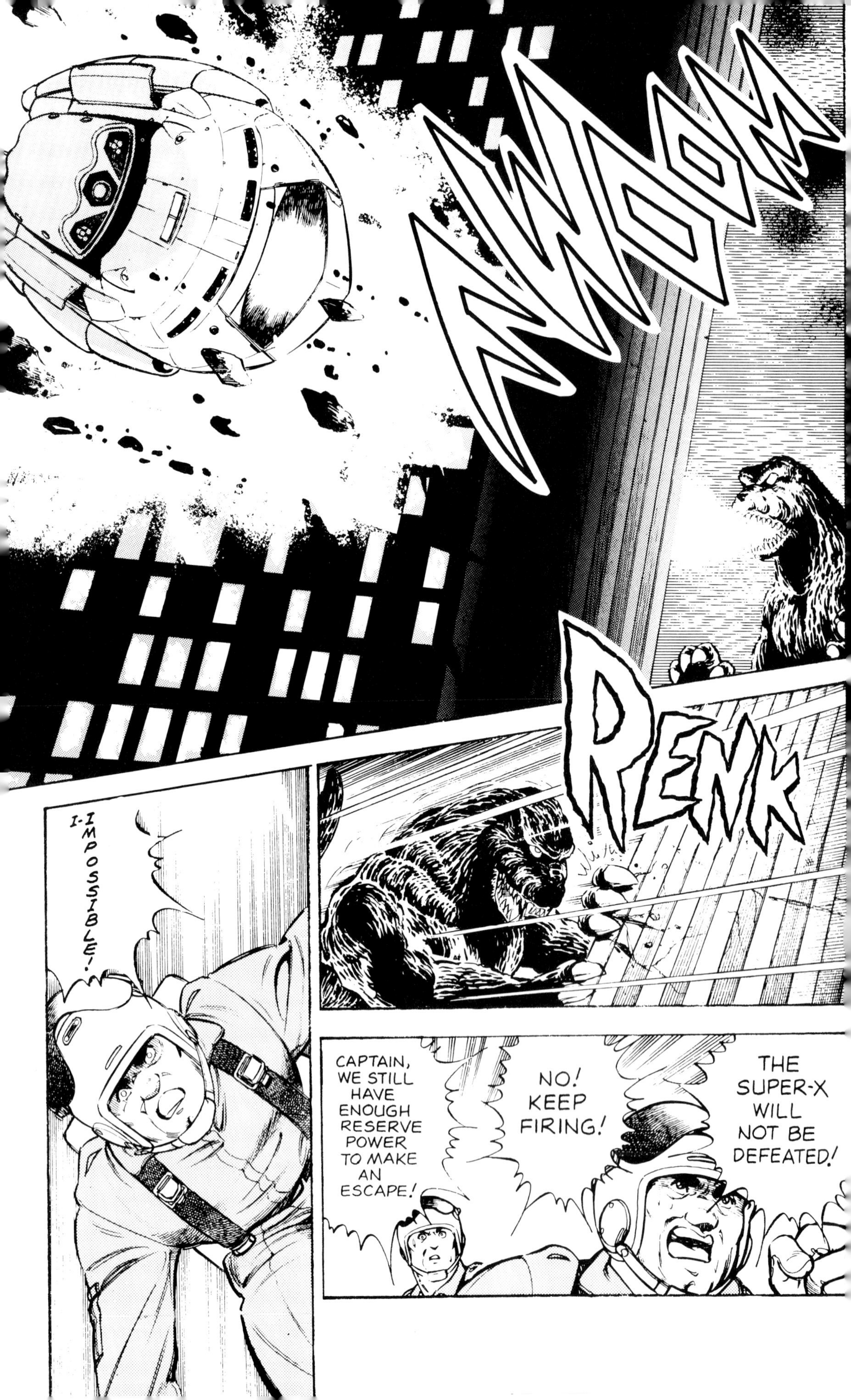

WHOOM
RENK
I-IMPOSSIBLE!
CAPTAIN, WE STILL HAVE ENOUGH RESERVE POWER TO MAKE AN ESCAPE!
NO! KEEP FIRING!
THE SUPER-X WILL NOT BE DEFEATED!

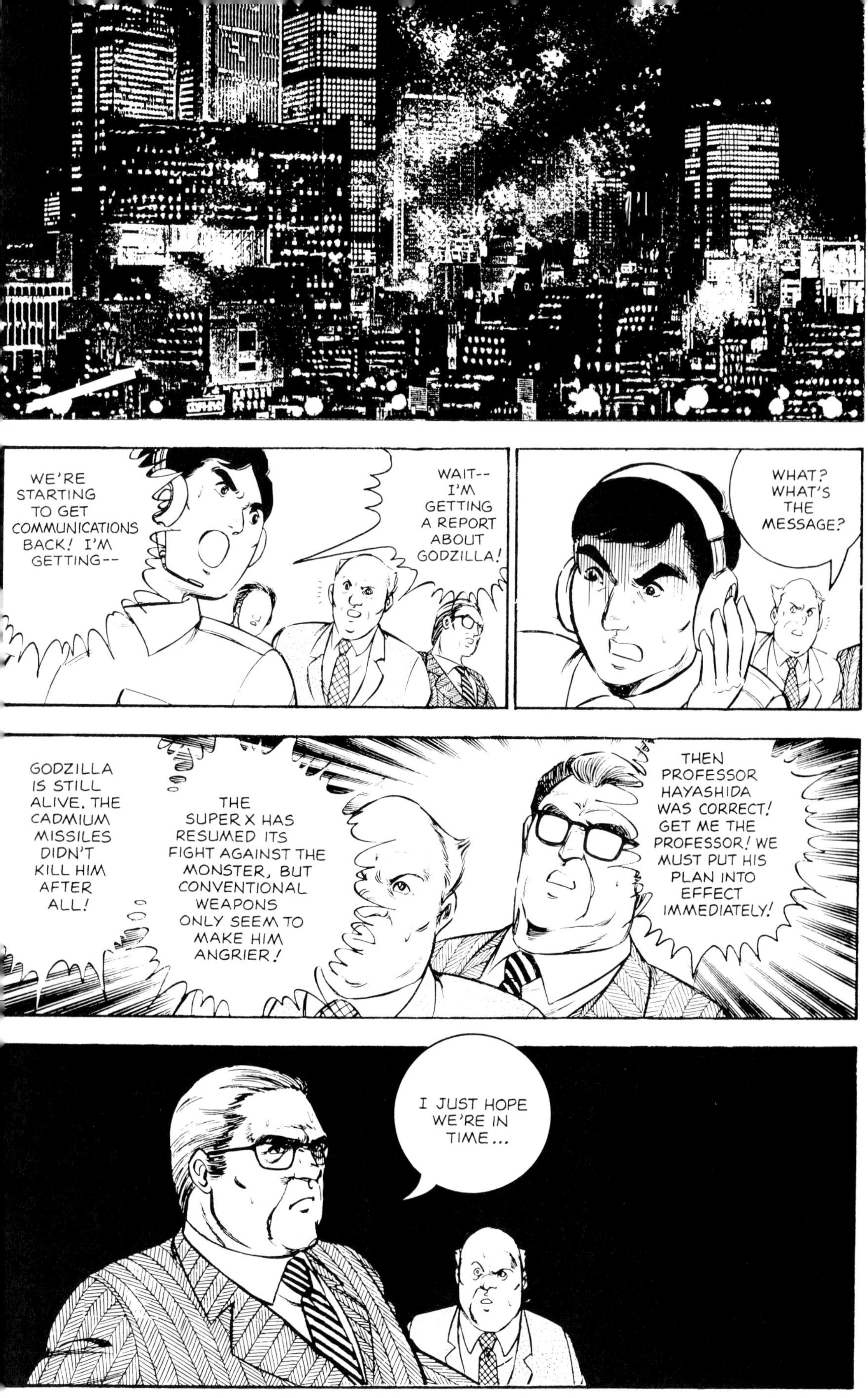
WE'RE STARTING TO GET COMMUNICATIONS BACK! I'M GETTING--
WAIT-- I'M GETTING A REPORT ABOUT GODZILLA!
WHAT? WHAT'S THE MESSAGE?
GODZILLA IS STILL ALIVE. THE CADMIUM MISSILES DIDN'T KILL HIM AFTER ALL!
THE SUPER X HAS RESUMED ITS FIGHT AGAINST THE MONSTER, BUT CONVENTIONAL WEAPONS ONLY SEEM TO MAKE HIM ANGRIER!
THEN PROFESSOR HAYASHIDA WAS CORRECT! GET ME THE PROFESSOR! WE MUST PUT HIS PLAN INTO EFFECT IMMEDIATELY!
I JUST HOPE WE'RE IN TIME...

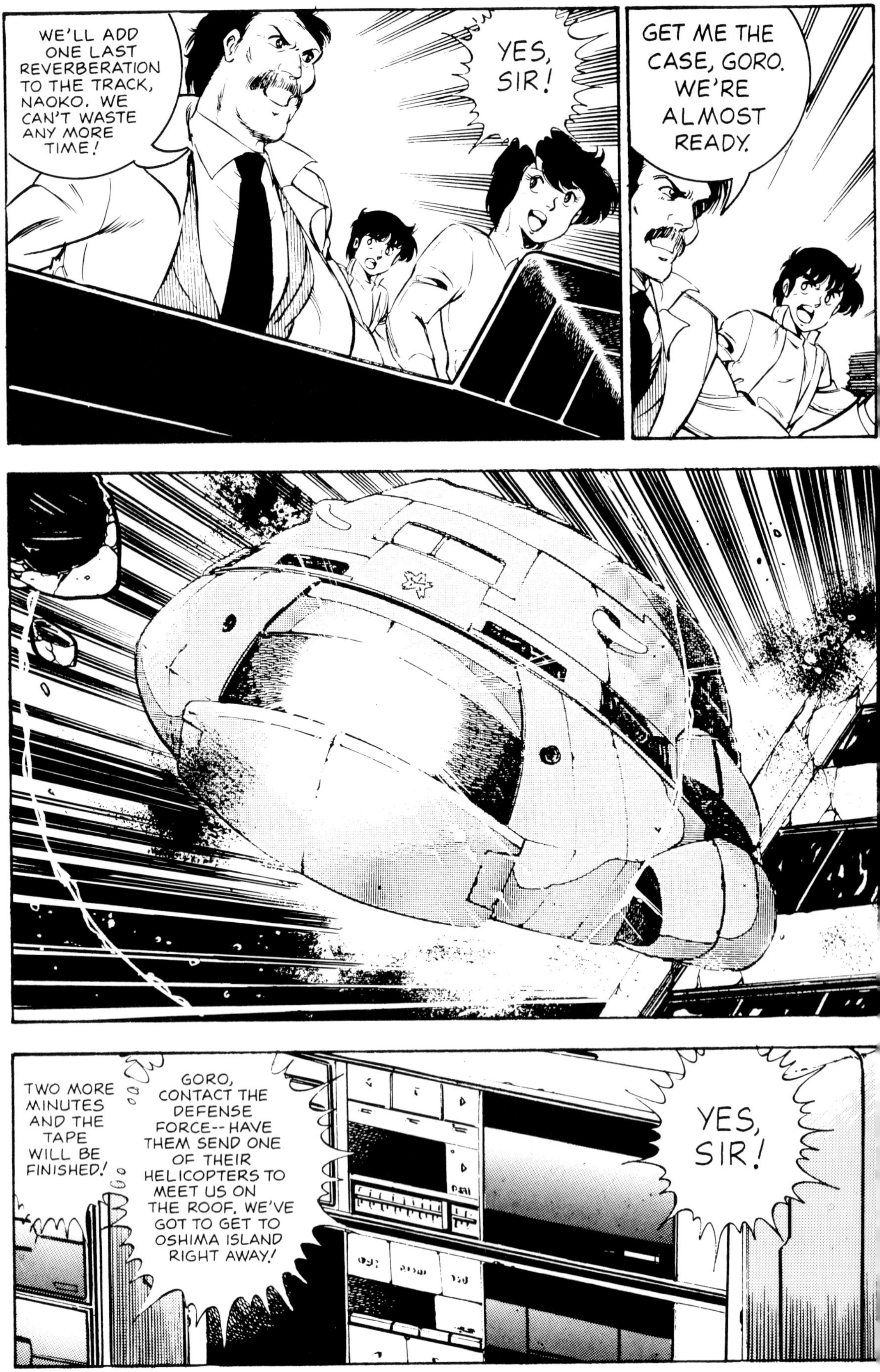
WE'LL ADD ONE LAST REVERBERATION TO THE TRACK, NAOKO. WE CAN'T WASTE ANY MORE TIME!
YES, SIR!
GET ME THE CASE, GORO. WE'RE ALMOST READY.
TWO MORE MINUTES AND THE TAPE WILL BE FINISHED!
GORO, CONTACT THE DEFENSE FORCE-- HAVE THEM SEND ONE OF THEIR HELICOPTERS TO MEET US ON THE ROOF. WE'VE GOT TO GET TO OSHIMA ISLAND RIGHT AWAY!
YES, SIR!

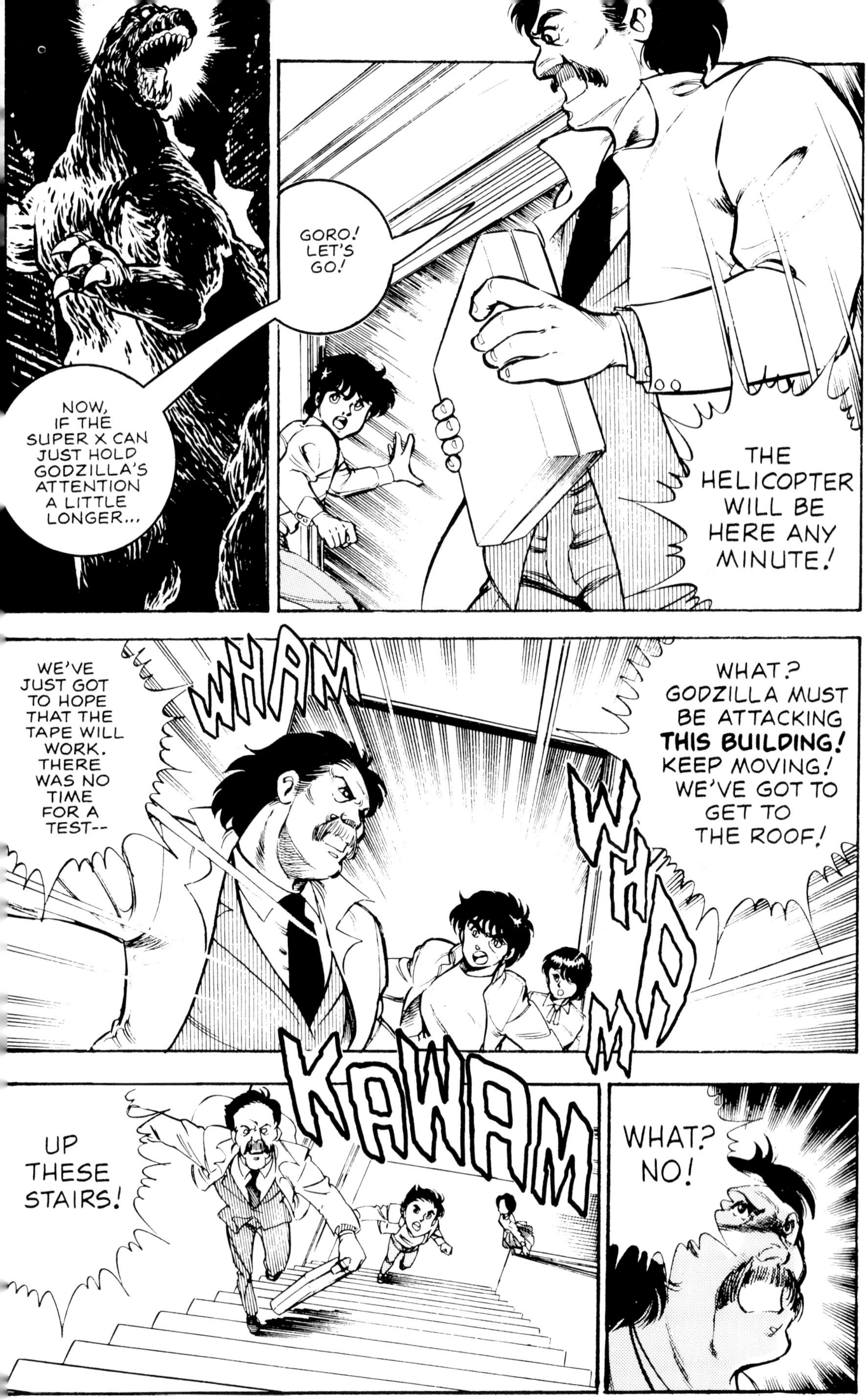
GORO! LET'S GO!
NOW, IF THE SUPER X CAN JUST HOLD GODZILLA'S ATTENTION A LITTLE LONGER...
THE HELICOPTER WILL BE HERE ANY MINUTE!
WHAM
WHAM
WE'VE JUST GOT TO HOPE THAT THE TAPE WILL WORK. THERE WAS NO TIME FOR A TEST--
WHAT? GODZILLA MUST BE ATTACKING **THIS BUILDING!** KEEP MOVING! WE'VE GOT TO GET TO THE ROOF!
KAWAM
UP THESE STAIRS!
WHAT? NO!

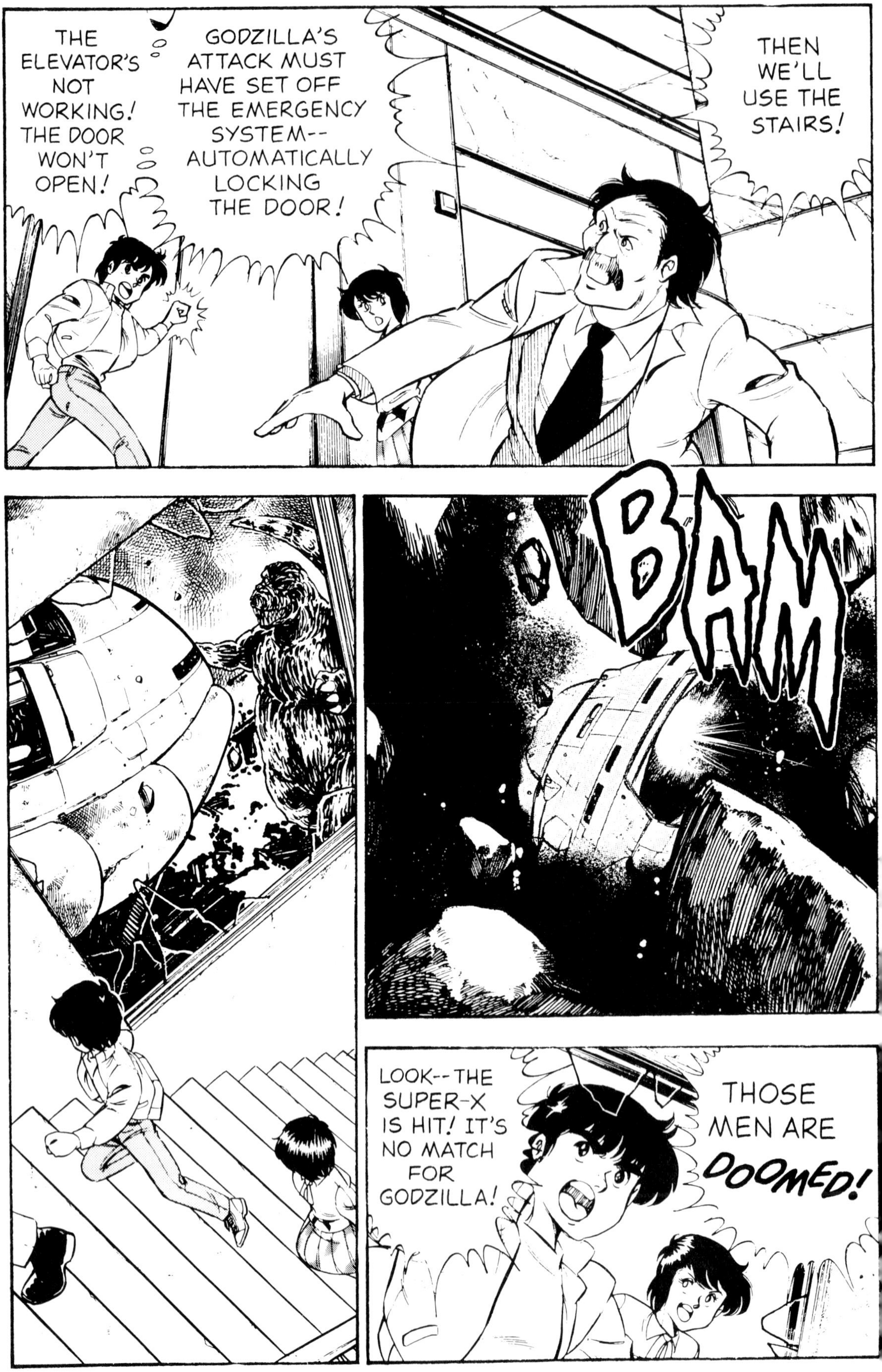
THE ELEVATOR'S NOT WORKING! THE DOOR WON'T OPEN!
GODZILLA'S ATTACK MUST HAVE SET OFF THE EMERGENCY SYSTEM-- AUTOMATICALLY LOCKING THE DOOR!
THEN WE'LL USE THE STAIRS!
BAM
LOOK--THE SUPER-X IS HIT! IT'S NO MATCH FOR GODZILLA!
THOSE MEN ARE DOOMED!

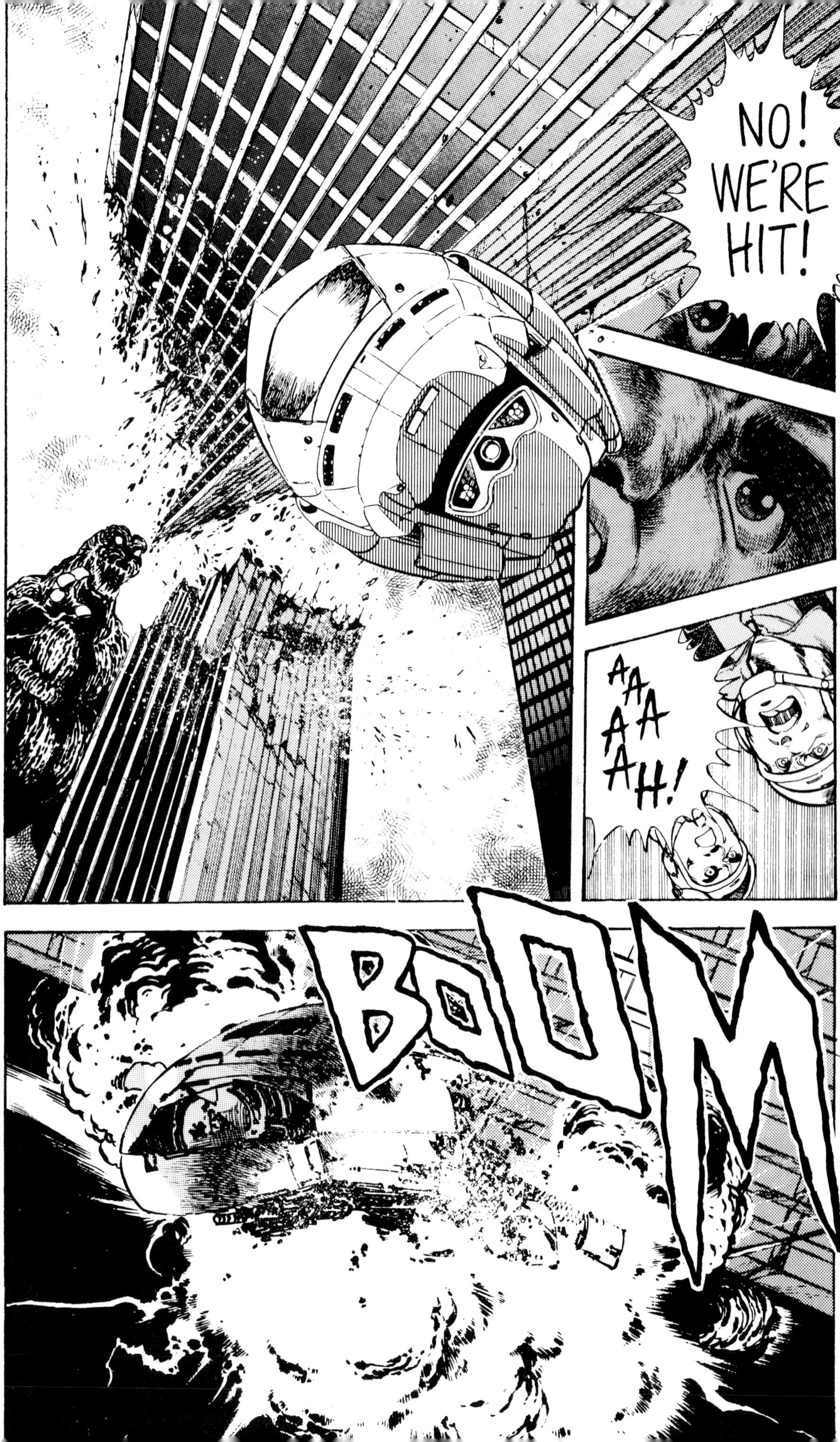
NO! WE'RE HIT!
AAAAAAH!
BOOM

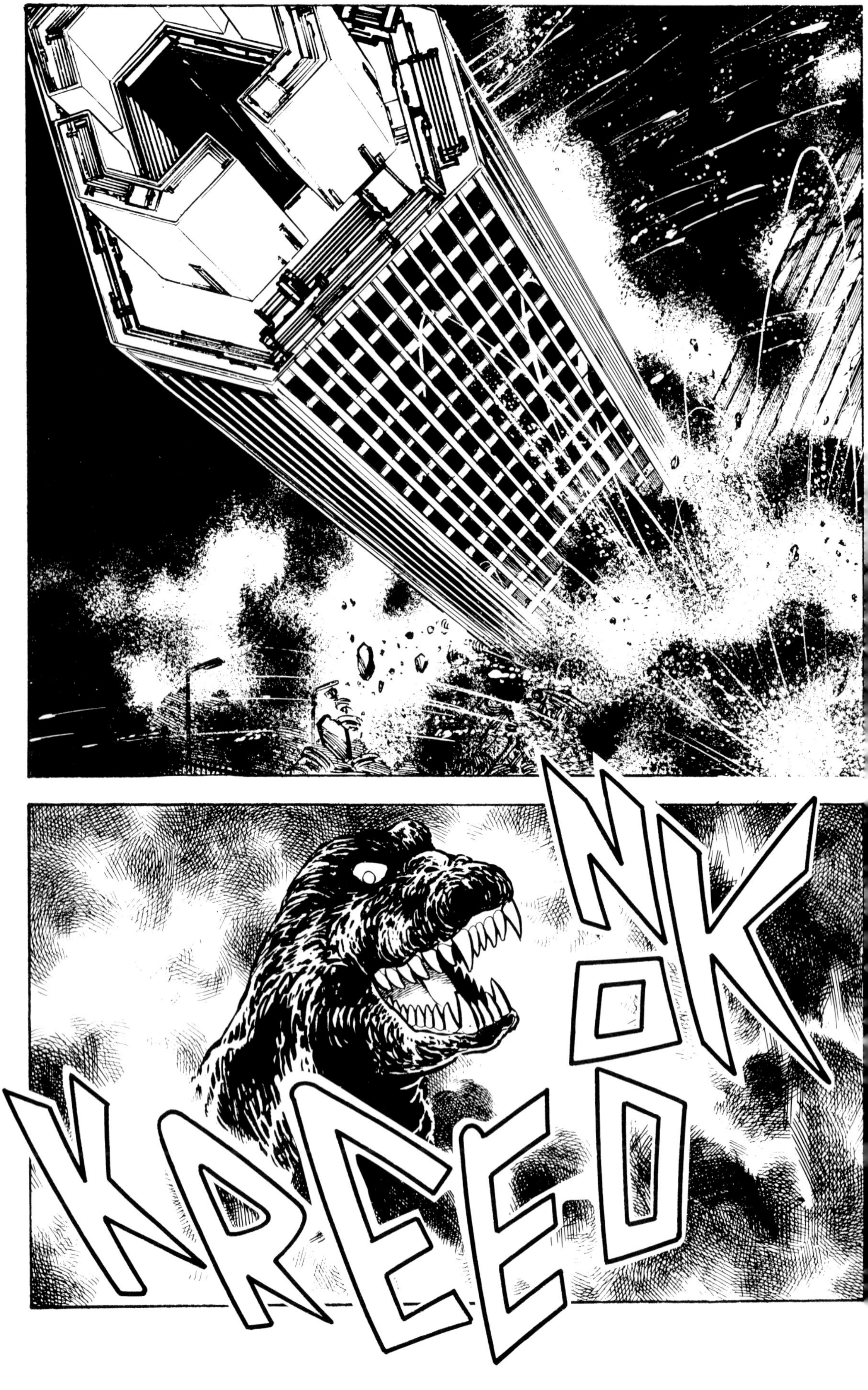
KREE-DONK

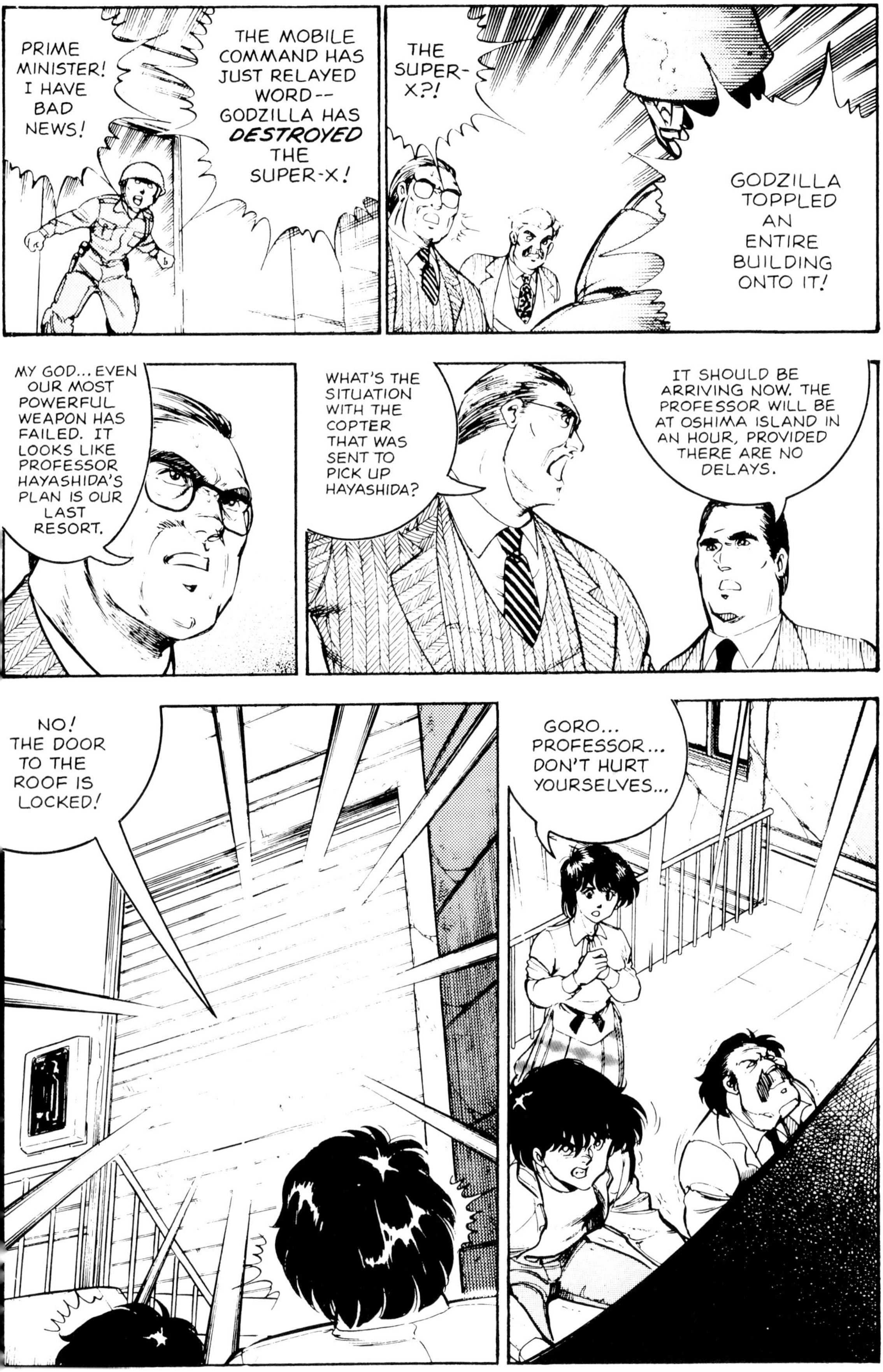
PRIME MINISTER! I HAVE BAD NEWS!
THE MOBILE COMMAND HAS JUST RELAYED WORD-- GODZILLA HAS DESTROYED THE SUPER-X!
THE SUPER-X?!
GODZILLA TOPPLED AN ENTIRE BUILDING ONTO IT!
MY GOD... EVEN OUR MOST POWERFUL WEAPON HAS FAILED. IT LOOKS LIKE PROFESSOR HAYASHIDA'S PLAN IS OUR LAST RESORT.
WHAT'S THE SITUATION WITH THE COPTER THAT WAS SENT TO PICK UP HAYASHIDA?
IT SHOULD BE ARRIVING NOW. THE PROFESSOR WILL BE AT OSHIMA ISLAND IN AN HOUR, PROVIDED THERE ARE NO DELAYS.
NO! THE DOOR TO THE ROOF IS LOCKED!
GORO... PROFESSOR... DON'T HURT YOURSELVES...

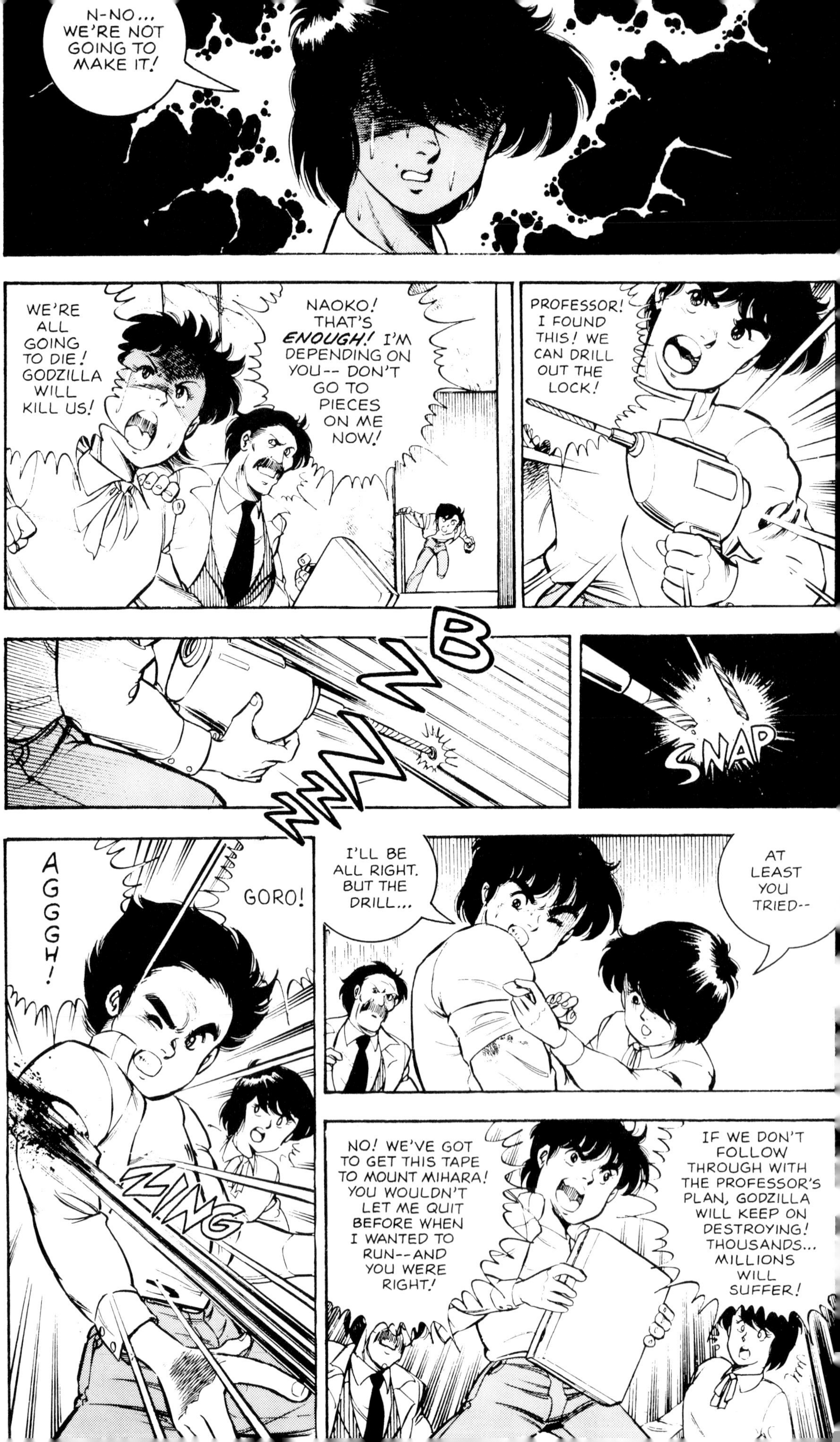
N-NO... WE'RE NOT GOING TO MAKE IT!
WE'RE ALL GOING TO DIE! GODZILLA WILL KILL US!
NAOKO! THAT'S ENOUGH! I'M DEPENDING ON YOU-- DON'T GO TO PIECES ON ME NOW!
PROFESSOR! I FOUND THIS! WE CAN DRILL OUT THE LOCK!
BZZZZ
SNAP
AGGGH!
GORO!
ZING
I'LL BE ALL RIGHT. BUT THE DRILL...
AT LEAST YOU TRIED--
NO! WE'VE GOT TO GET THIS TAPE TO MOUNT MIHARA! YOU WOULDN'T LET ME QUIT BEFORE WHEN I WANTED TO RUN--AND YOU WERE RIGHT!
IF WE DON'T FOLLOW THROUGH WITH THE PROFESSOR'S PLAN, GODZILLA WILL KEEP ON DESTROYING! THOUSANDS... MILLIONS WILL SUFFER!

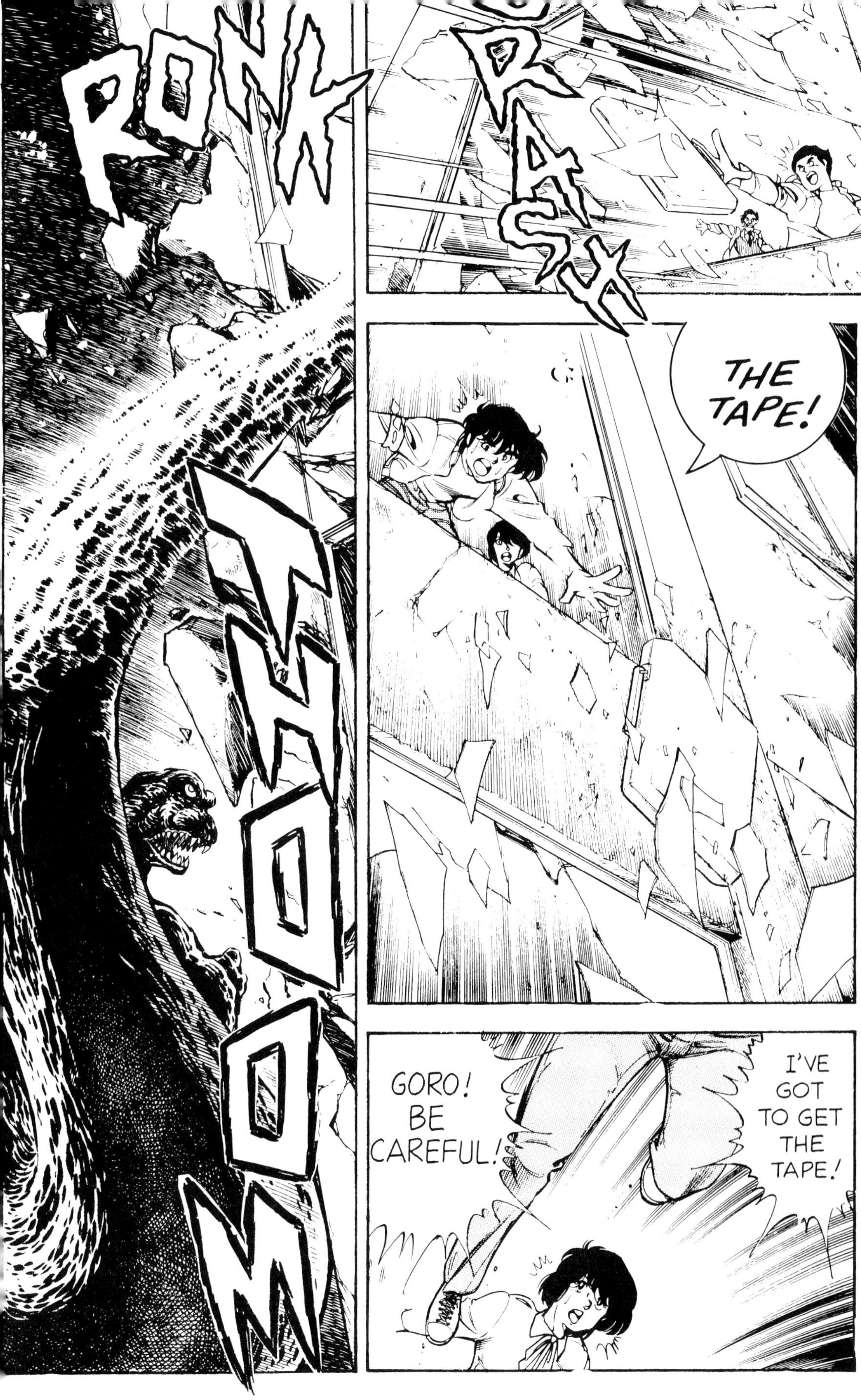
THE TAPE!
GORO! BE CAREFUL!
I'VE GOT TO GET THE TAPE!

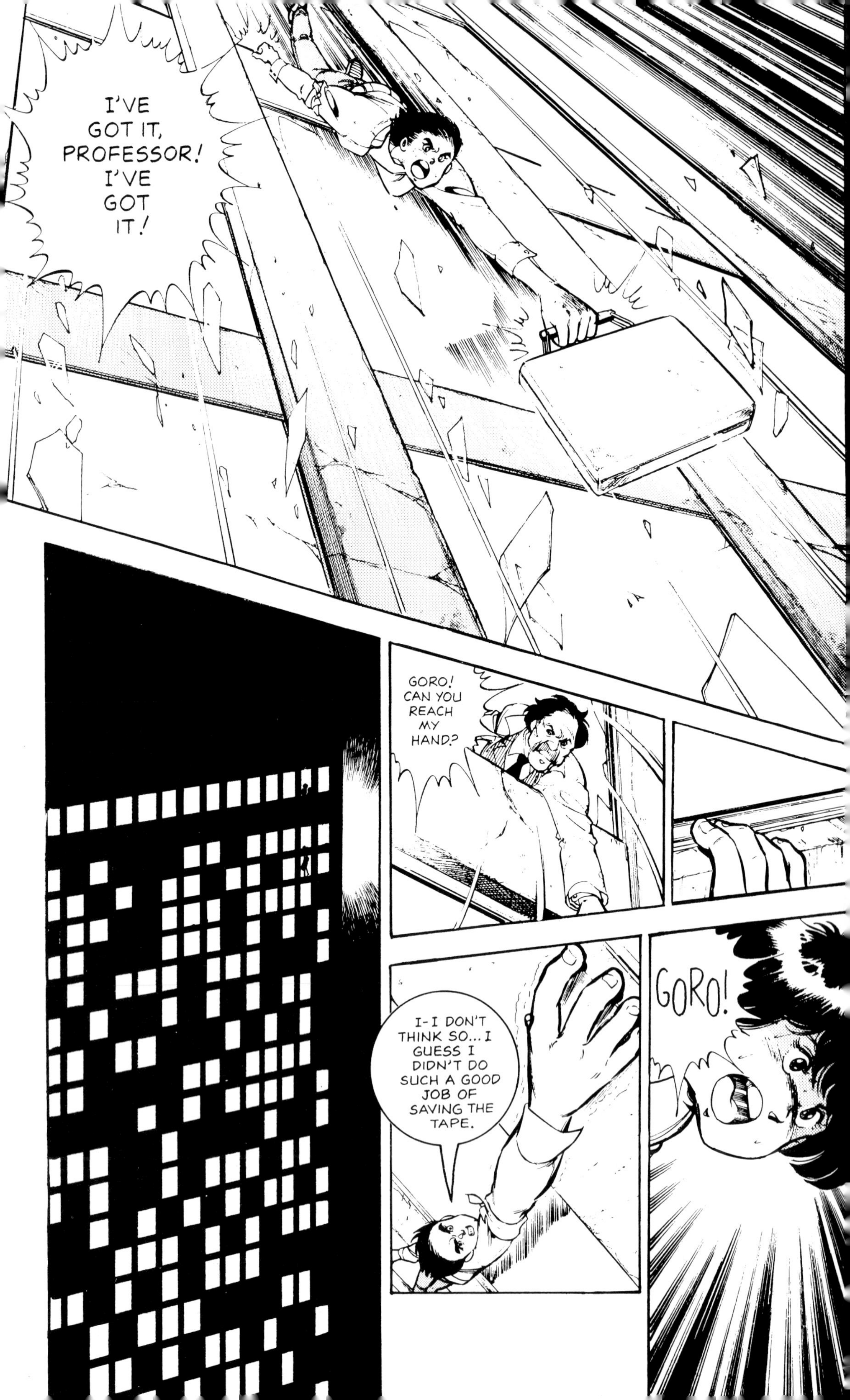
I'VE GOT IT, PROFESSOR! I'VE GOT IT!
GORO! CAN YOU REACH MY HAND?
I-I DON'T THINK SO... I GUESS I DIDN'T DO SUCH A GOOD JOB OF SAVING THE TAPE.
GORO!

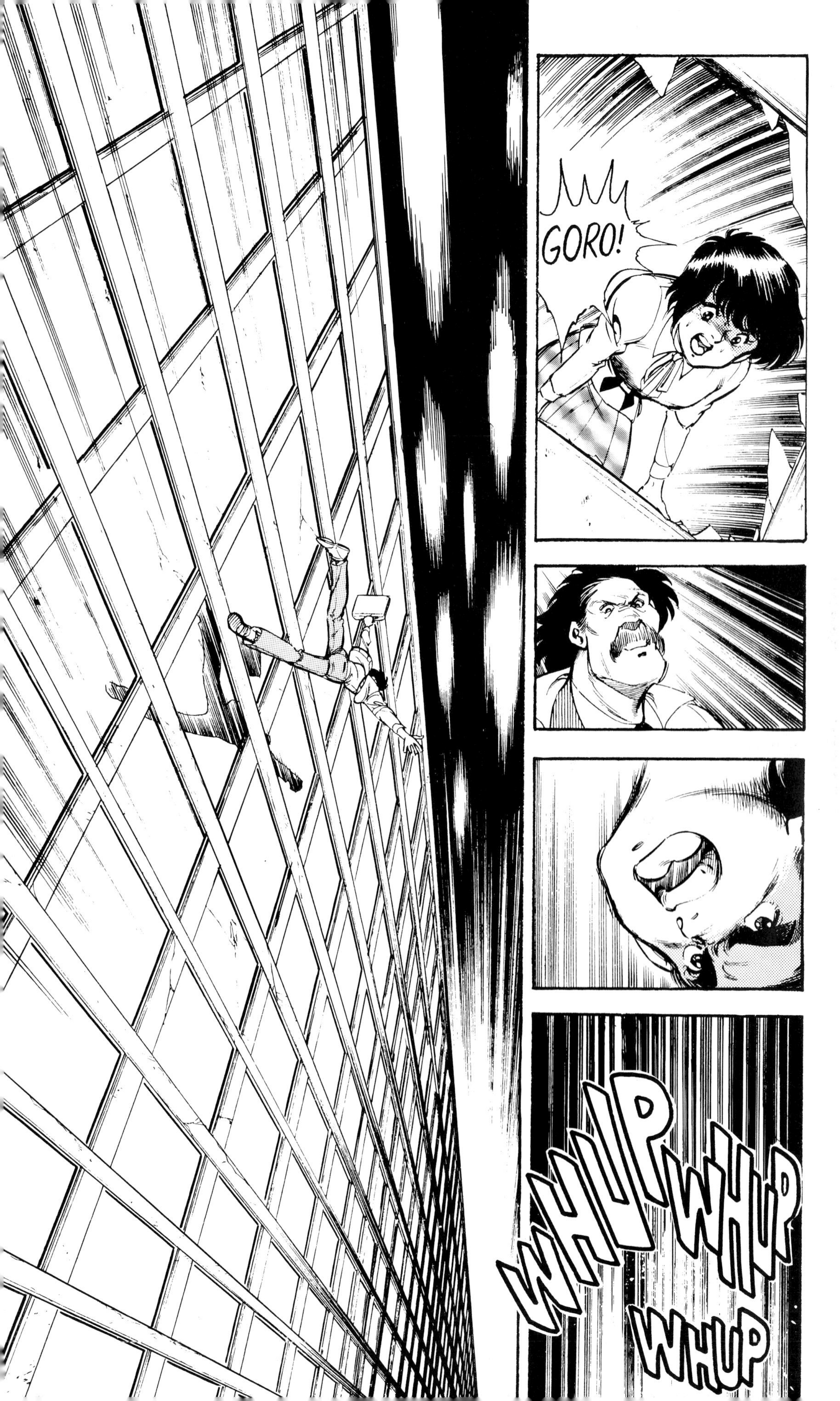
GORO!
WHIP WHIP
WHUP

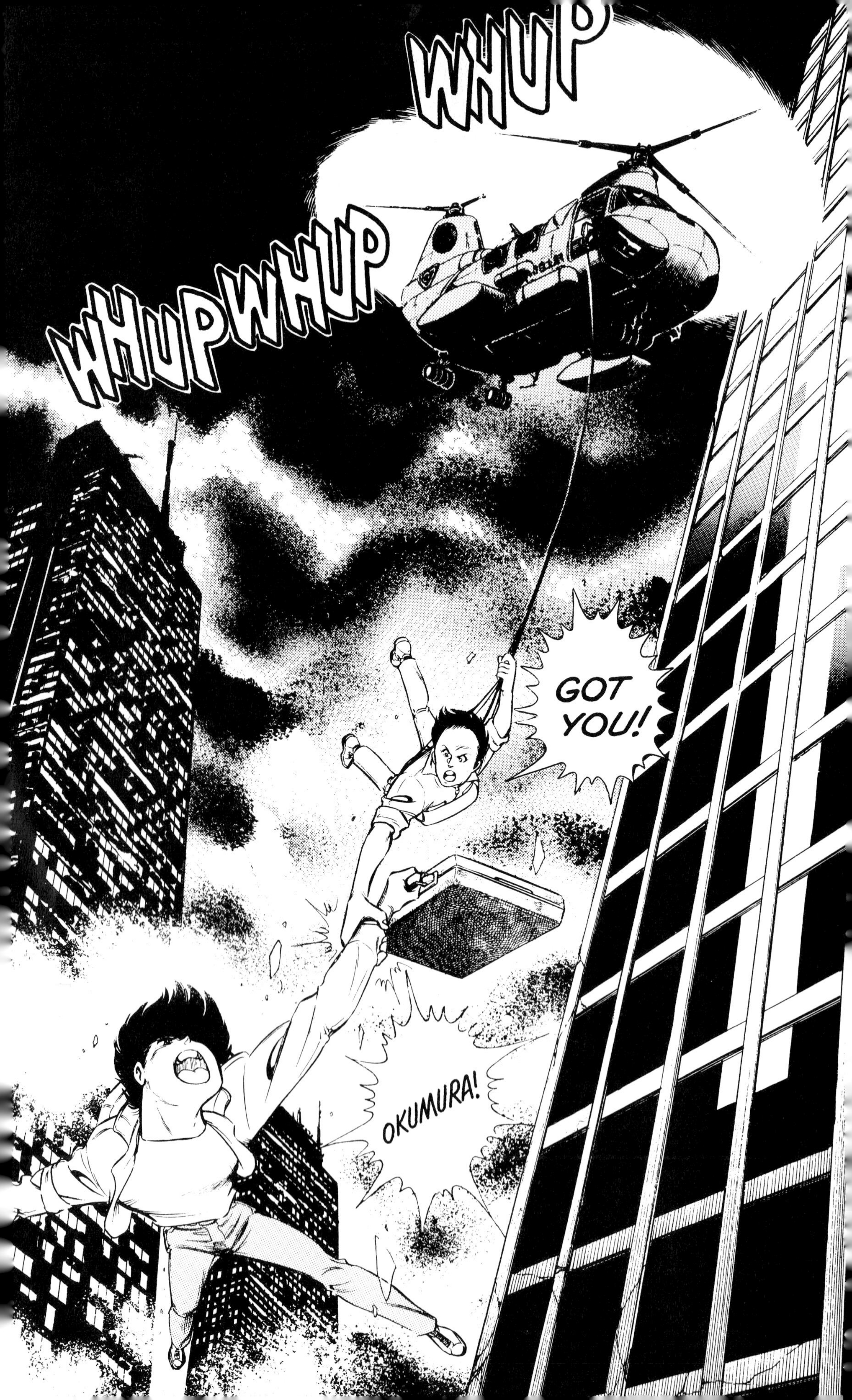
WHUP
WHUPWHUP
GOT YOU!
OKUMURA!

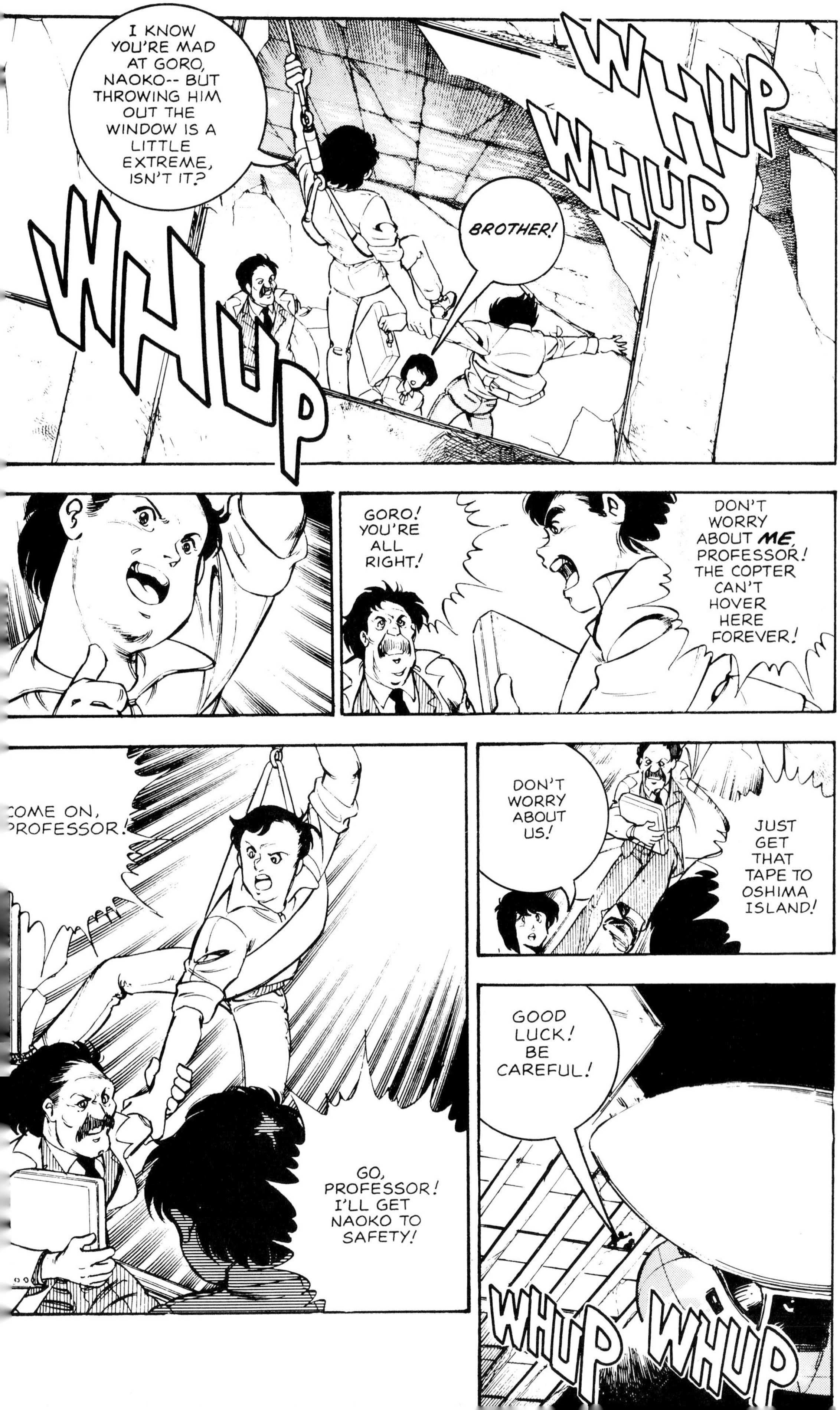
I KNOW YOU'RE MAD AT GORO, NAOKO-- BUT THROWING HIM OUT THE WINDOW IS A LITTLE EXTREME, ISN'T IT?
WHUP WHUP
BROTHER!
WHUP
GORO! YOU'RE ALL RIGHT!
DON'T WORRY ABOUT *ME*, PROFESSOR! THE COPTER CAN'T HOVER HERE FOREVER!
COME ON, PROFESSOR!
GO, PROFESSOR! I'LL GET NAOKO TO SAFETY!
DON'T WORRY ABOUT US!
JUST GET THAT TAPE TO OSHIMA ISLAND!
GOOD LUCK! BE CAREFUL!
WHUP WHUP

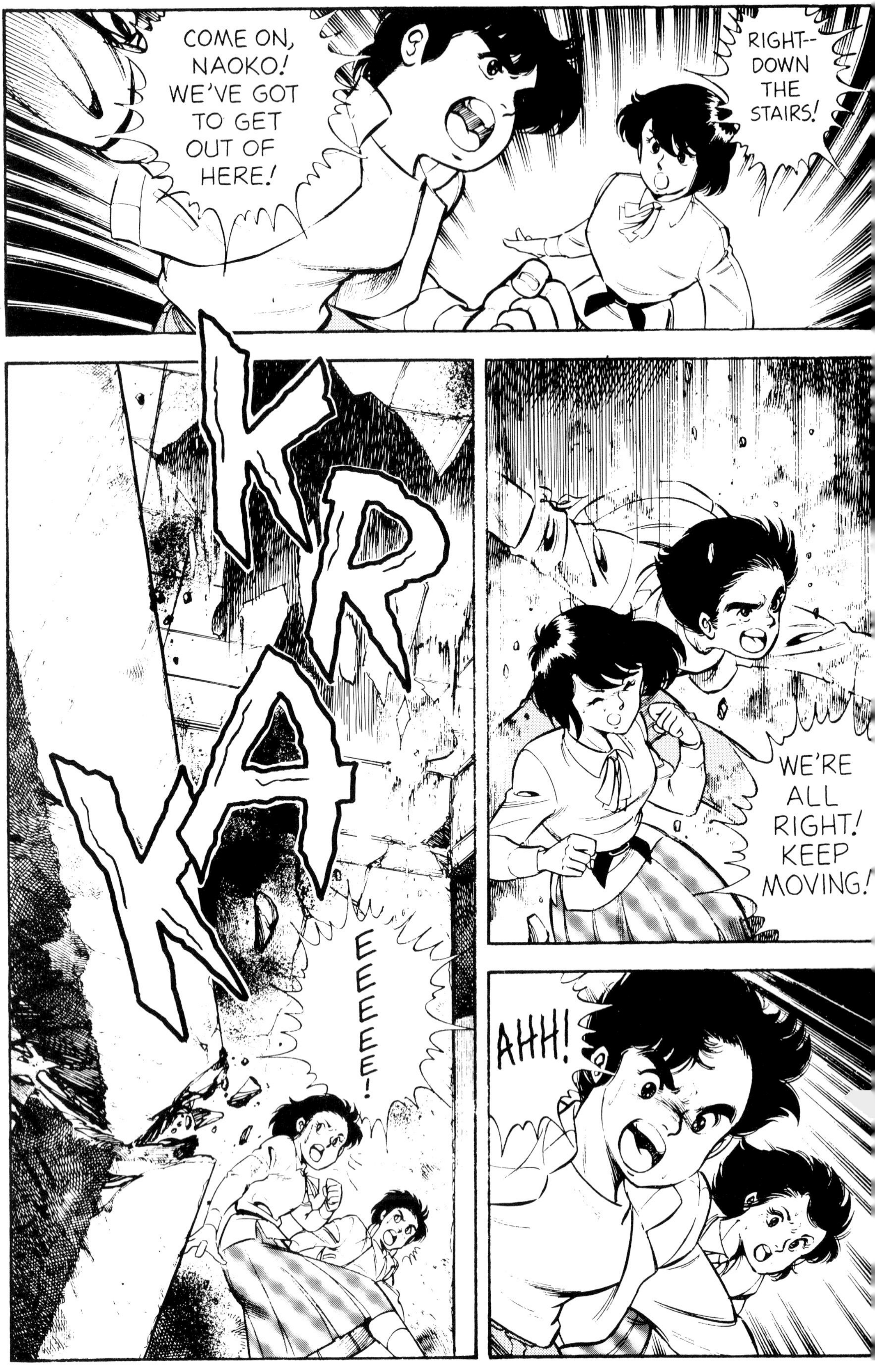
COME ON, NAOKO! WE'VE GOT TO GET OUT OF HERE!
RIGHT-- DOWN THE STAIRS!
KRAKA
EEEEEE!
WE'RE ALL RIGHT! KEEP MOVING!
AHH!

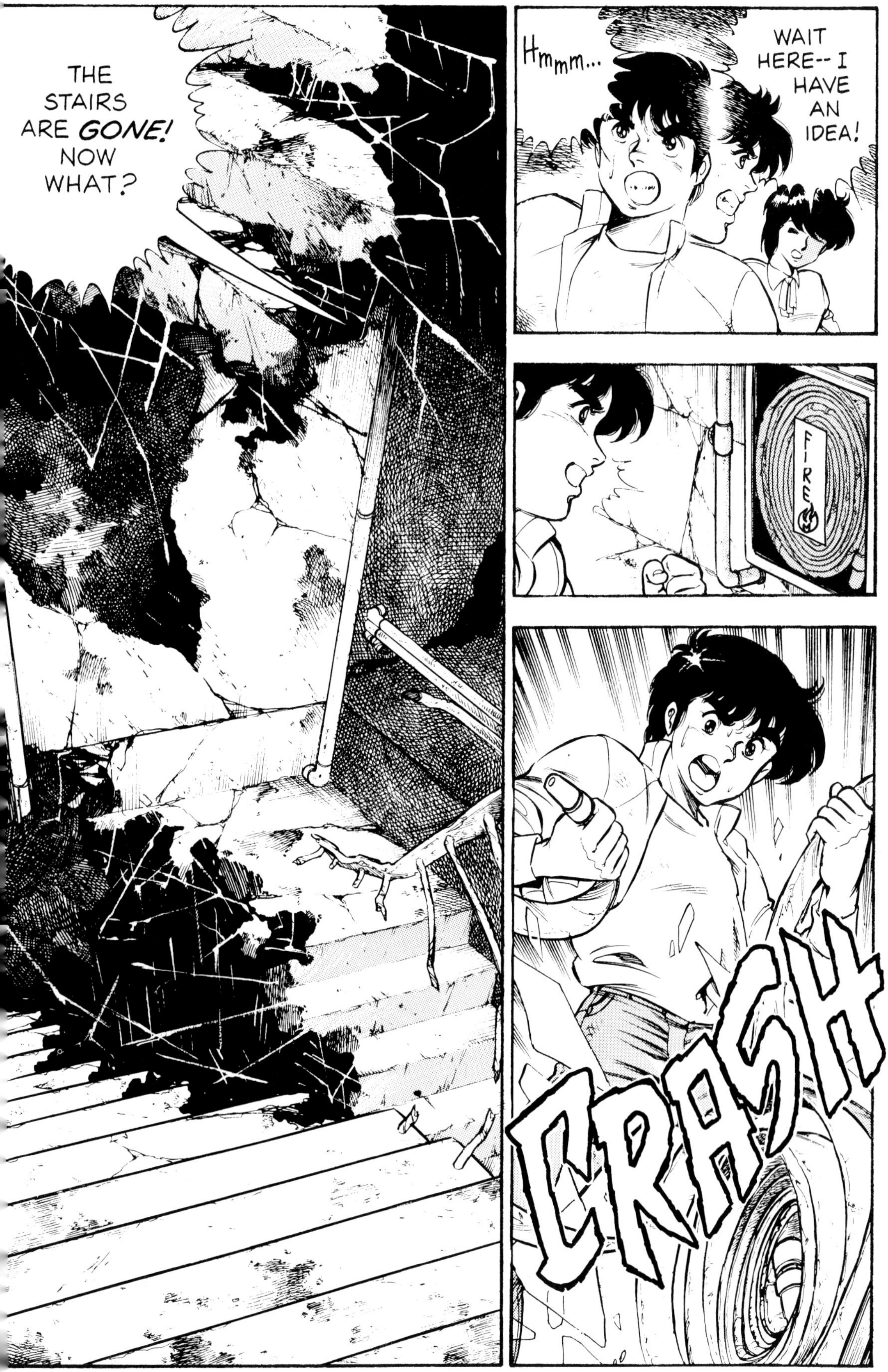

WAIT HERE-- I HAVE AN IDEA!
Hmmm...
FIRE
CRASH
THE STAIRS ARE GONE! NOW WHAT?

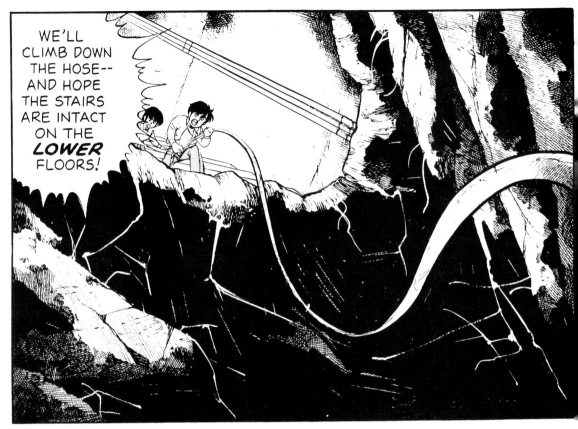

WE'LL CLIMB DOWN THE HOSE-- AND HOPE THE STAIRS ARE INTACT ON THE **LOWER** FLOORS!

CAREFUL, NAOKO!

TAP

OKAY! NOW, LET'S FIND SOMEWHERE SAFE TO HIDE UNTIL THE PROFESSOR'S TAPE LURES GODZILLA AWAY FROM TOKYO!

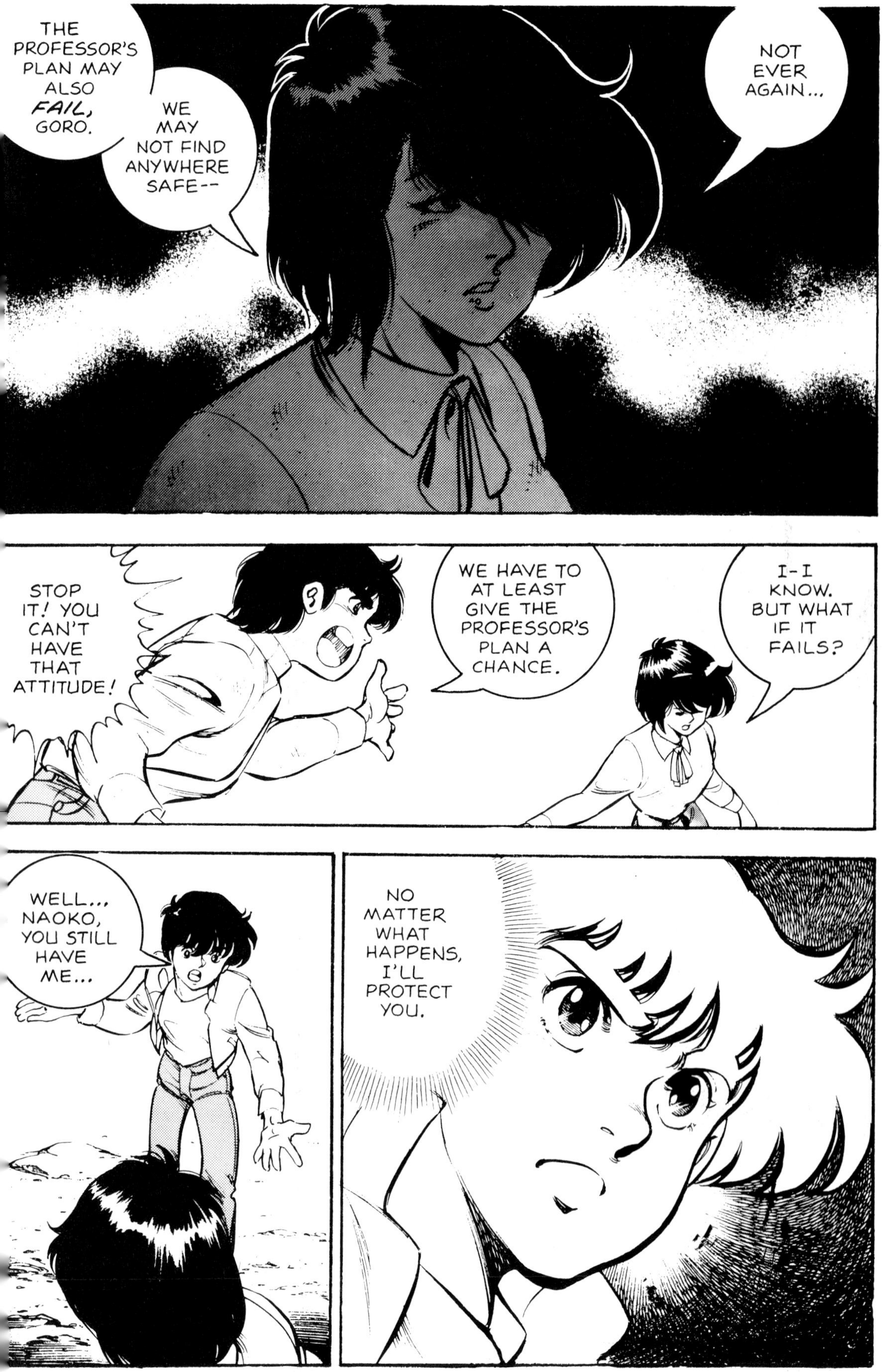
THE PROFESSOR'S PLAN MAY ALSO FAIL, GORO.
WE MAY NOT FIND ANYWHERE SAFE--
NOT EVER AGAIN...
STOP IT! YOU CAN'T HAVE THAT ATTITUDE!
WE HAVE TO AT LEAST GIVE THE PROFESSOR'S PLAN A CHANCE.
I-I KNOW. BUT WHAT IF IT FAILS?
WELL... NAOKO, YOU STILL HAVE ME...
NO MATTER WHAT HAPPENS, I'LL PROTECT YOU.

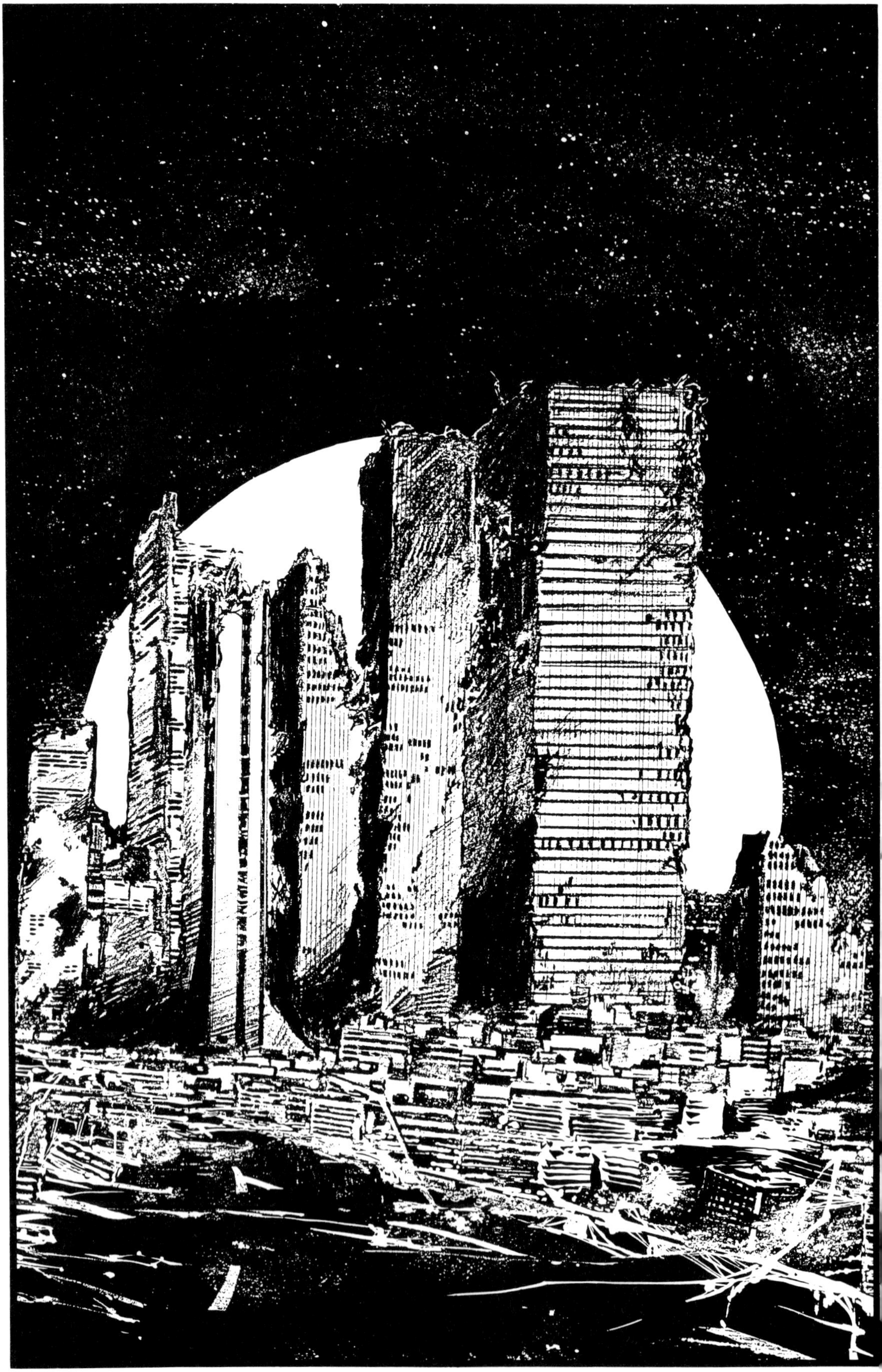

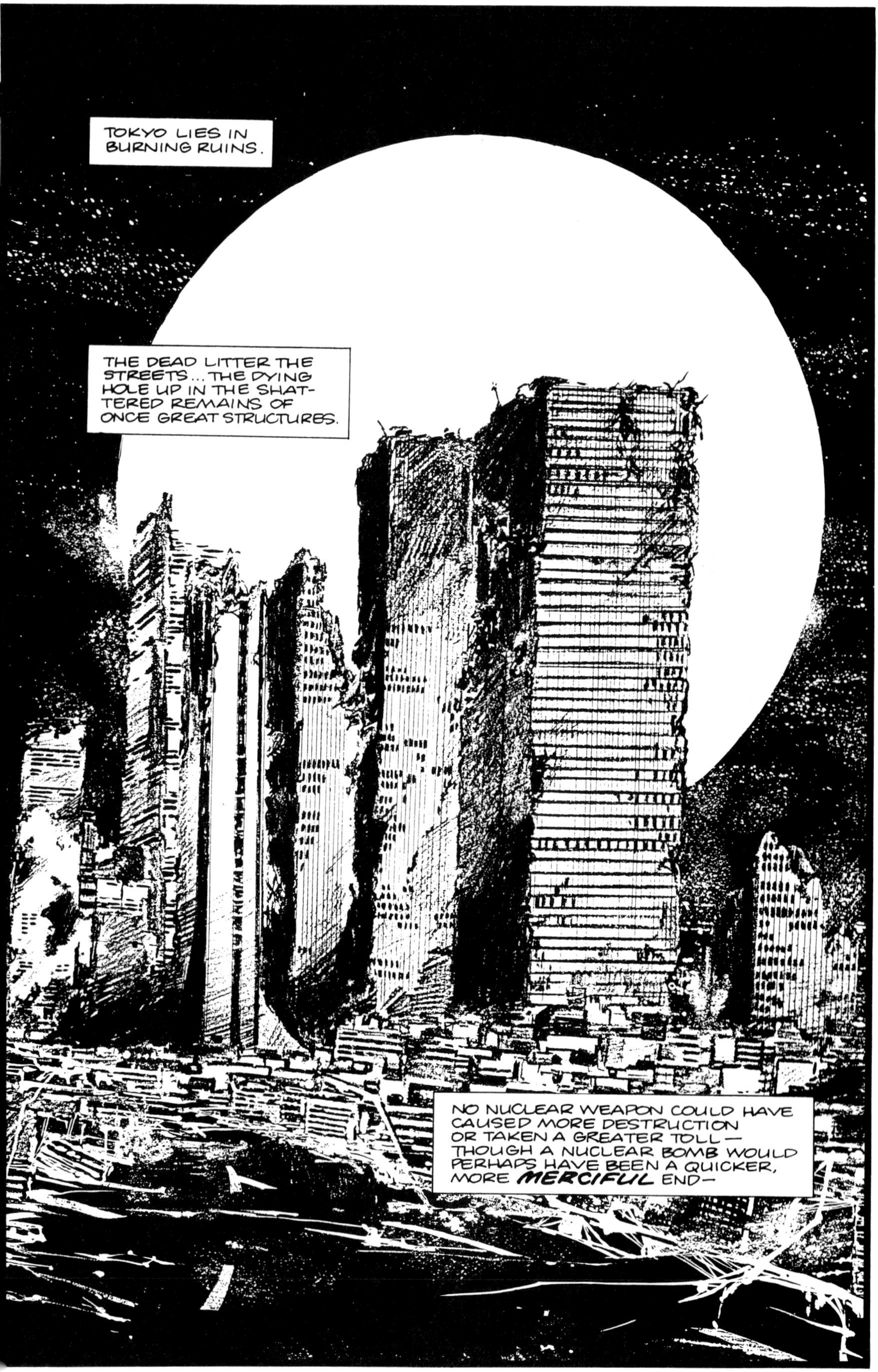
TOKYO LIES IN BURNING RUINS.
THE DEAD LITTER THE STREETS... THE DYING HOLE UP IN THE SHATTERED REMAINS OF ONCE GREAT STRUCTURES.
NO NUCLEAR WEAPON COULD HAVE CAUSED MORE DESTRUCTION OR TAKEN A GREATER TOLL— THOUGH A NUCLEAR BOMB WOULD PERHAPS HAVE BEEN A QUICKER, MORE MERCIFUL END—

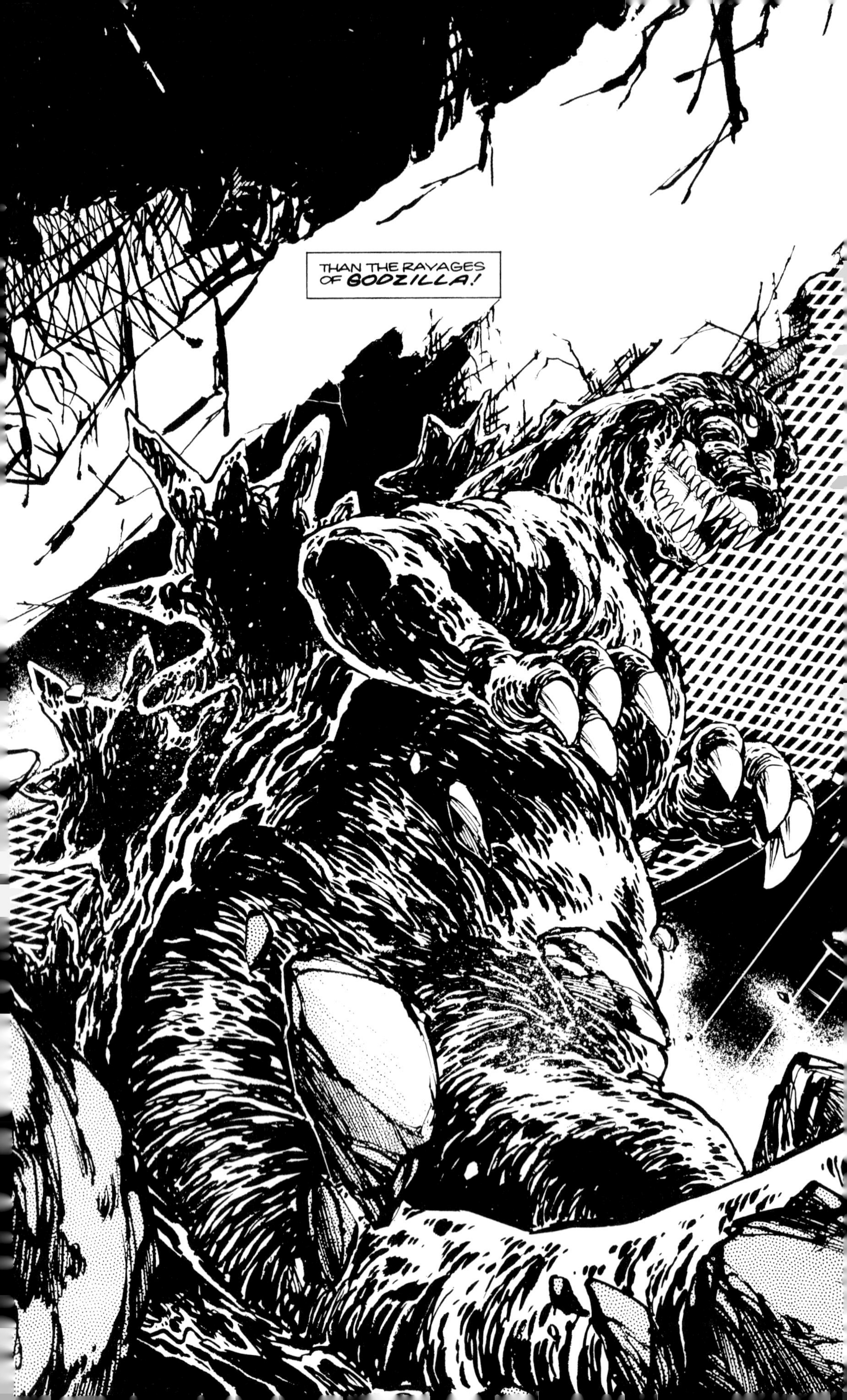
THAN THE RAVAGES OF GODZILLA!

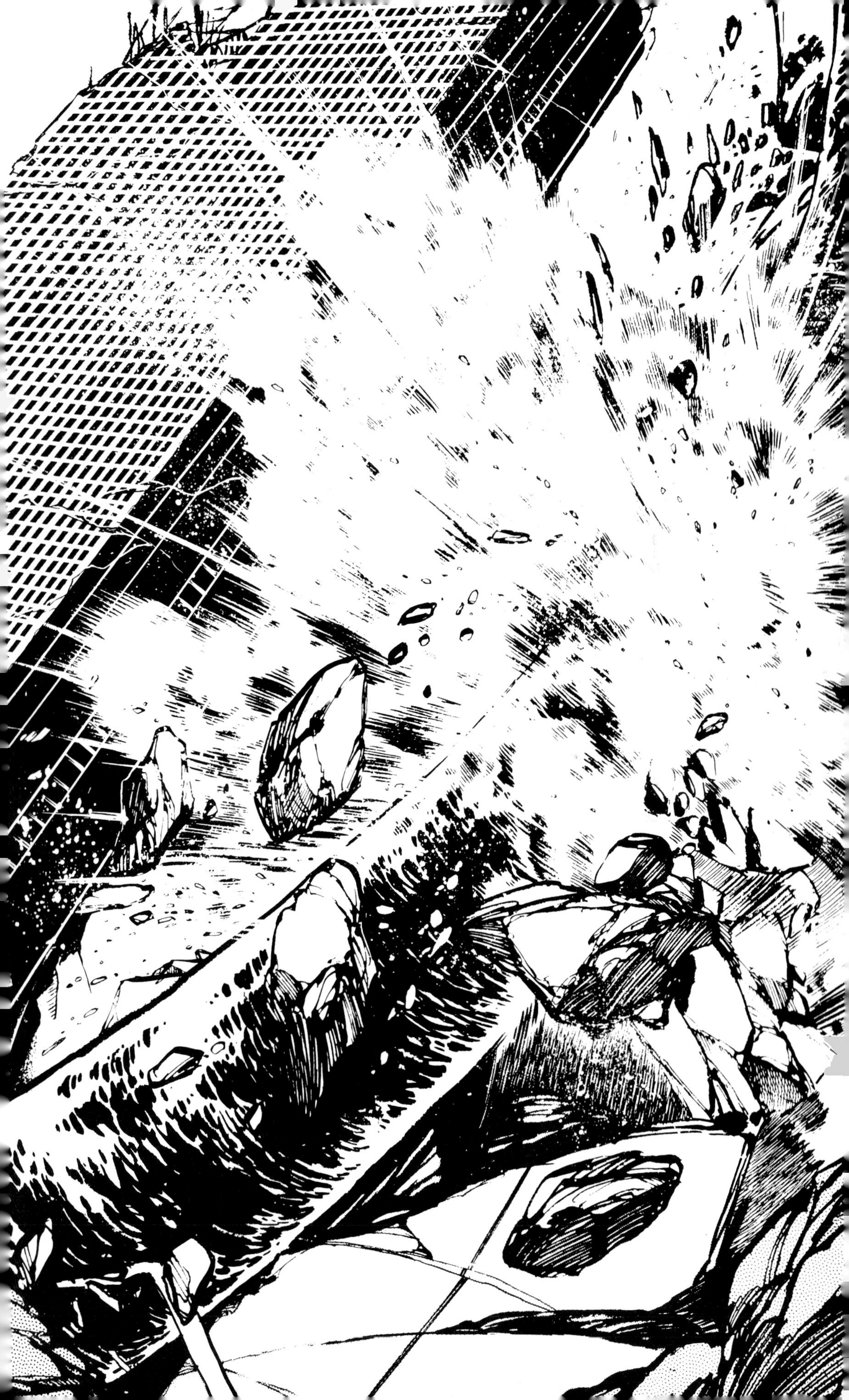

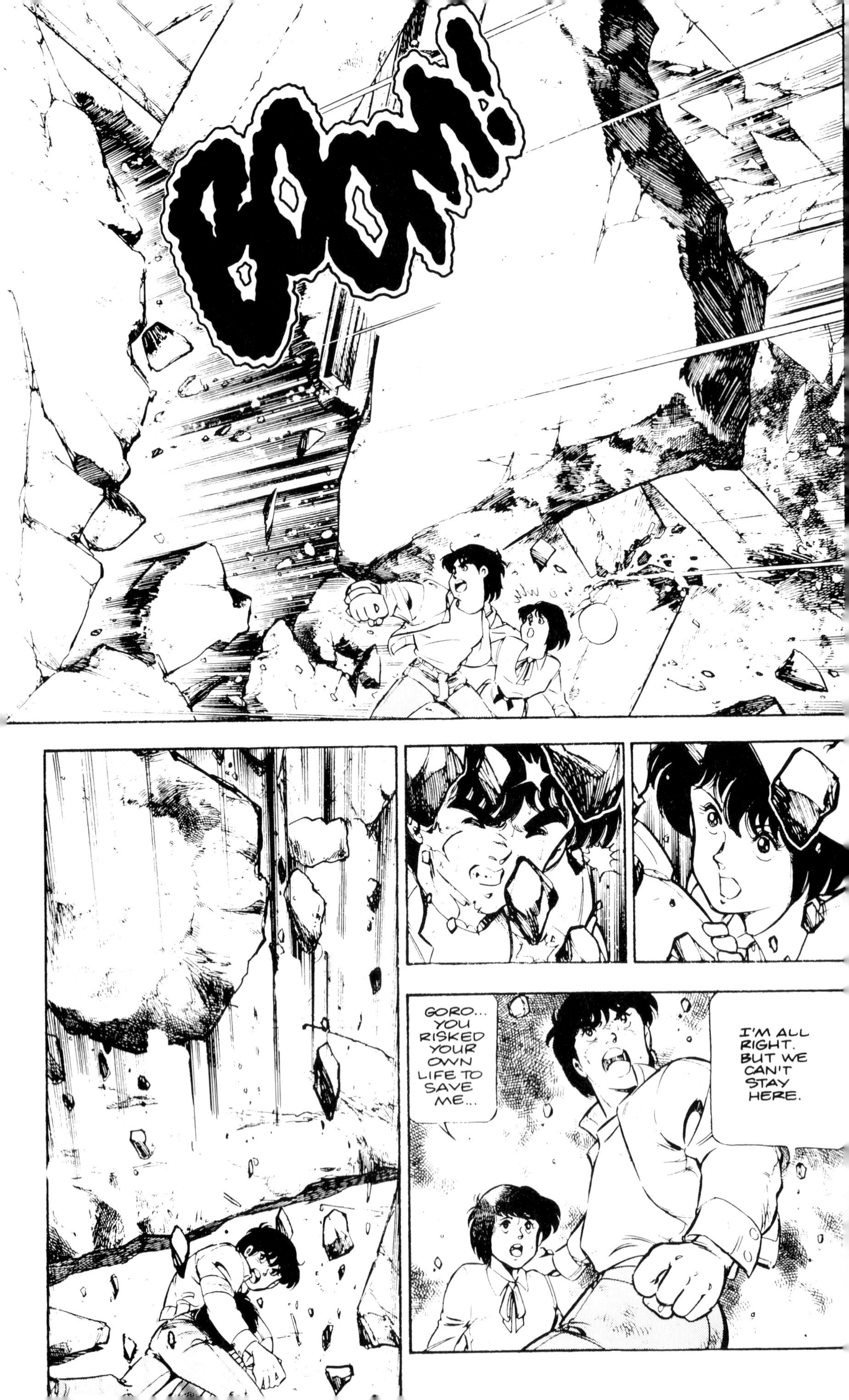
BOOM!
GORO... YOU RISKED YOUR OWN LIFE TO SAVE ME...
I'M ALL RIGHT. BUT WE CAN'T STAY HERE.

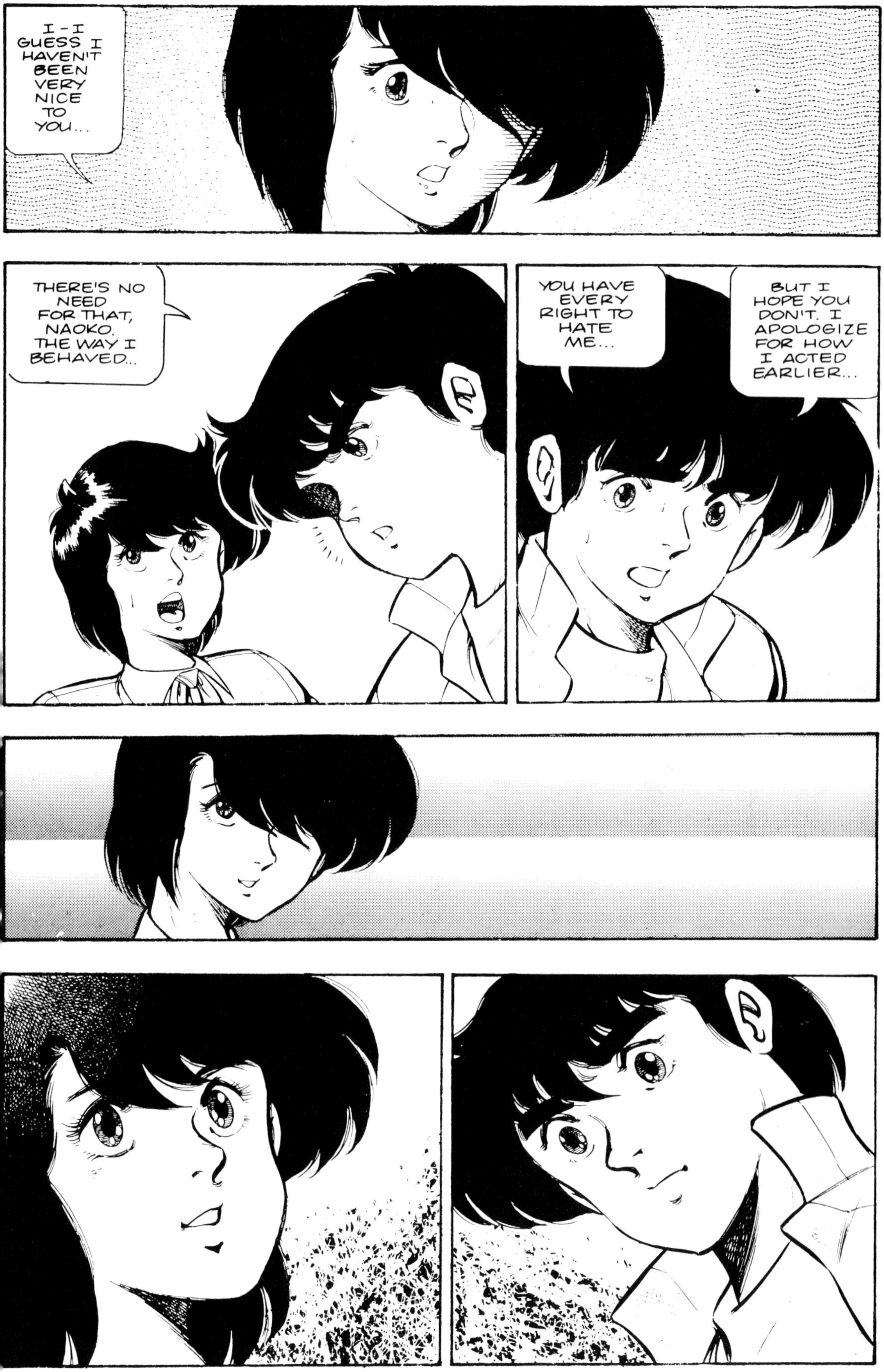
I-I GUESS I HAVEN'T BEEN VERY NICE TO YOU...
THERE'S NO NEED FOR THAT, NAOKO. THE WAY I BEHAVED...
YOU HAVE EVERY RIGHT TO HATE ME...
BUT I HOPE YOU DON'T. I APOLOGIZE FOR HOW I ACTED EARLIER...

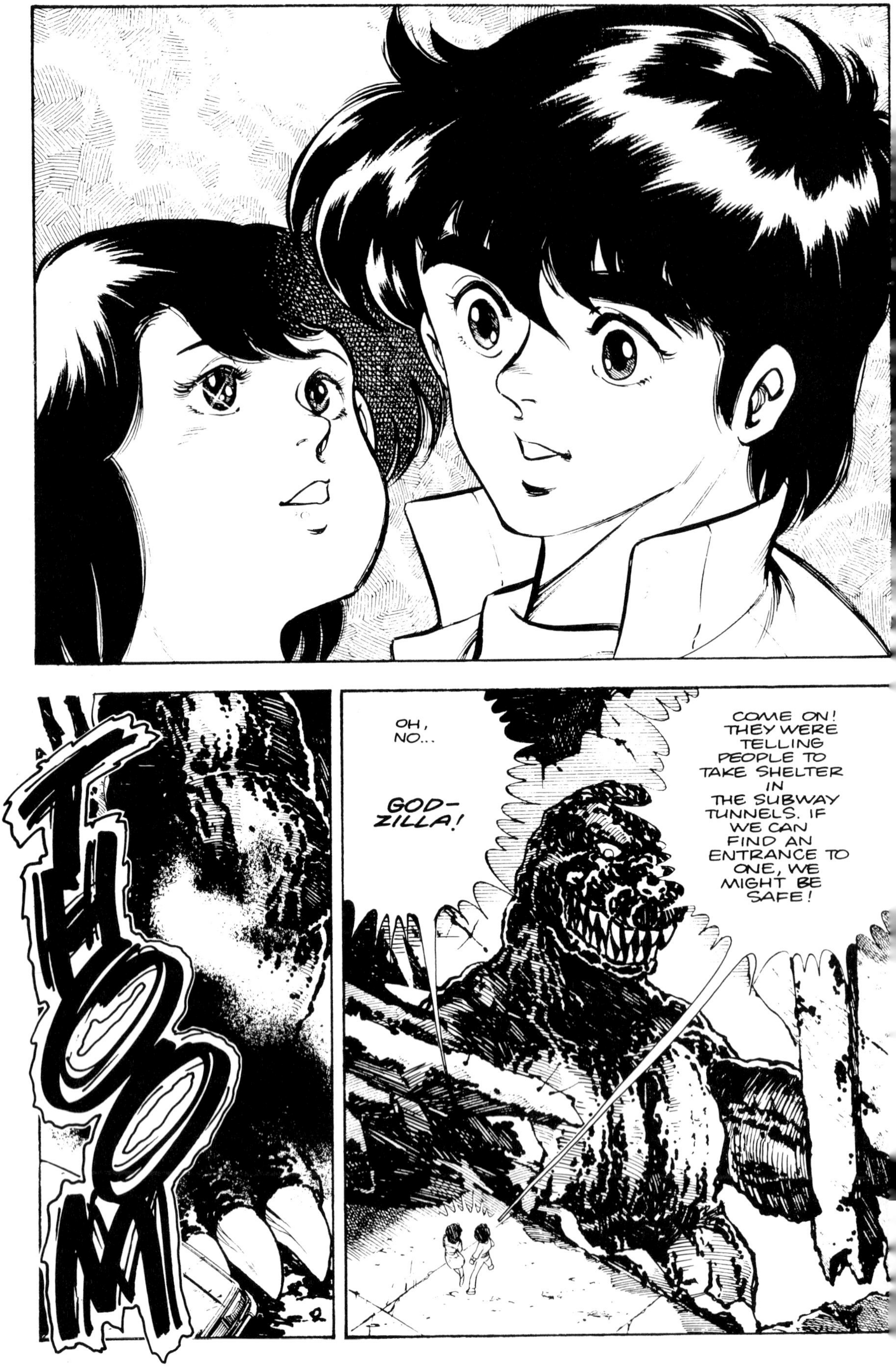
THOOM
OH, NO...
GOD-ZILLA!
COME ON! THEY WERE TELLING PEOPLE TO TAKE SHELTER IN THE SUBWAY TUNNELS. IF WE CAN FIND AN ENTRANCE TO ONE, WE MIGHT BE SAFE!

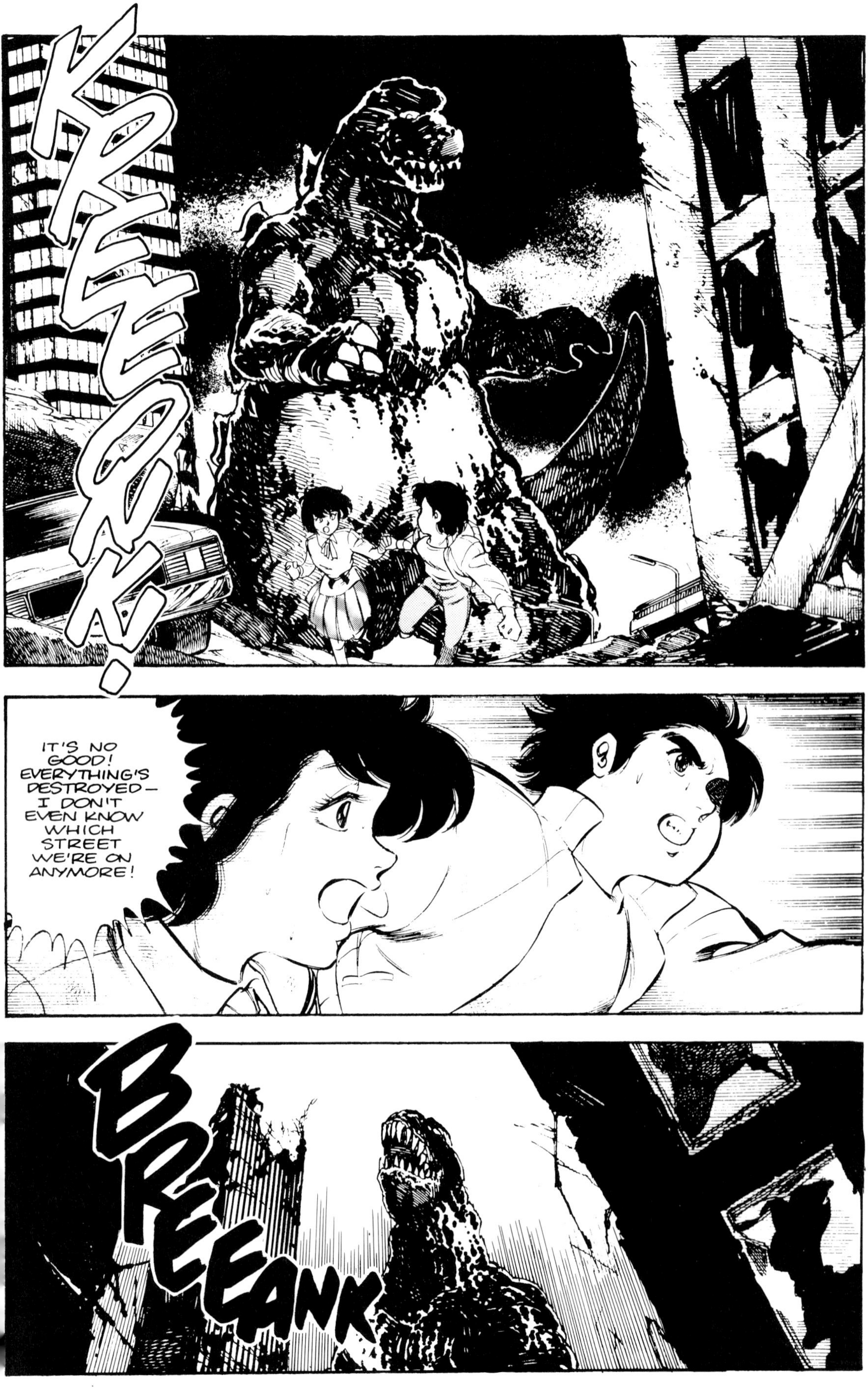
KYEOONK!
IT'S NO GOOD! EVERYTHING'S DESTROYED— I DON'T EVEN KNOW WHICH STREET WE'RE ON ANYMORE!
BREEEANK

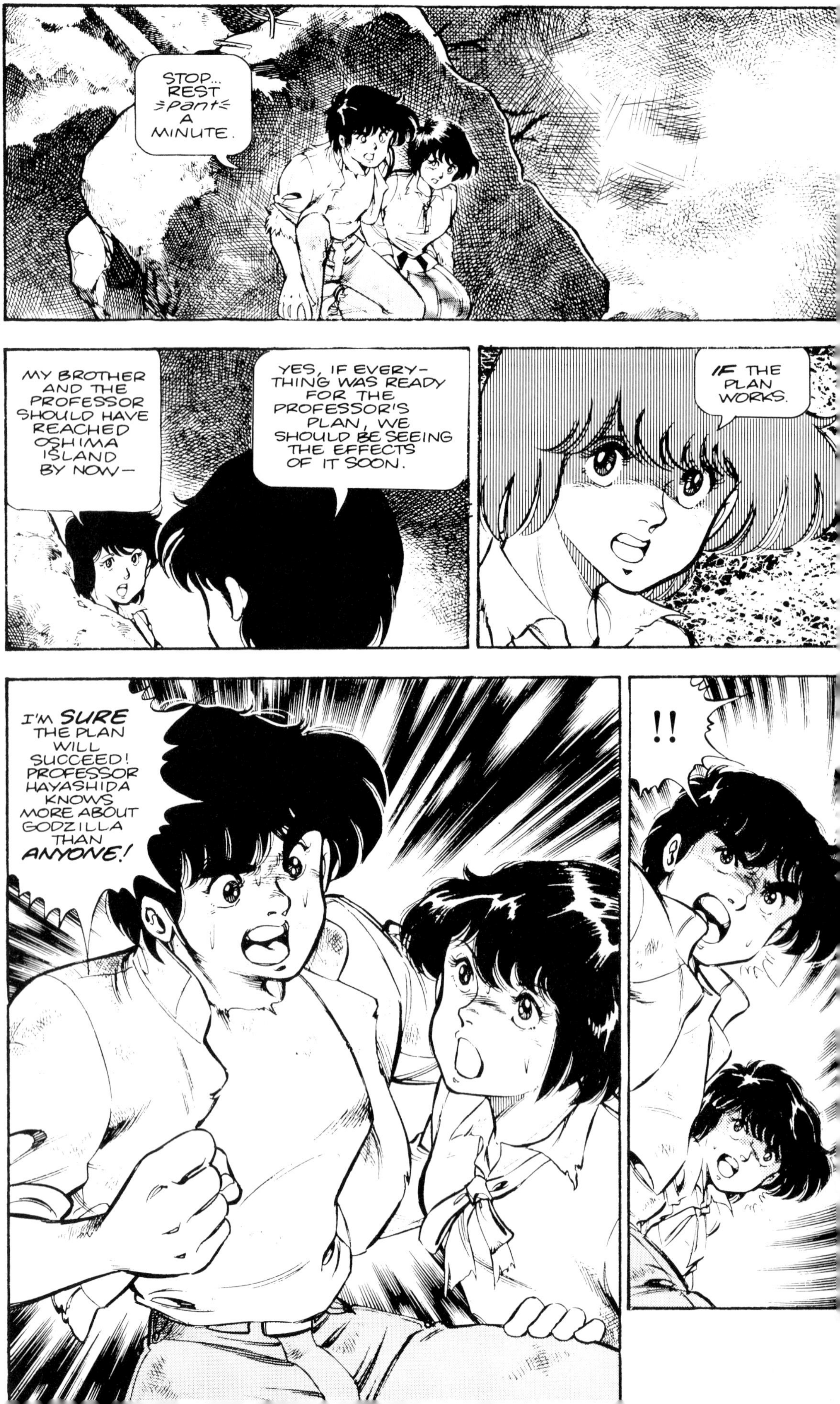
STOP... REST *pant* A MINUTE.
MY BROTHER AND THE PROFESSOR SHOULD HAVE REACHED OSHIMA ISLAND BY NOW—
YES, IF EVERY-THING WAS READY FOR THE PROFESSOR'S PLAN, WE SHOULD BE SEEING THE EFFECTS OF IT SOON.
IF THE PLAN WORKS.
I'M **SURE** THE PLAN WILL SUCCEED! PROFESSOR HAYASHIDA KNOWS MORE ABOUT GODZILLA THAN **ANYONE!**
!!

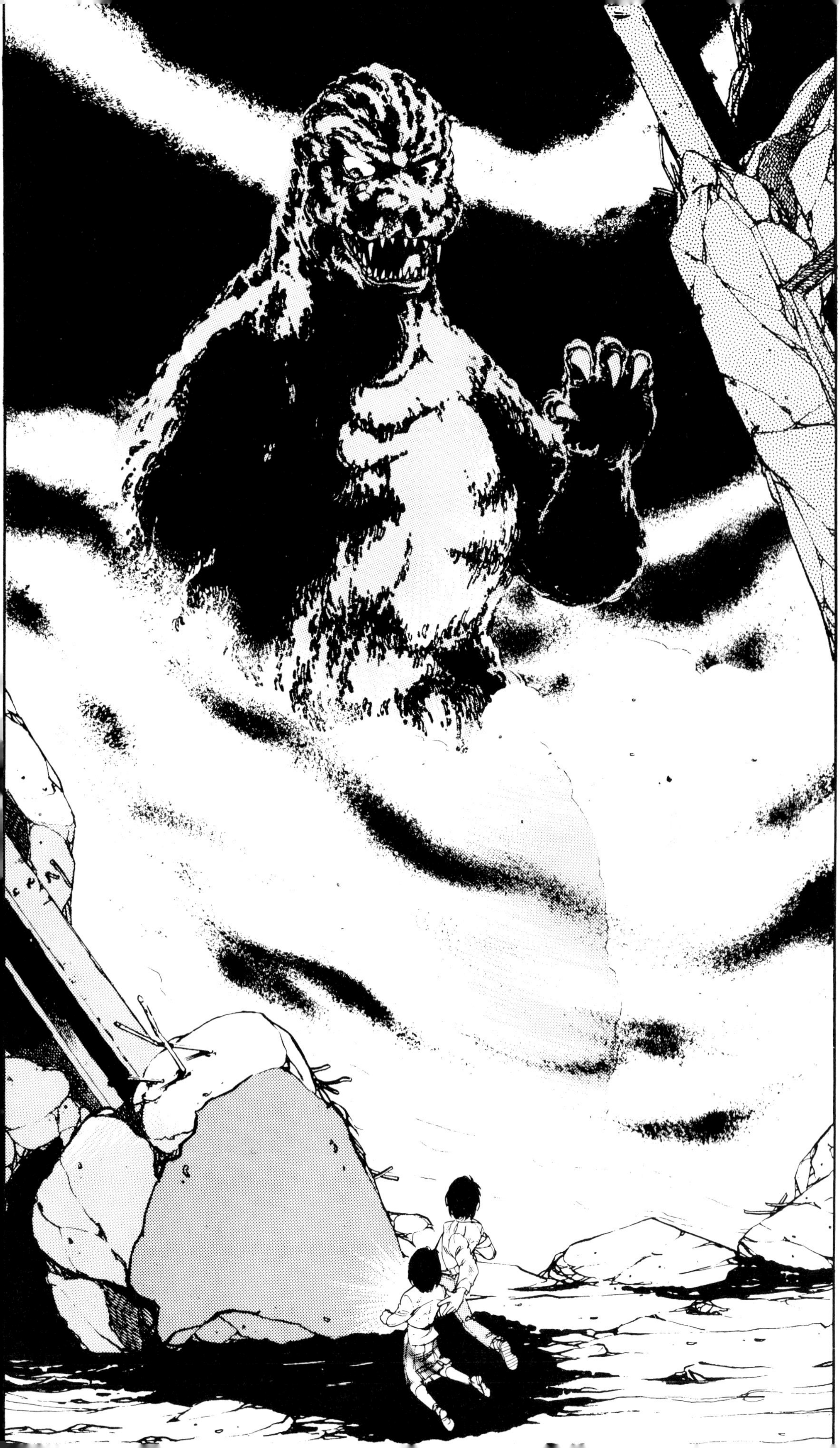

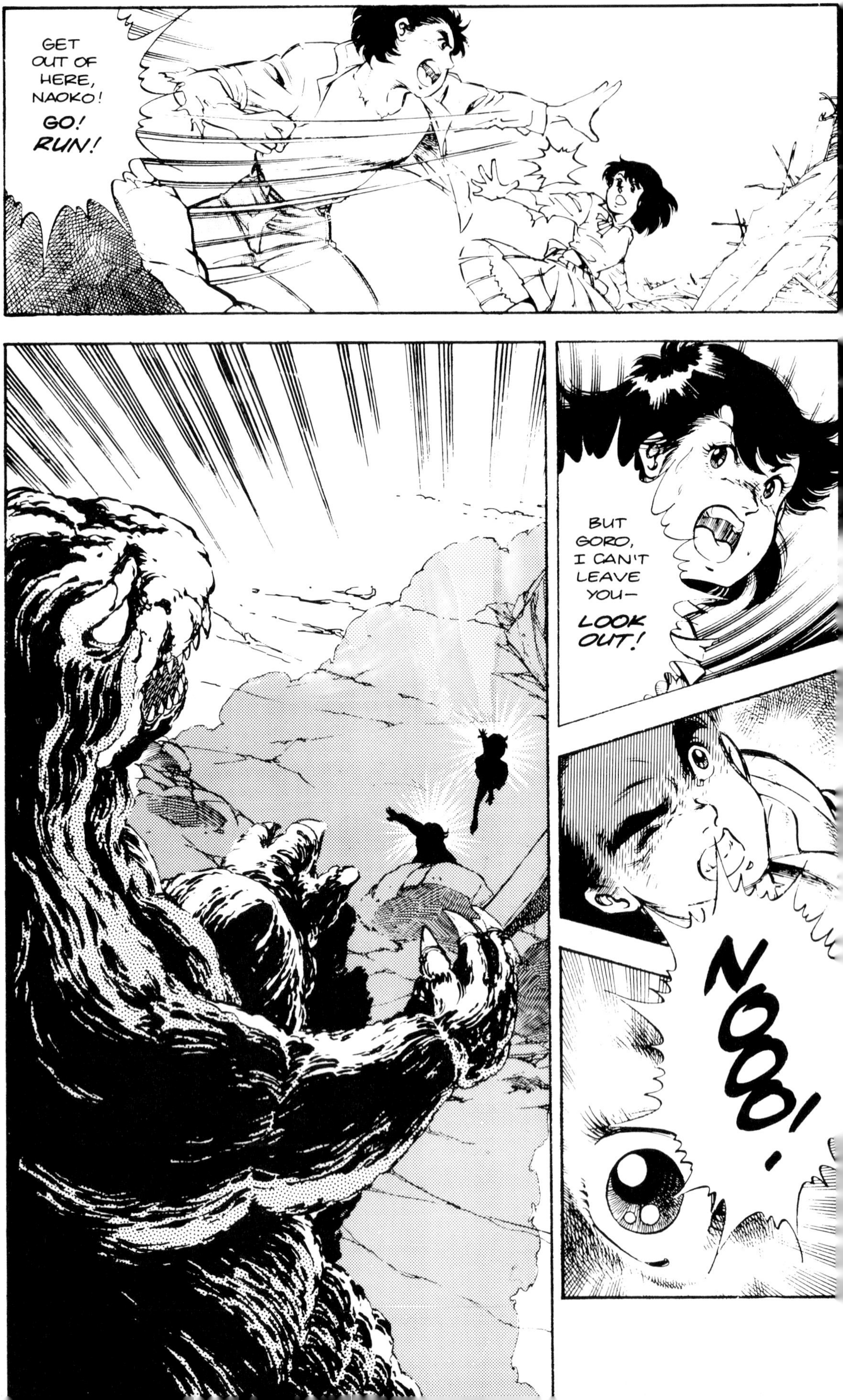
GET OUT OF HERE, NAOKO! GO! RUN!
BUT GORO, I CAN'T LEAVE YOU— LOOK OUT!
NOOO!!

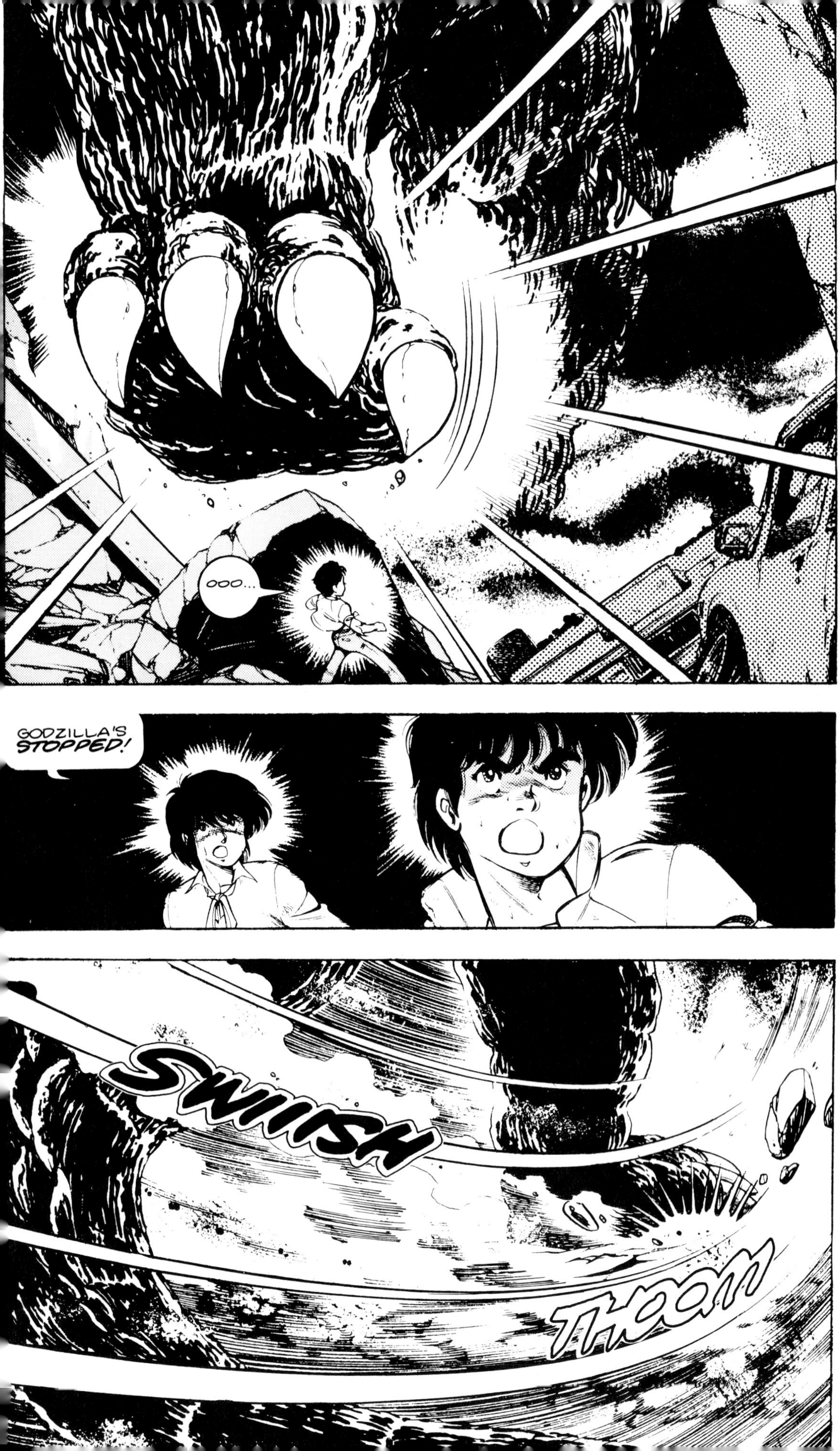
Ooo...
GODZILLA'S STOPPED!
SWISH
THOOM

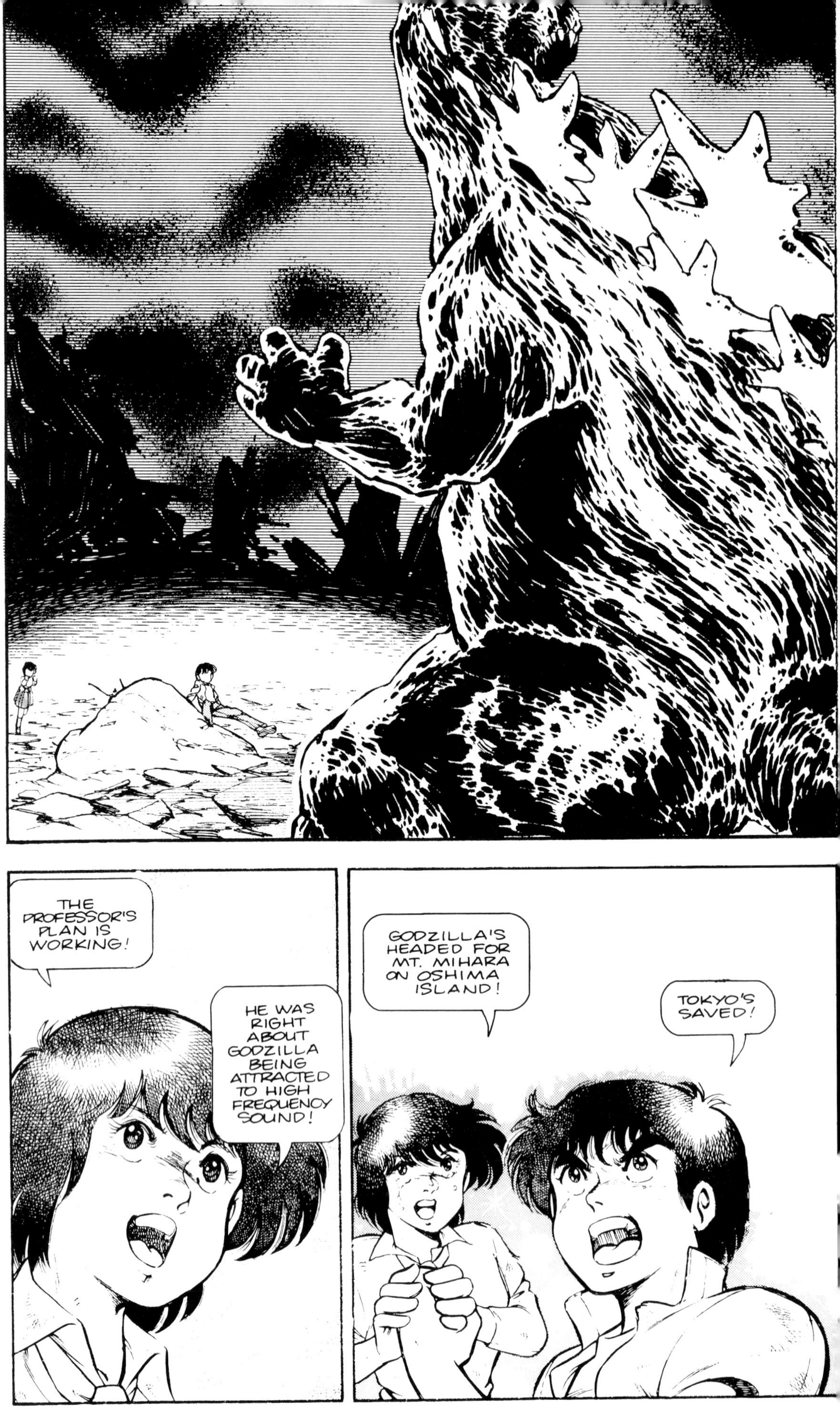
THE PROFESSOR'S PLAN IS WORKING!
HE WAS RIGHT ABOUT GODZILLA BEING ATTRACTED TO HIGH FREQUENCY SOUND!
GODZILLA'S HEADED FOR MT. MIHARA ON OSHIMA ISLAND!
TOKYO'S SAVED!

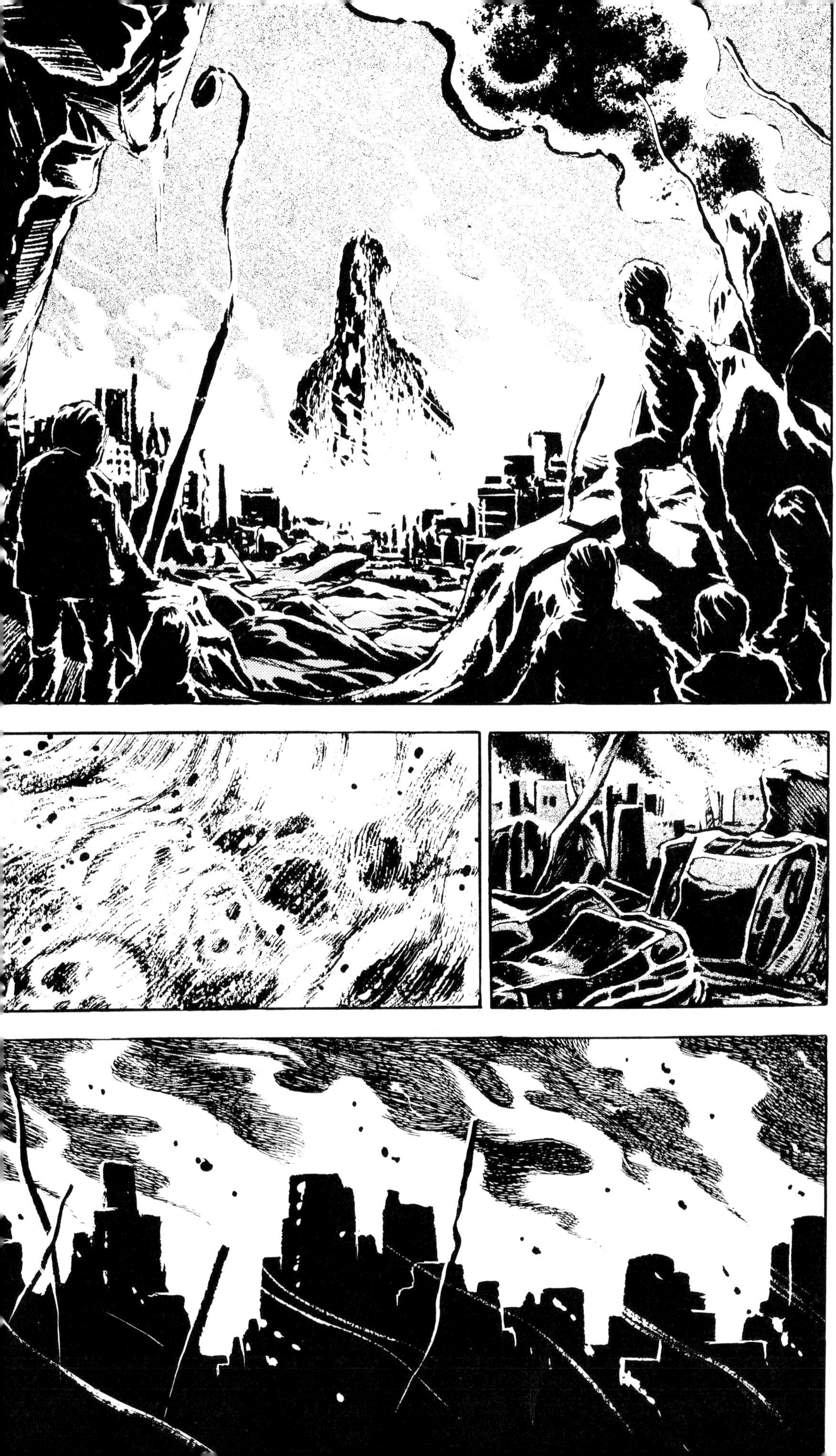

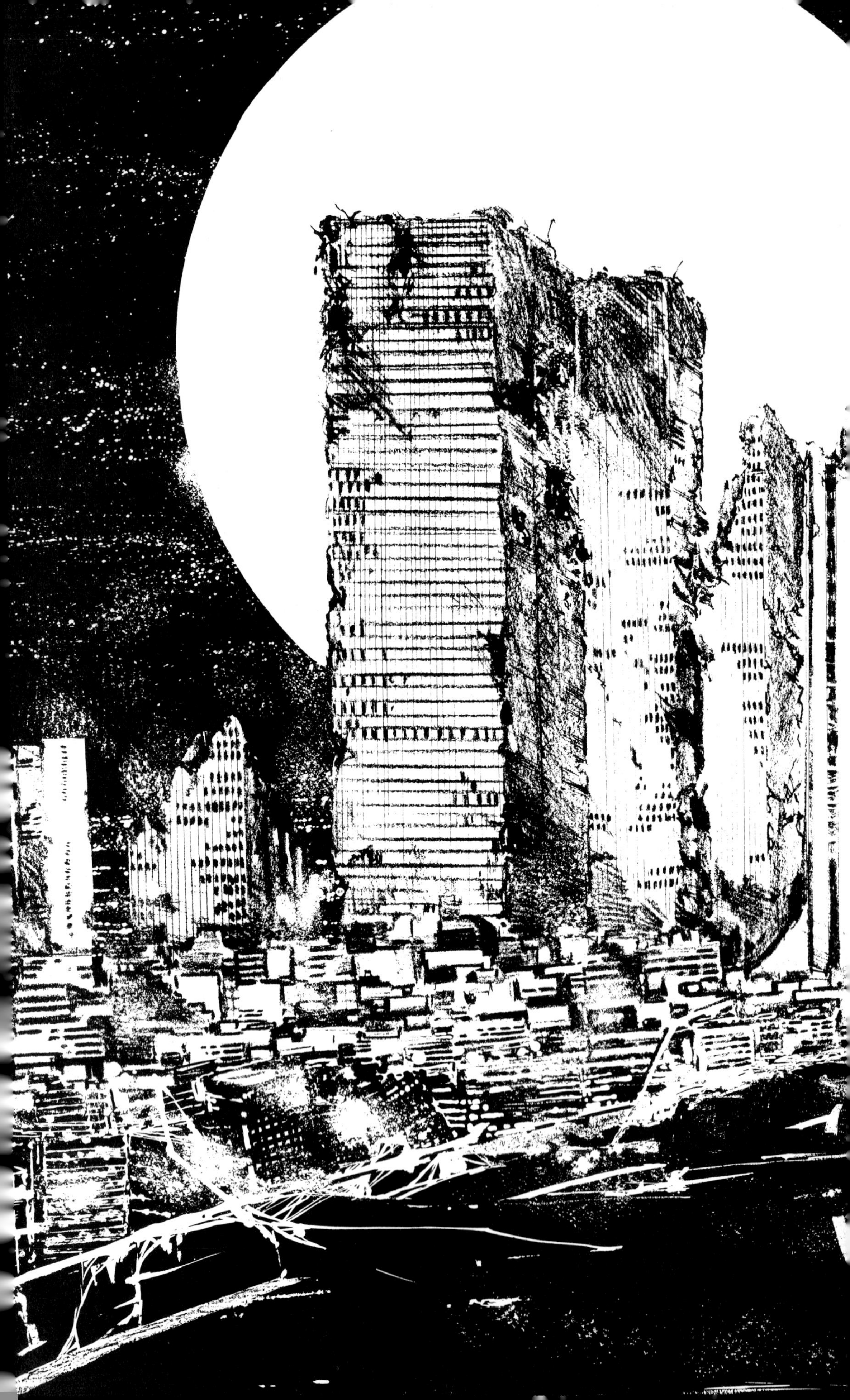

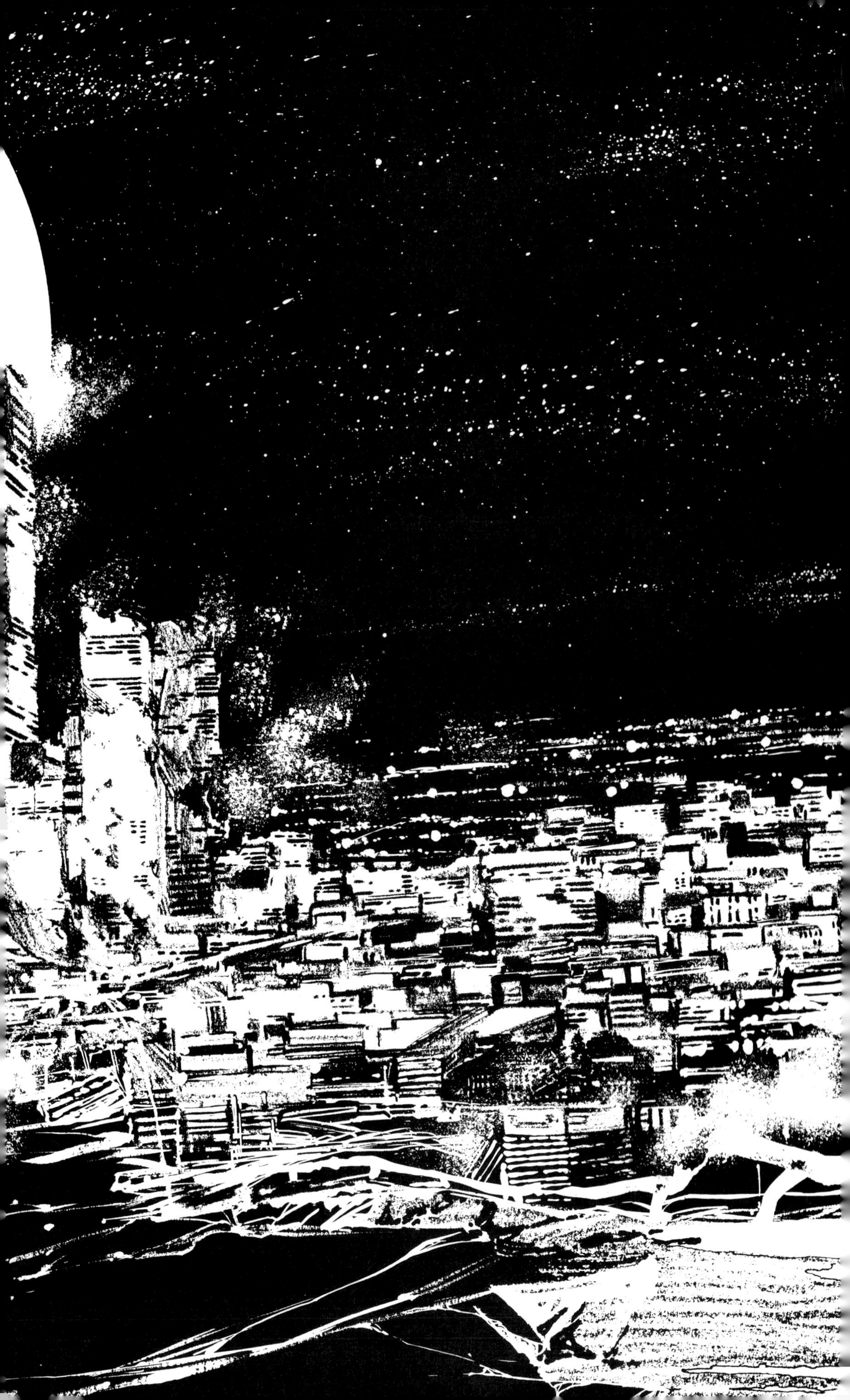

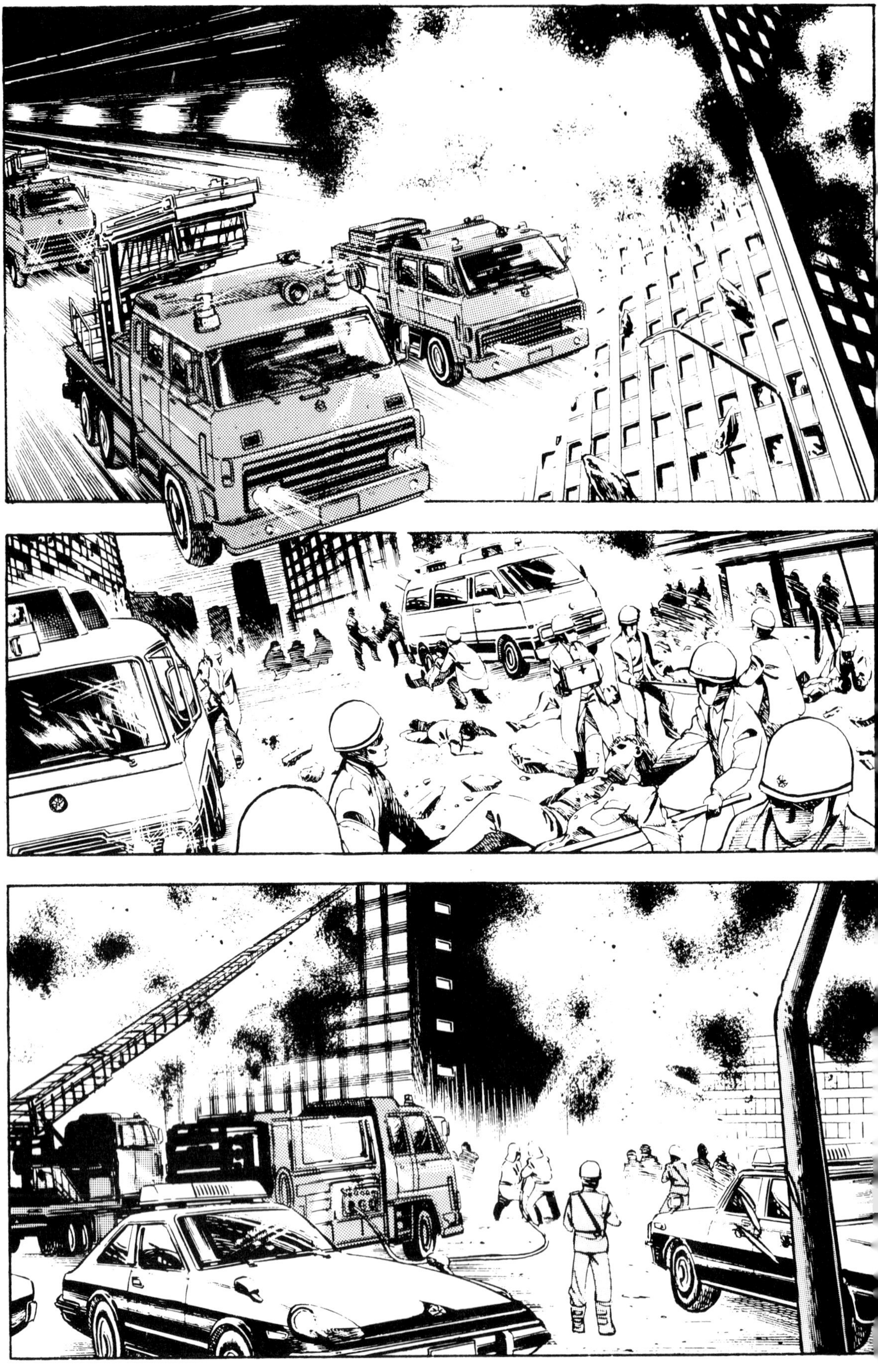

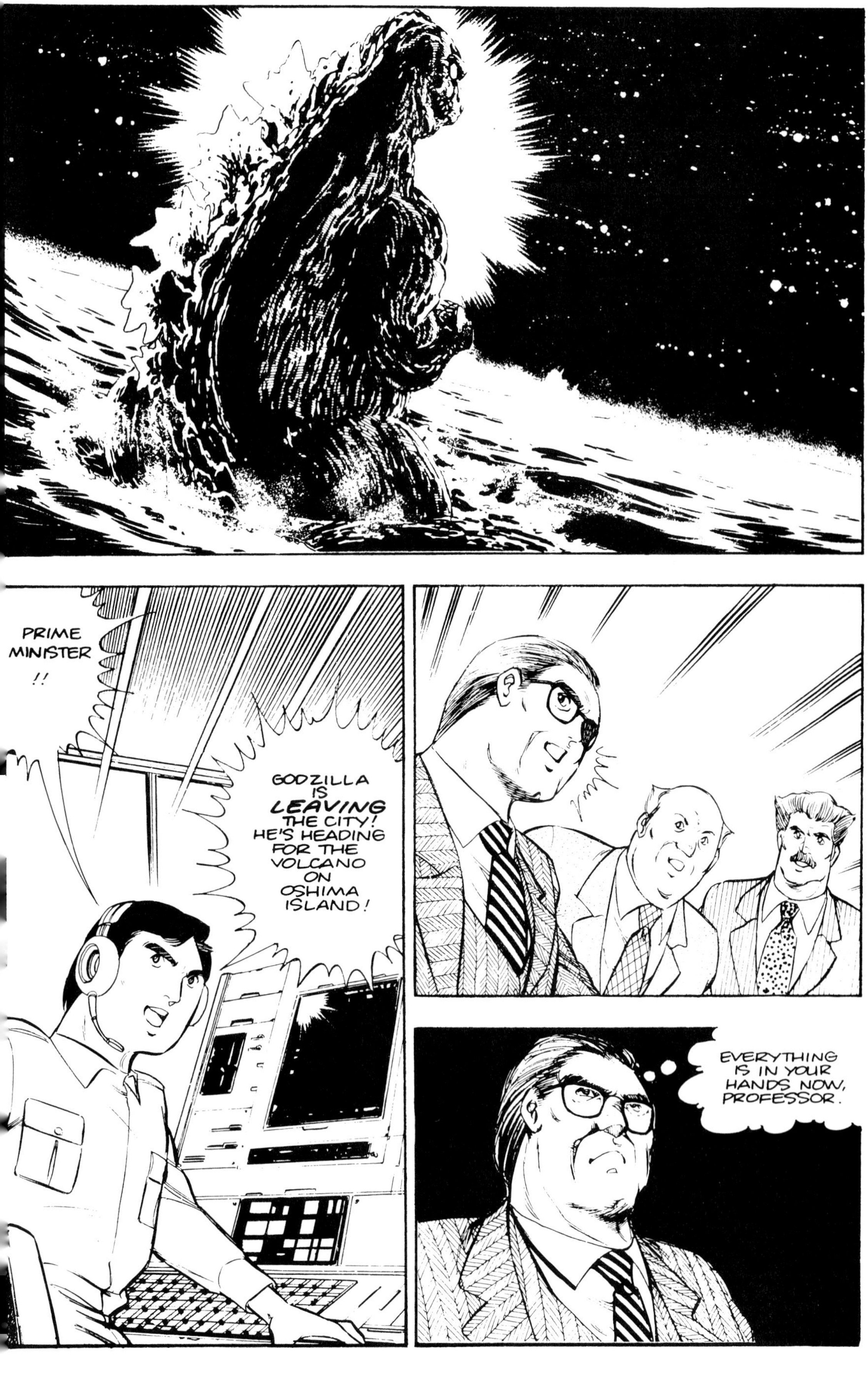
PRIME MINISTER !!
GODZILLA IS LEAVING THE CITY! HE'S HEADING FOR THE VOLCANO ON OSHIMA ISLAND!
EVERYTHING IS IN YOUR HANDS NOW, PROFESSOR.

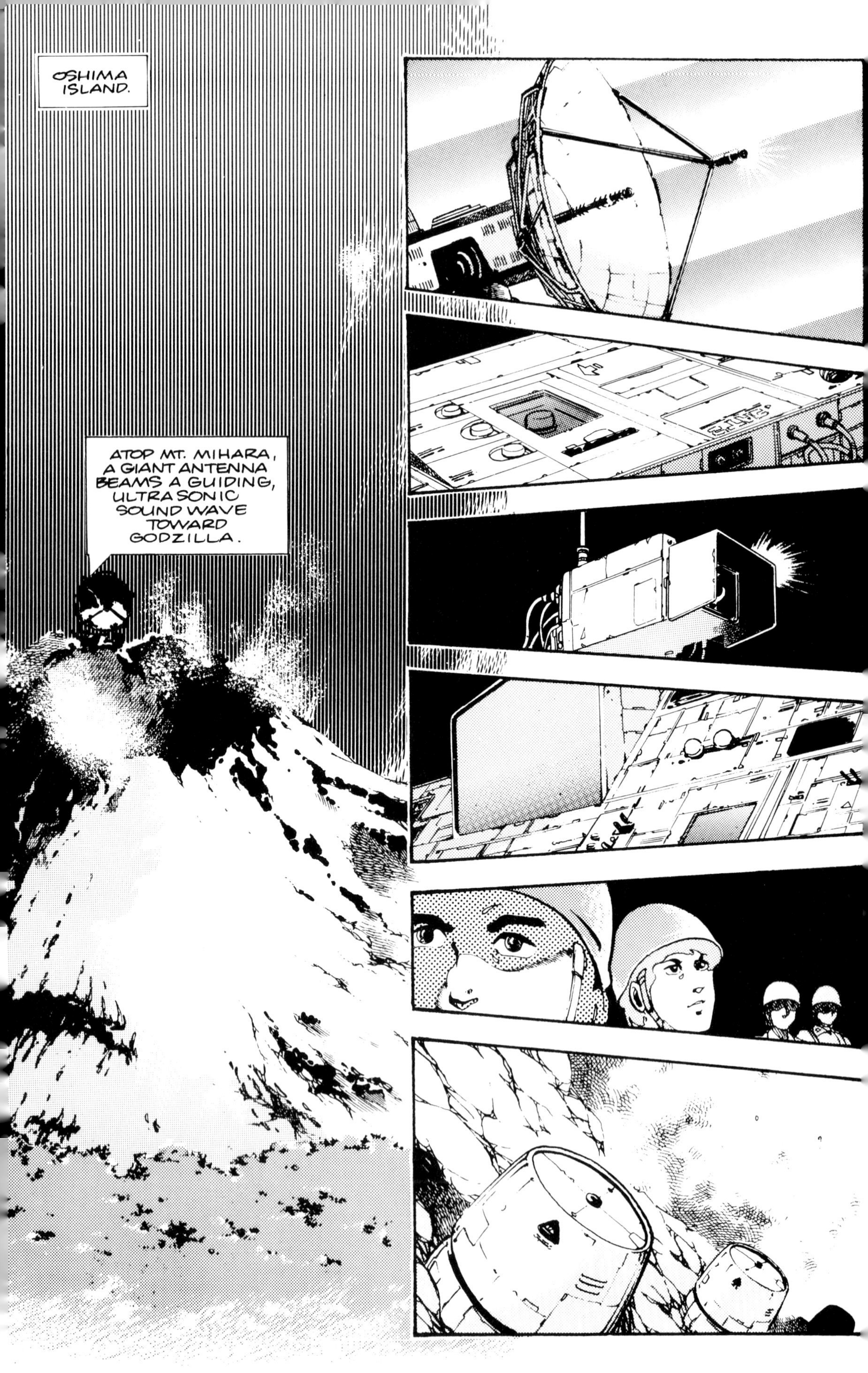
OSHIMA ISLAND.
ATOP MT. MIHARA, A GIANT ANTENNA BEAMS A GUIDING, ULTRASONIC SOUND WAVE TOWARD GODZILLA.

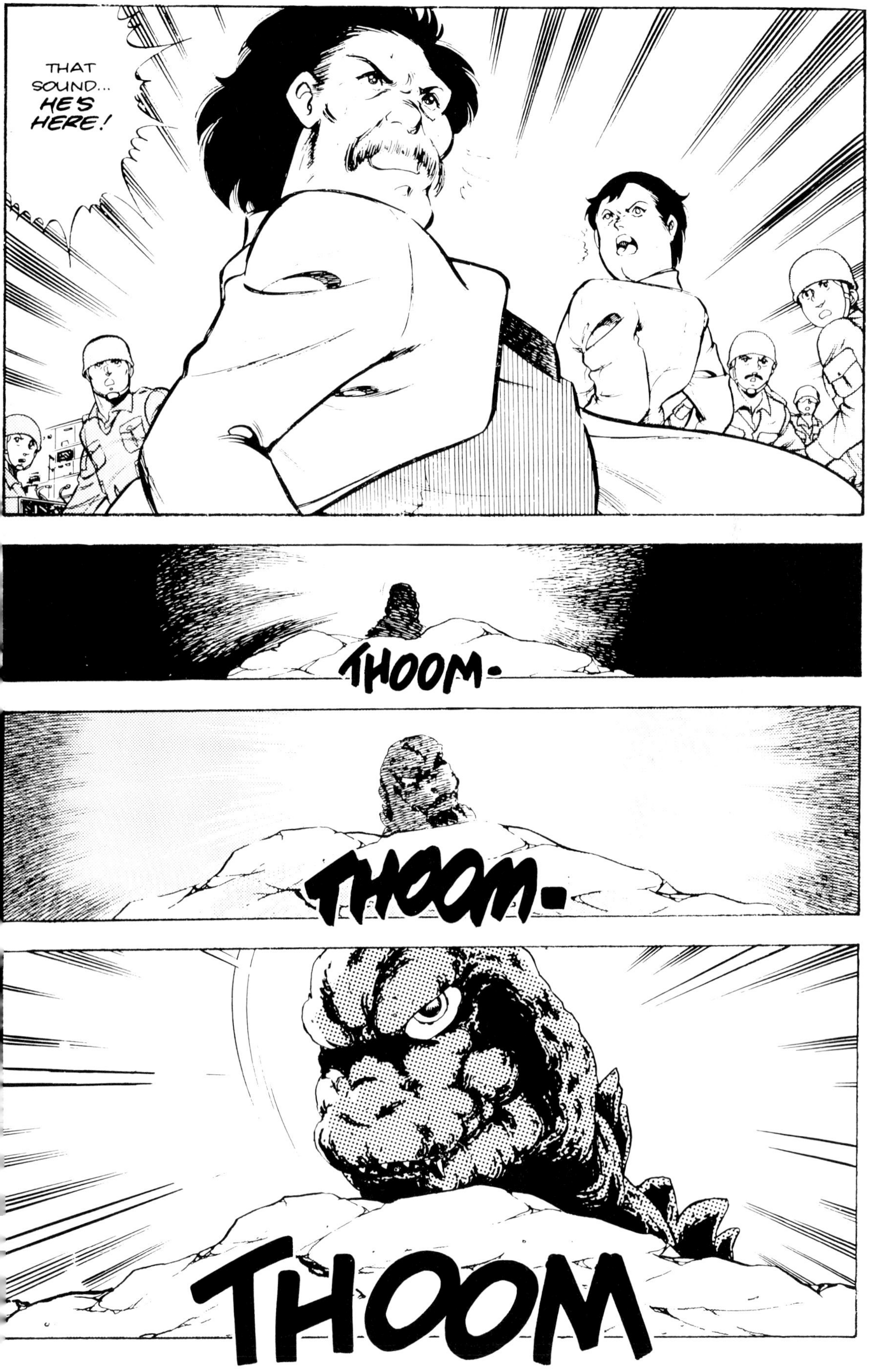
THAT SOUND... HE'S HERE!
THOOM-
THOOM-
THOOM

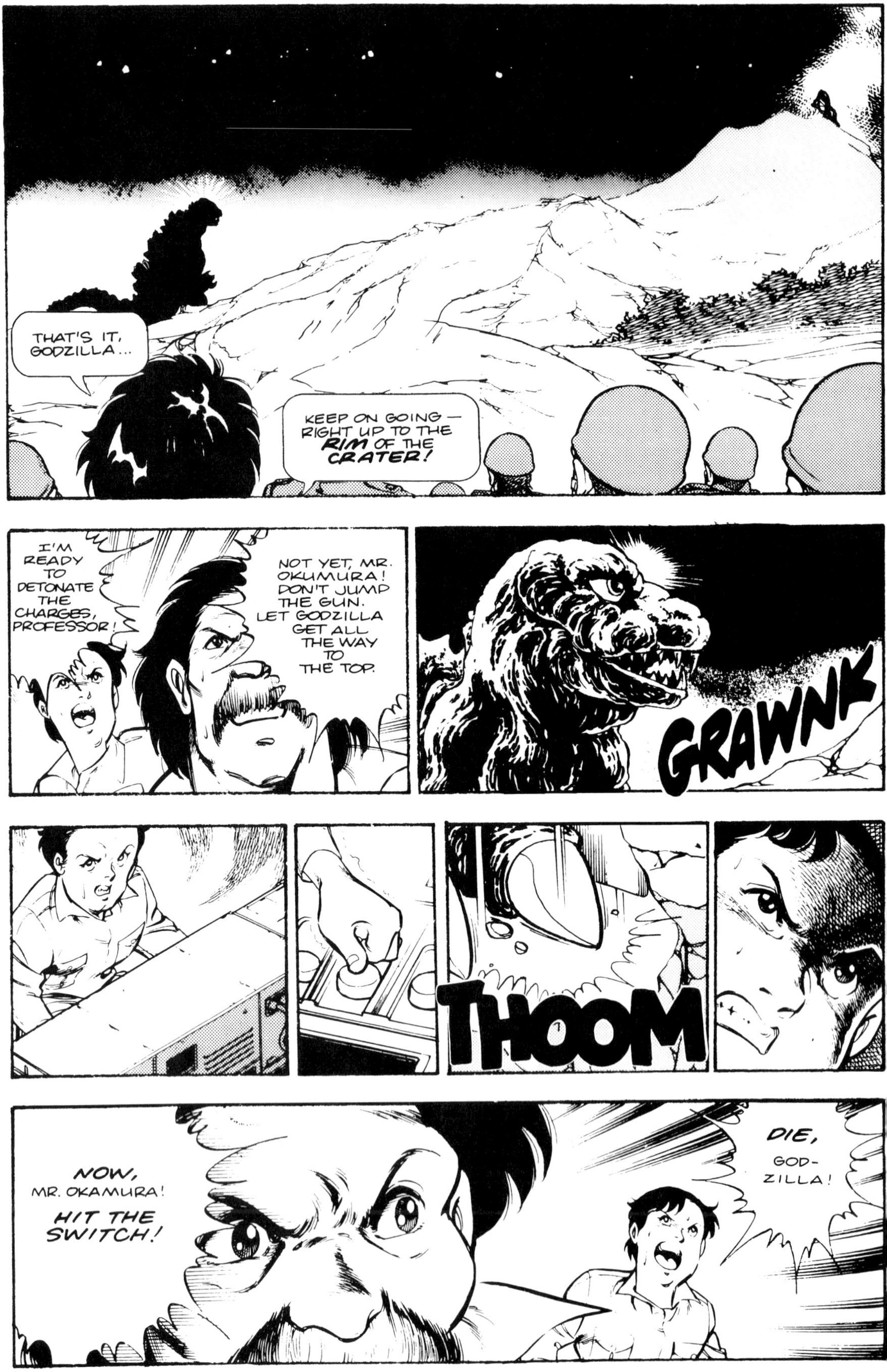
THAT'S IT, GODZILLA...
KEEP ON GOING — RIGHT UP TO THE RIM OF THE CRATER!
I'M READY TO DETONATE THE CHARGES, PROFESSOR!
NOT YET, MR. OKUMURA! DON'T JUMP THE GUN. LET GODZILLA GET ALL THE WAY TO THE TOP.
GRAWNK
THOOM
NOW, MR. OKAMURA! HIT THE SWITCH!
DIE, GOD-ZILLA!

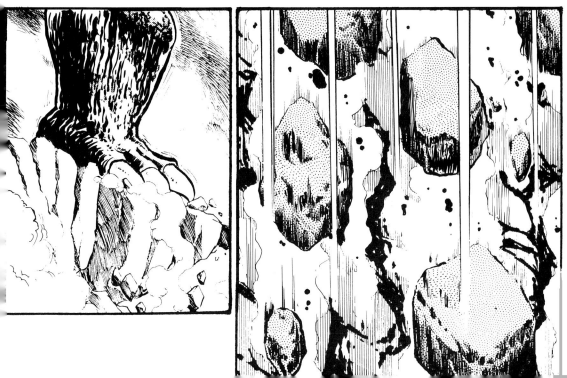

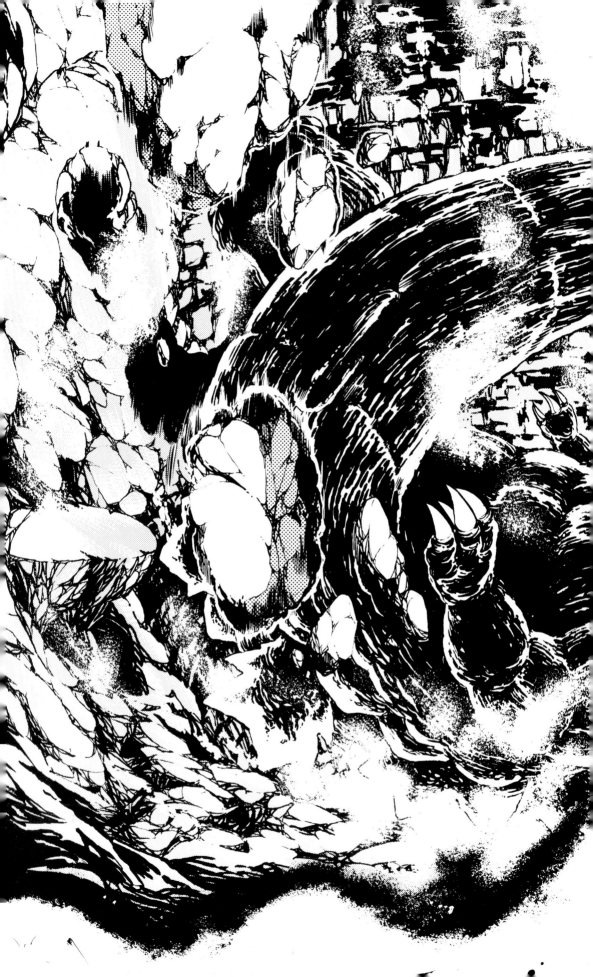

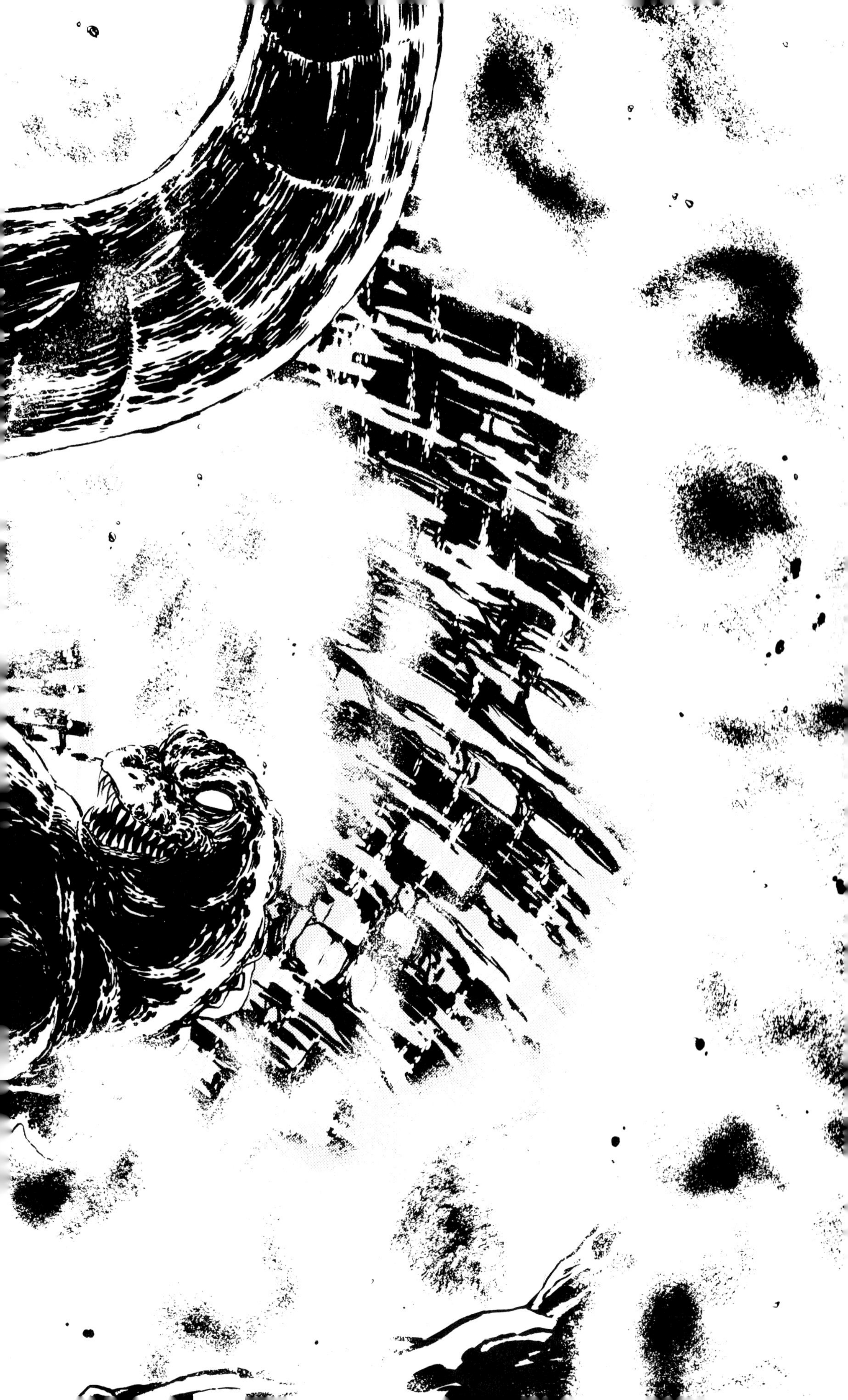

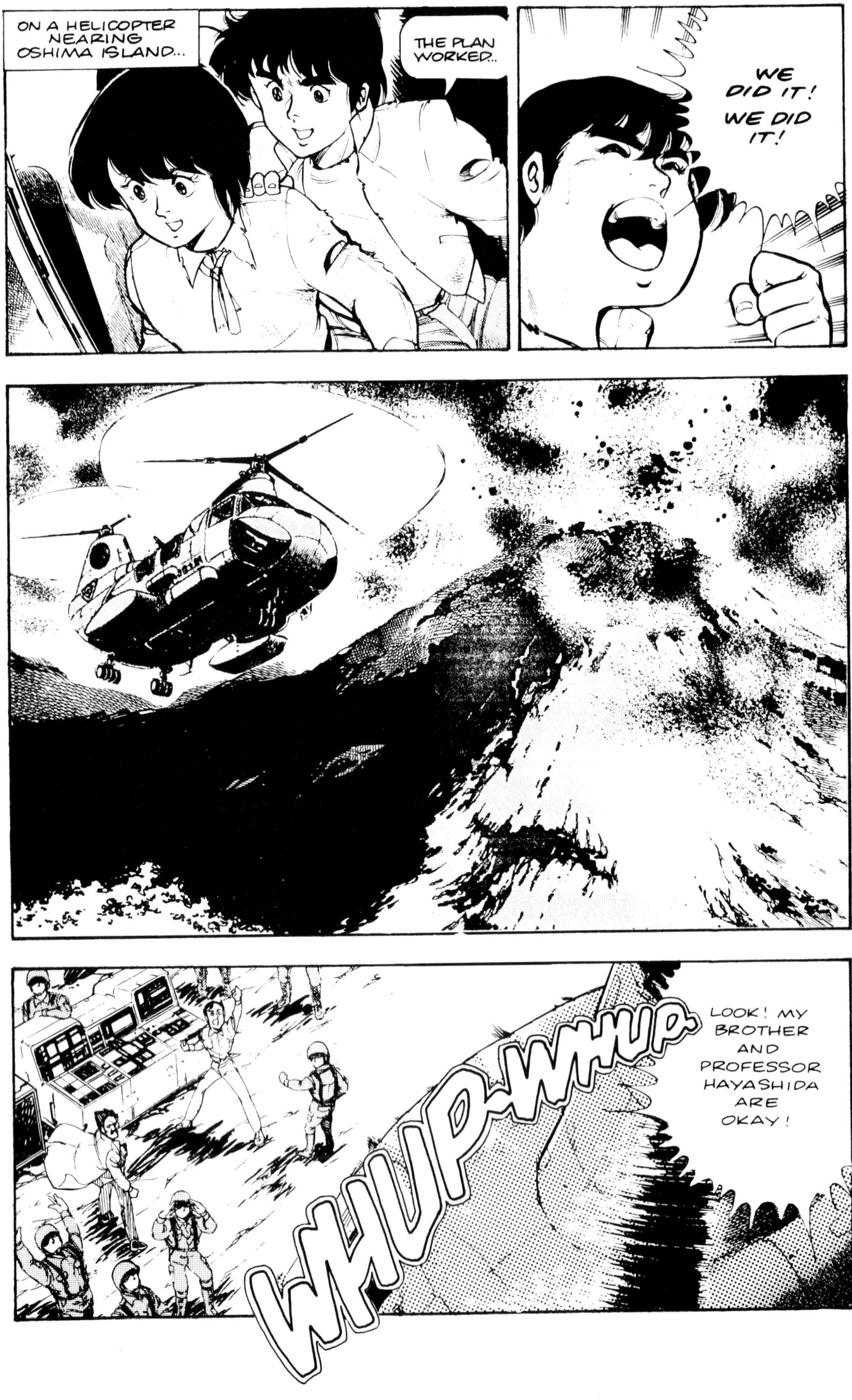
ON A HELICOPTER NEARING OSHIMA ISLAND...
THE PLAN WORKED...
WE DID IT! WE DID IT!
WHUP WHUP
LOOK! MY BROTHER AND PROFESSOR HAYASHIDA ARE OKAY!

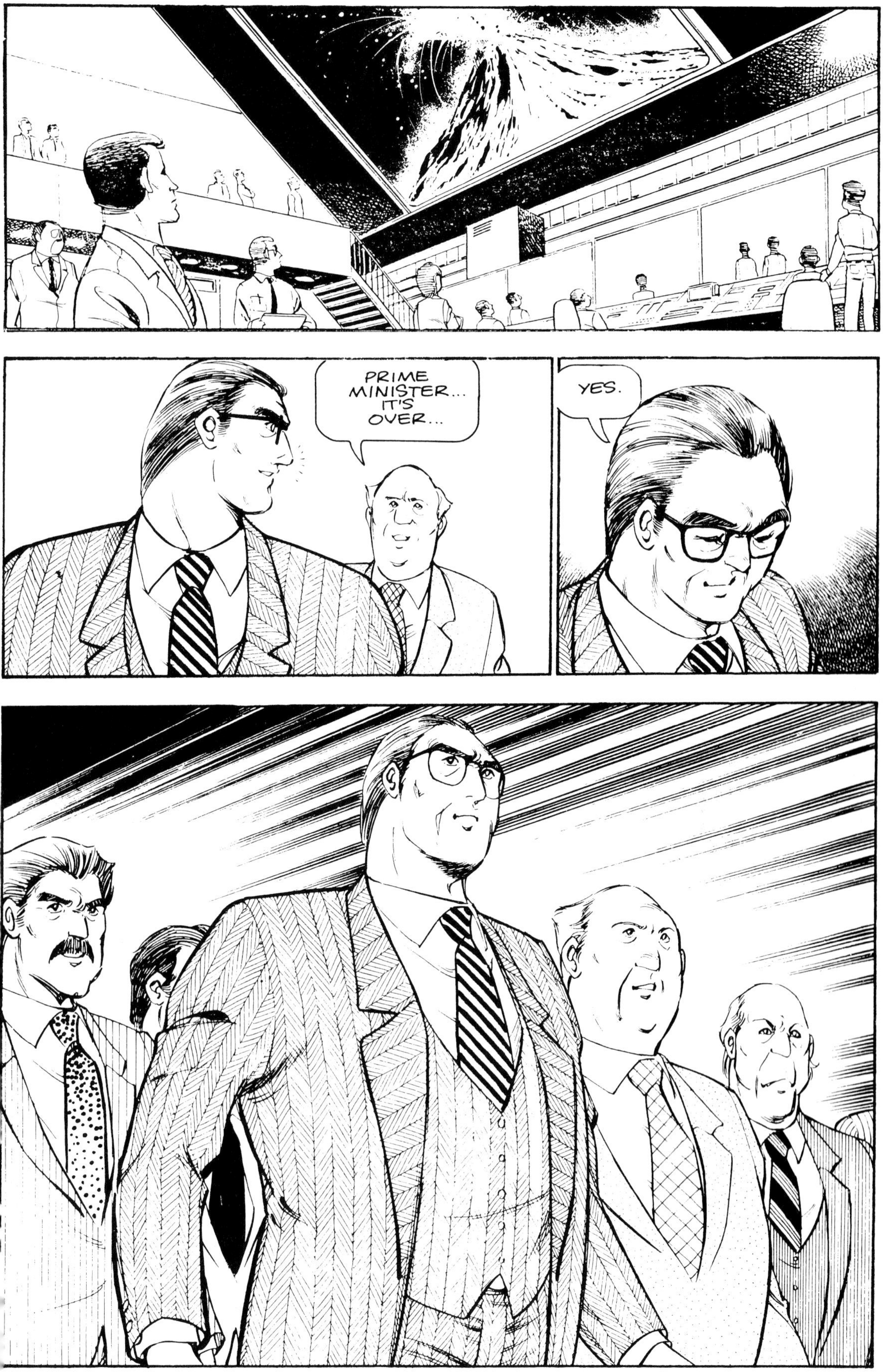
PRIME MINISTER... IT'S OVER...
YES.

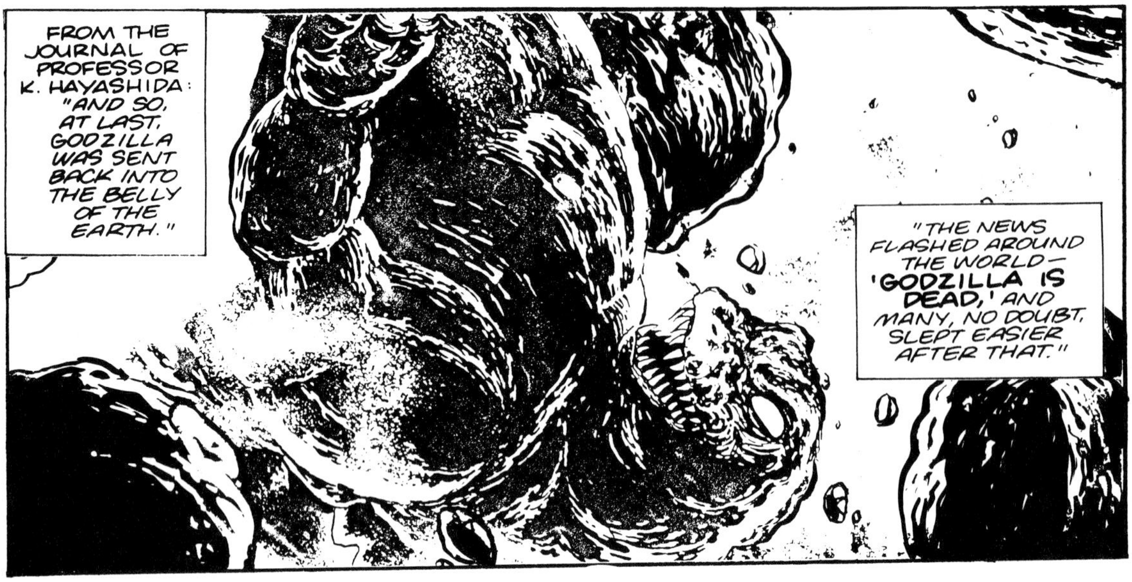
FROM THE JOURNAL OF PROFESSOR K. HAYASHIDA: "AND SO, AT LAST, GODZILLA WAS SENT BACK INTO THE BELLY OF THE EARTH."
"THE NEWS FLASHED AROUND THE WORLD-- 'GODZILLA IS DEAD,' AND MANY, NO DOUBT, SLEPT EASIER AFTER THAT."

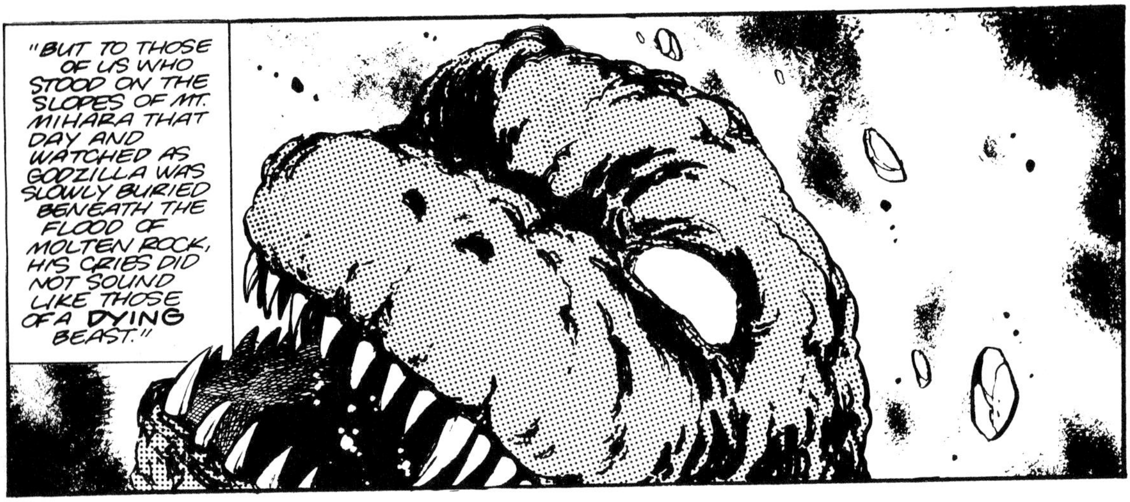
"BUT TO THOSE OF US WHO STOOD ON THE SLOPES OF MT. MIHARA THAT DAY AND WATCHED AS GODZILLA WAS SLOWLY BURIED BENEATH THE FLOOD OF MOLTEN ROCK, HIS CRIES DID NOT SOUND LIKE THOSE OF A DYING BEAST."

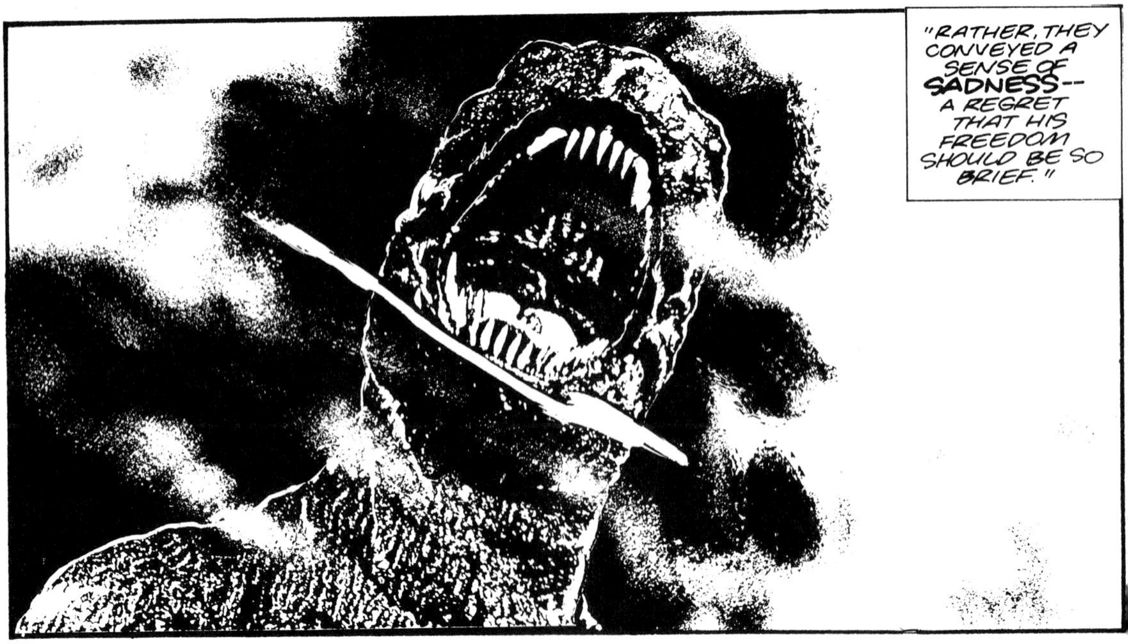
"RATHER, THEY CONVEYED A SENSE OF SADNESS-- A REGRET THAT HIS FREEDOM SHOULD BE SO BRIEF."

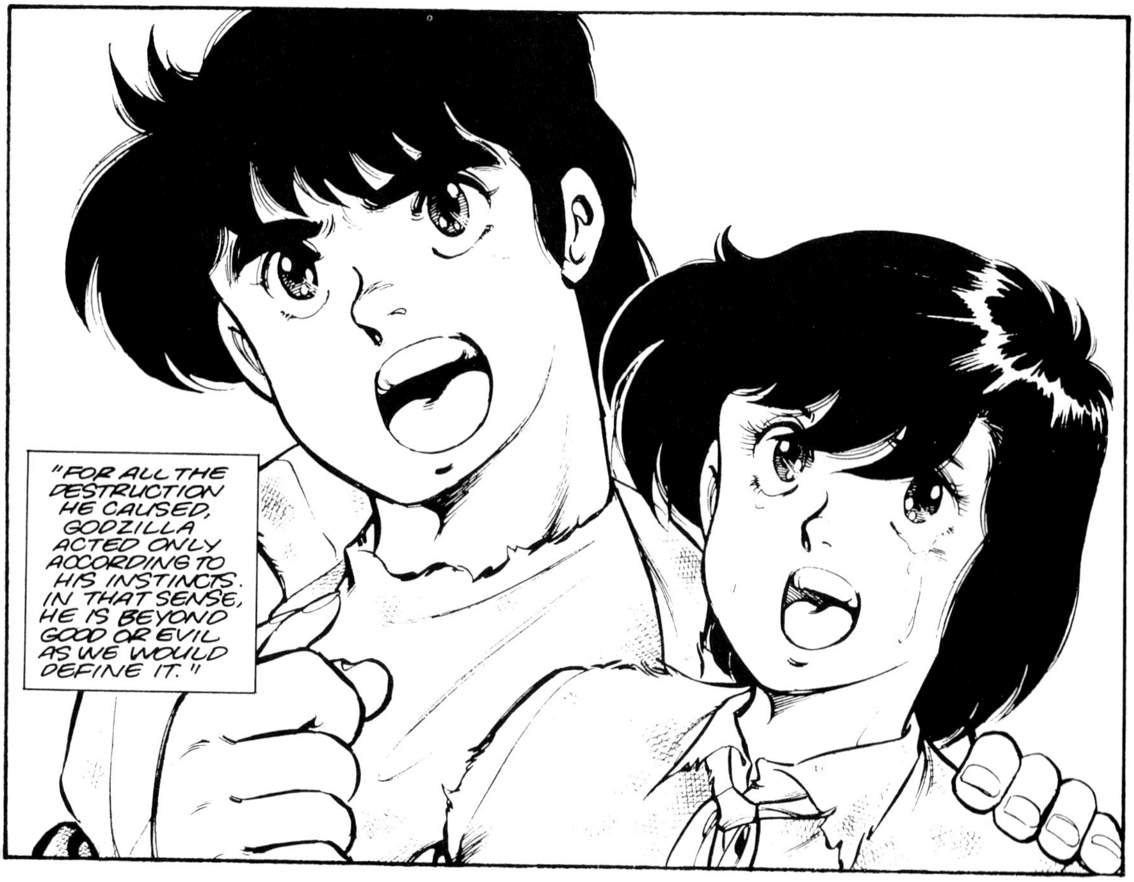
"FOR ALL THE DESTRUCTION HE CAUSED, GODZILLA ACTED ONLY ACCORDING TO HIS INSTINCTS. IN THAT SENSE, HE IS BEYOND GOOD OR EVIL AS WE WOULD DEFINE IT."

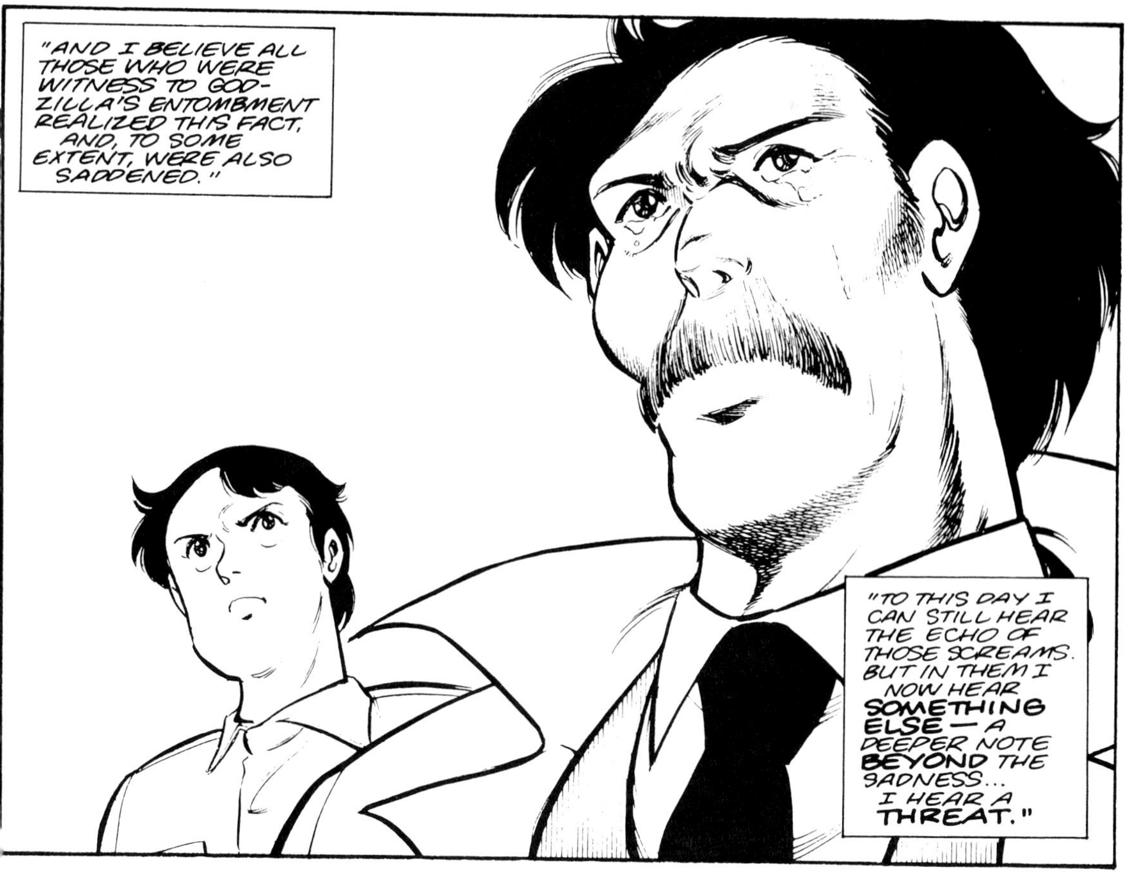
"AND I BELIEVE ALL THOSE WHO WERE WITNESS TO GOD-ZILLA'S ENTOMBMENT REALIZED THIS FACT, AND, TO SOME EXTENT, WERE ALSO SADDENED."
"TO THIS DAY I CAN STILL HEAR THE ECHO OF THOSE SCREAMS. BUT IN THEM I NOW HEAR SOMETHING ELSE — A DEEPER NOTE BEYOND THE SADNESS... I HEAR A THREAT."

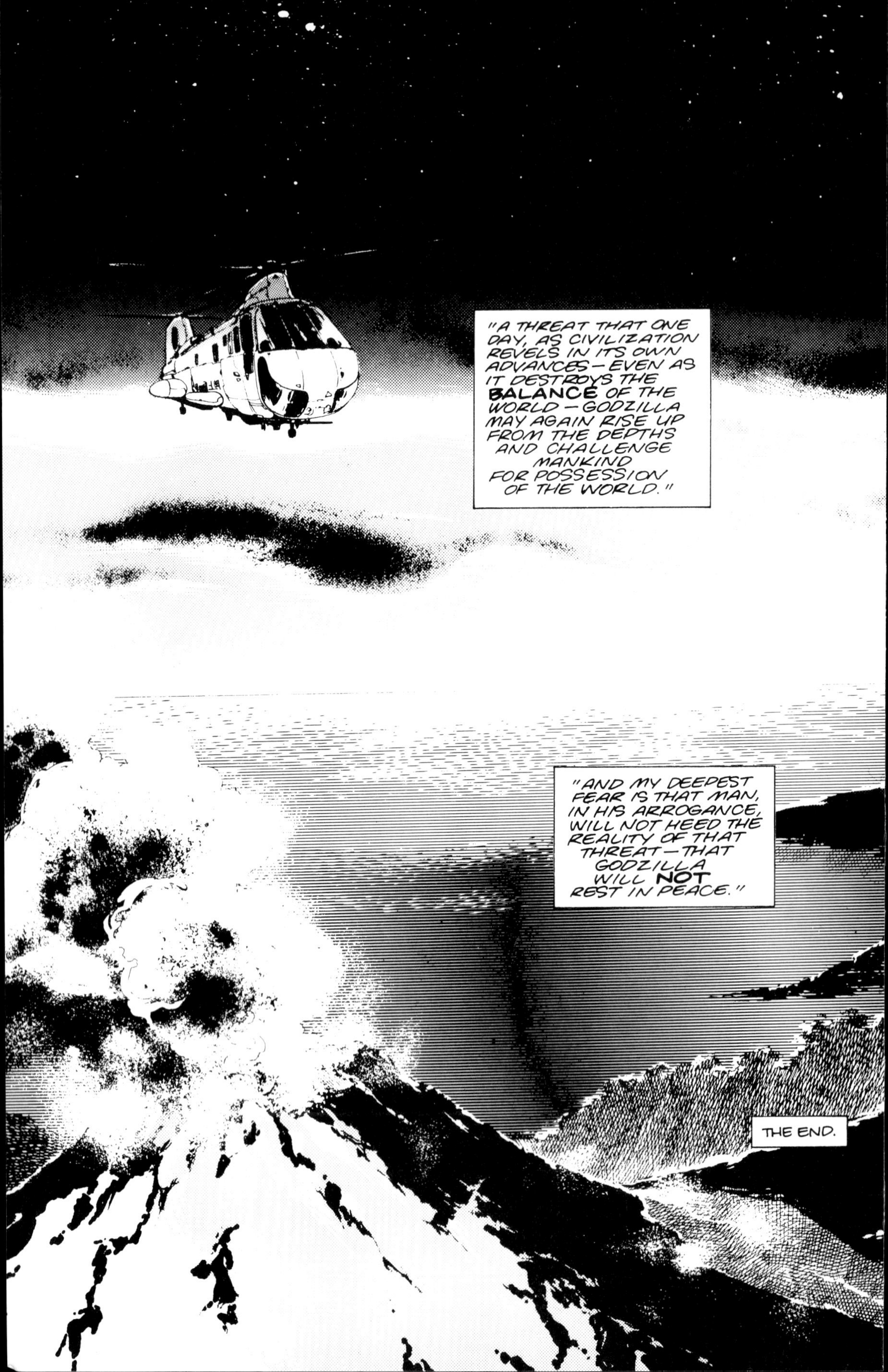
"A THREAT THAT ONE DAY, AS CIVILIZATION REVELS IN ITS OWN ADVANCES—EVEN AS IT DESTROYS THE **BALANCE** OF THE WORLD—GODZILLA MAY AGAIN RISE UP FROM THE DEPTHS AND CHALLENGE MANKIND FOR POSSESSION OF THE WORLD."
"AND MY DEEPEST FEAR IS THAT MAN, IN HIS ARROGANCE, WILL NOT HEED THE REALITY OF THAT THREAT—THAT GODZILLA WILL **NOT** REST IN PEACE."
THE END.

It was winter of 1975. Ah, yes, the good ol' seventies — a time of free love; Watergate; TV game shows like "The Dating Game" and "Name That Tune"; "Supermax"-ed afros; wide-collar shirts; great music from Pink Floyd, Funkadelic, Genesis, Kiss, Earth Wind and Fire, and Blue Oyster Cult; bell-bottom jeans and platform shoes; and polyester suits. Unfortunately, I was only aware of some of the above; I was only five years old.

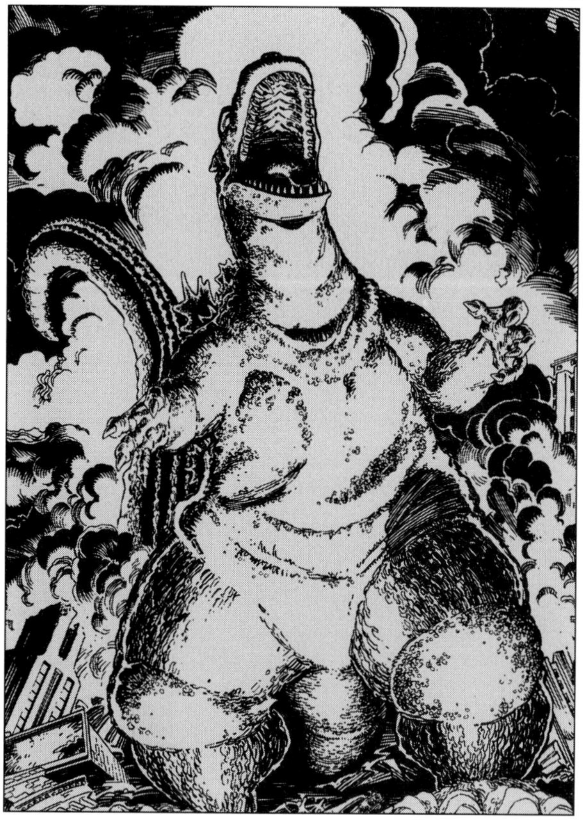
ART ADAMS

Even though this was before kindergarten, the days seemed to progress in a regular session: Mondays through Thursdays were spent learning reading, writing, and arithmetic (thanks, Mom!); catching the weekly Disney flick in town; eating wonderfully prepared meals (and stealing my younger brothers' jars of Gerber baby food — yum!); and watching "The Tom and Jerry Hour," "Batman," "Superman," "The Lone Ranger," "Eyewitness News" with Roger Grimsby and Bill Beutel, and "Carol Burnett." But Fridays were different — Fridays were *special*.

On Fridays, my father took our family out on the town. Boy, those were the days — first we'd go to Play-World or Toys 'R' Us, which introduced me to cool (or should I say "groovy"?) toys like View-Master reels, Show 'N' Tell Picturesound Programs, Weebles (remember that nifty song, "Weebles wobble but they don't fall down"?), Crazy Straws, Mego action figures, See & Say, Fisher-Price playsets, Legos, etc. After that excursion into toyland, we'd go through our dinner ritual, which synonymously meant going to either Tina's Pizza, Kim-Wah's Chinese Kitchen, Kentucky Fried Chicken (not KFC as it is appropriately known in a healthier, more educated American society that dreads the word "fried"), or the favorite of children everywhere: McDonald's.

And this Friday night was virtually no different — off we went to McDonald's for dinner. But the fine cuisine that ol' Ronald the Clown offered didn't appeal to Mom that night, so she suggested that she and Dad have a meal elsewhere after my brothers and I ate. I remember thinking it strange that Dad was so eager to please Mom and was willing to give up the succulent taste of a Big Mac for the sake of a pastrami-on-rye sandwich.

As for myself, after eating a double cheeseburger, small fries, and a Coke, my stomach was satisfied.

But *I* wasn't.

After my parents went to a local delicatessen and purchased the pastrami sandwiches they craved, I, wanting to taste the finer things in life, requested a sample of this new food.

"Mommy, can I have some a' your sandwich?"

"Oh, no, Bobby," said my mother. "You'll get sick if you eat too much."

"Are you *still* hungry, Robert?" my father said. "I'd swear you have a tapeworm or something inside you."

"Oh, come on, Daddy, let me just taste it — pleeeeeeze!"

After taking a bite or two of this sandwich

dressed in mustard, I wasn't all that impressed. I guess five-year-old children don't acquire a taste for corned pastrami on rye with mustard the first time they taste it. But I finished what my parents gave me on the way home.

"I don't know," Dad said. "I'd give any-thing you're gonna be sick tomorrow."

"Uh-uh, Daddy. I'll be just fine!" I said as we went home.

Guess what, true believers?

I got sick.

The next morning, a pain shot throughout my stomach (which I would later find out is called indigestion). I watched my mother dress my brothers as I lay in bed in my red pajamas (with booties) under my blankets. I looked at my mom with a sympathetic tear in my eye and asked, "Where ya goin', Mommy?"

"Your brothers and I are going shopping with your uncle," said Mom, knowing I wasn't going to like the sound of that.

"Can't you go later?" I asked with enthusiasm. "I'll be feeling better; then I can come, too."

"I'm sorry, Bobby, but your father and I told you not to eat that sandwich. Now watch TV and be good while your grand-mother takes care of you."

Grrrrrr.

As my brothers left our bedroom, I started crying; I really wanted to go. But, oh, well — even at that young age, I knew it was indeed my fault I was ill; I should've lis-tened to my parents. There was little I could do to let my stomach pain subside before my uncle's car left our driveway.

My grandmother came in my room and after administering some Pepto-Bismol, asked if I wanted to watch television. As I nodded my head in the "yes" mode, she pressed the "on" button and left the room.

As the televison set warmed up, WOR channel 9 blared across the screen with the end credits of a program titled "Dr.

Who." While I was staring at this show's colorful psychedelic images, an announcer stated that Godzilla, King of the Monsters would air next on its "Horror Double-Feature Theatre."

The program's introduction featured a sinister blinking eye that encompassed the entire television screen. What followed was the film that would change my life forever. I sat in bed fevered with curiosity as the television's speaker emitted several "THOOM" sounds before the movie's title appeared with three deafening roars. Enthralled, I watched and listened as actor Raymond Burr told the story of how Tokyo, Japan was ravaged by a monster awakened by hydrogen bomb testing. I nervously stared in awe as this huge, almost 400-foot-tall lizard rose above Tokyo Bay and destroyed everything in sight. Ships burned, buildings crumbled, electrical towers snapped like sticks, trains were wrecked, but most frightening of all, millions of people perished under this behemoth's might and radioactive, fiery breath.

But what scared me most about Godzilla was his origin; the human race created him. Even though I couldn't put my feel-ings into words, I knew that Godzilla's destructive warpath was somehow nature's revenge against man for defiling its environment. At that point, I believed Armageddon was here, and not knowing what to do, I yelled for my grandmother. "Grandma! Grandmaaaa!!"

My grandmother ran into the bedroom in what seemed to be an instant.

"What is it, Robert?!" she said with a tinge of concern. "Are you still in pain?"

"No, Grandma!" I said as I hastily pointed to the television with a shaking forefinger. "People in Toe-kee-o are dyin', Grandma! We gotta save 'em!"

My grandmother looked at the screen with one of those "What the heck are you watching?" expressions. After she realized it was "one of those monster movies," she gazed upon me with an emotion I would categorize as a hybrid between anger and annoyance.

"Oh, stop that, Robert! That's not real!"

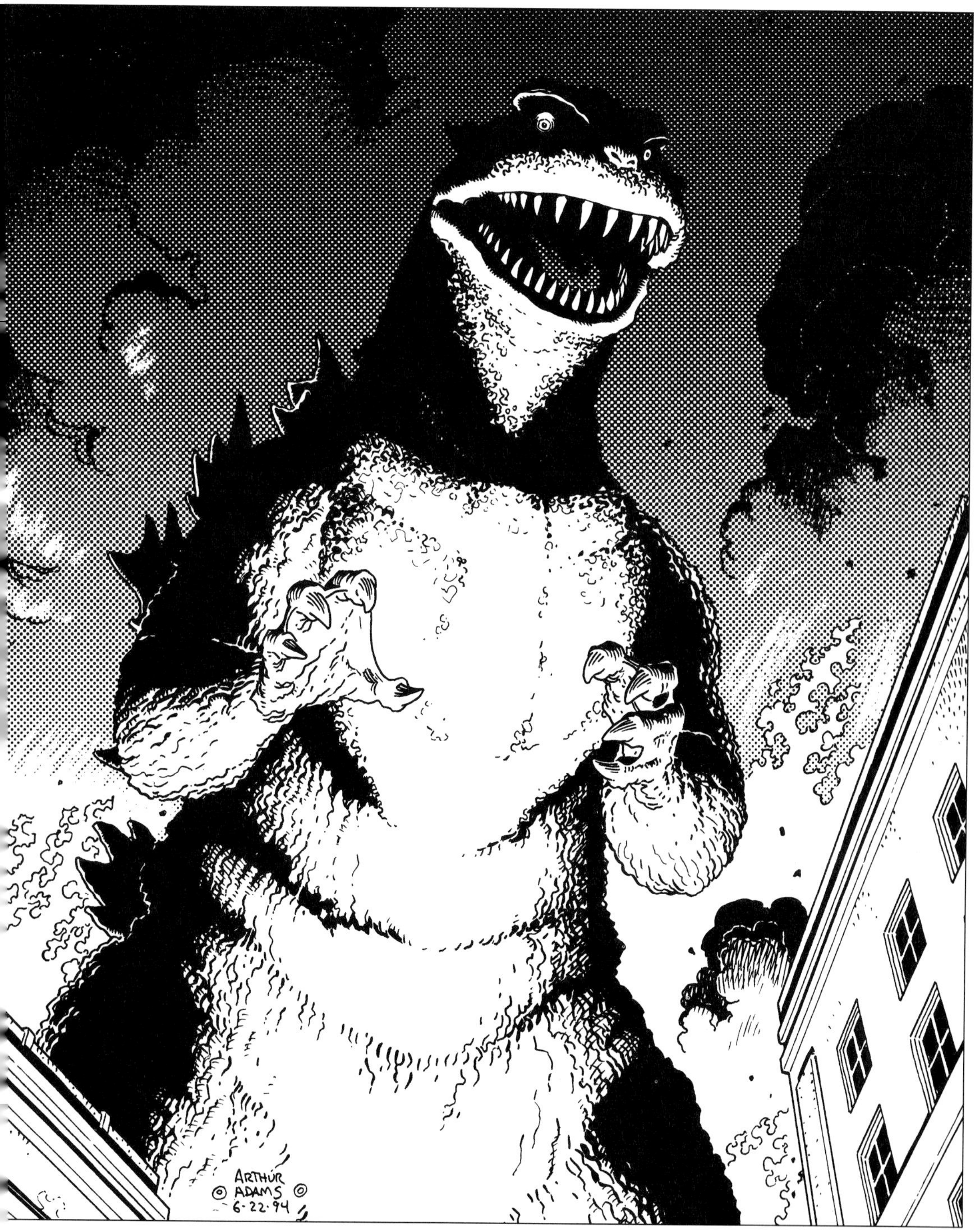
ARTHUR
© ADAMS ©
6-22-94

ART ADAMS

My world suddenly stopped; time seemed to pause as I looked at her with utter confusion.

"Whaddayamean, 'That's not real!'?"

"I mean this movie's fictional."

"*Fictional*?!"

"You know, *make-believe*? Now if you're scared, I can turn it — "

"Oh, no, Grandma!" I quickly interjected. "I'm, uh, not scared."

"Okay, then. Now finish watching television, and I'll see how you're doing later."

I watched the rest of *Godzilla, King of the Monsters*, not quite understanding or believing Godzilla wasn't real; he seemed real enough. And boy, did I faint a sigh of relief when Dr. Serizawa and Ogata killed the beast with the Oxygen Destroyer. Whether my grandmother thought Godzilla existed or not, I knew that somehow, he did, and I was happy he was defeated.

The film ended with one more "THOOM" sound before the next feature aired, hinting that Godzilla would return; "If The Blob, Dracula, and Frankenstein could come back from the dead, why not Godzilla?" I thought. Within seconds, my thought became reality when, sure enough, the second feature was *Godzilla's Revenge*.

I had great expectations for this film; I was curious to know how Godzilla came back to life to threaten the world once again. But *Godzilla's Revenge*, to say the least, was something . . . different. Godzilla was green (I couldn't tell the difference between black-and-white and color film back then; I thought Godzilla was brown!), and had a son named Minya (who spoke English, no less!). Minya joined forces with a human child to defeat a bully-of-a-monster named Gaborah. As the story progressed, I realized major developments in the Godzilla saga were missing, but that didn't matter; everything soon faded away.

"Bobby! Bobby! Wake up!"

Next thing I knew, I awoke to see my mother and brothers in my bedroom, freshly home from their shopping spree. My mother gave me a Mego Shazam action figure and smiled at me, knowing I was feeling much better. While she was correct about my physical health, I was somewhat mentally troubled.

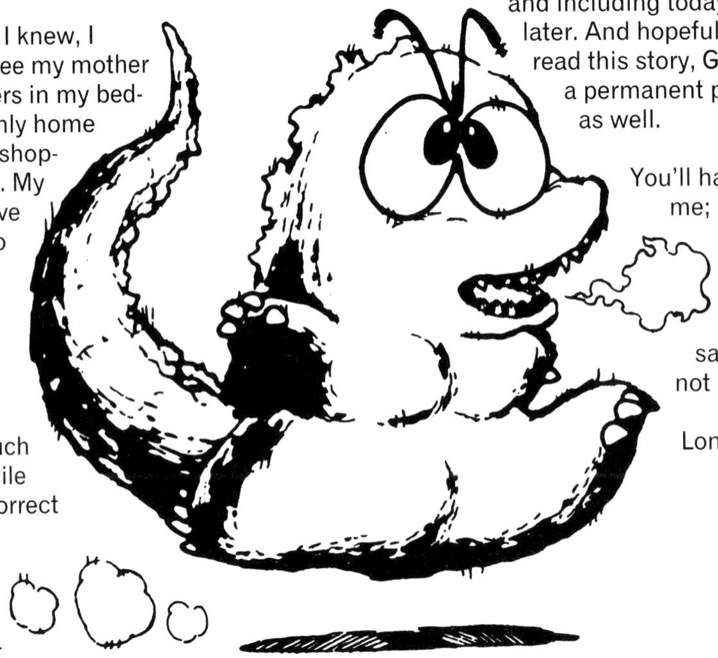

"Mom! Is Godzilla real?" I asked in great anticipation.

"Godzilla?" she said, looking at me strangely as if she knew something I didn't.

"Yeah, Mommy, look!" I turned to the television set to show her the horror I had witnessed earlier that day, but instead, exposed her to an episode of "Tarzan."

"Oh, no, it's not on anymore," I said in sheer disappointment. "Godzilla destroyed Toe-kee-o right in front of me."

"Oh, I see what you mean," Mom said. "I think we have to have a talk about television."

After having the difference between film fantasy and news reality explained, I grew to stop fearing Godzilla and started appreciating him. Before long, my room was covered in Godzilla comic books, View-Master reels, Shogun Warrior figures, bendables, movie stills and posters, records, and other paraphernalia. I sat glued to the television set every time ABC featured "Monster Week" on its daily 4:30 movie and every Saturday when NBC aired the "Godzilla/Jana of the Jungle Hour" cartoon show.

Godzilla became a part of my life up to and including today, twenty years later. And hopefully, after you've read this story, Godzilla will be a permanent part of yours as well.

You'll have to excuse me; my parents are coming over to have dinner. And no, pastrami sandwiches will not be on the menu.

Long live the King!

IT'S GODZILLA'S 40th BIRTHDAY — LONG LIVE THE KING !!!

Since the release of Godzilla, King of the Monsters in both Japan and the United States, the giant, fire-breathing reptile has been the favorite of millions of moviegoers for forty years. But only few die-hard fans know all twenty-one silver-screen appearances Godzilla has made in his illustrious career. At right is a complete Japanese filmography of the King of Monsters with original release dates (courtesy of Toho Co., Ltd.).

Godzilla (a.k.a., *Gojira, Godzilla, King of the Monsters*) — 1954

Godzilla Raids Again (a.k.a., *Gigantis, the Fire Monster*) — 1955

King Kong vs. Godzilla — 1962

Mothra vs. Godzilla (a.k.a., *Godzilla vs. The Thing*) — 1964

Ghidorah, the Three-Headed Monster (a.k.a., *Ghidorah, Ghidora, King Ghidorah*) — 1964

Invasion of the Astro Monster (a.k.a., *Monster Zero, Godzilla vs. Monster Zero*) — 1965

Ebirah, Horror of the Deep (a.k.a., *Godzilla vs. the Sea Monster*) — 1966

Son of Godzilla — 1967

Destroy All Monsters — 1968

All Monsters Attack (a.k.a., *Godzilla's Revenge*) — 1969

Godzilla vs. Hedorah (a.k.a., *Godzilla vs. the Smog Monster*) — 1971

Godzilla vs. Gigan (a.k.a., *Godzilla on Monster Island*) — 1972

Godzilla vs. Megalon — 1973

Godzilla vs. Mechagodzilla (a.k.a., *Godzilla vs. the Cosmic Monster, Godzilla vs. the Bionic Monster*) — 1974

Terror of Mechagodzilla (a.k.a., *Revenge of Mechagodzilla*) — 1975

The Return of Godzilla (a.k.a., *Godzilla 1985*) — 1984

Godzilla vs. Biollante — 1989

Godzilla vs. King Ghidorah (a.k.a., *Godzilla vs. Ghidorah*) — 1991

Godzilla vs. Mothra (a.k.a., *Godzilla and Mothra: The Battle for Earth*) — 1992

Godzilla vs. Mechagodzilla II (a.k.a., *Godzilla vs. Super-Mechagodzilla*) — 1993

Godzilla vs. Space Godzilla (a.k.a., *Godzilla vs. Space Monster*) — 1994

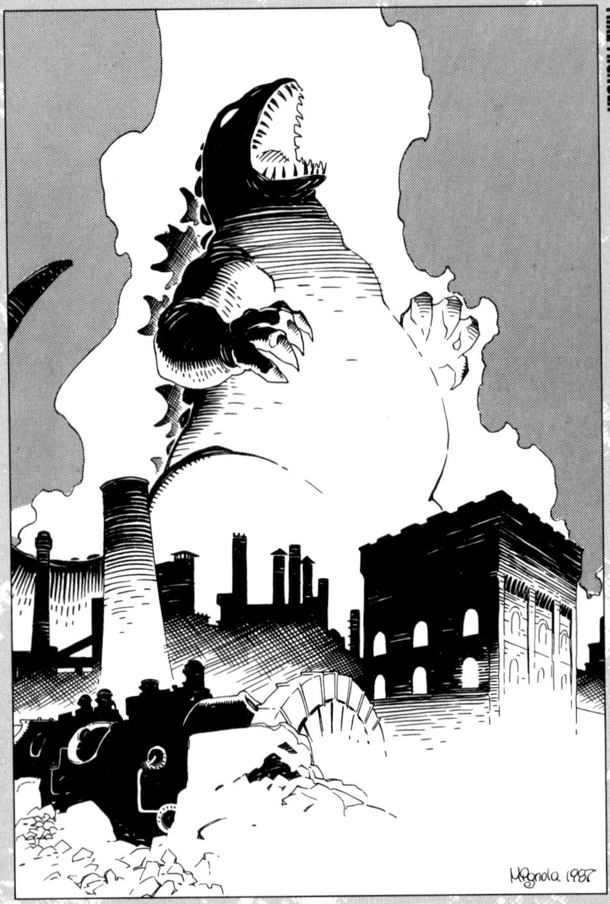
Mignola 1987

MIKE MIGNOLA

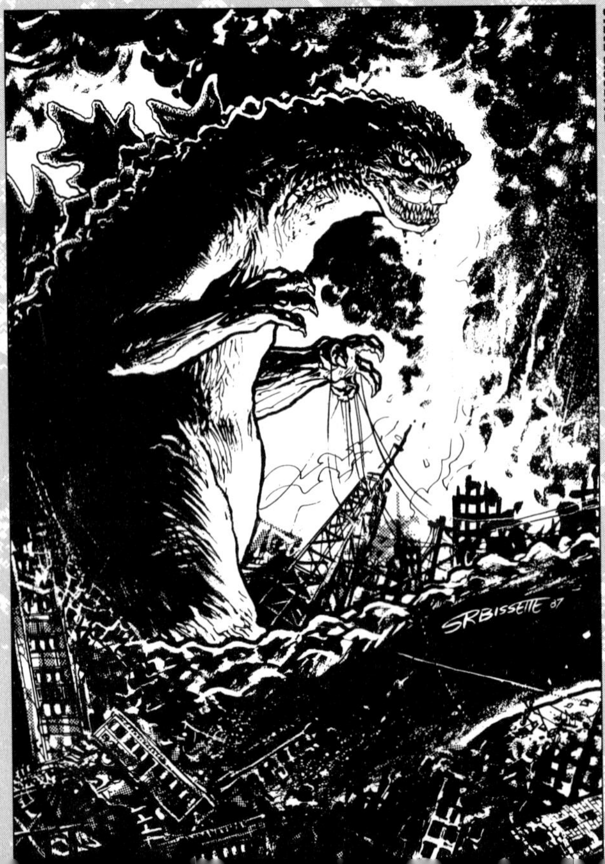
SRBISSETTE '87

STEVE BISSETTE

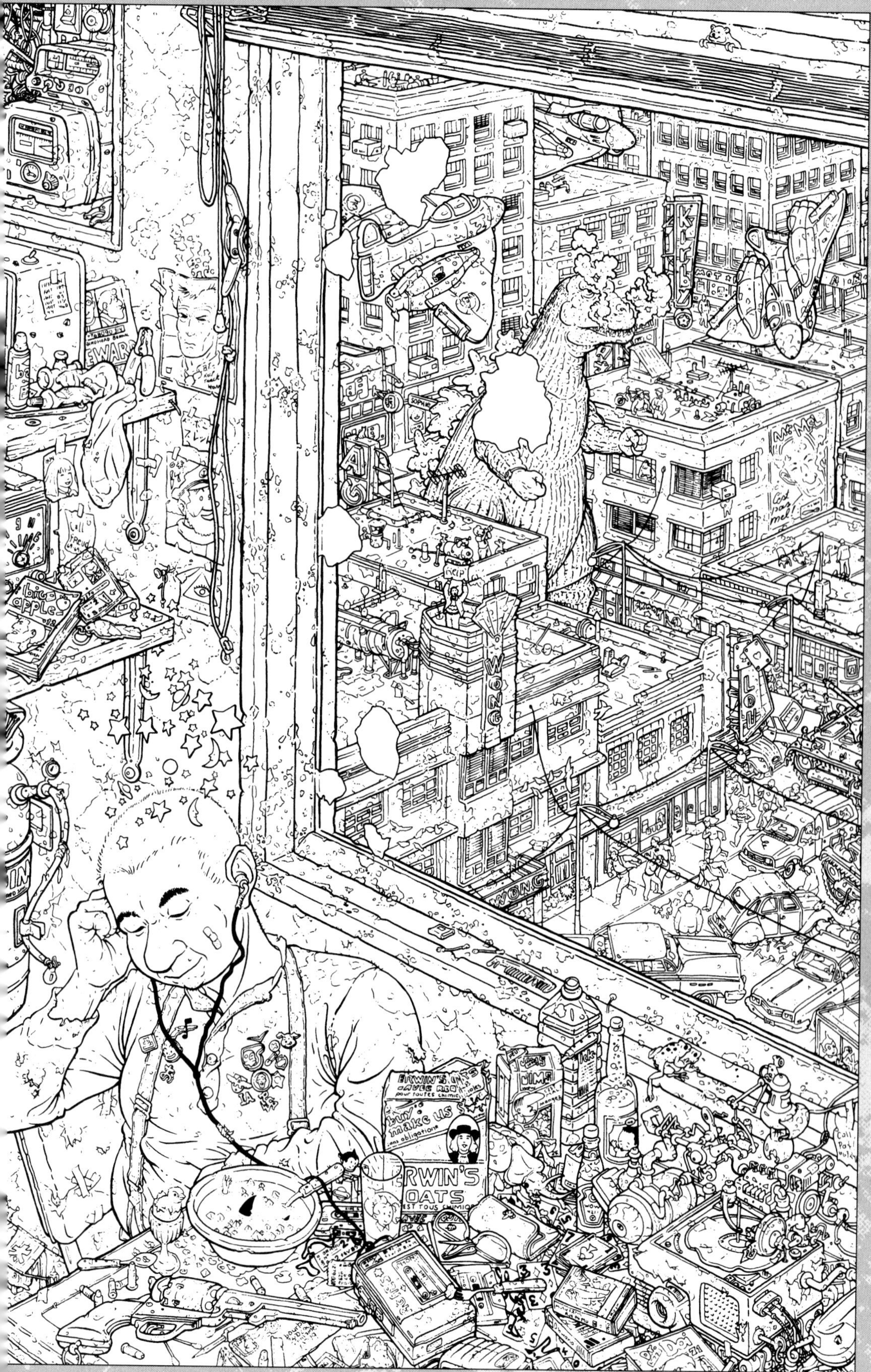

WONG
WONG
HELP
big apple
buy make us
sans obligations
RWIN'S
OATS

GEOF DARROW

ゴジラと産業化
日本の精神

CYNTHIA MARTIN

GOJIRA TO SANGYŌKA NIHON NO SEISHIN.
GODZILLA AND THE SPIRIT OF INDUSTRIAL-
IZED JAPAN. By Cynthia Martin

MARK A. NELSON

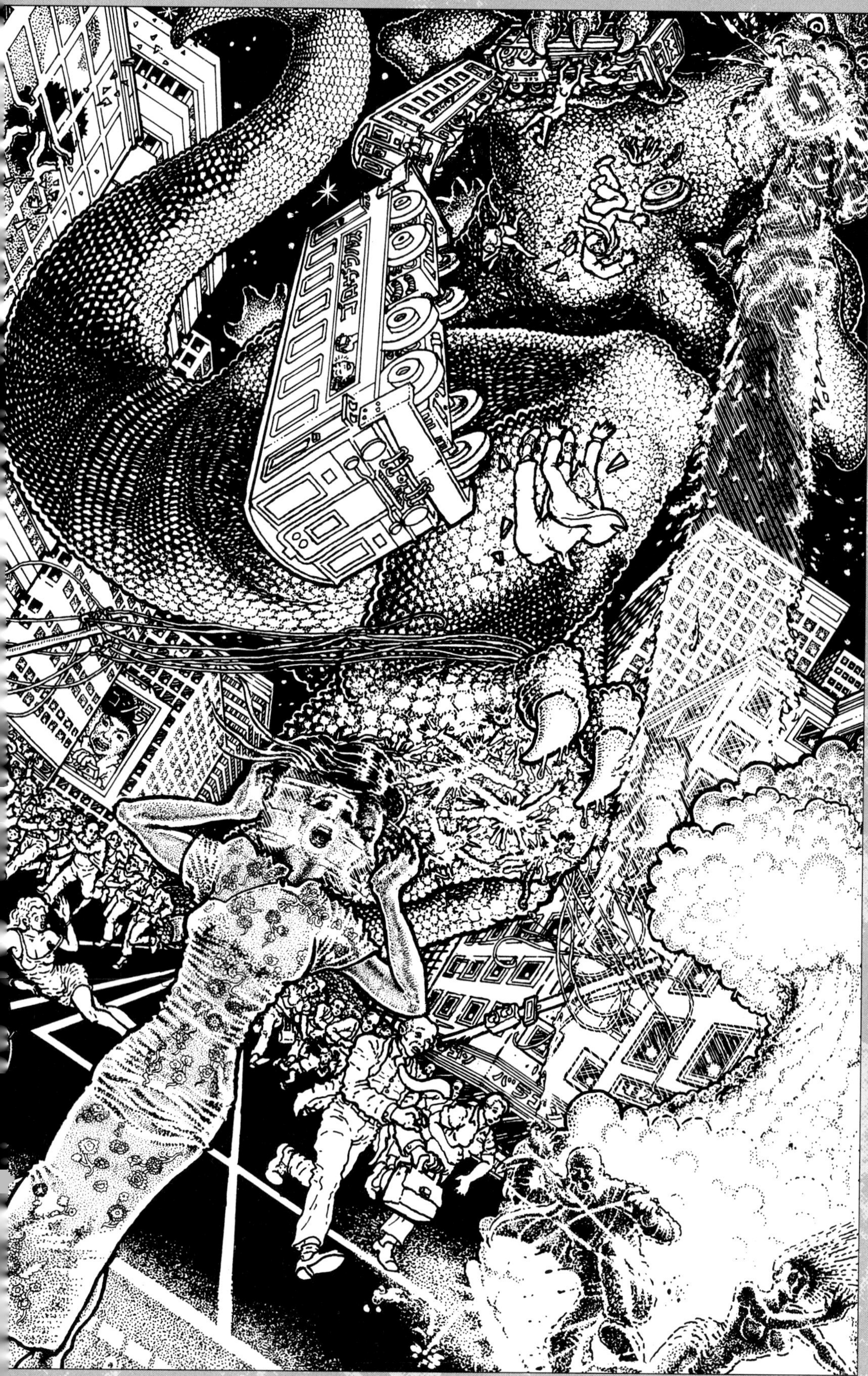

ALAN MOORE